FAIRY TAIL

49

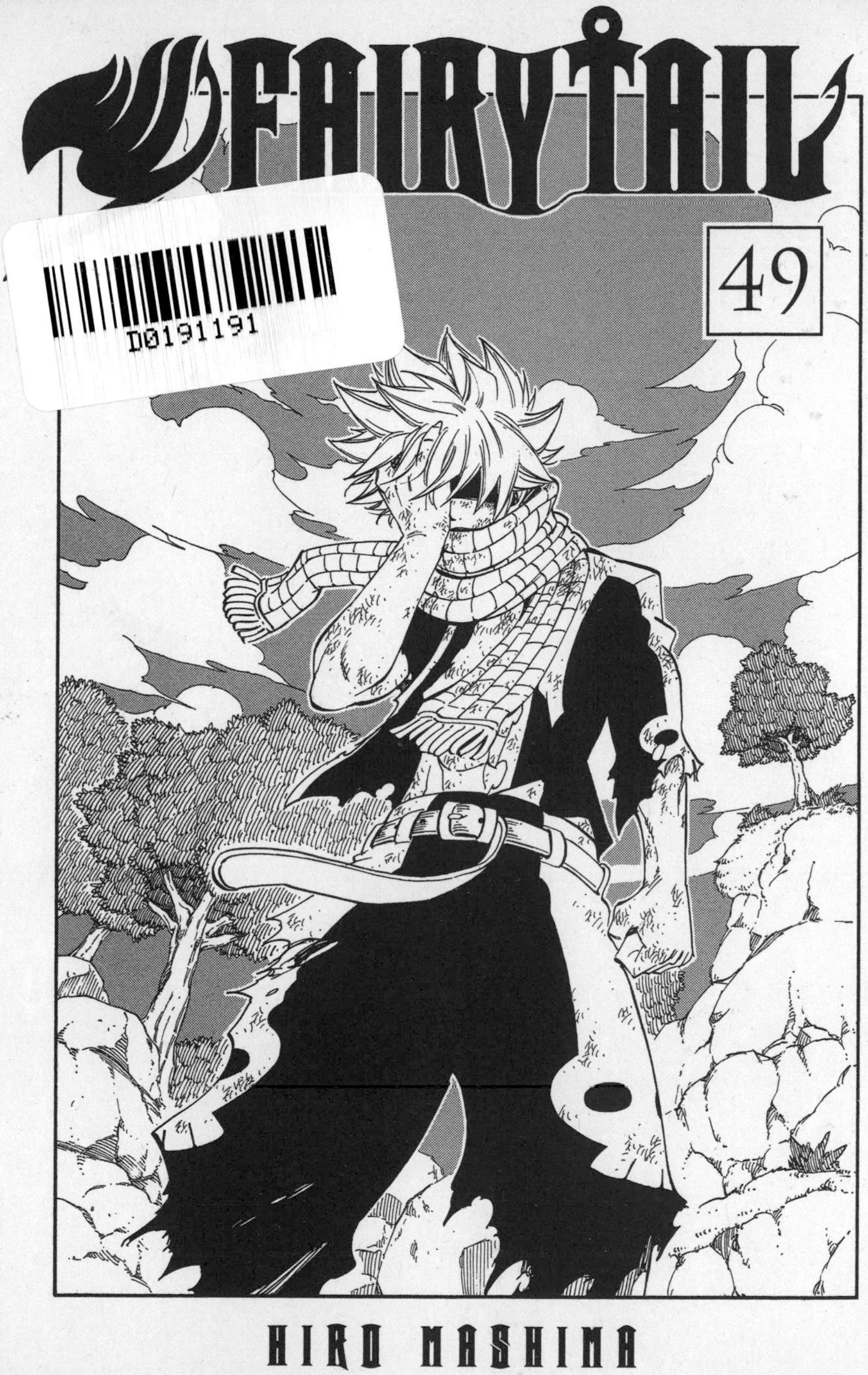

HIRO MASHIMA

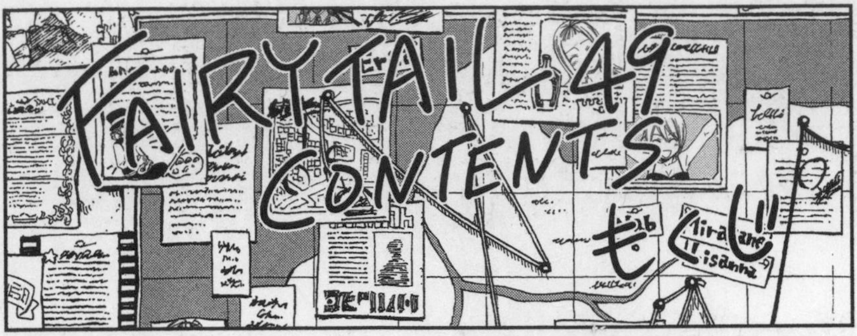
FAIRY TAIL 49
CONTENTS
もくじ
Mirajane
Lisanna

FAIRY TAIL

フェアリーテイル

Chapter 413: The Tome of END

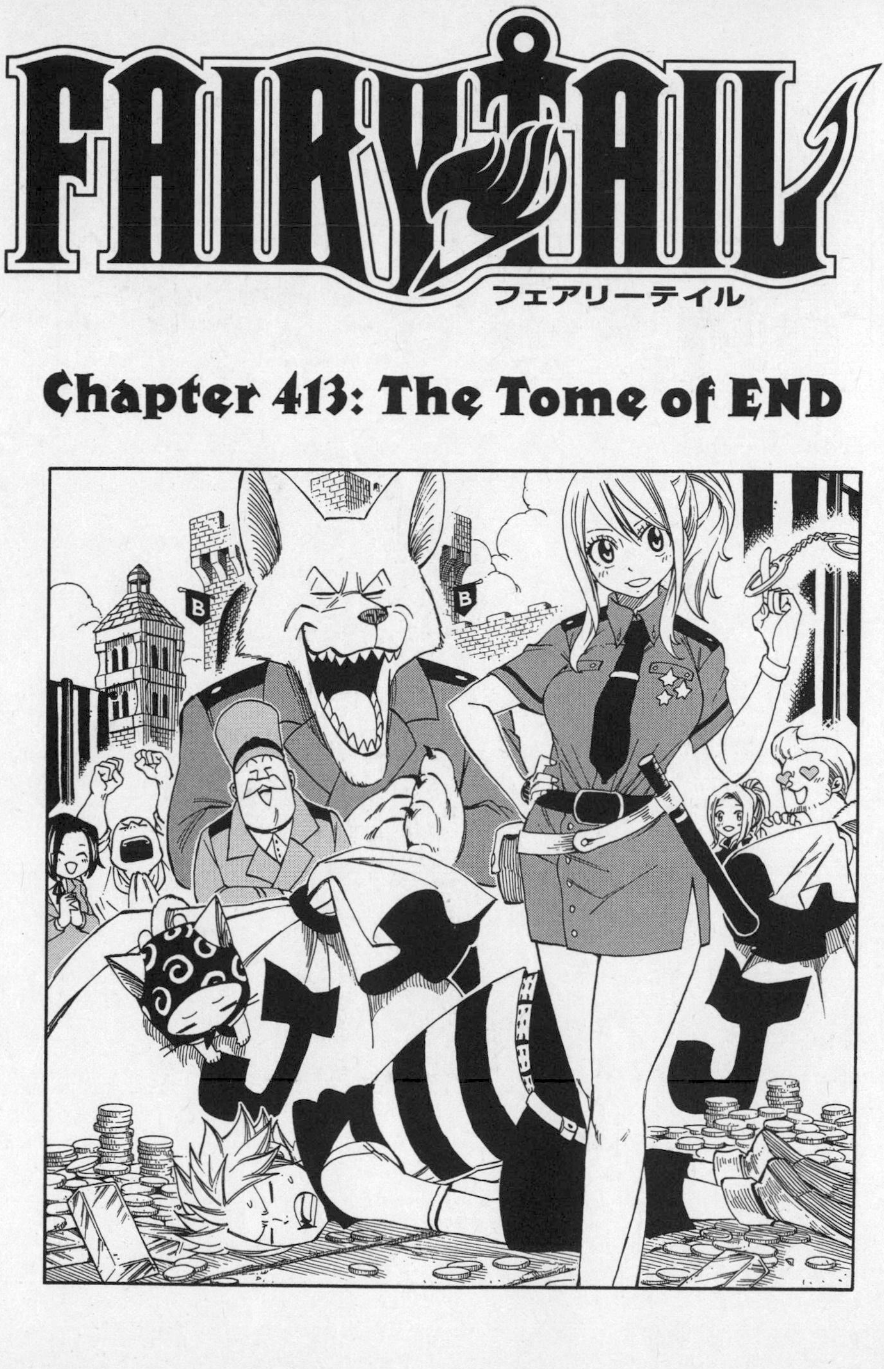

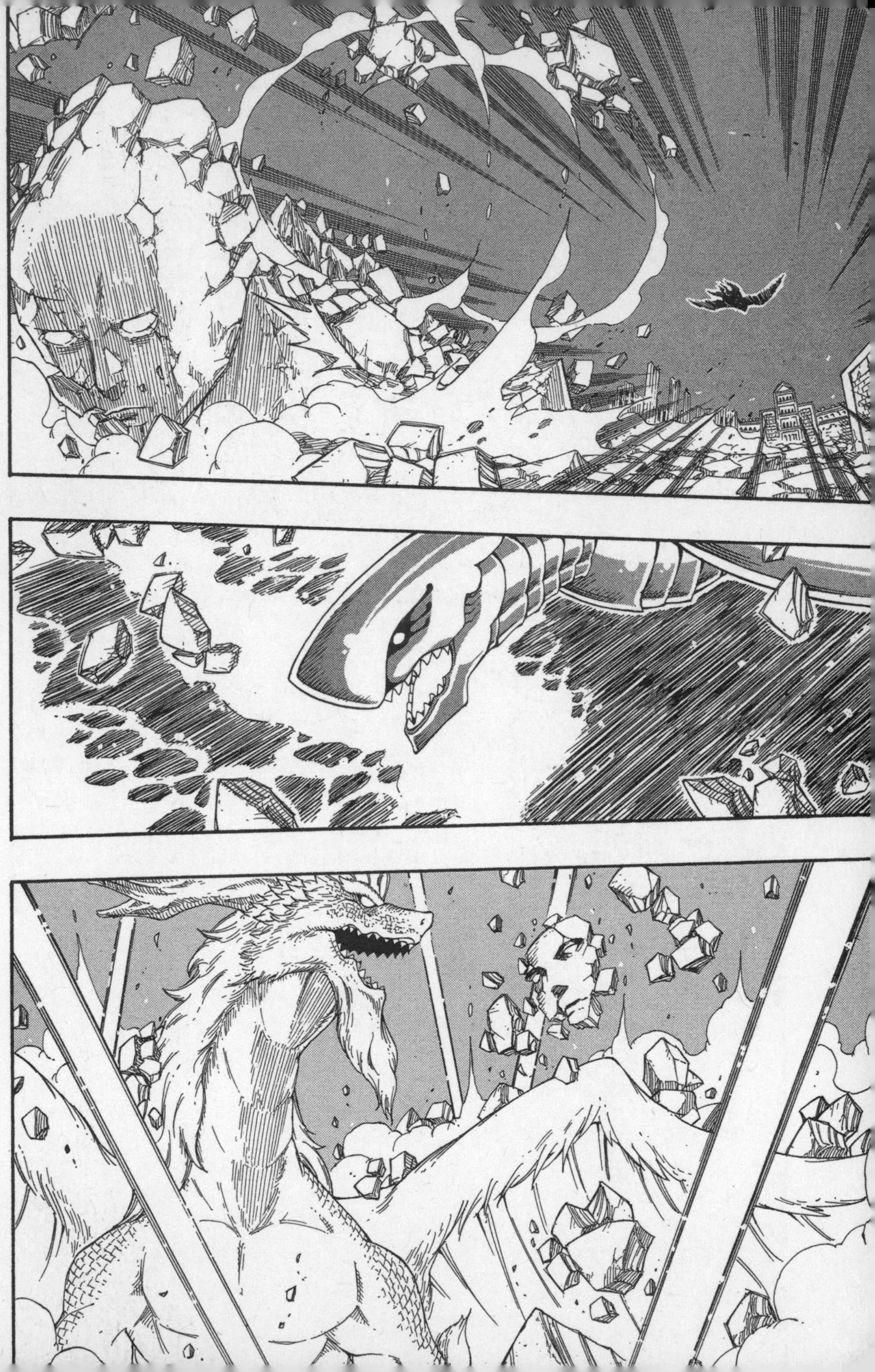

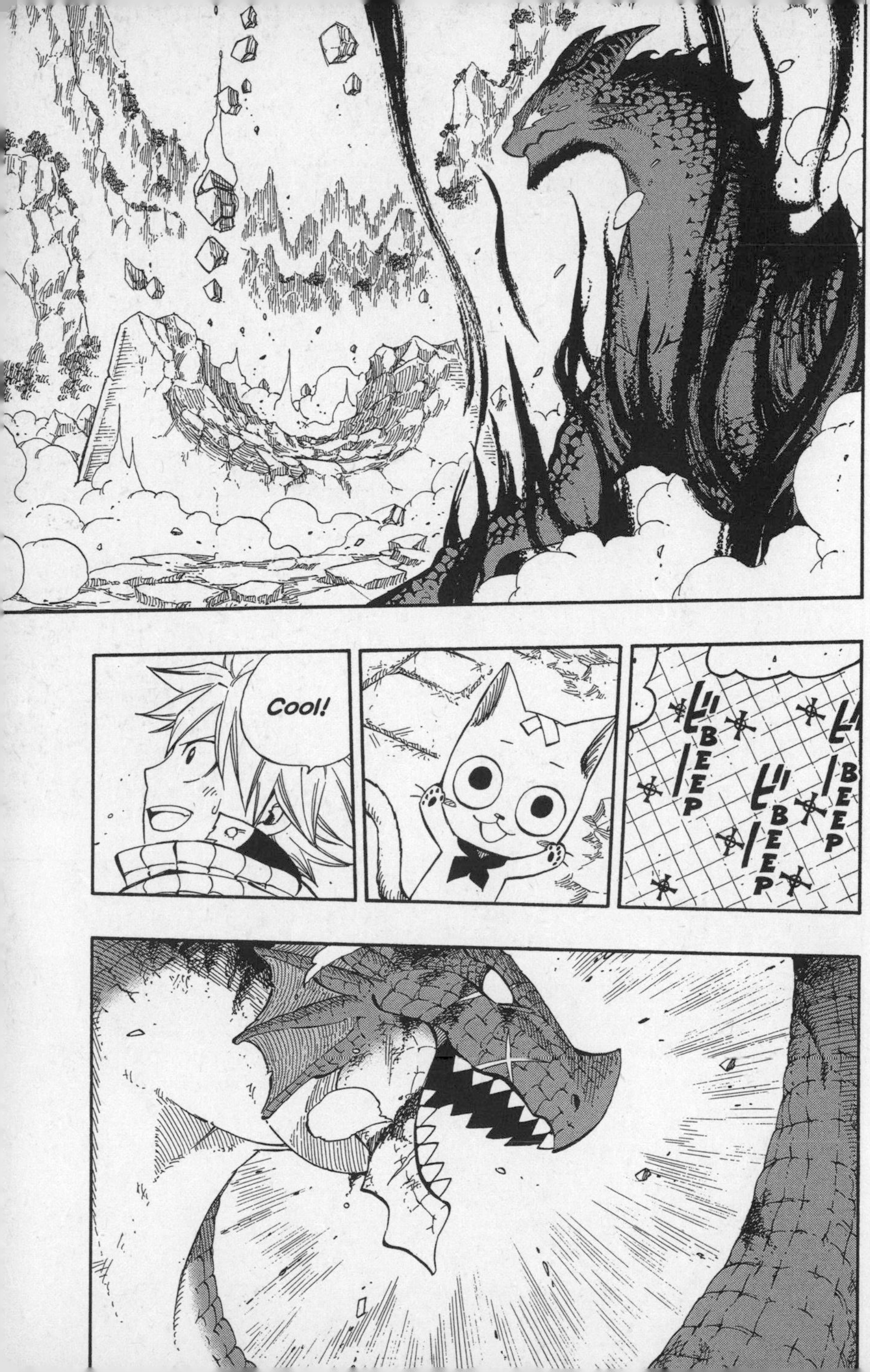
BEEP
BEEP
BEEP
Cool!

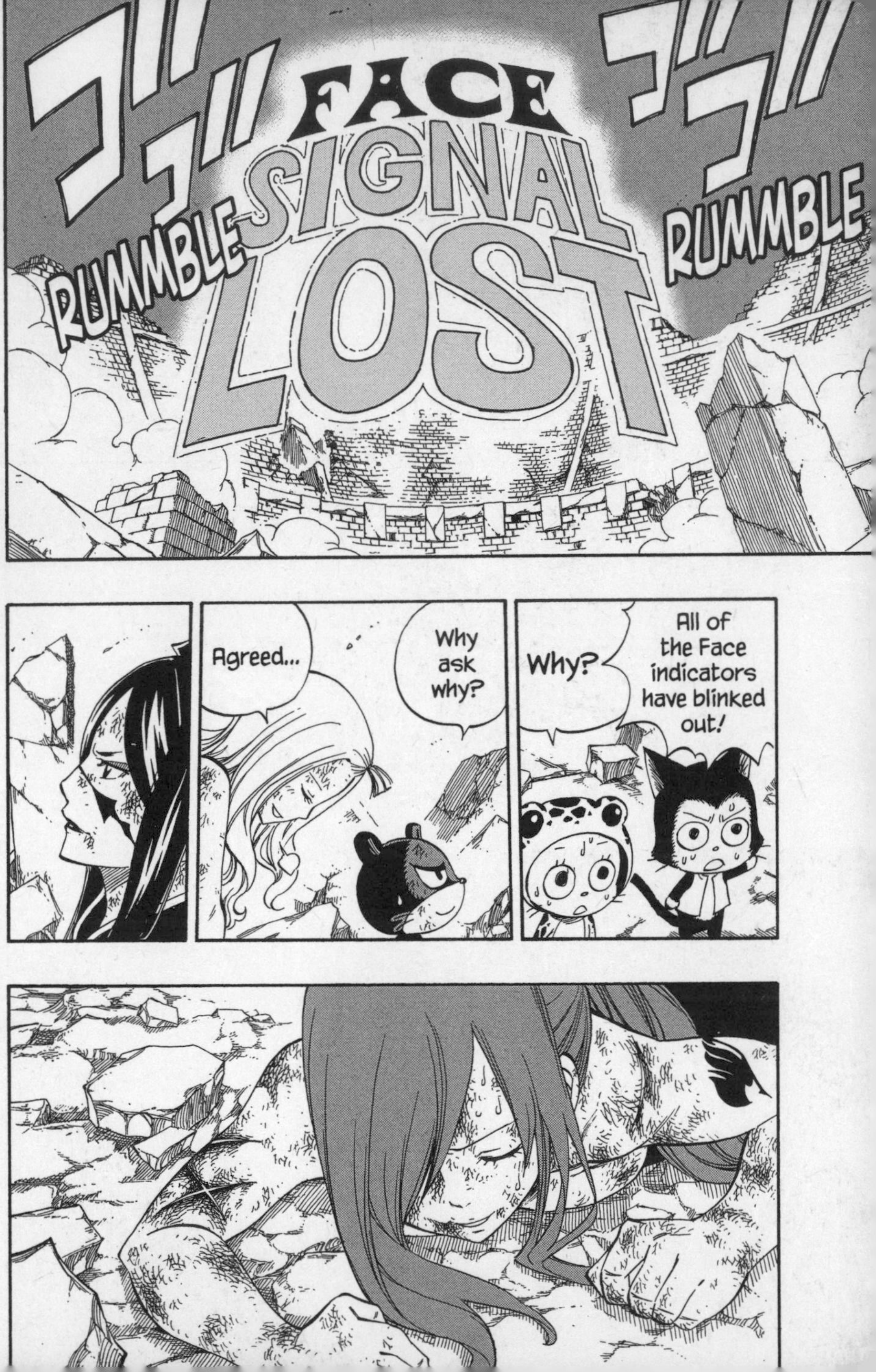

FACE SIGNAL LOST
RUMMBLE
RUMMBLE
All of the Face indicators have blinked out!
Why?
Why ask why?
Agreed...

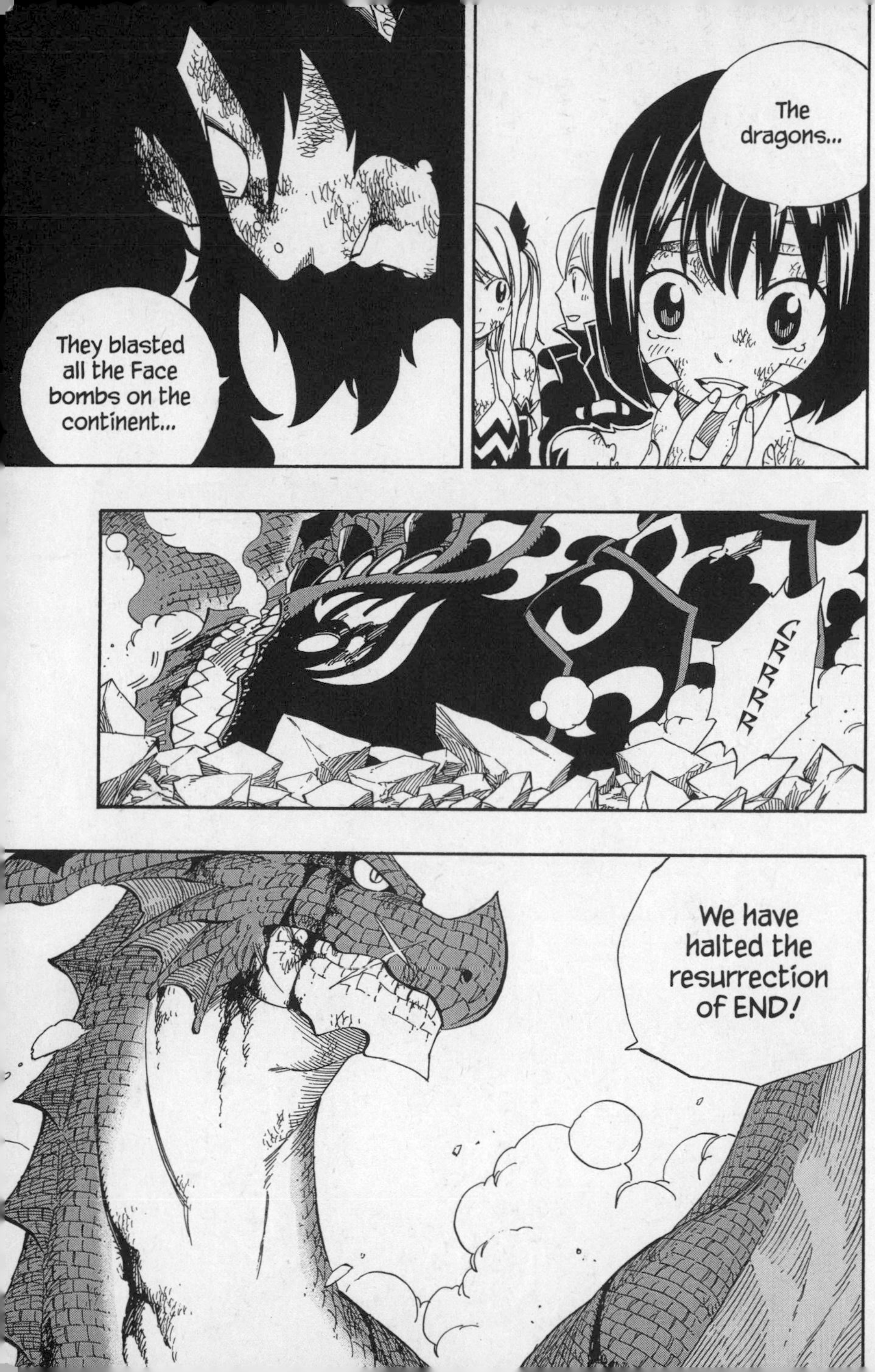
The dragons...
They blasted all the Face bombs on the continent...
GRRRRR
We have halted the resurrection of END!

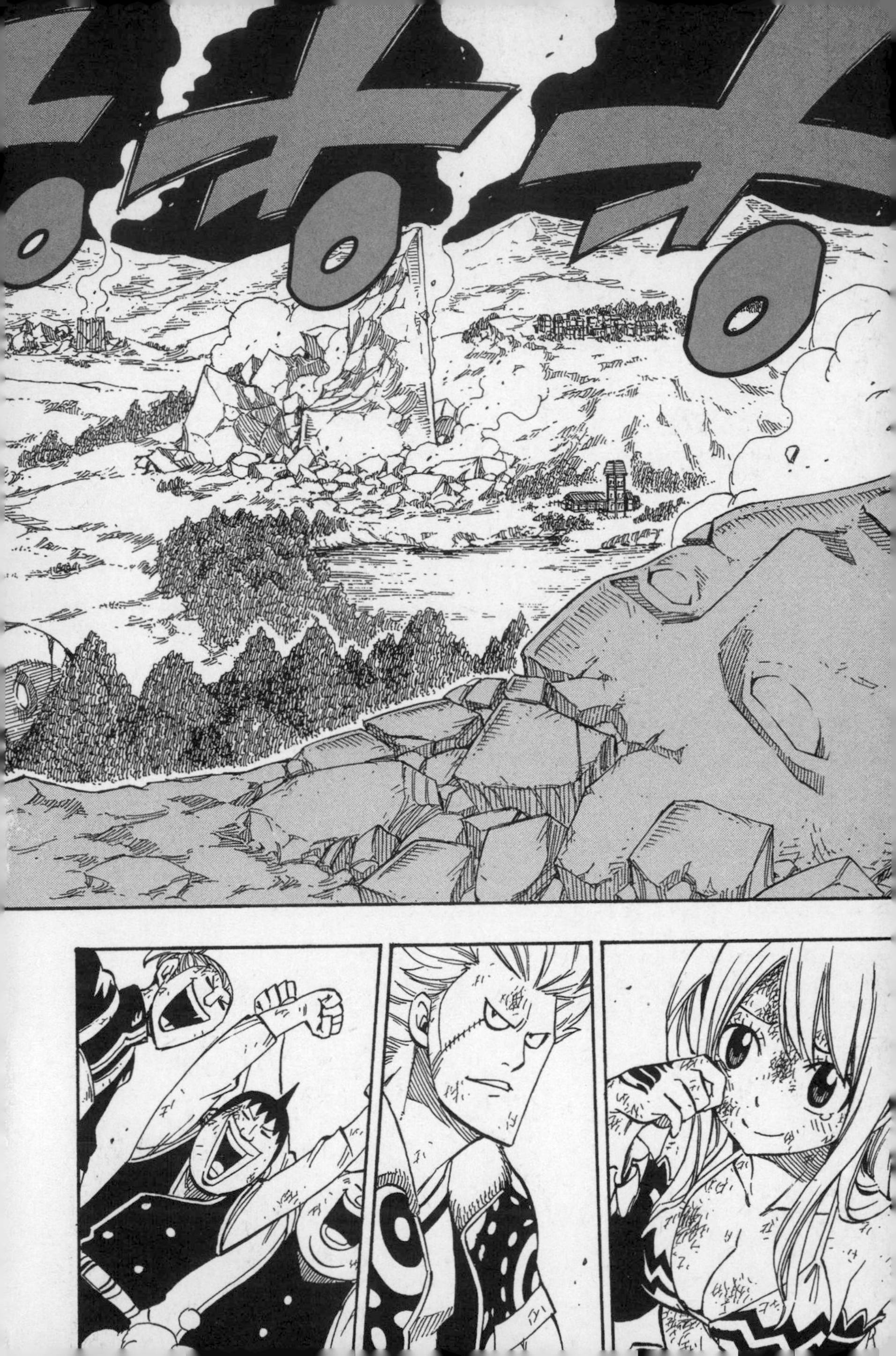

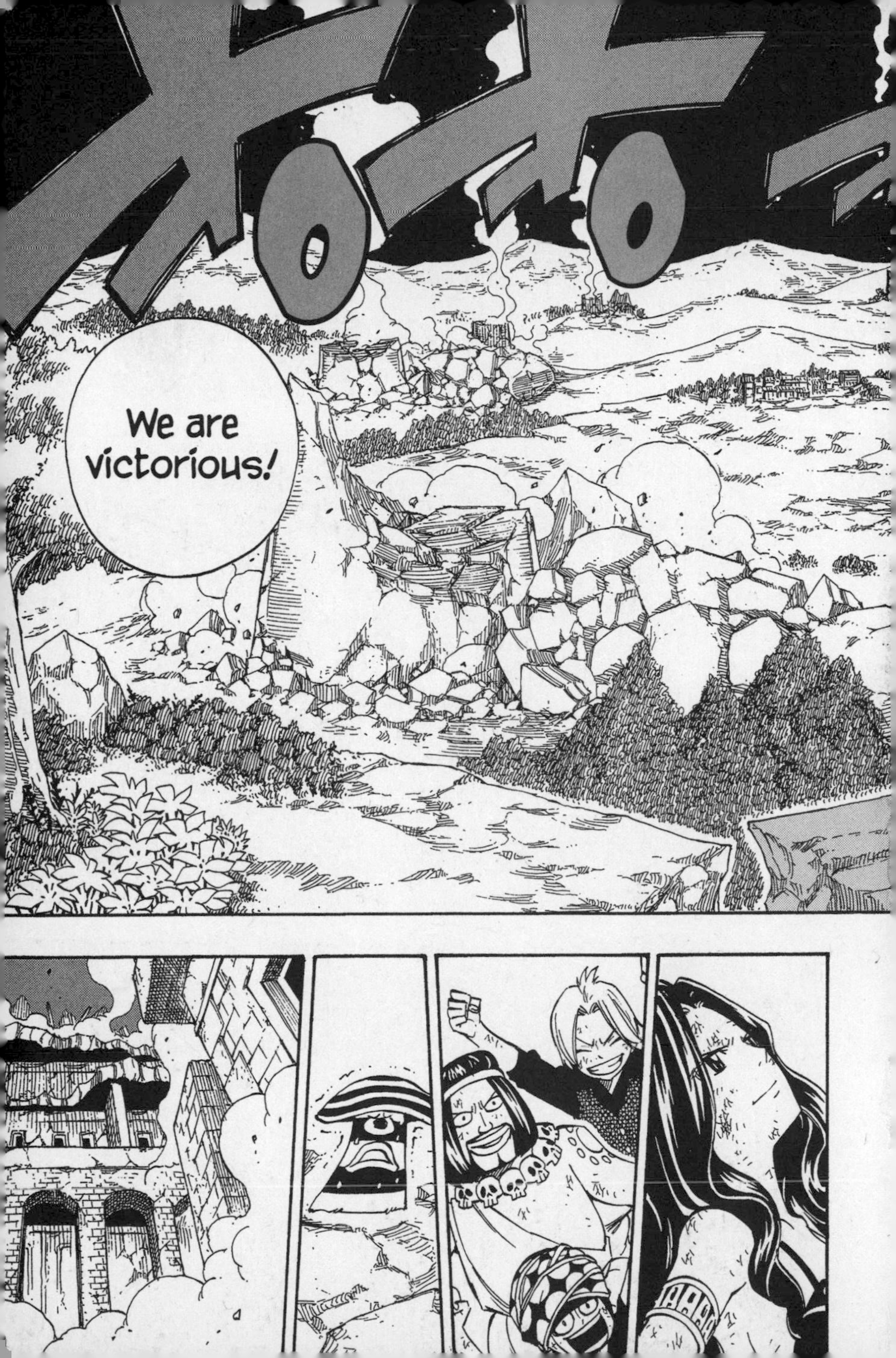
We are victorious!

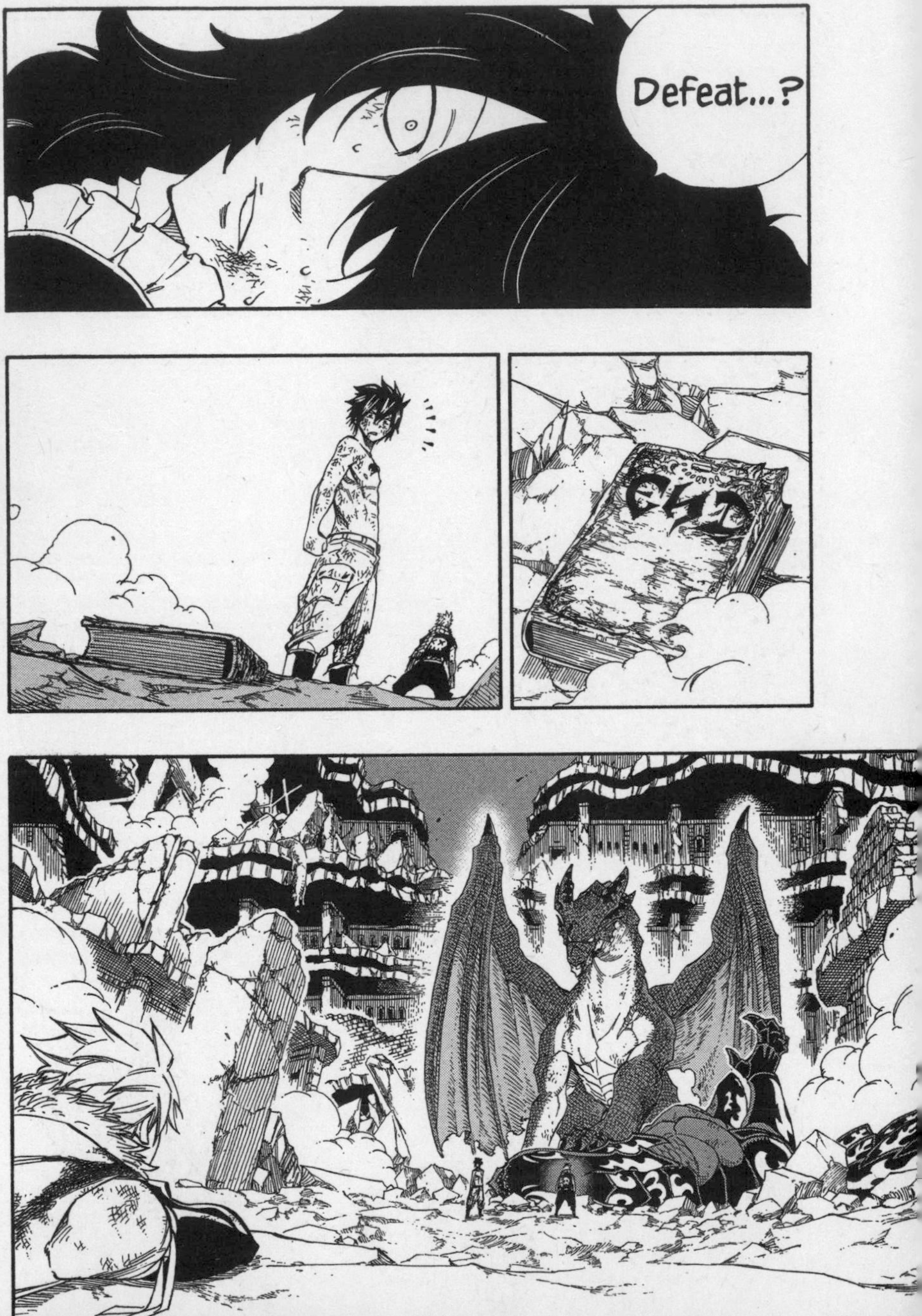
Defeat...?

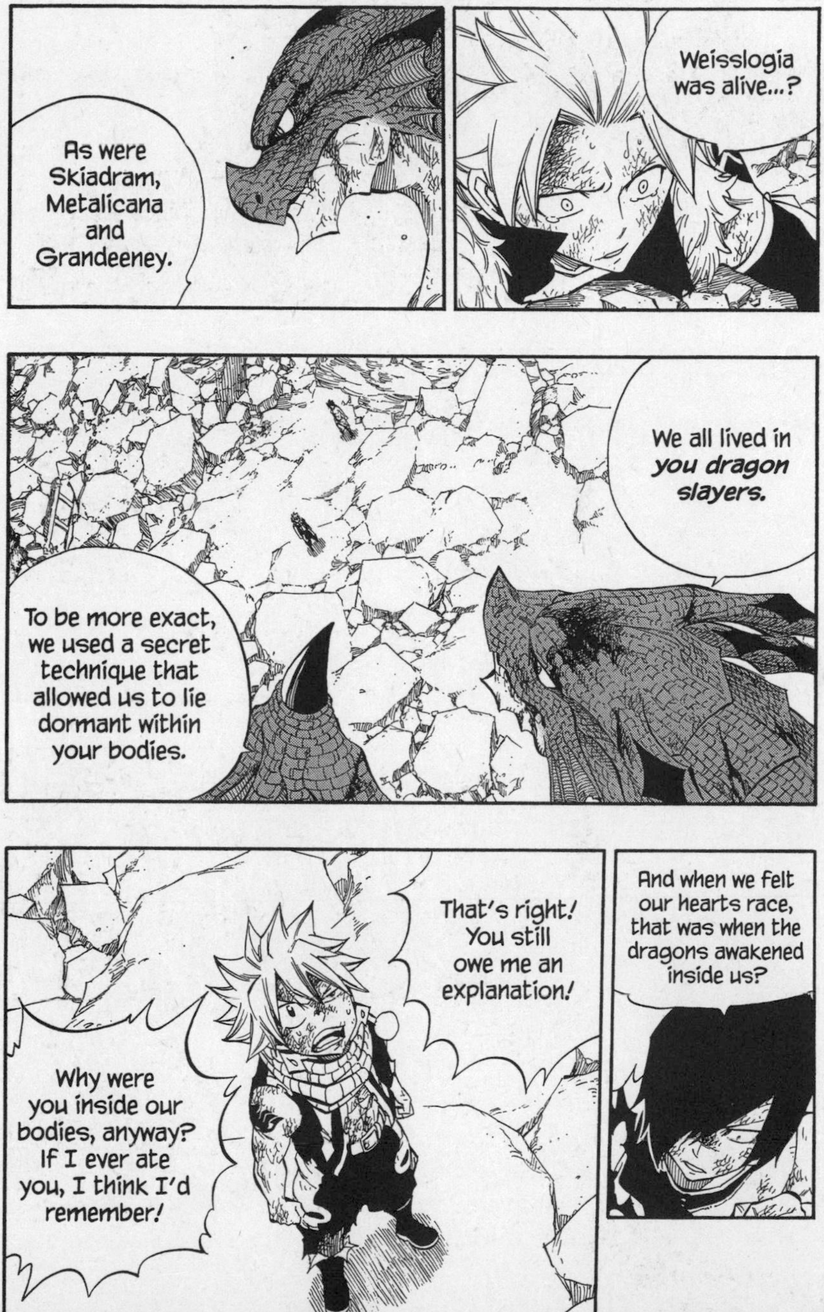
Weisslogia was alive...?
As were Skiadram, Metalicana and Grandeeney.
We all lived in *you dragon slayers.*
To be more exact, we used a secret technique that allowed us to lie dormant within your bodies.
And when we felt our hearts race, that was when the dragons awakened inside us?
That's right! You still owe me an explanation!
Why were you inside our bodies, anyway? If I ever ate you, I think I'd remember!

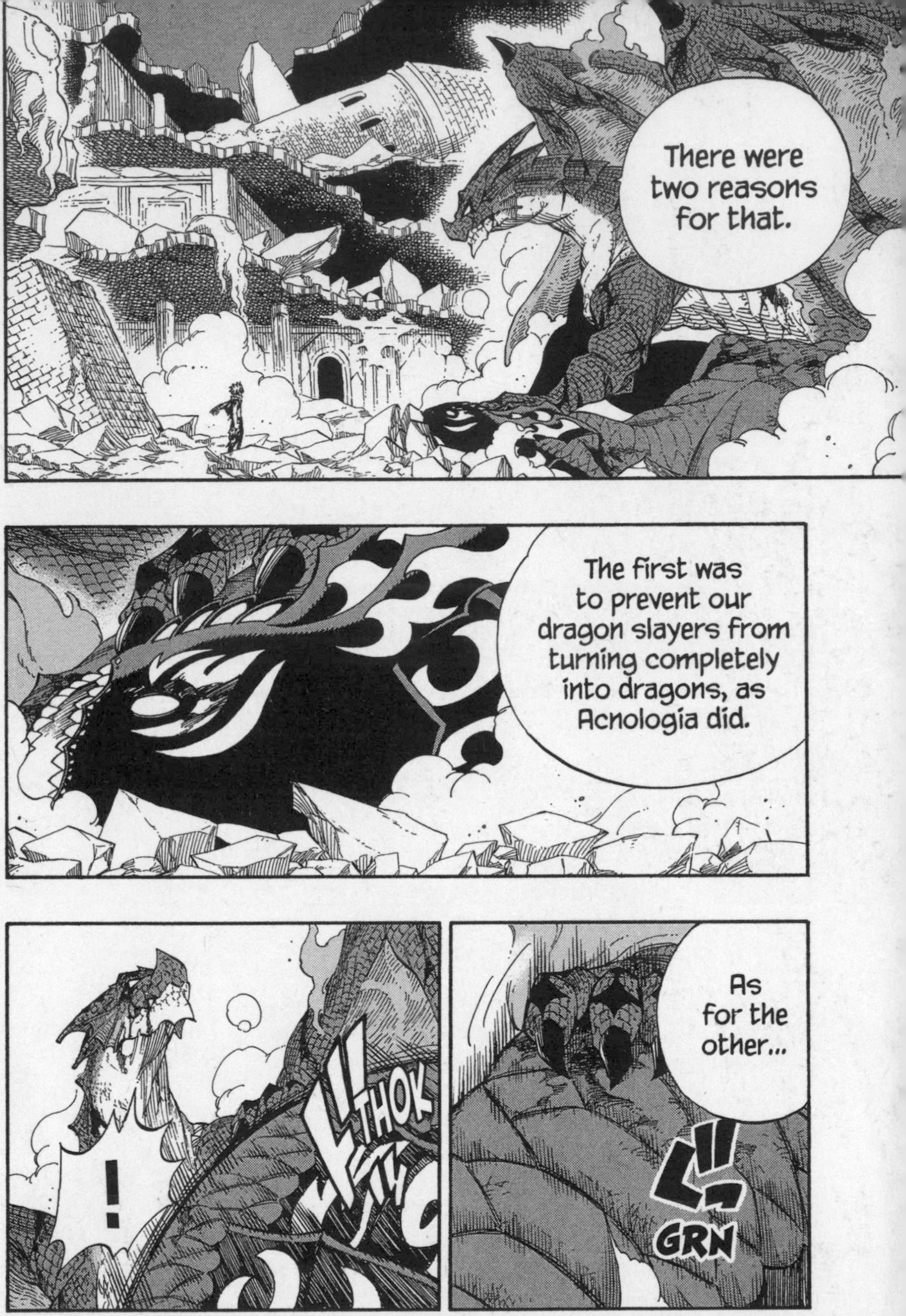
There were two reasons for that.
The first was to prevent our dragon slayers from turning completely into dragons, as Acnologia did.
As for the other...
GRN
THOK
!

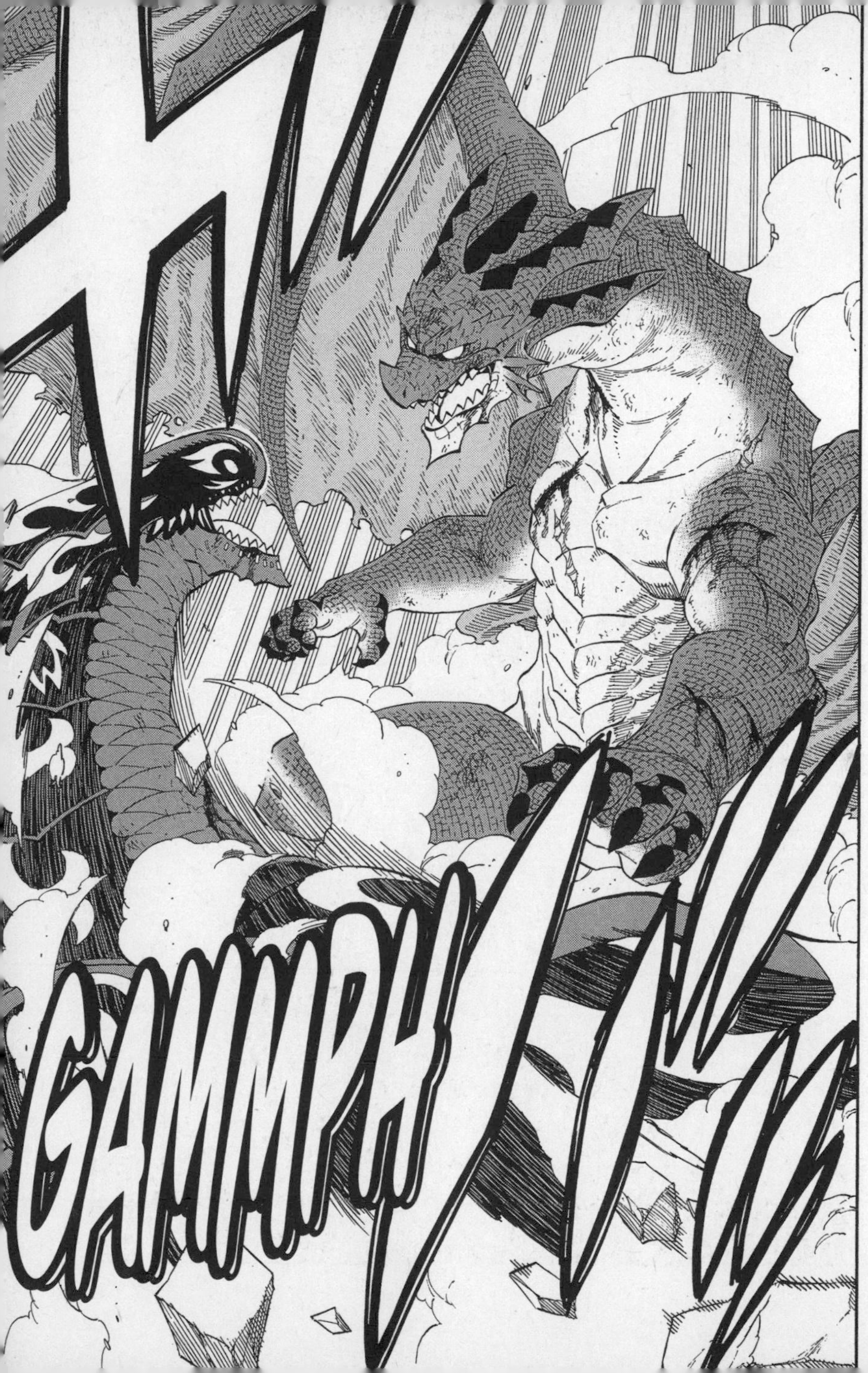
GAMMPH!!!

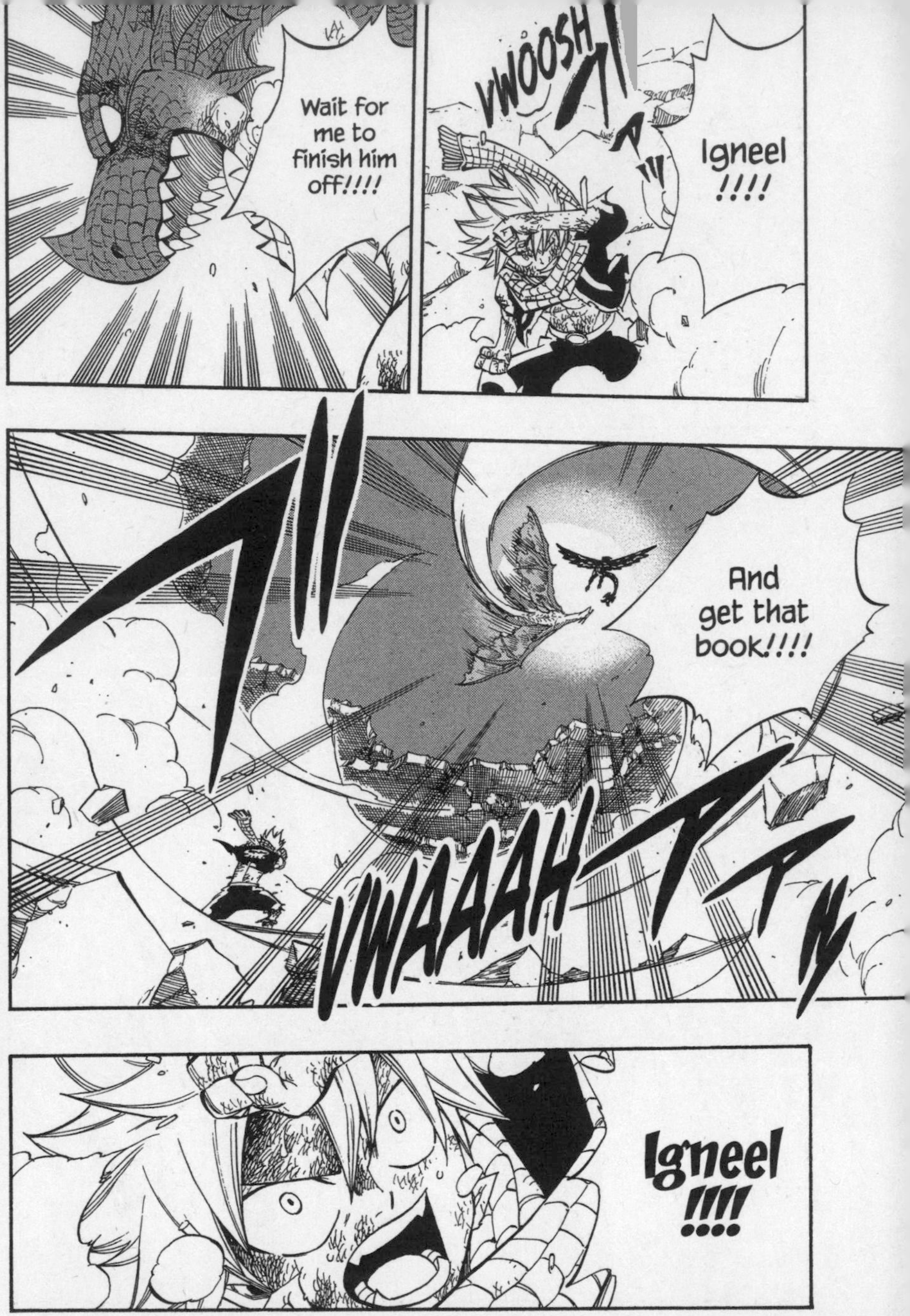
VWOOSH
Igneel !!!!
Wait for me to finish him off!!!!
And get that book!!!!
VWAAAH
Igneel !!!!

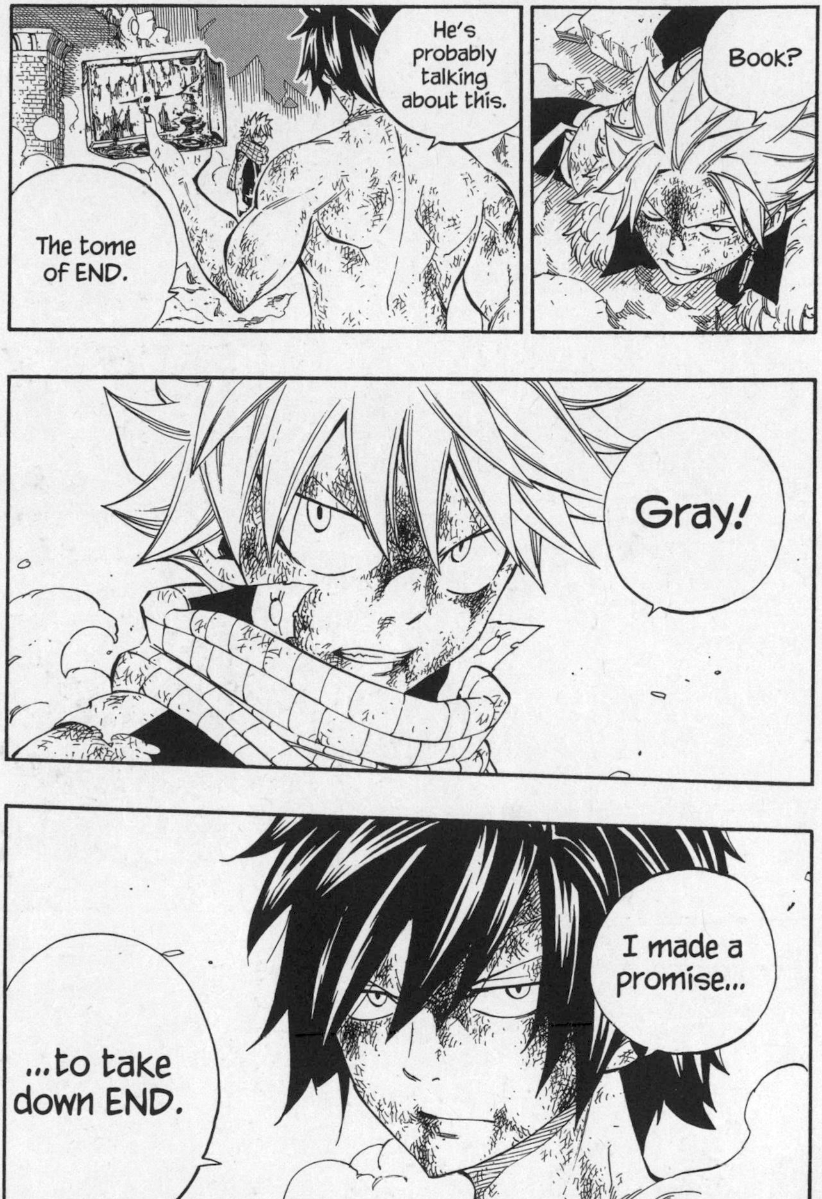
Book?
He's probably talking about this.
The tome of END.
Gray!
I made a promise...
...to take down END.

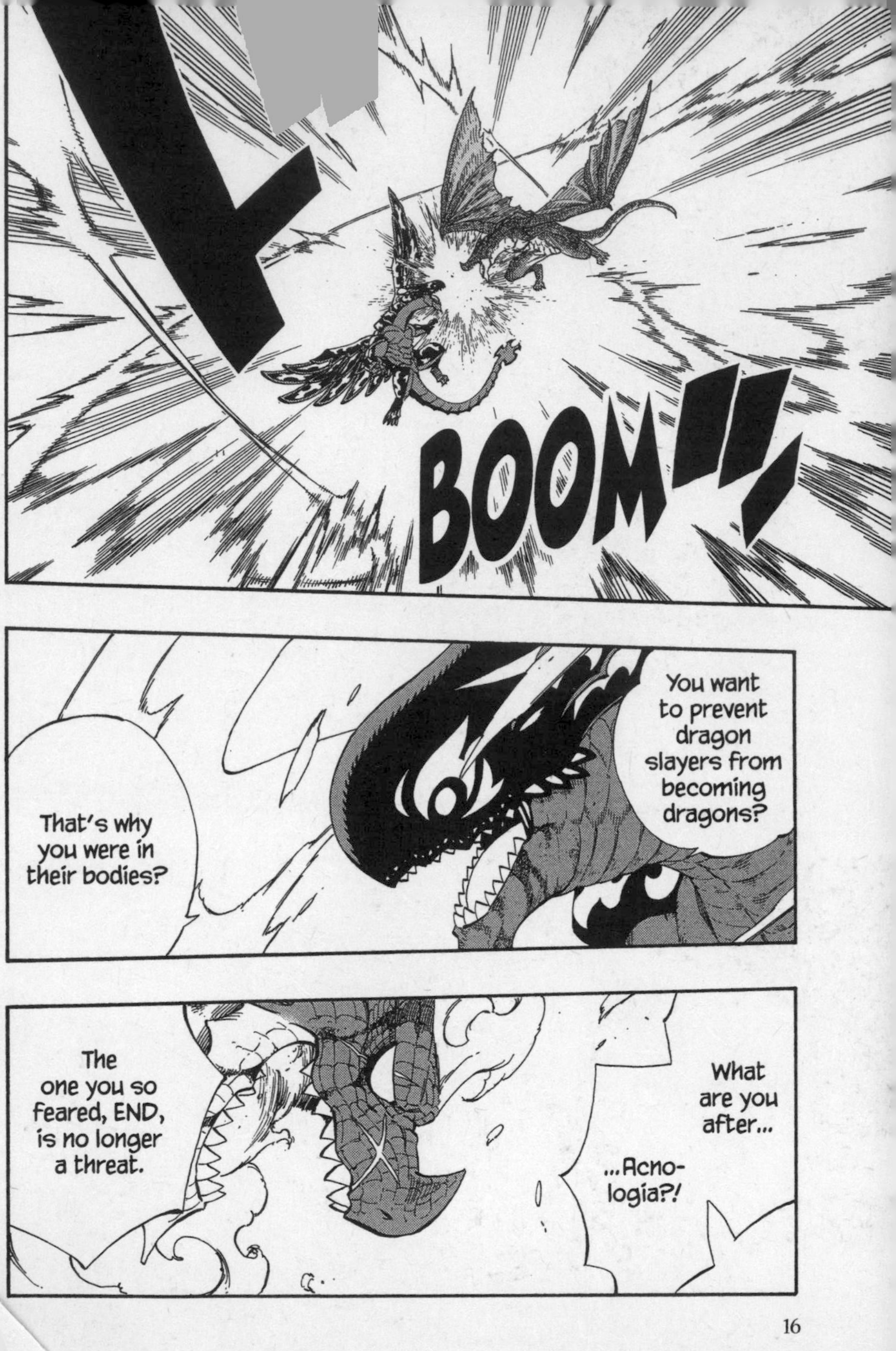
BOOM!!
You want to prevent dragon slayers from becoming dragons?
That's why you were in their bodies?
What are you after...
...Acnologia?!
The one you so feared, END, is no longer a threat.

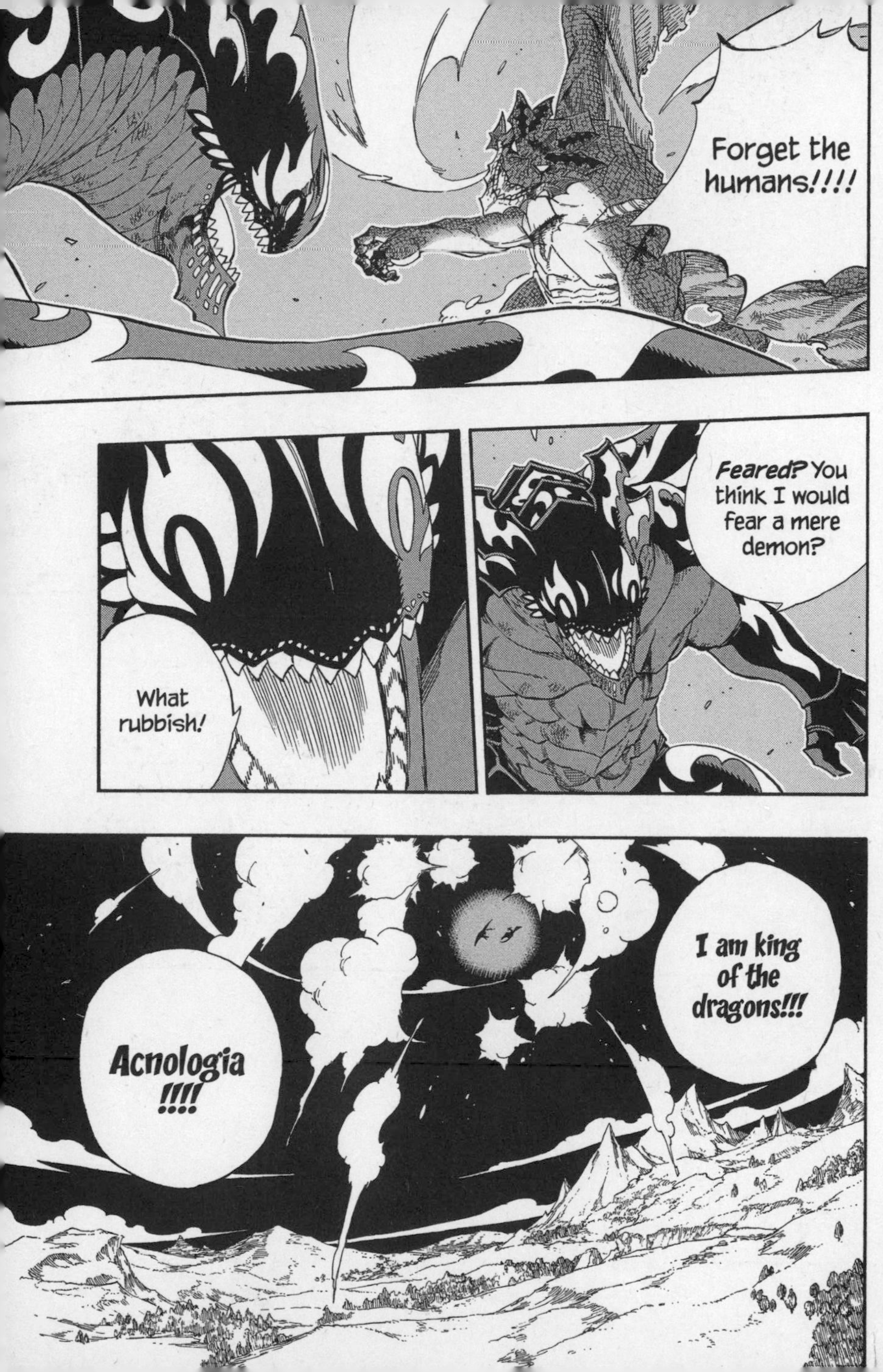
Forget the humans!!!!
Feared? You think I would fear a mere demon?
What rubbish!
I am king of the dragons!!!
Acnologia!!!!

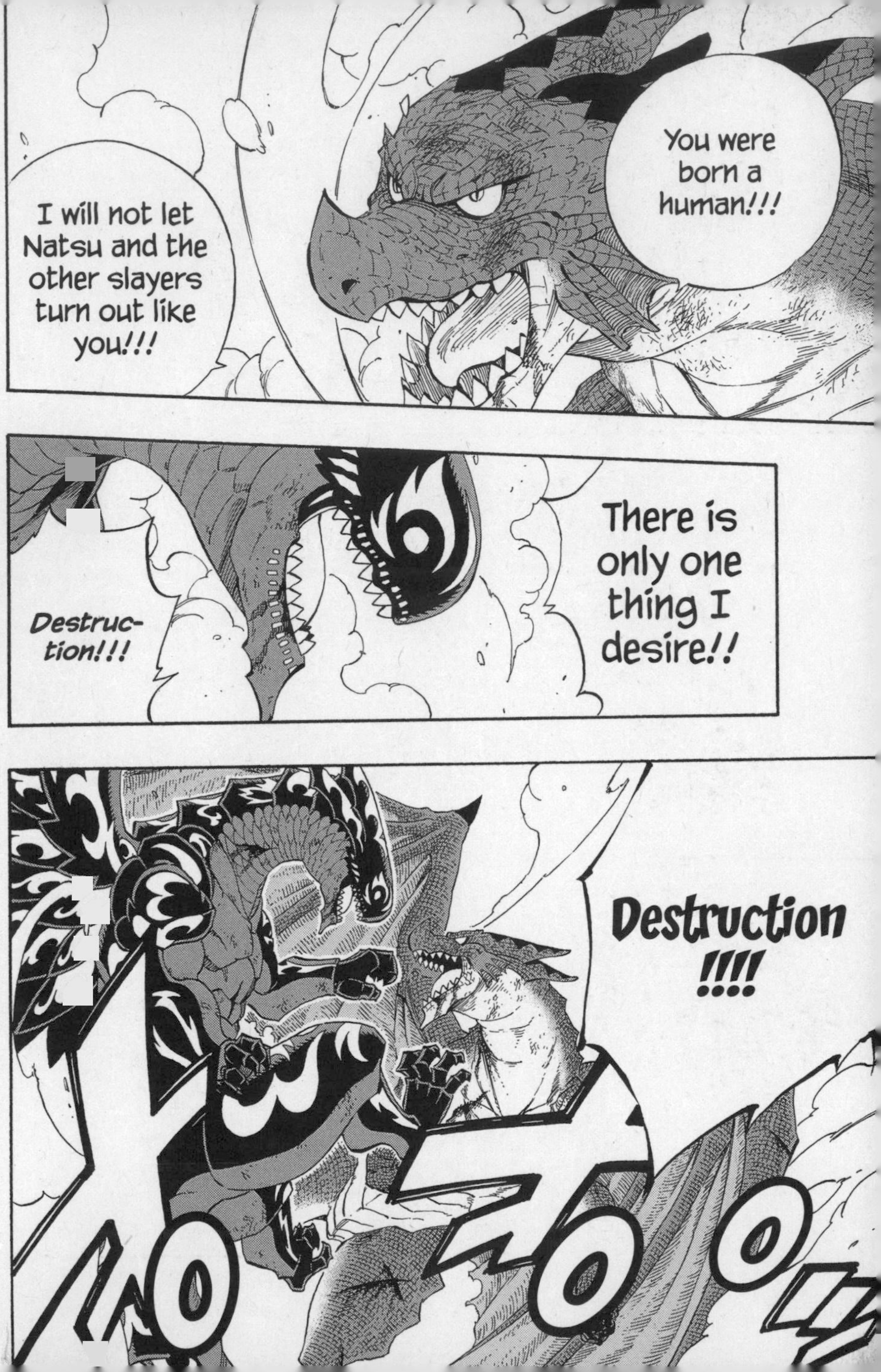
You were born a human!!!
I will not let Natsu and the other slayers turn out like you!!!
There is only one thing I desire!!
Destruction!!!
Destruction!!!!

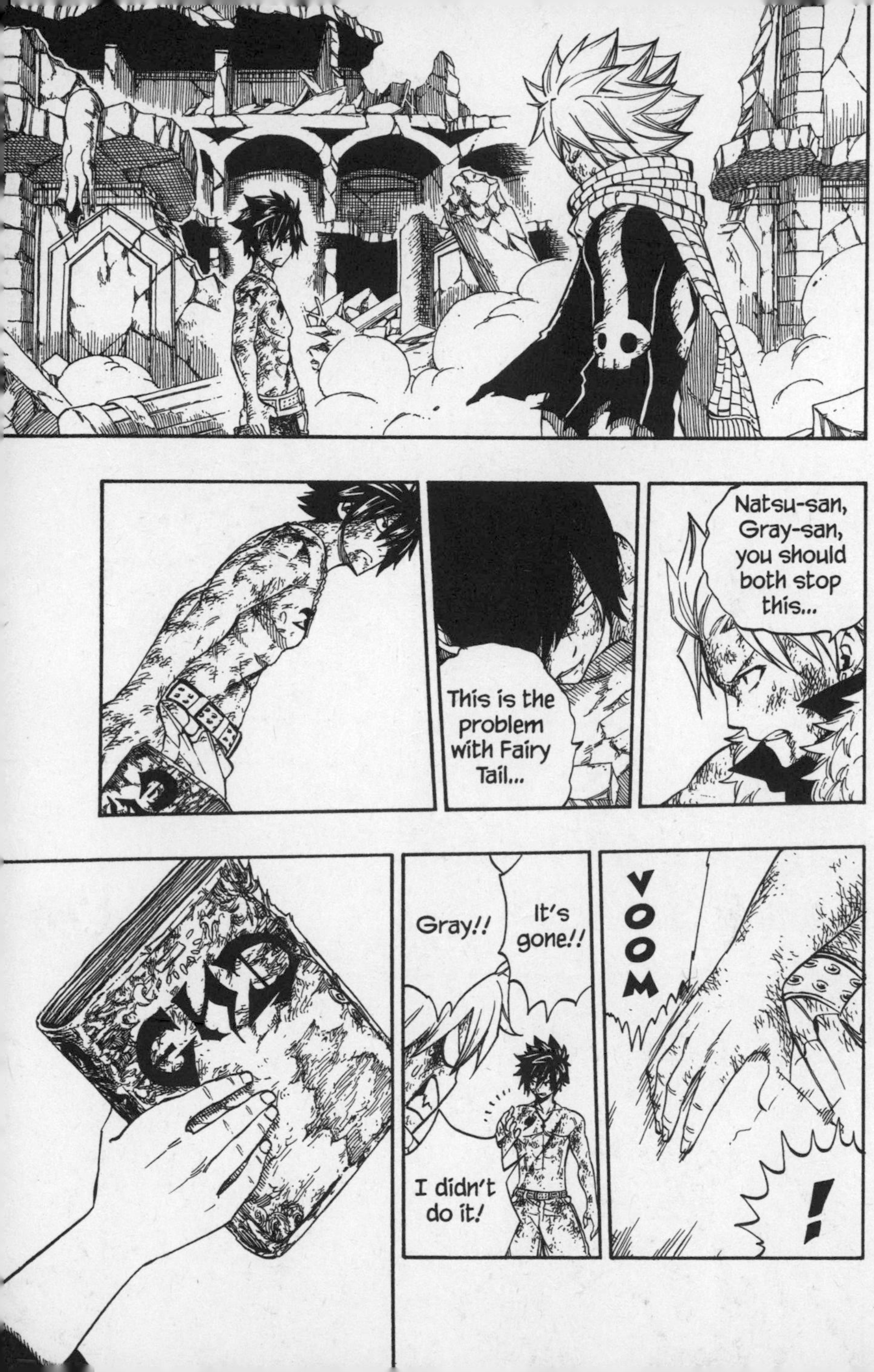
Natsu-san, Gray-san, you should both stop this...
This is the problem with Fairy Tail...
VOOM
!
It's gone!!
Gray!!
I didn't do it!

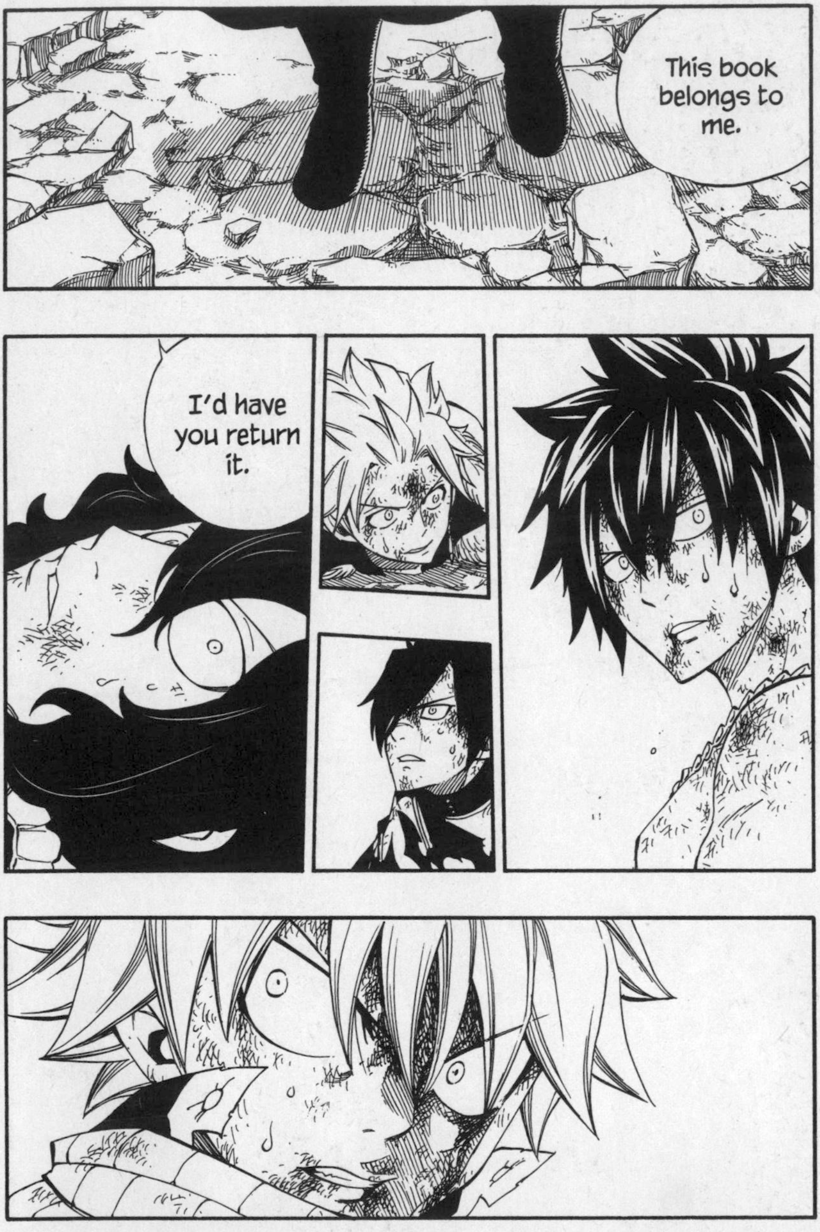
This book belongs to me.
I'd have you return it.

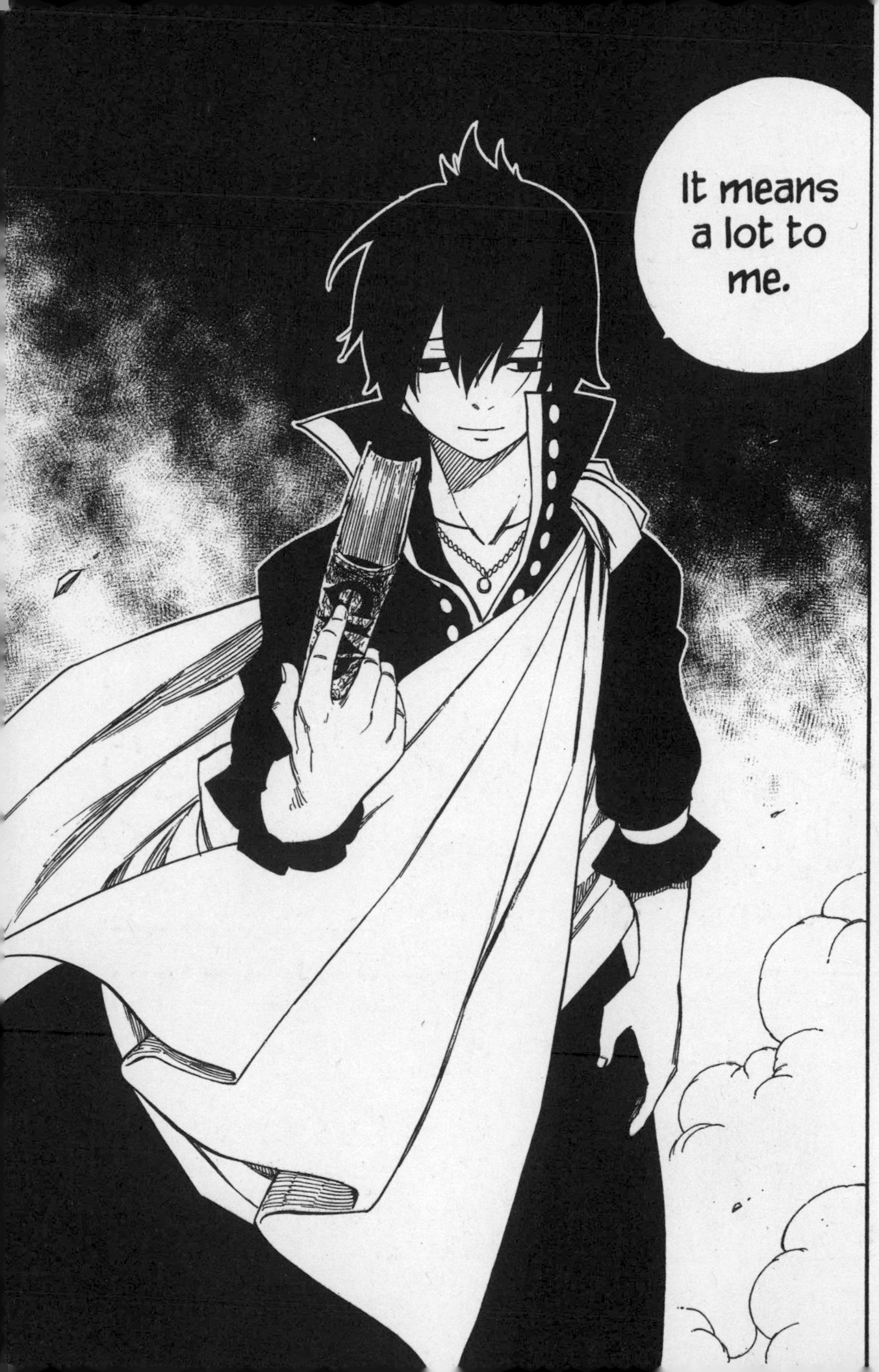
It means a lot to me.

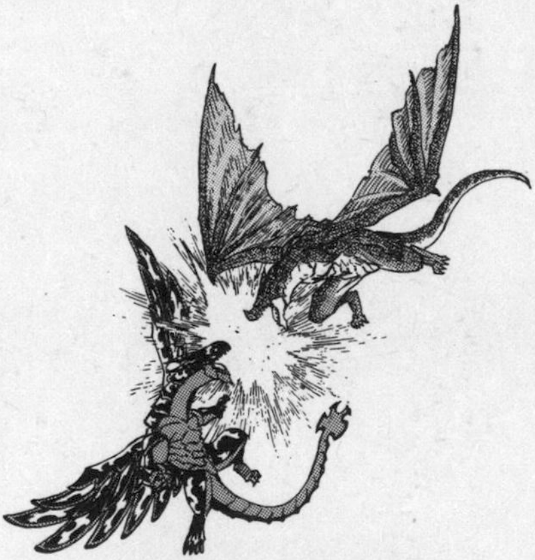

FAIRY TAIL

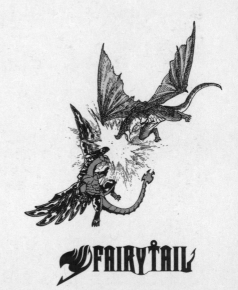

FAIRY TAIL
フェアリーテイル

Chapter 414: Drops of Fire

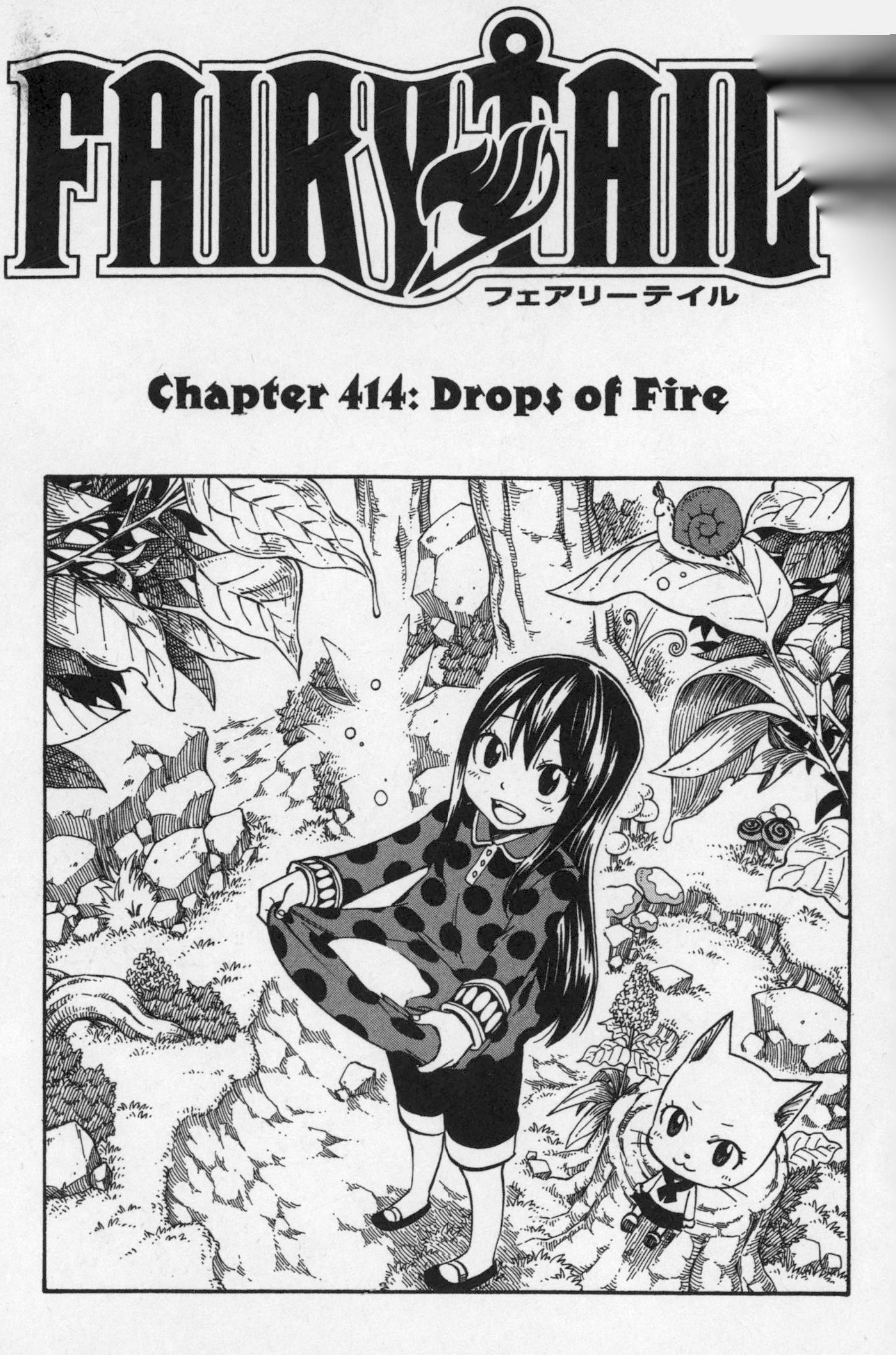

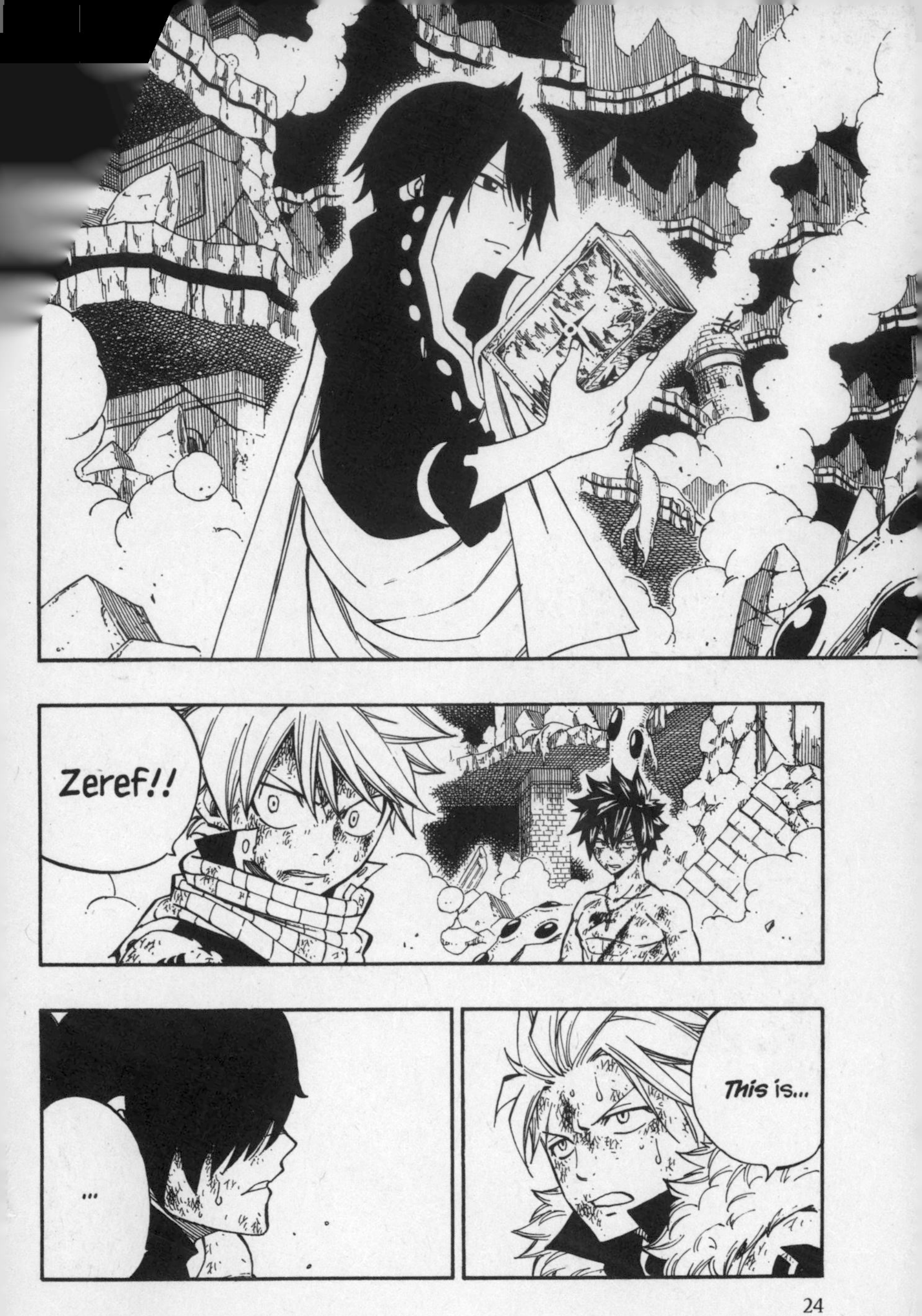
Zeref!!
This is...
...

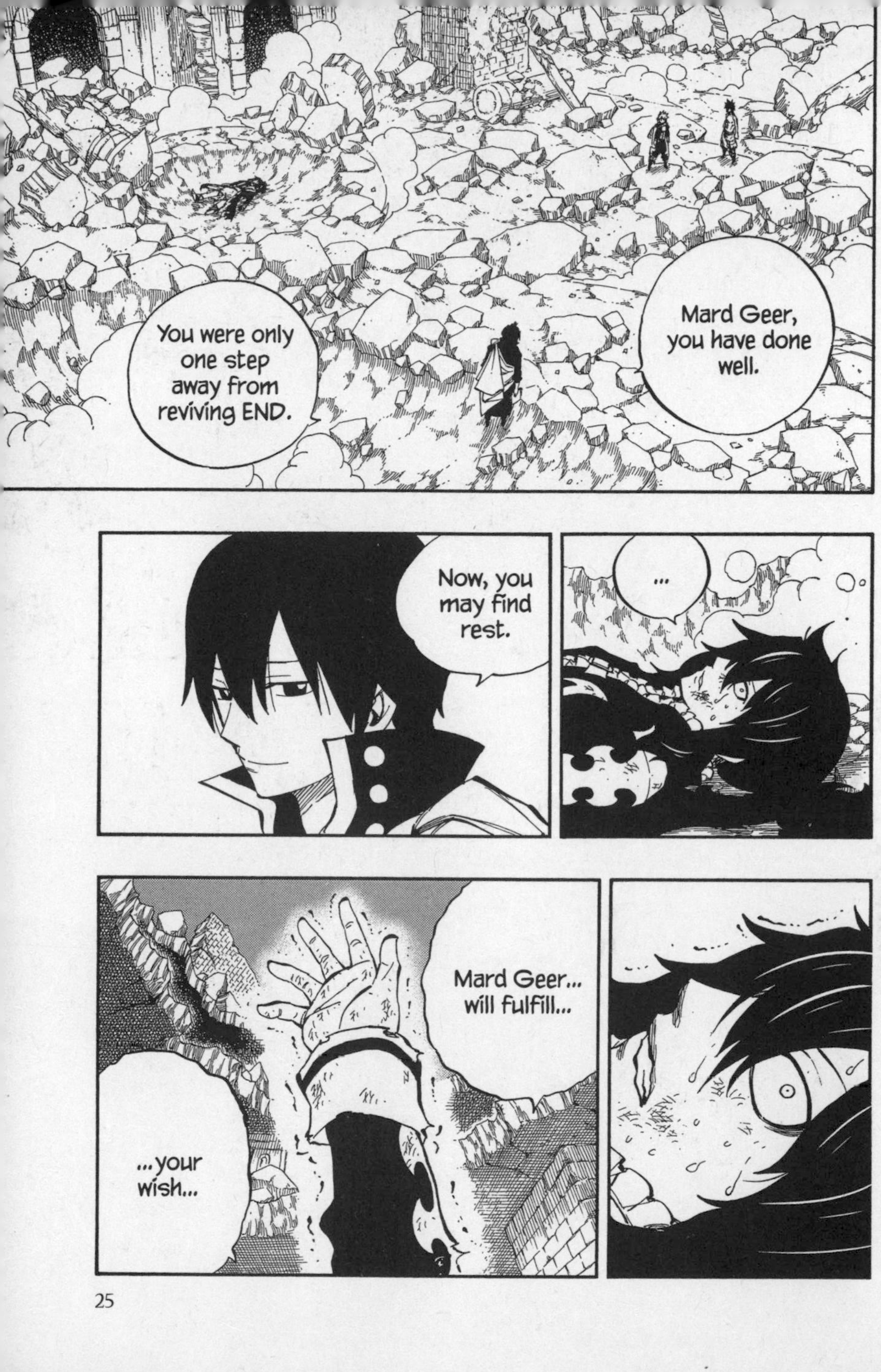

Mard Geer, you have done well.
You were only one step away from reviving END.
...
Now, you may find rest.
Mard Geer... will fulfill...
...your wish...

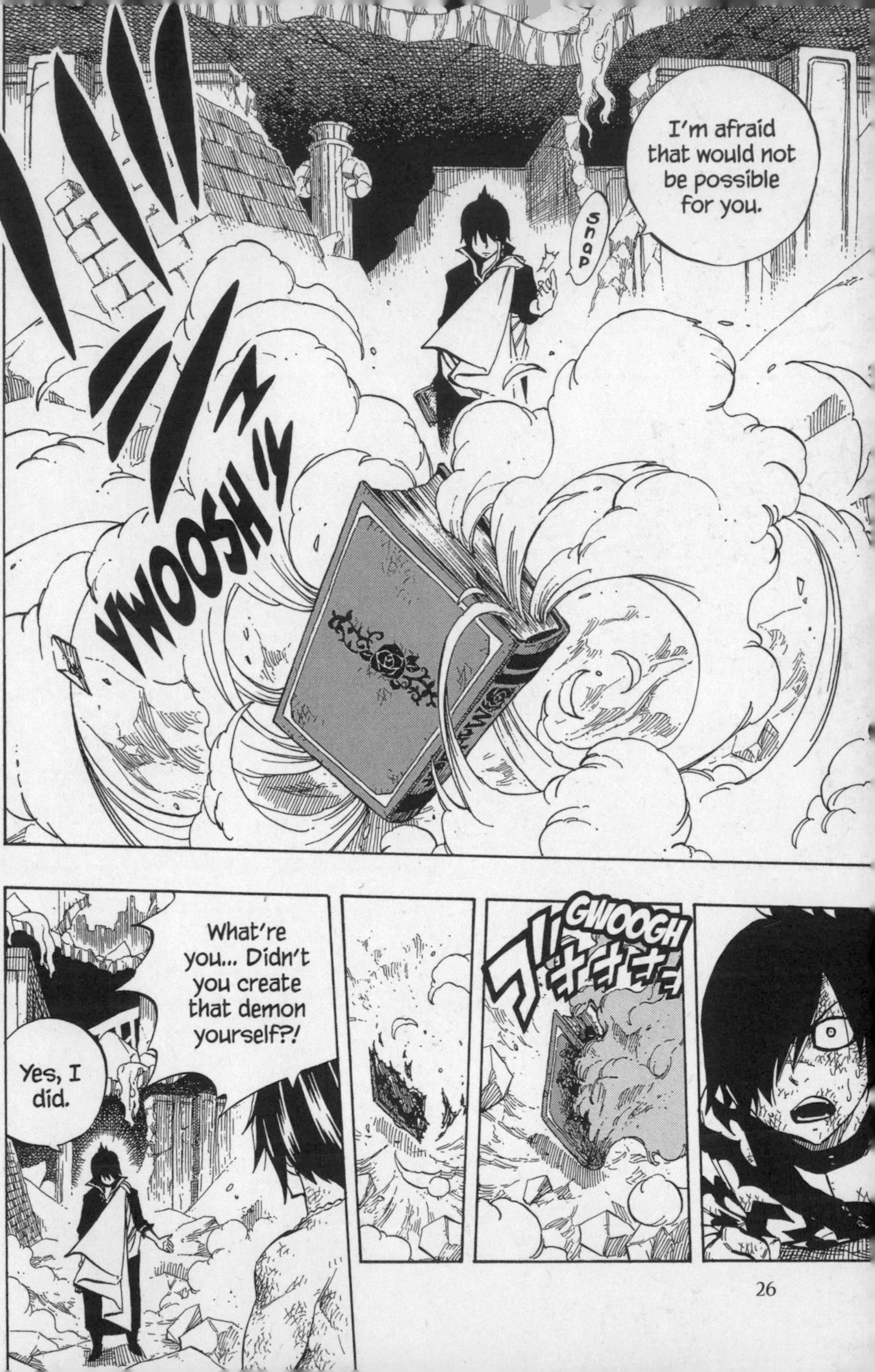
I'm afraid that would not be possible for you.
snap
VWOOSH
GWOOGH
What're you... Didn't you create that demon yourself?!
Yes, I did.

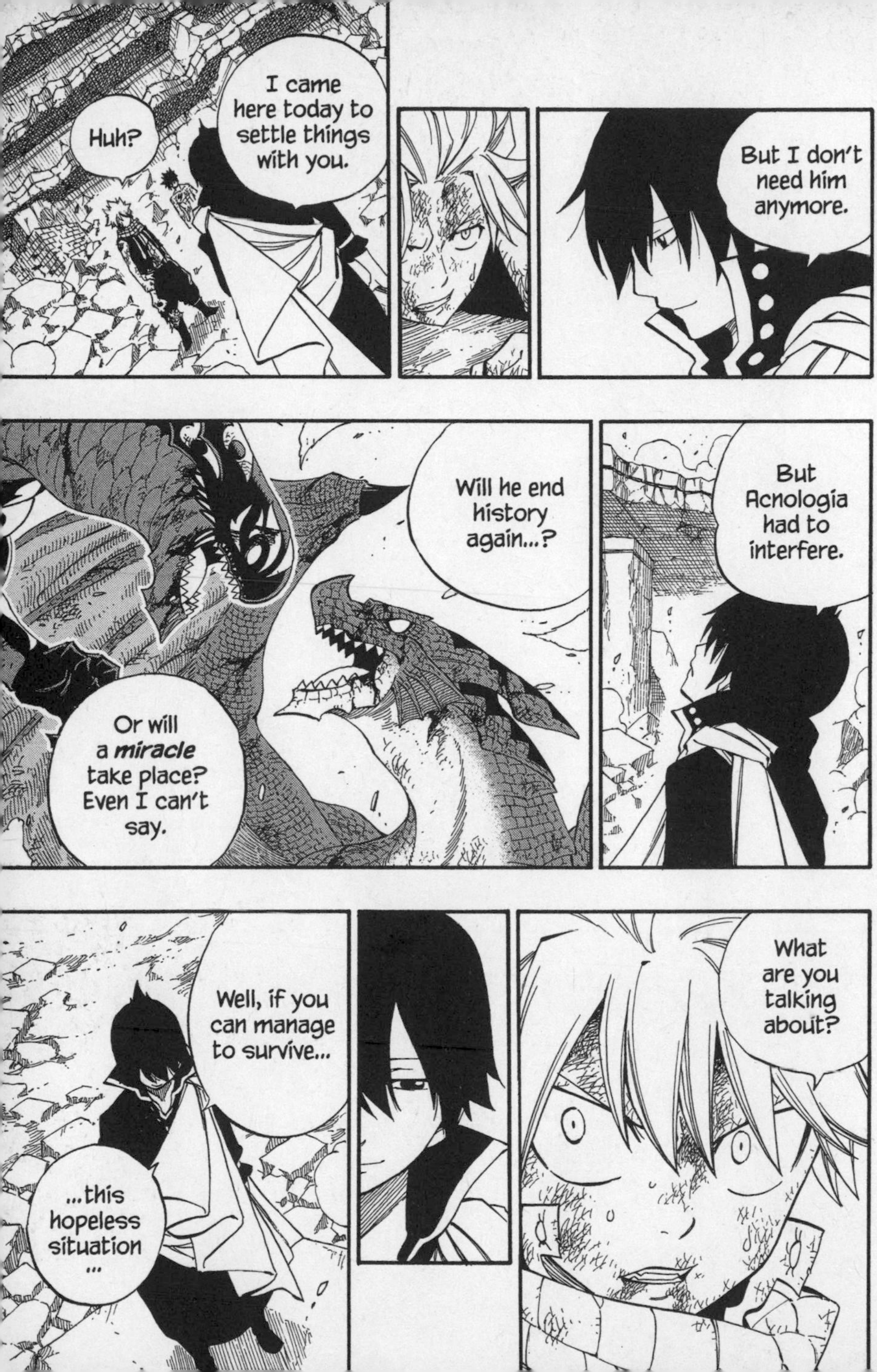
But I don't need him anymore.
I came here today to settle things with you.
Huh?
But Acnologia had to interfere.
Will he end history again...?
Or will a *miracle* take place? Even I can't say.
What are you talking about?
Well, if you can manage to survive...
...this hopeless situation ...

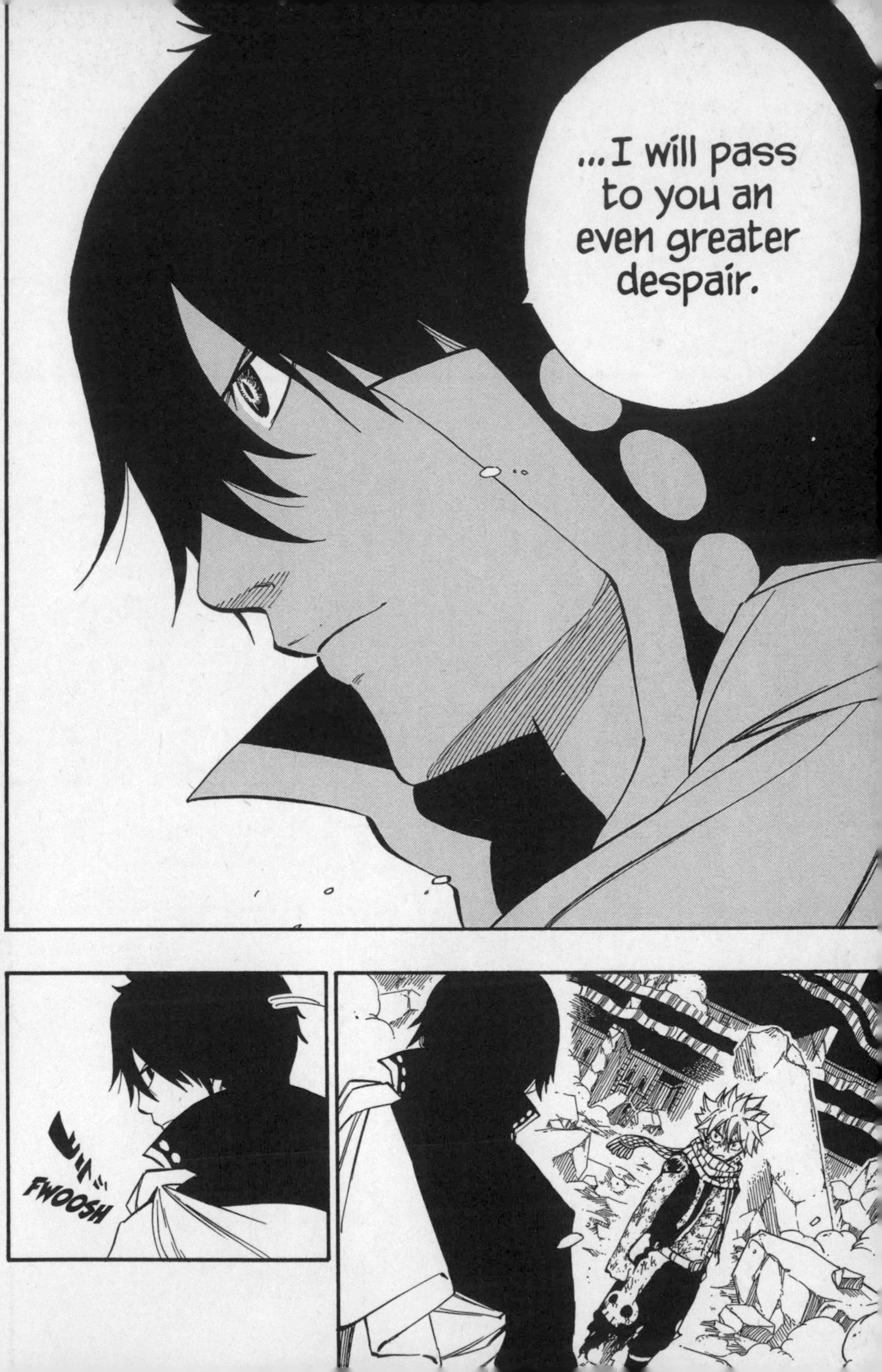
...I will pass to you an even greater despair.
FWOOSH

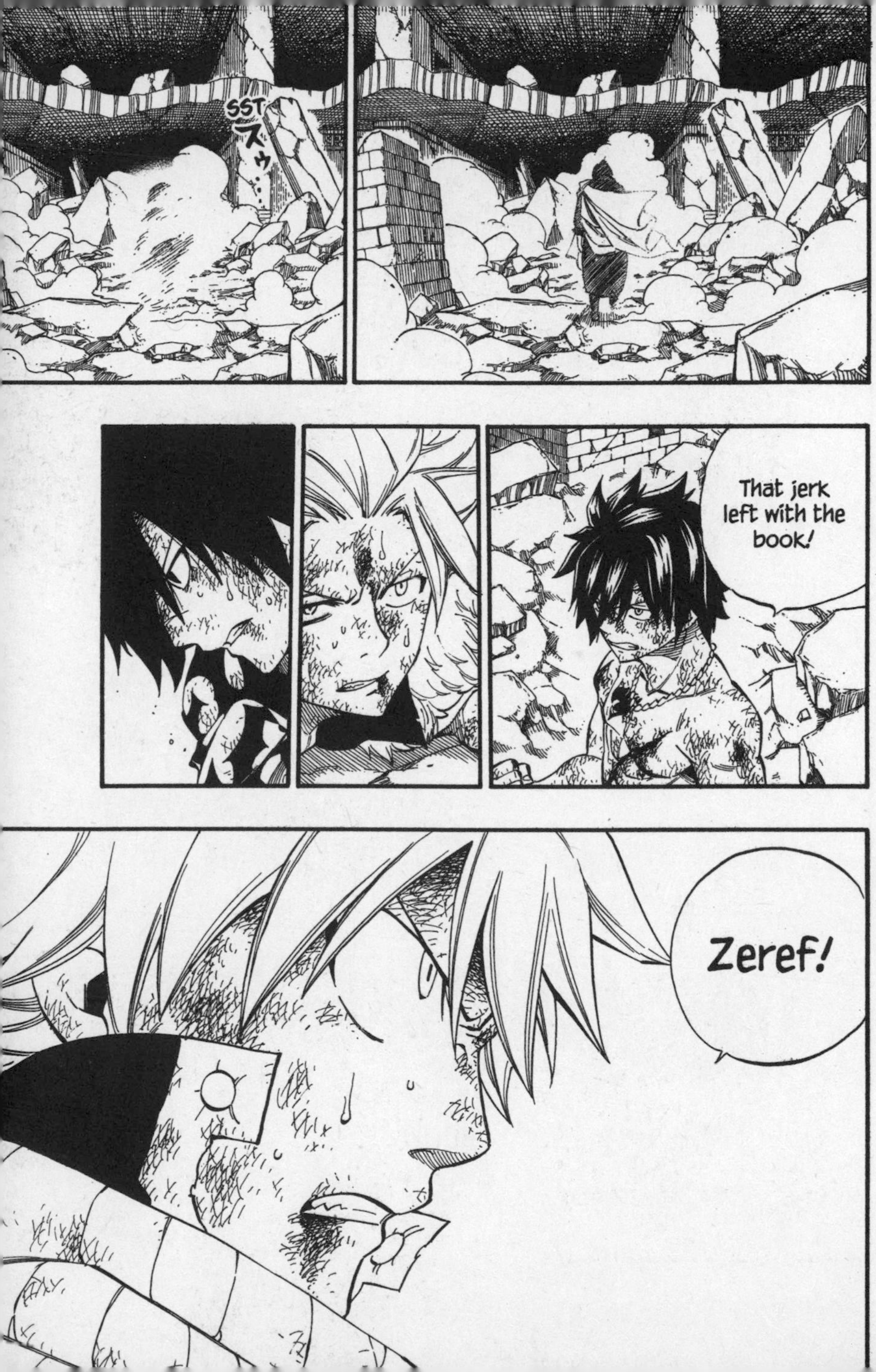
SST スゥ…
That jerk left with the book!
Zeref!

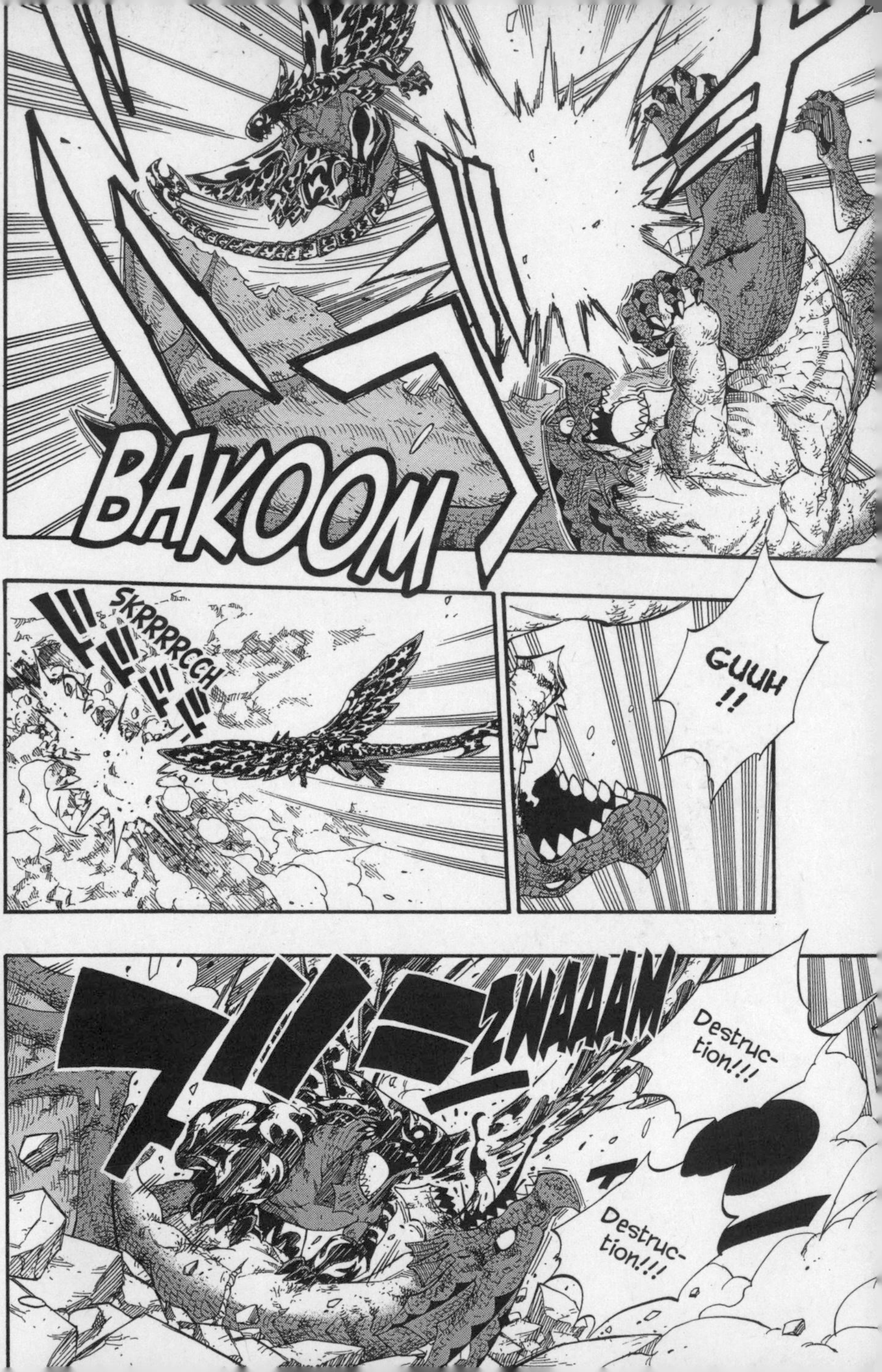
BAKOOM
GUUH!!
SKRRRRRCCH
ZWAAAM
Destruc-tion!!!
Destruc-tion!!!

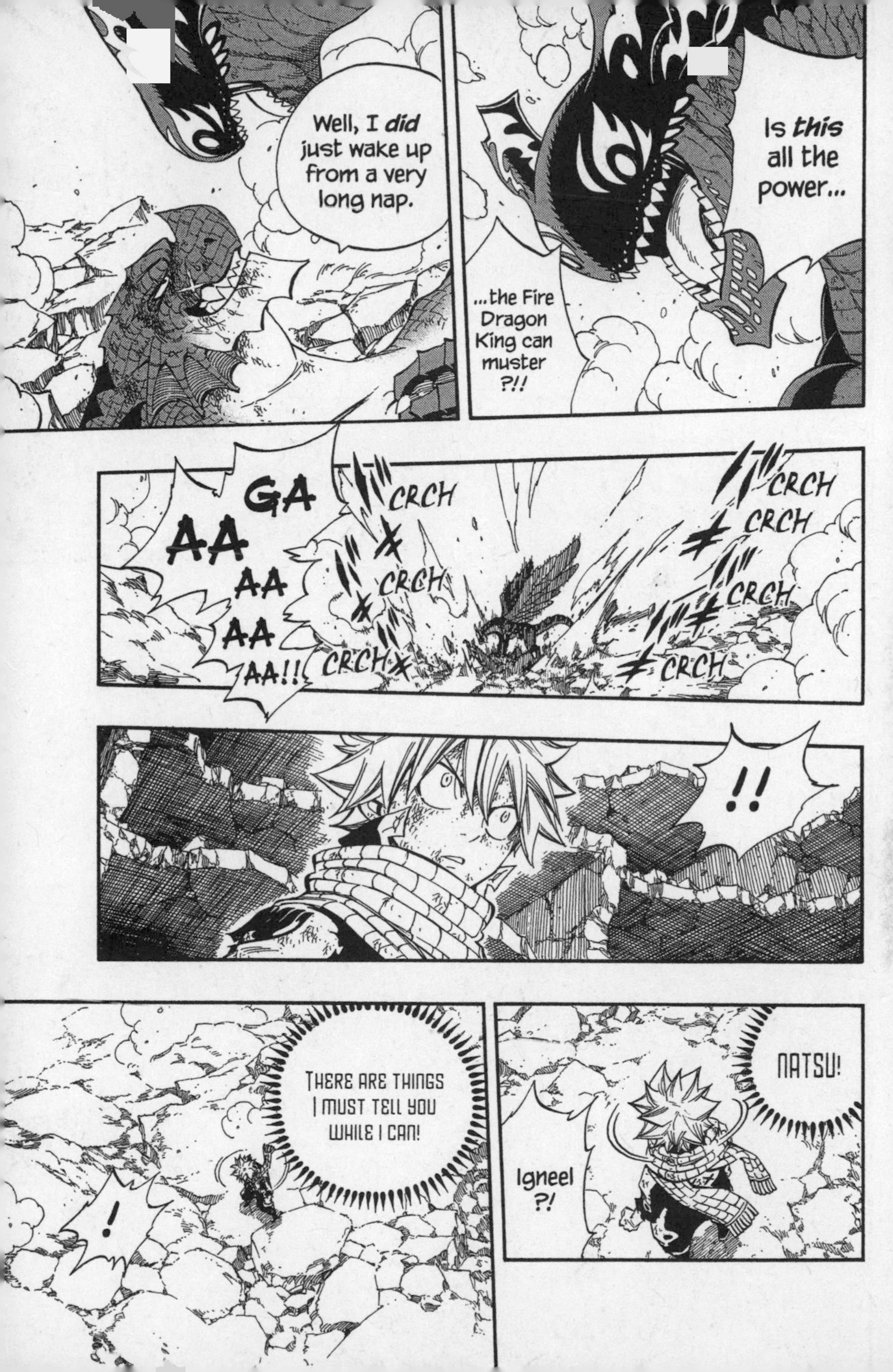

Is *this* all the power...
...the Fire Dragon King can muster ?!!
Well, I *did* just wake up from a very long nap.
CRCH
CRCH
CRCH
CRCH
GA AA AA AA AA!!!
CRCH
CRCH
CRCH
!!
NATSU!
Igneel ?!
There are things I must tell you while I can!
!

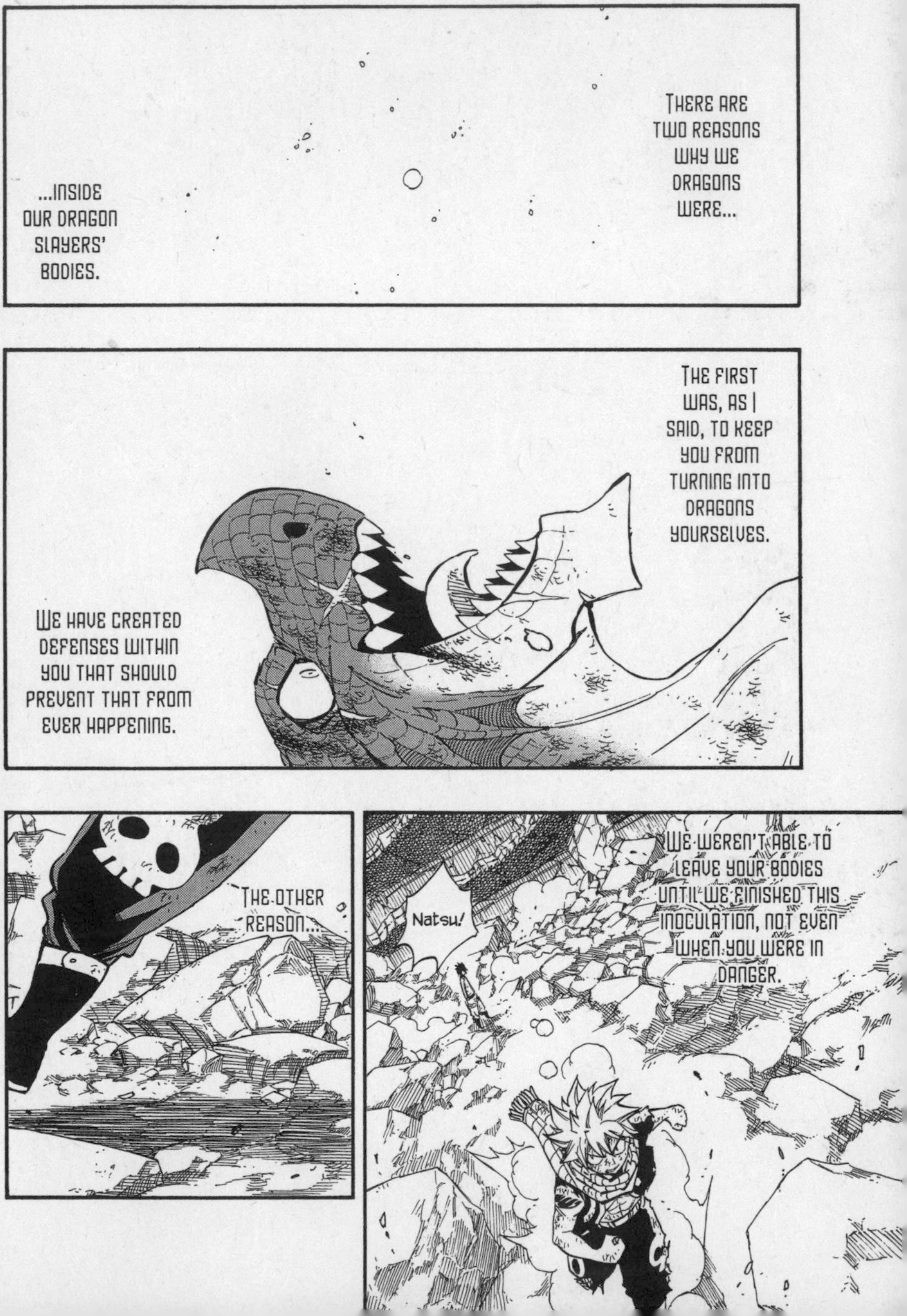
THERE ARE TWO REASONS WHY WE DRAGONS WERE...
...INSIDE OUR DRAGON SLAYERS' BODIES.
THE FIRST WAS, AS I SAID, TO KEEP YOU FROM TURNING INTO DRAGONS YOURSELVES.
WE HAVE CREATED DEFENSES WITHIN YOU THAT SHOULD PREVENT THAT FROM EVER HAPPENING.
WE WEREN'T ABLE TO LEAVE YOUR BODIES UNTIL WE FINISHED THIS INOCULATION, NOT EVEN WHEN YOU WERE IN DANGER.
Natsu!
THE OTHER REASON...

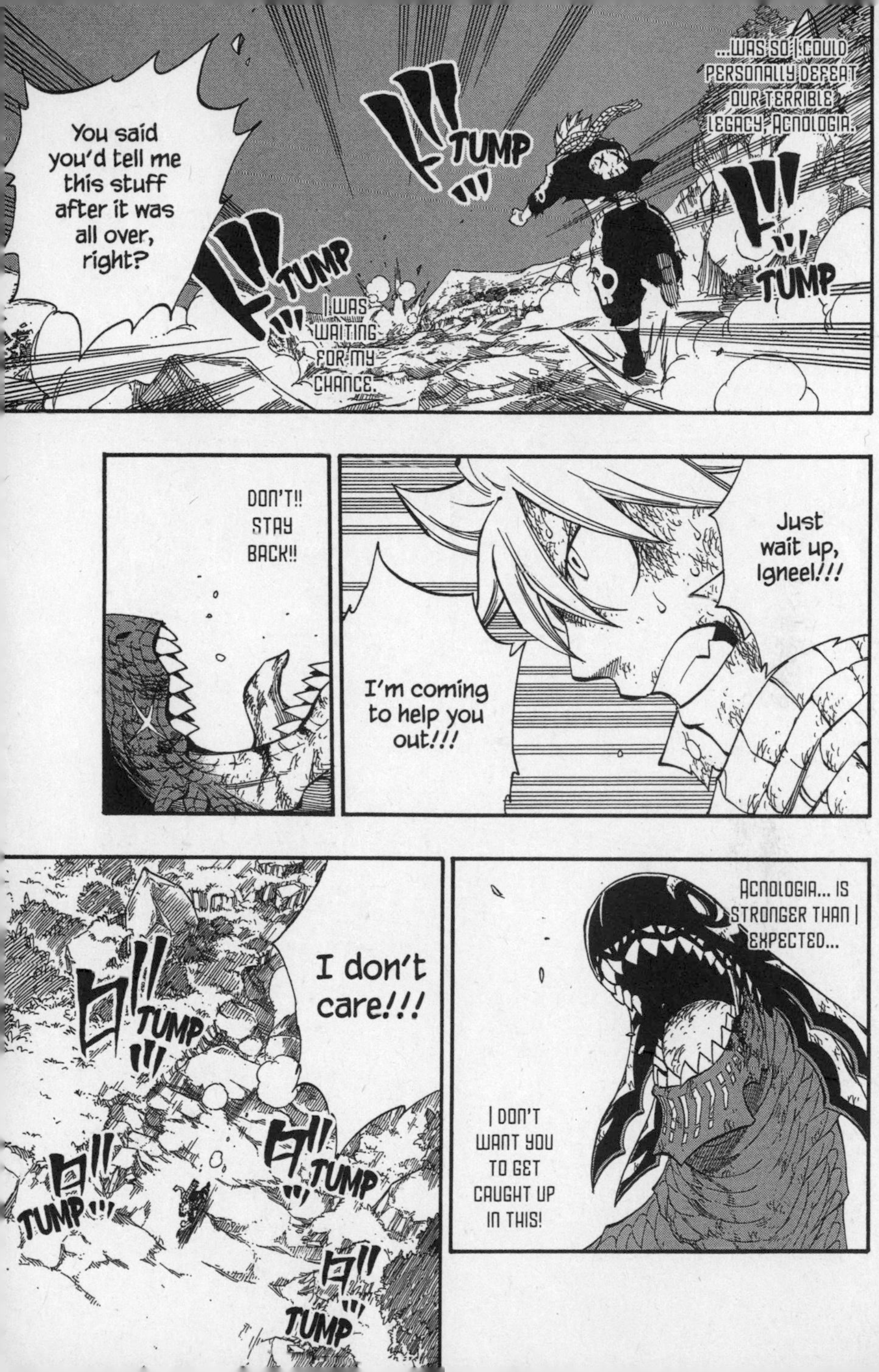

...WAS SO I COULD PERSONALLY DEFEAT OUR TERRIBLE LEGACY, ACNOLOGIA.
TUMP
TUMP
You said you'd tell me this stuff after it was all over, right?
TUMP
I WAS WAITING FOR MY CHANCE.
Just wait up, Igneel!!!
I'm coming to help you out!!!
DON'T!! STAY BACK!!
ACNOLOGIA... IS STRONGER THAN I EXPECTED...
I DON'T WANT YOU TO GET CAUGHT UP IN THIS!
I don't care!!!
TUMP
TUMP
TUMP
TUMP

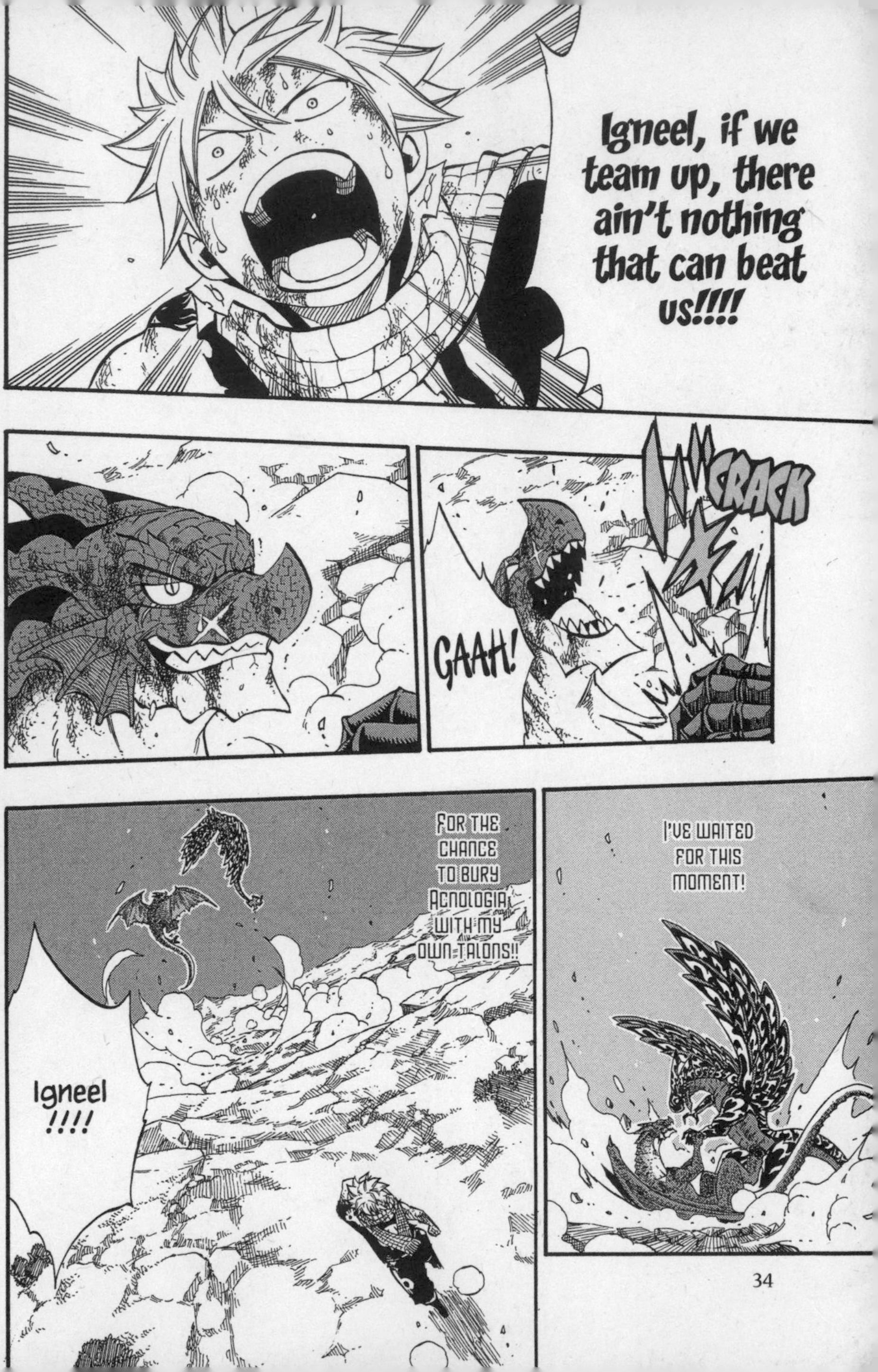

Igneel, if we team up, there ain't nothing that can beat us!!!!
CRACK
GAAH!
I'VE WAITED FOR THIS MOMENT!
FOR THE CHANCE TO BURY ACNOLOGIA WITH MY OWN TALONS!!
Igneel !!!!

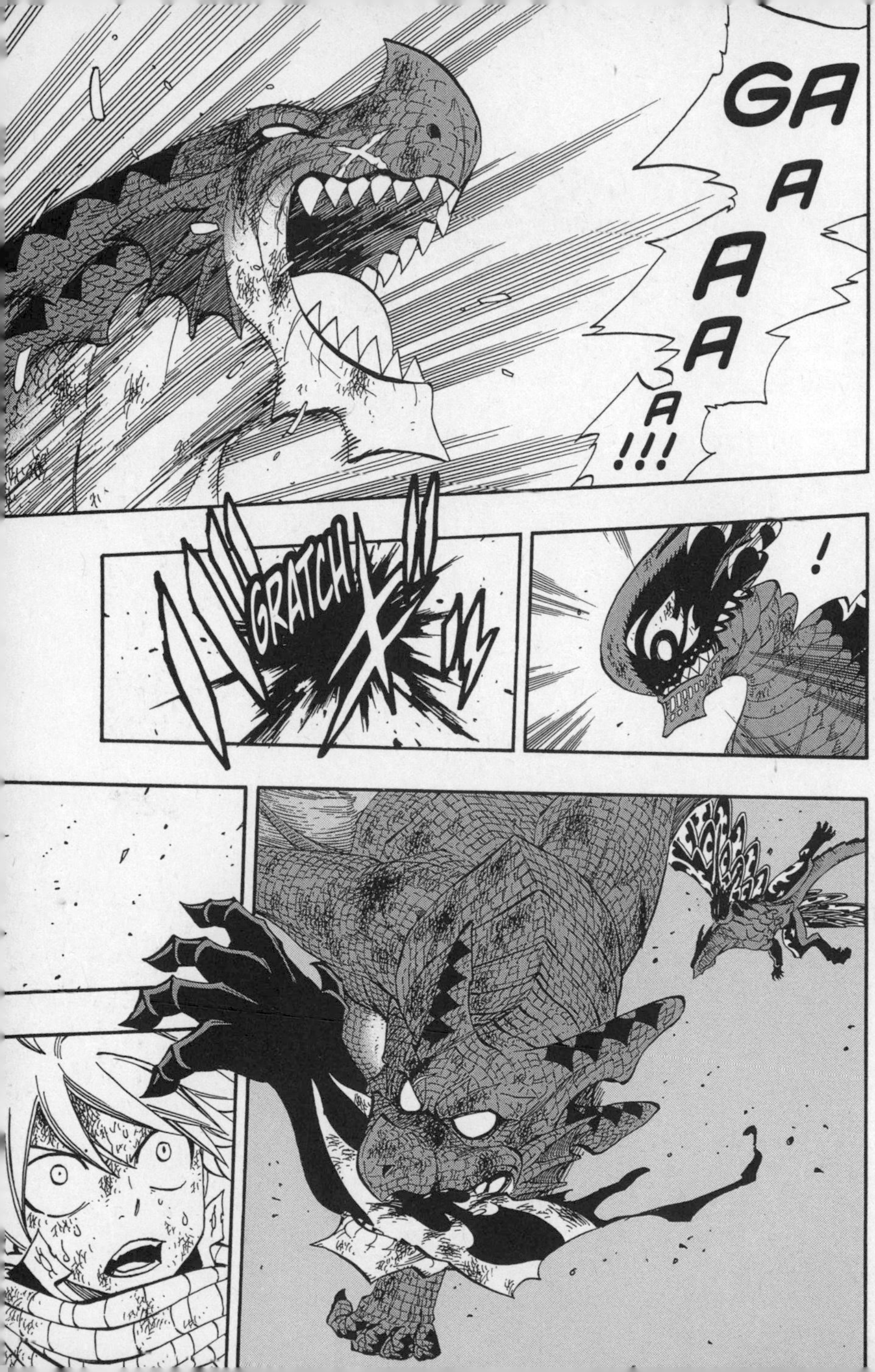
GAAAAA!!!
!
GRATCH

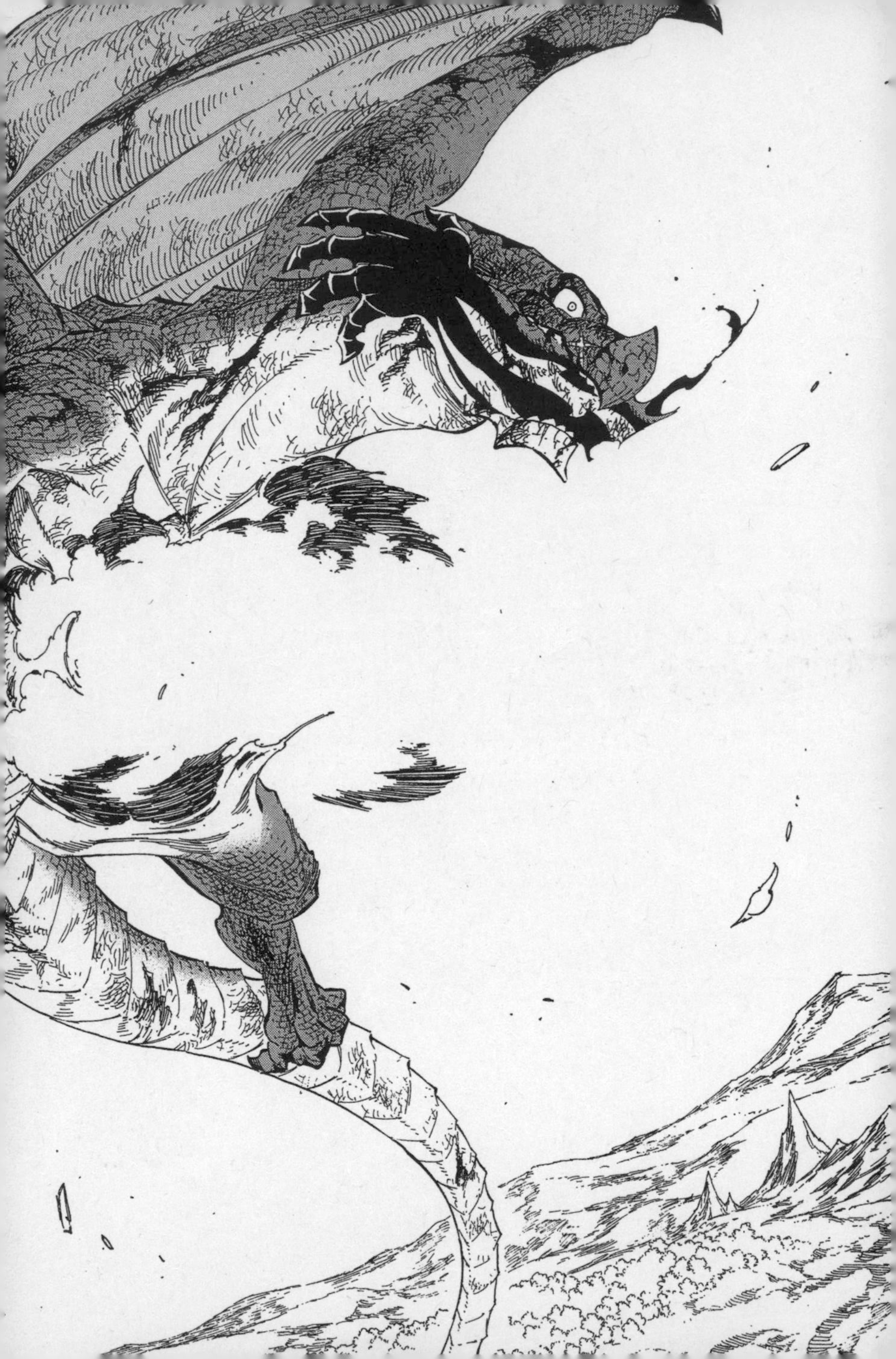

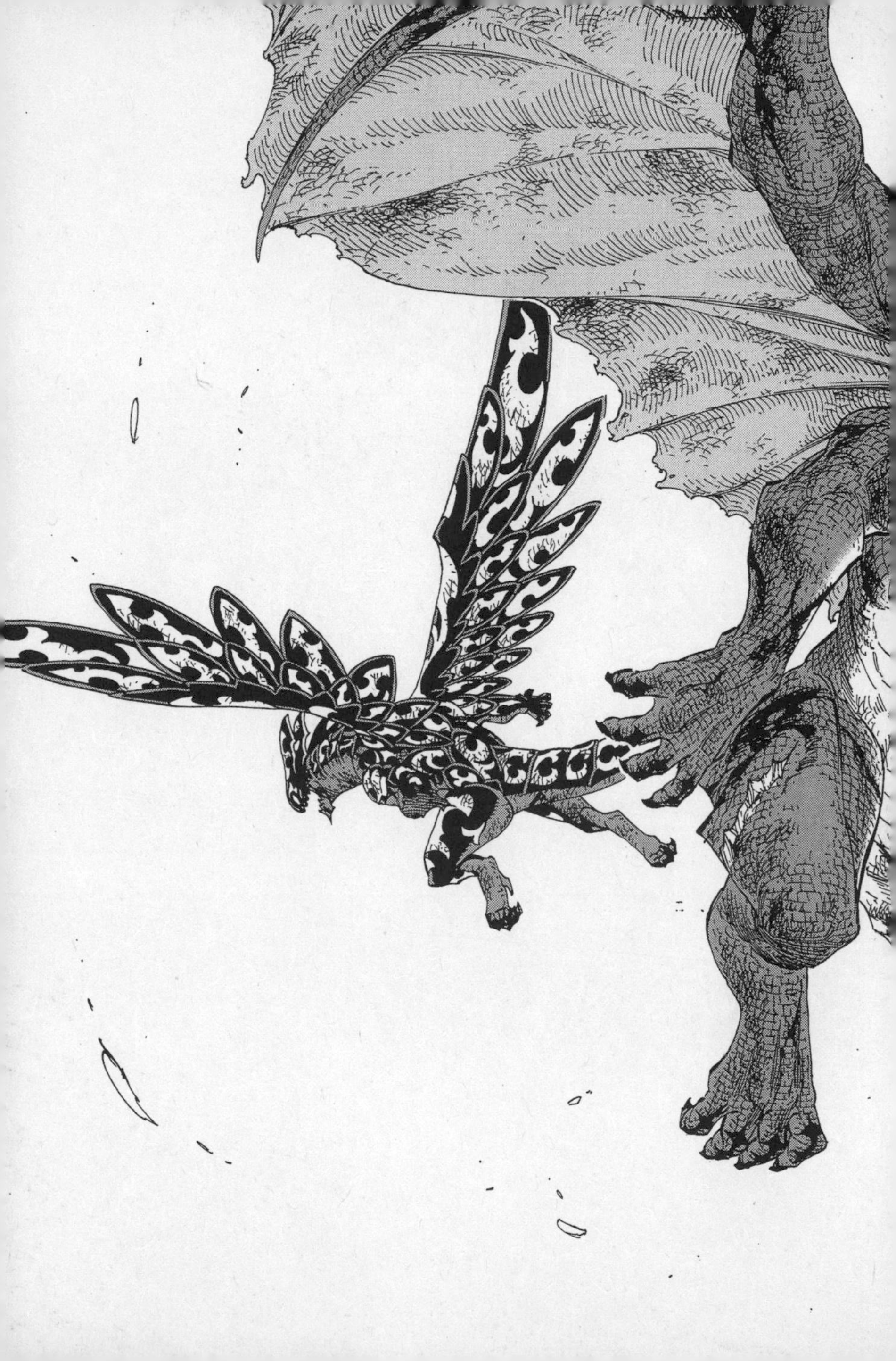

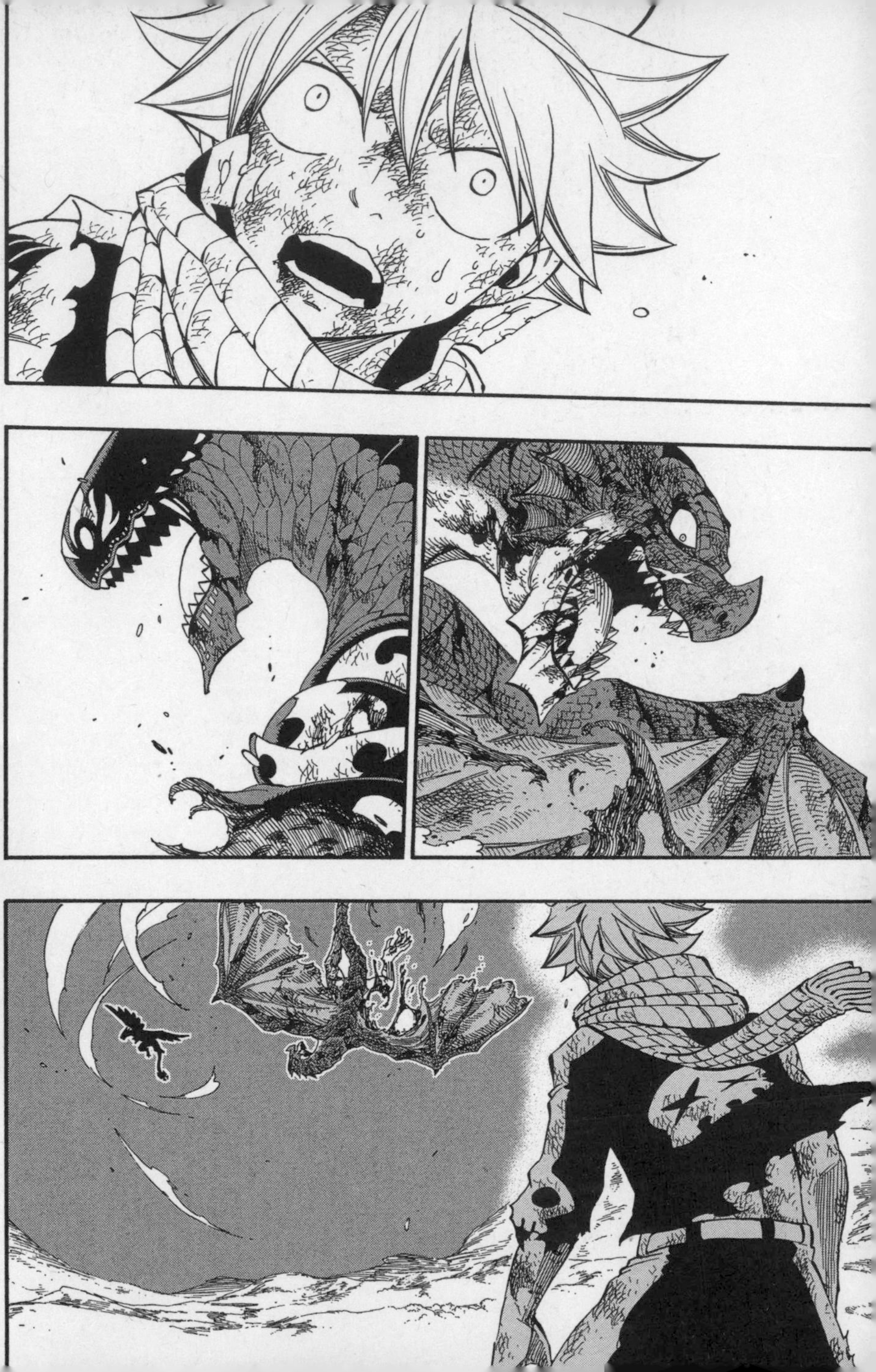

Natsu...

I was watching over you all along, as you grew up!

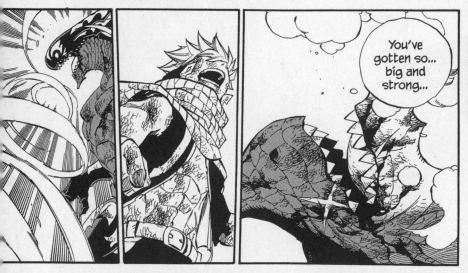

You've gotten so... big and strong...

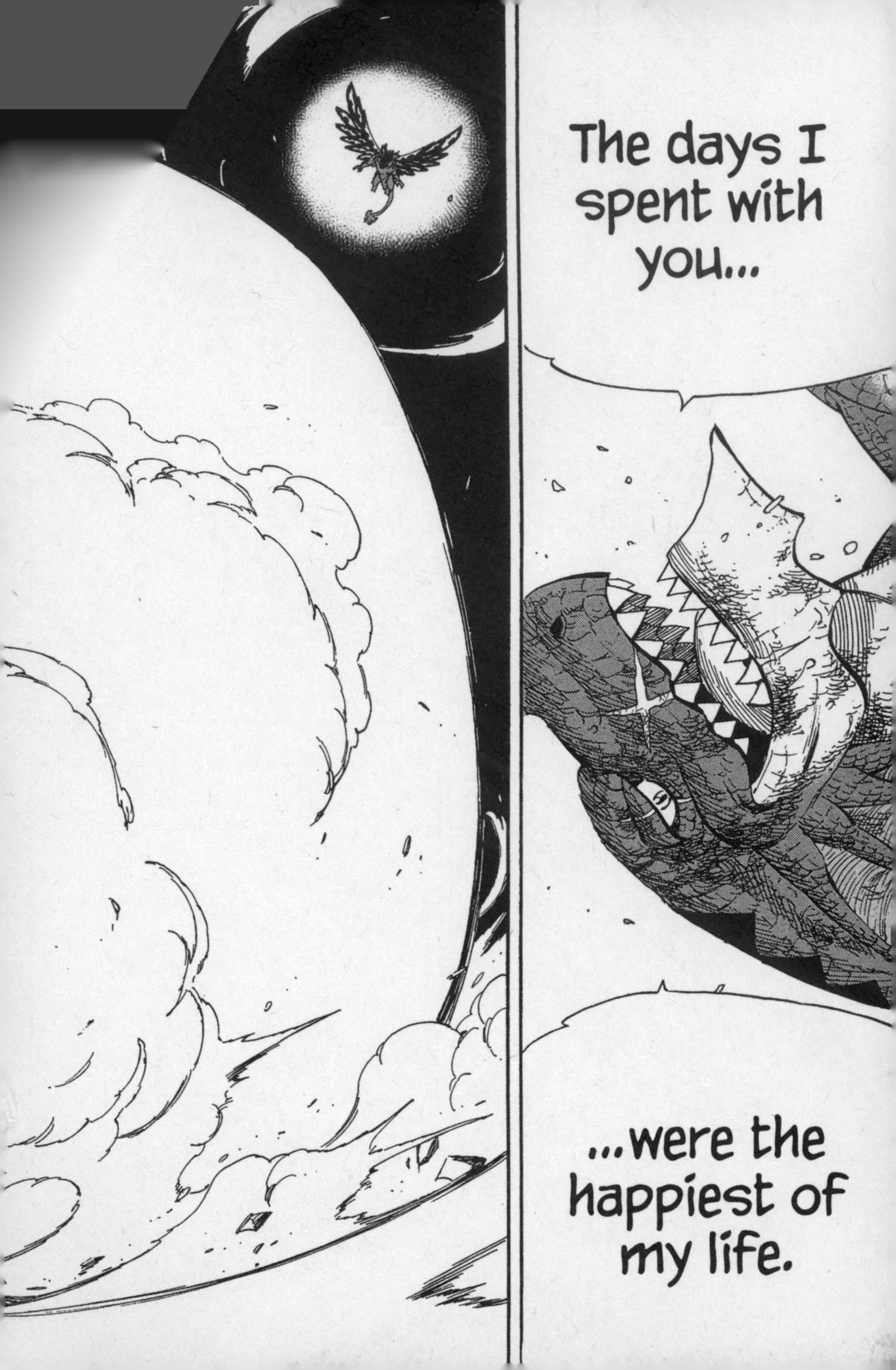
The days I spent with you...
...were the happiest of my life.

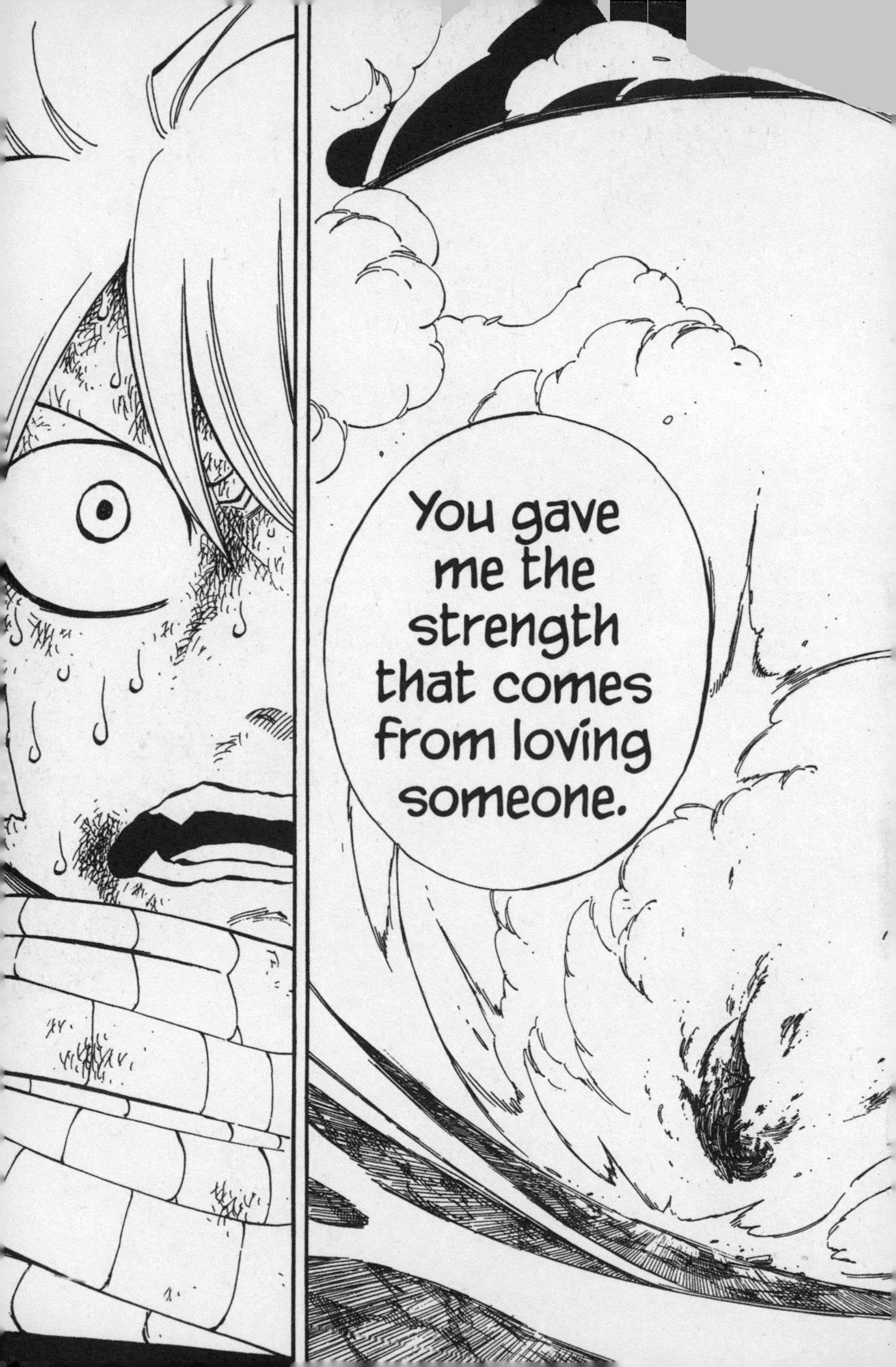
You gave me the strength that comes from loving someone.

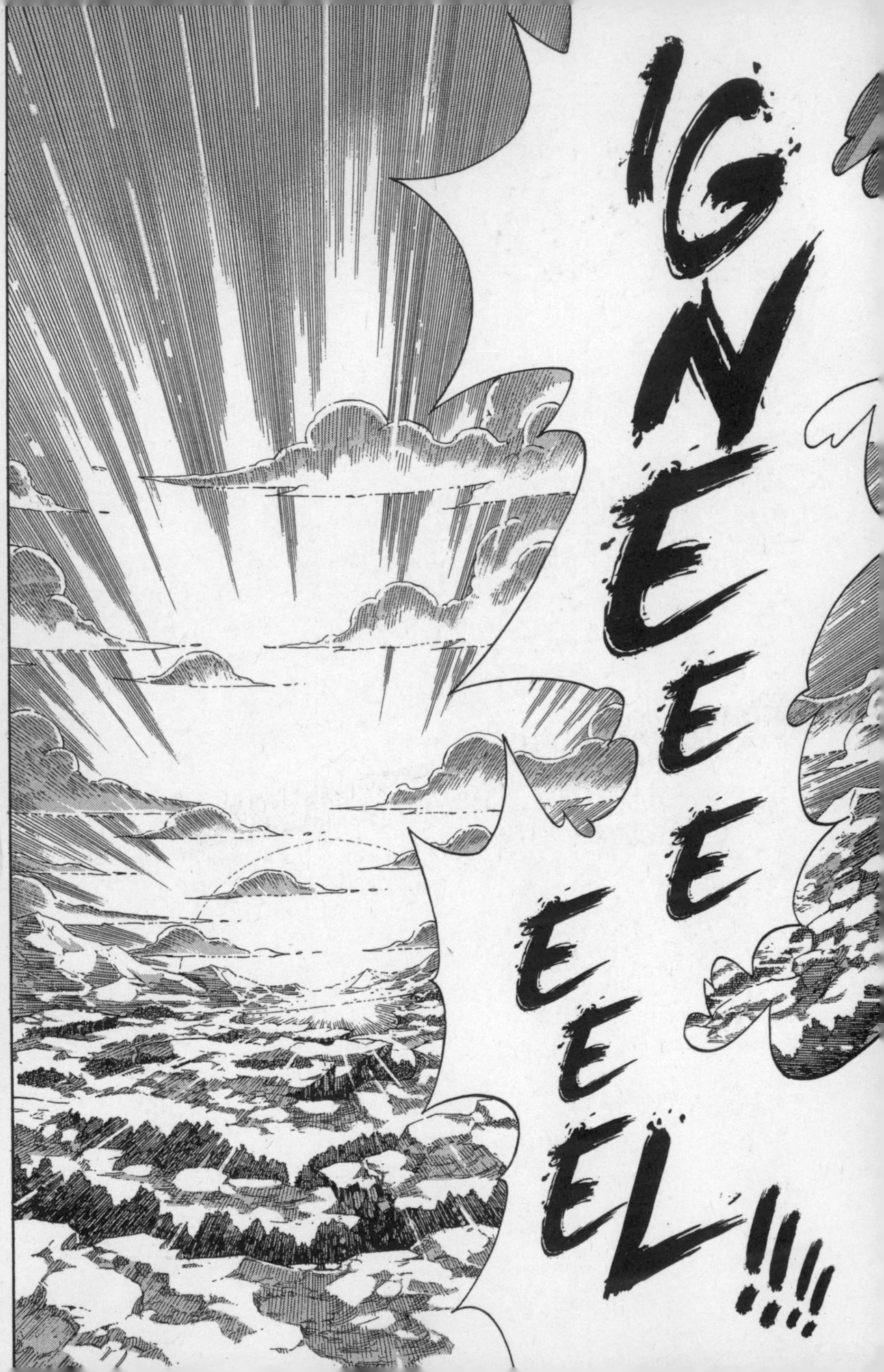
IGNEEEEEEL!!!!

Chapter 415: That Is the Power of Life

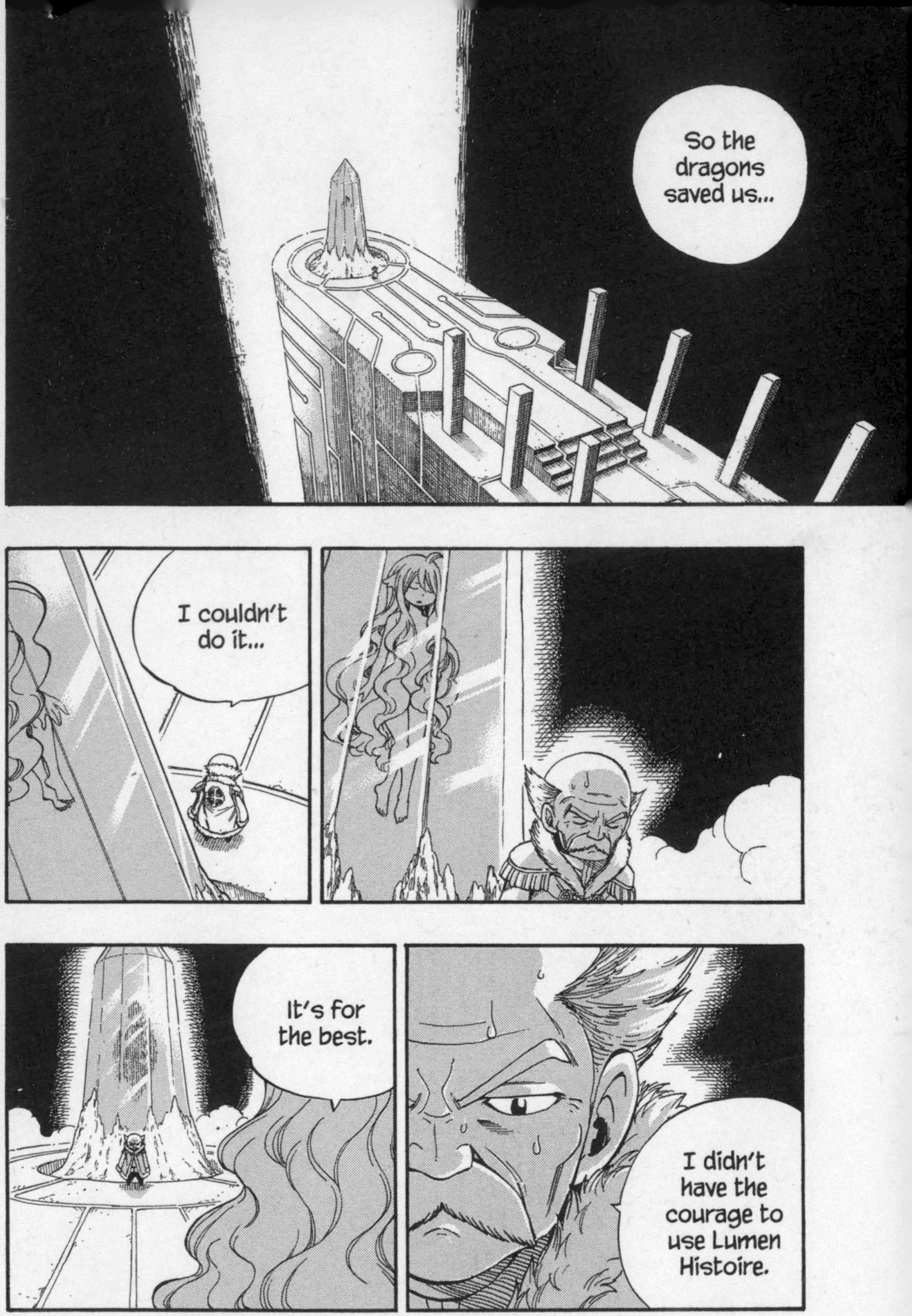
So the dragons saved us...
I couldn't do it...
I didn't have the courage to use Lumen Histoire.
It's for the best.

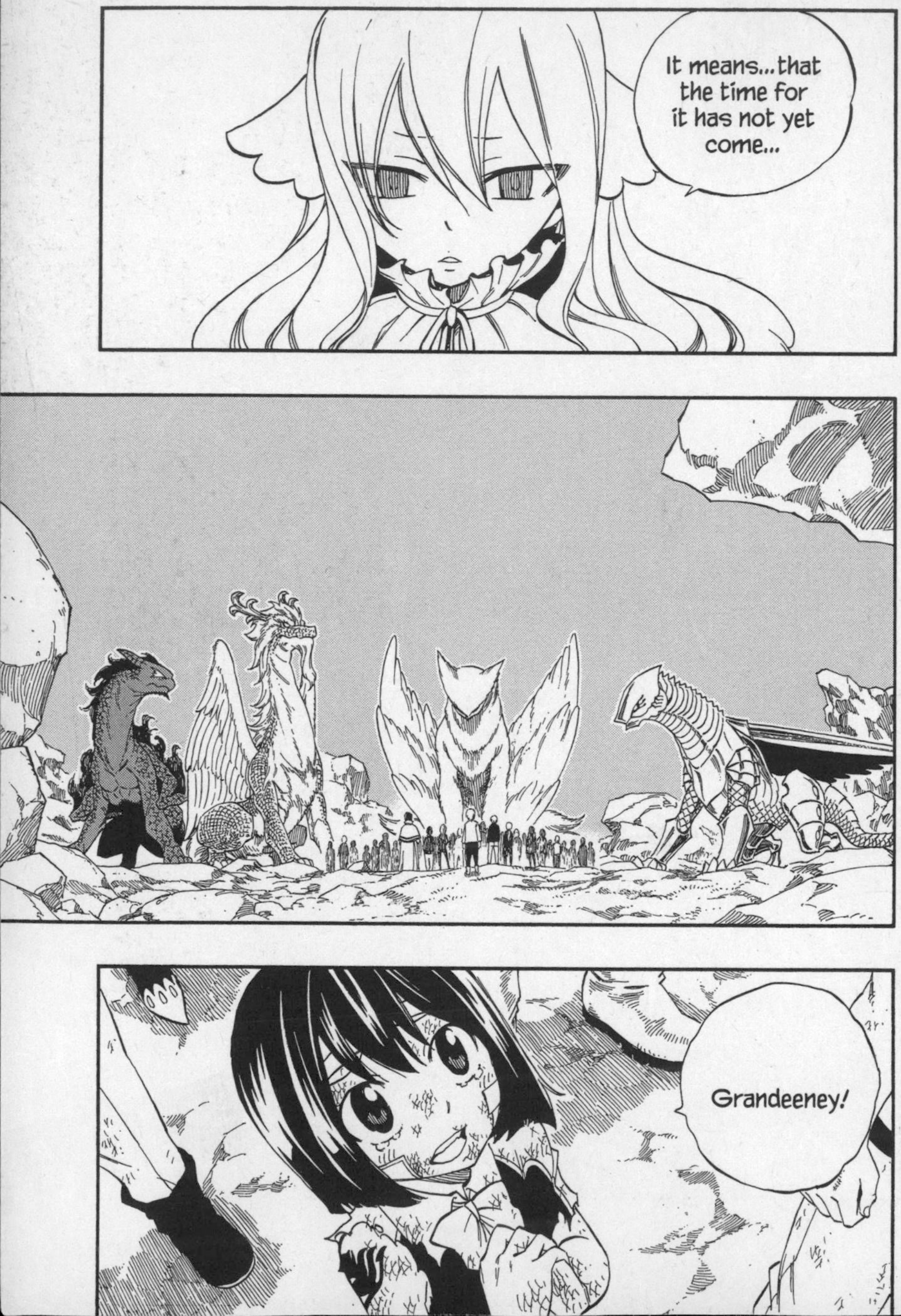
It means...that the time for it has not yet come...
Grandeeney!

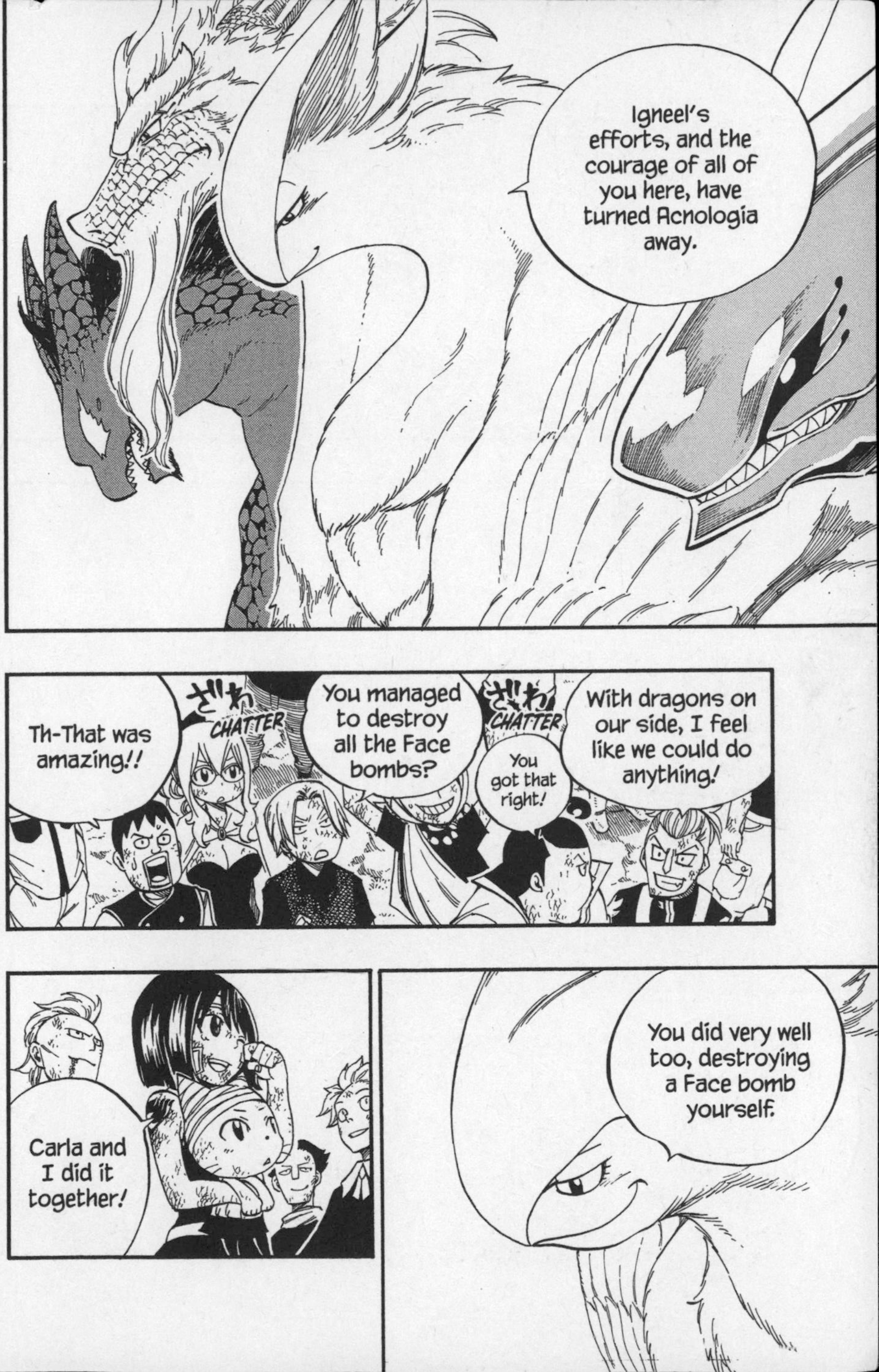
Igneel's efforts, and the courage of all of you here, have turned Acnologia away.
With dragons on our side, I feel like we could do anything!
You got that right!
CHATTER
You managed to destroy all the Face bombs?
CHATTER
Th-That was amazing!!
You did very well too, destroying a Face bomb yourself.
Carla and I did it together!

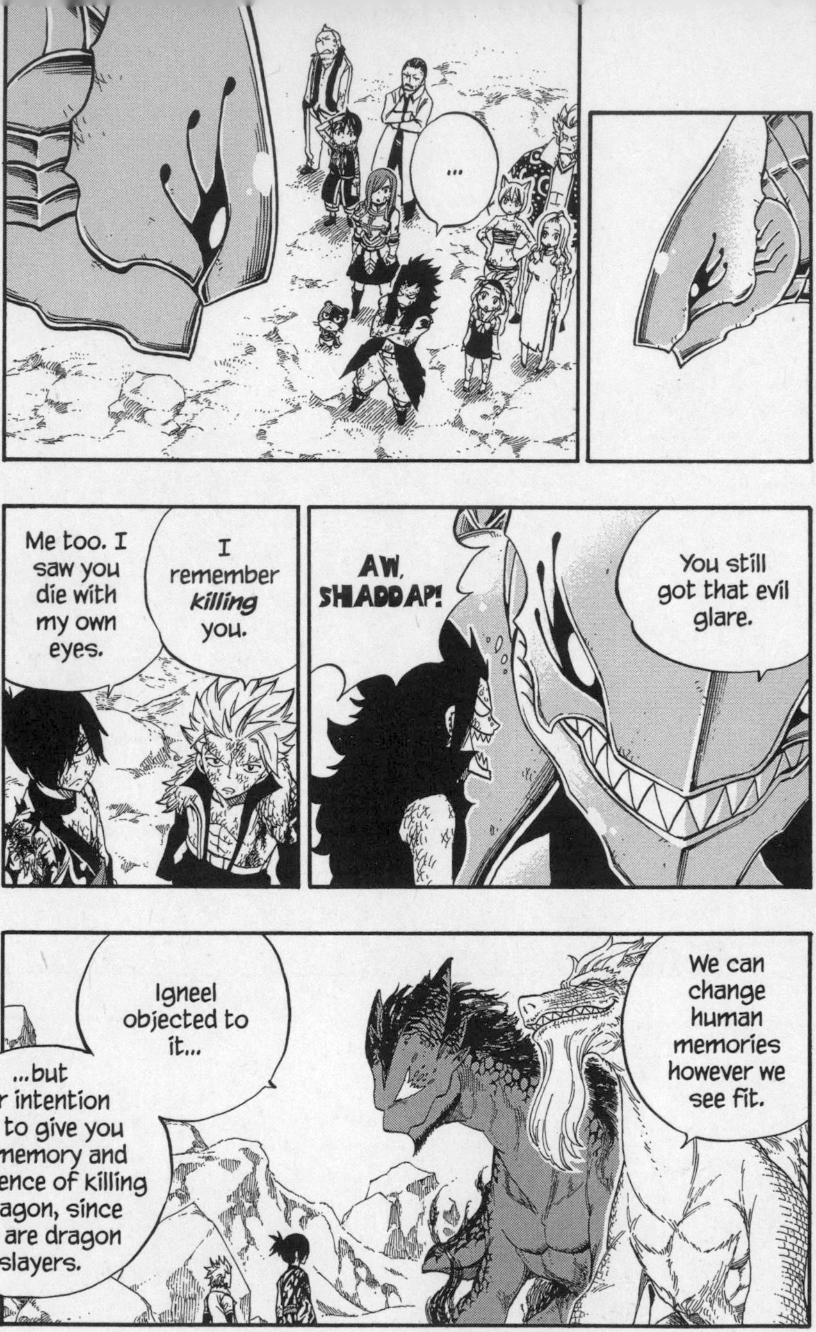
...
You still got that evil glare.
AW, SHADDAP!
I remember *killing* you.
Me too. I saw you die with my own eyes.
We can change human memories however we see fit.
Igneel objected to it...
...but our intention was to give you the memory and experience of killing a dragon, since you are dragon slayers.

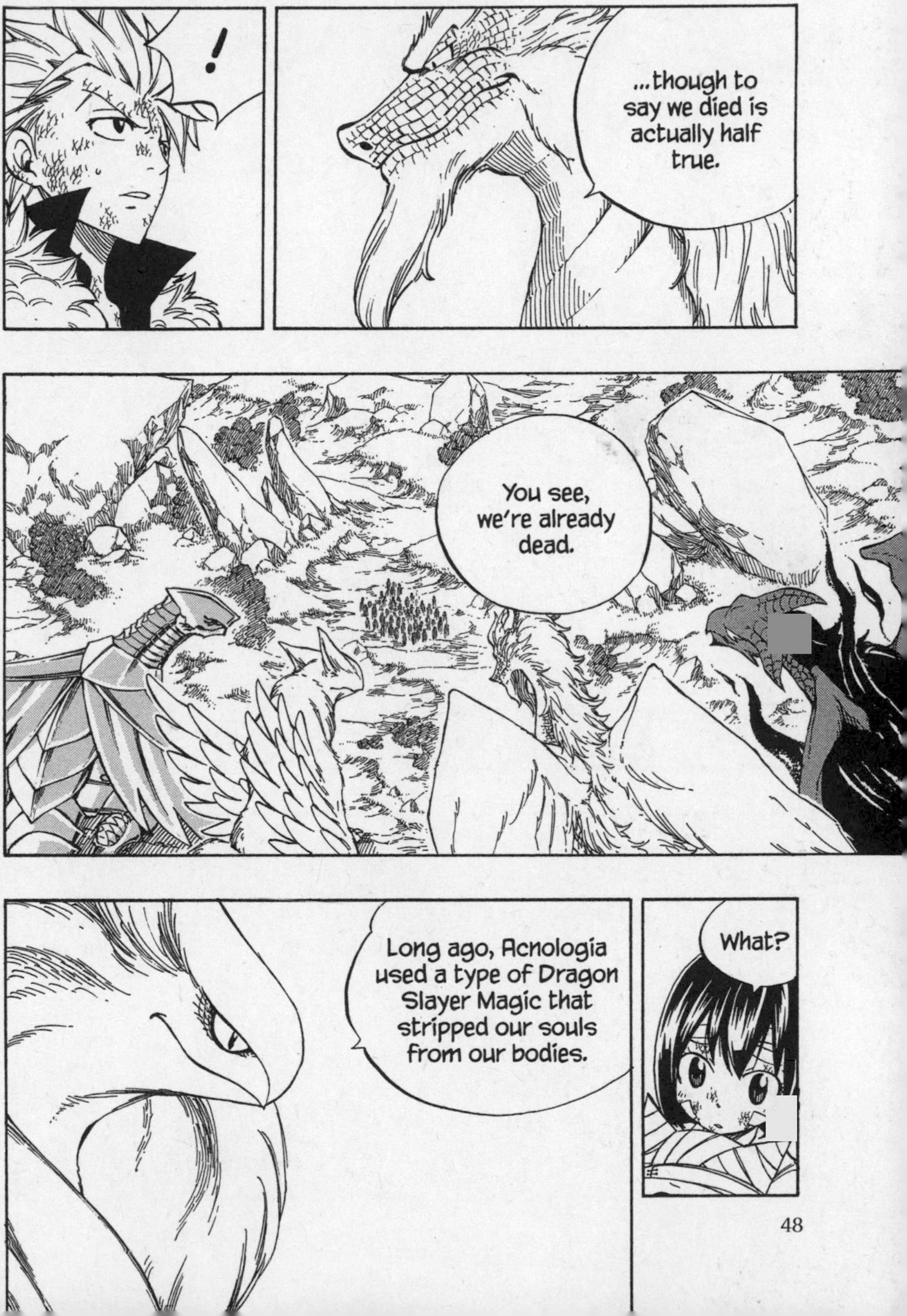
...though to say we died is actually half true.
!
You see, we're already dead.
What?
Long ago, Acnologia used a type of Dragon Slayer Magic that stripped our souls from our bodies.

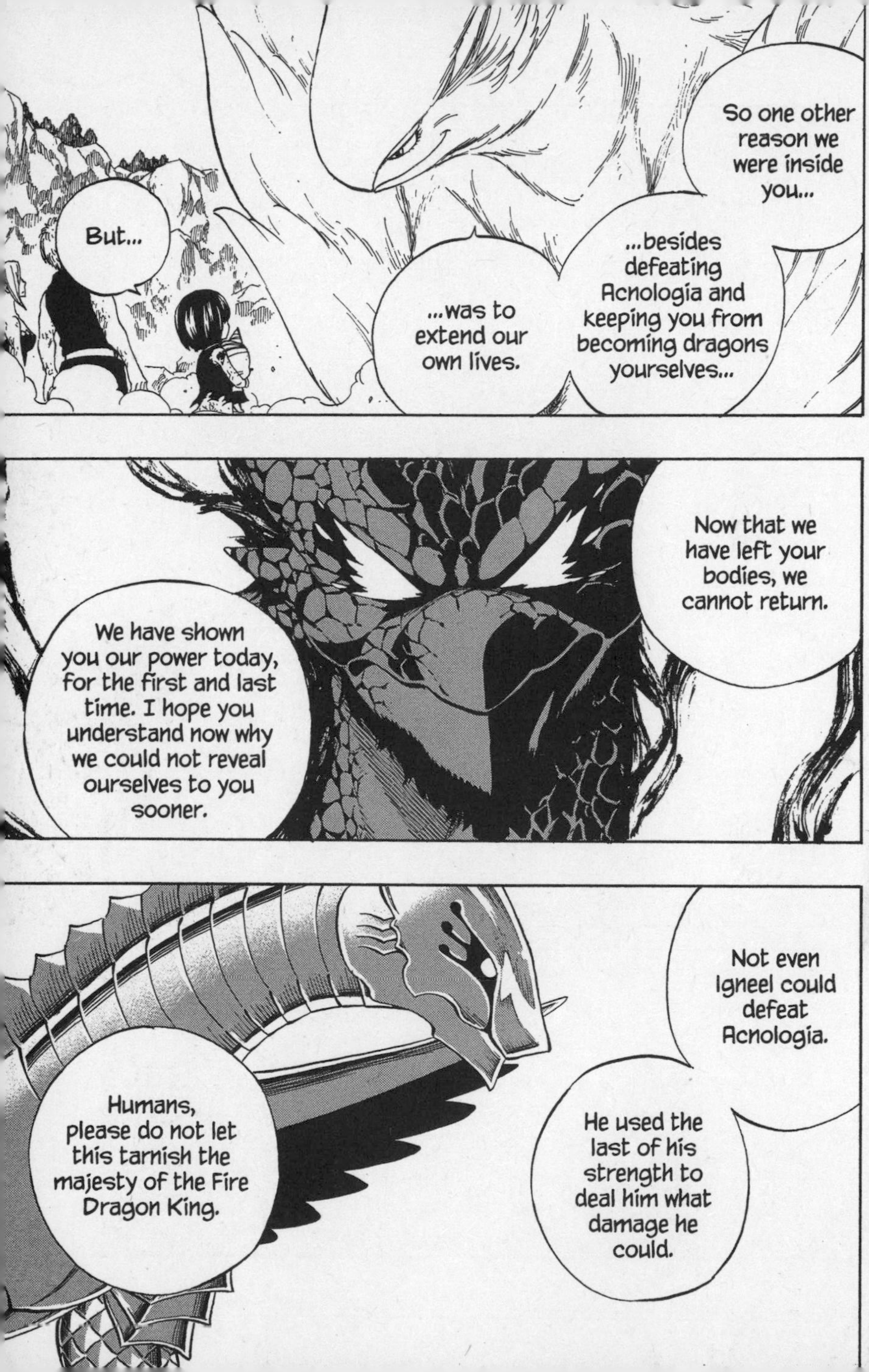

So one other reason we were inside you...
...besides defeating Acnologia and keeping you from becoming dragons yourselves...
...was to extend our own lives.
But...
Now that we have left your bodies, we cannot return.
We have shown you our power today, for the first and last time. I hope you understand now why we could not reveal ourselves to you sooner.
Not even Igneel could defeat Acnologia.
He used the last of his strength to deal him what damage he could.
Humans, please do not let this tarnish the majesty of the Fire Dragon King.

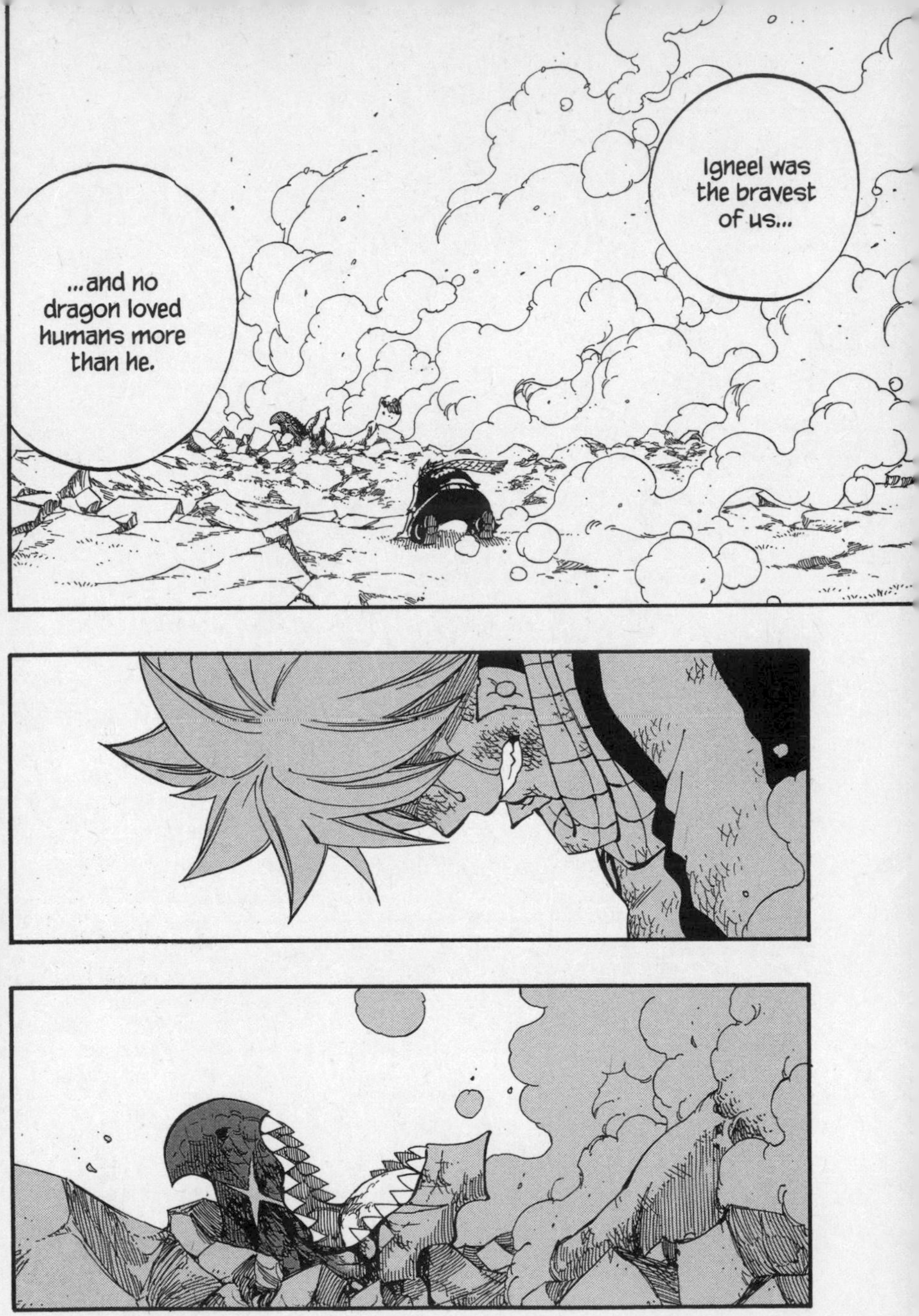
Igneel was the bravest of us...
...and no dragon loved humans more than he.

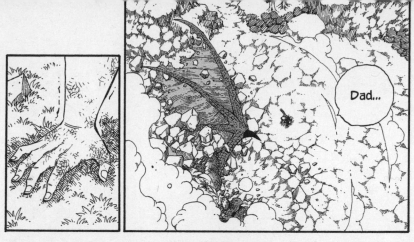

Dad...

You... promised... right?

That... you wouldn't... go anywhere...

You can't break your promise...

...I've been looking for you all this time...

SNIFF

I...

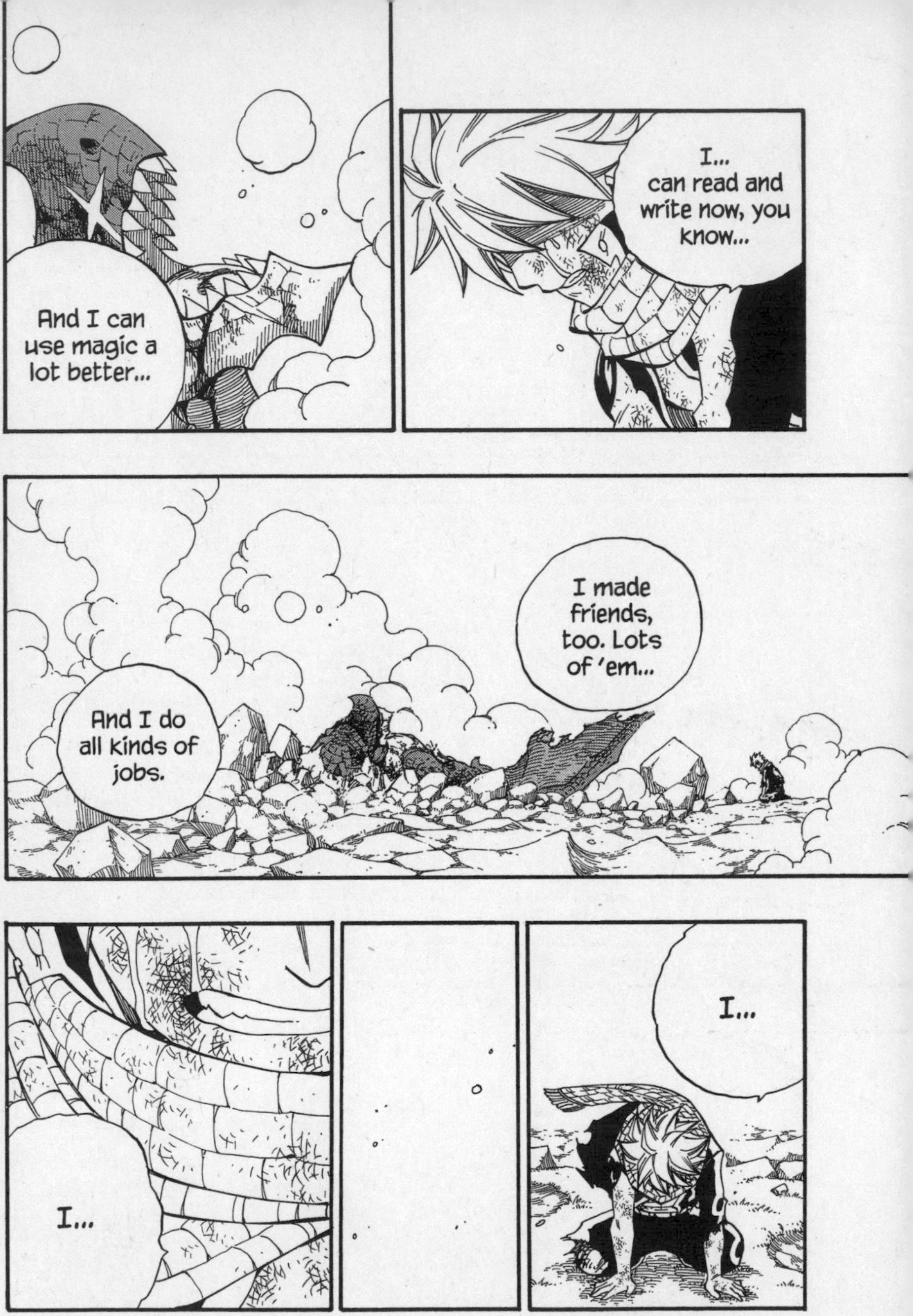
I... can read and write now, you know...
And I can use magic a lot better...
I made friends, too. Lots of 'em...
And I do all kinds of jobs.
I...
I...

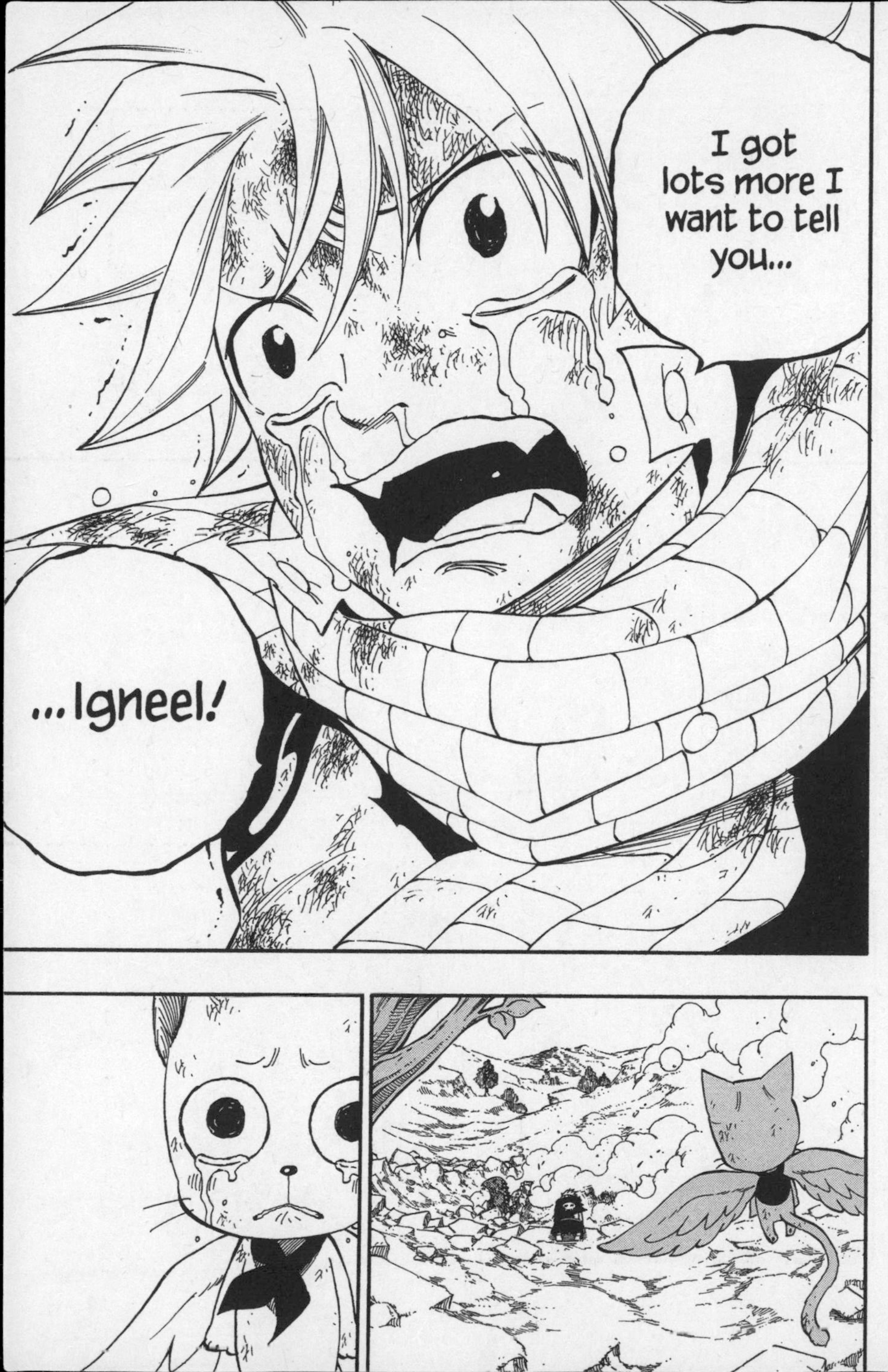
I got lots more I want to tell you...
...Igneel!

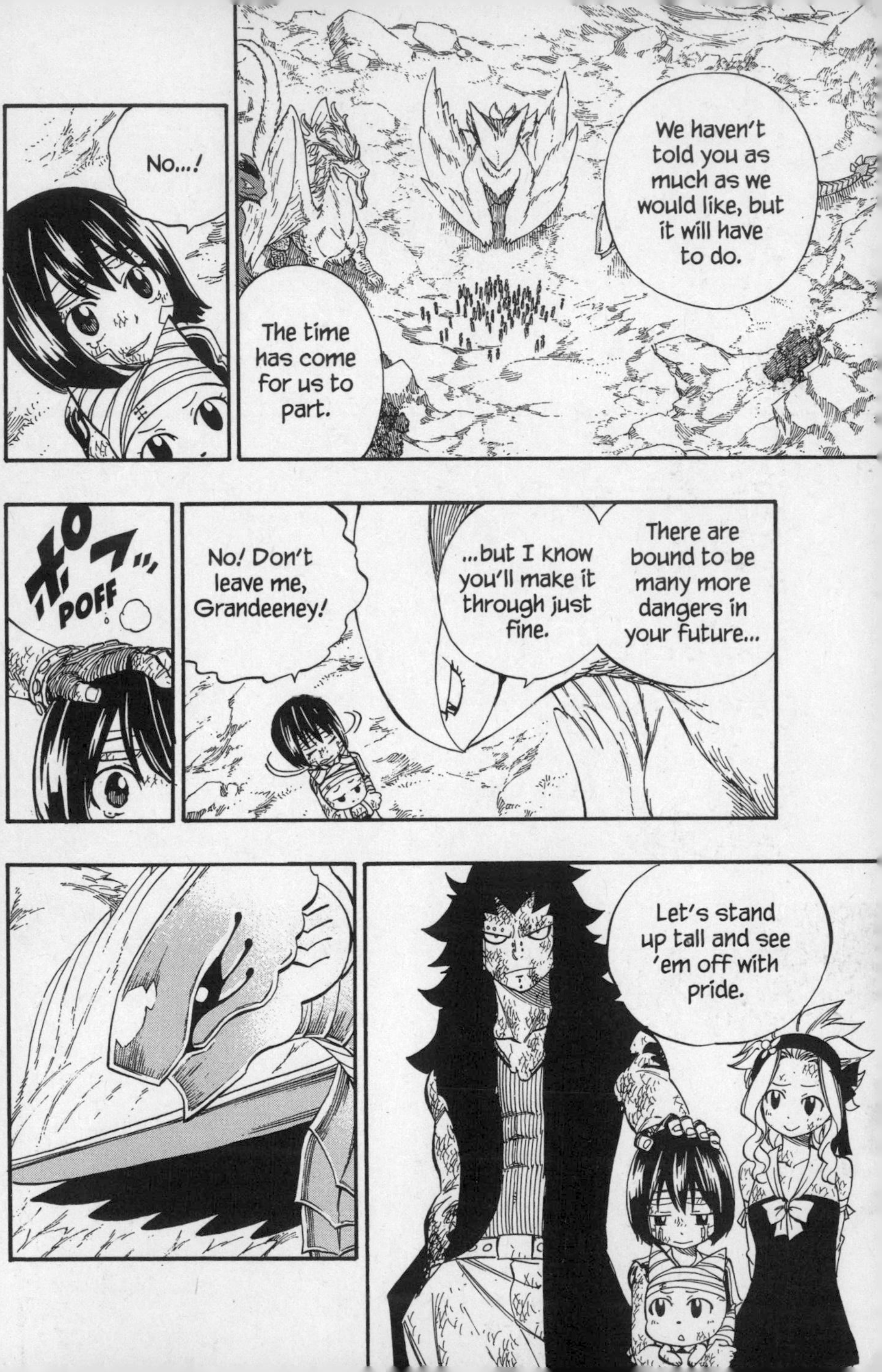
We haven't told you as much as we would like, but it will have to do.
The time has come for us to part.
No...!
There are bound to be many more dangers in your future...
...but I know you'll make it through just fine.
No! Don't leave me, Grandeeney!
POFF
Let's stand up tall and see 'em off with pride.

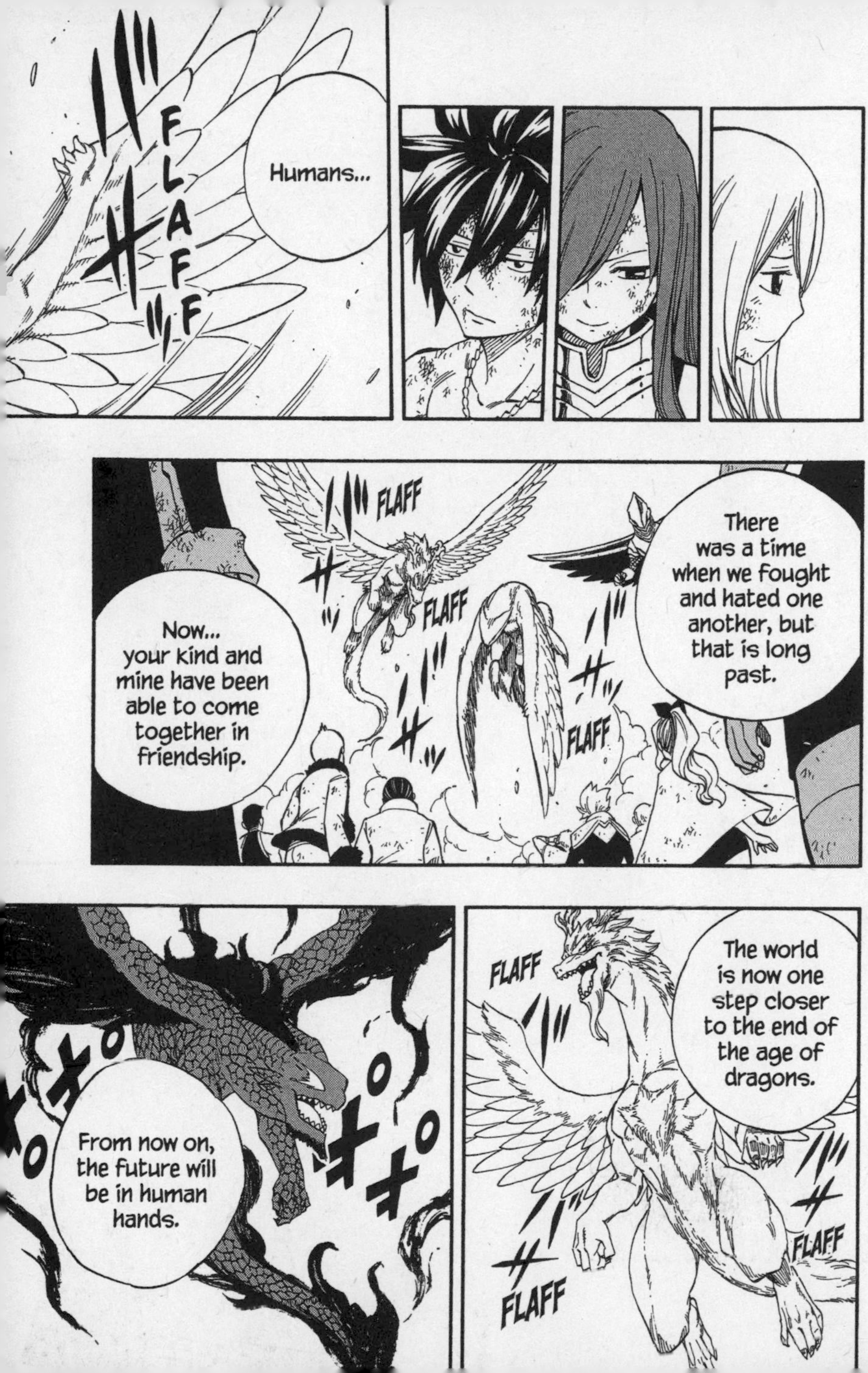
Humans...
FLAFF
There was a time when we fought and hated one another, but that is long past.
FLAFF
FLAFF
FLAFF
Now... your kind and mine have been able to come together in friendship.
The world is now one step closer to the end of the age of dragons.
FLAFF
FLAFF
FLAFF
From now on, the future will be in human hands.

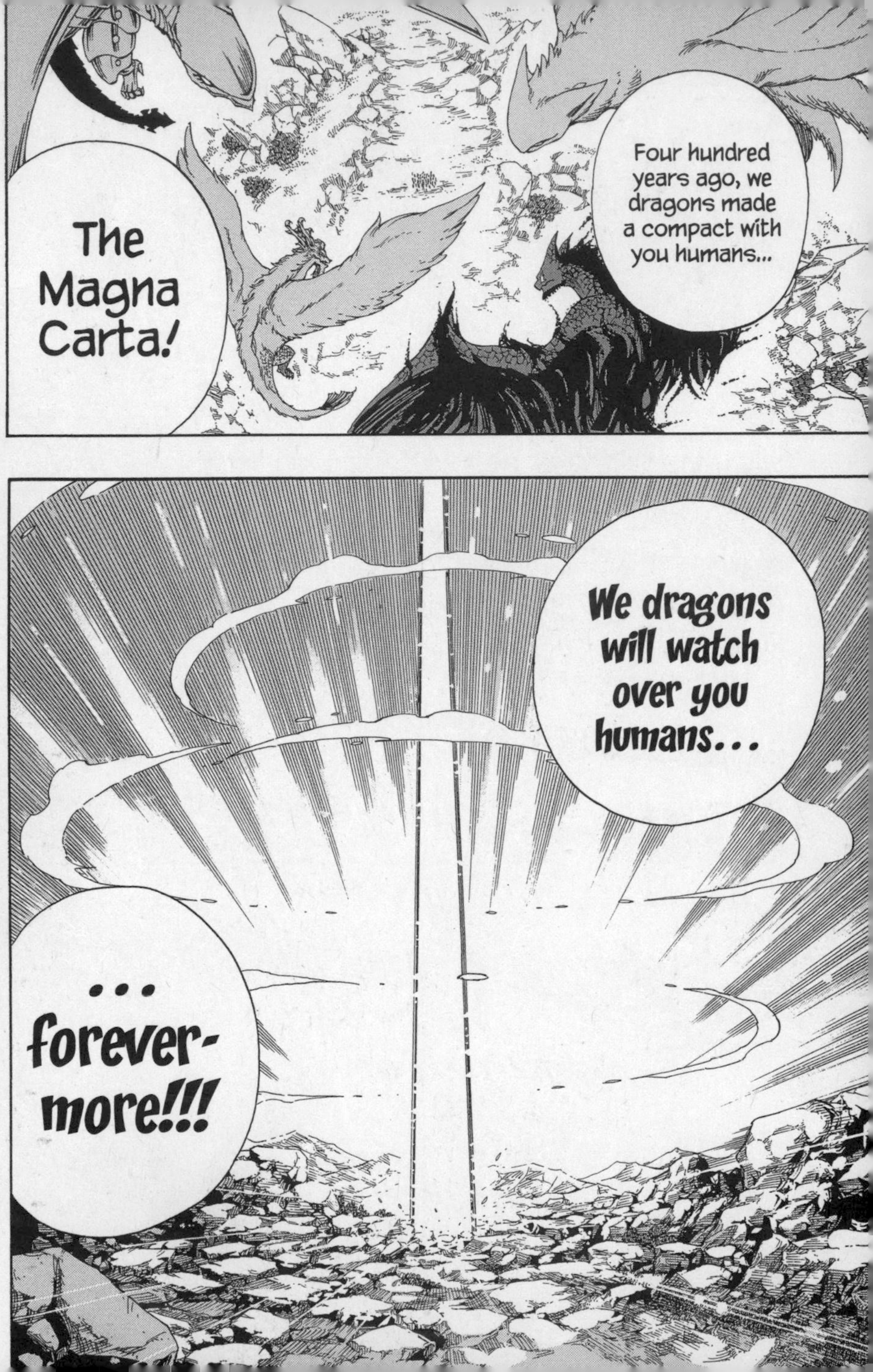
Four hundred years ago, we dragons made a compact with you humans...
The Magna Carta!
We dragons will watch over you humans...
...forever-more!!!

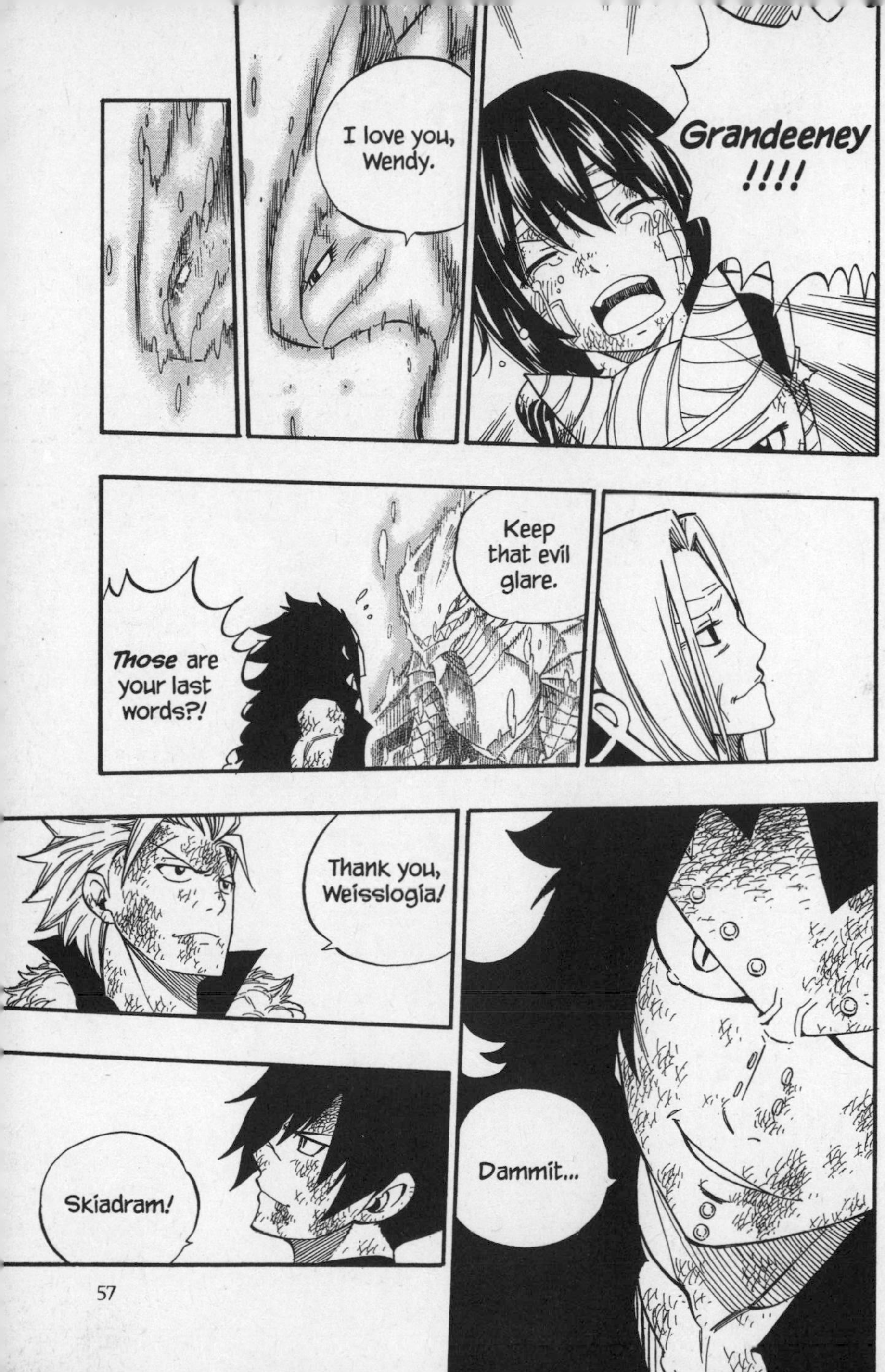
Grandeeney !!!!
I love you, Wendy.
Keep that evil glare.
Those are your last words?!
Dammit...
Thank you, Weisslogia!
Skiadram!

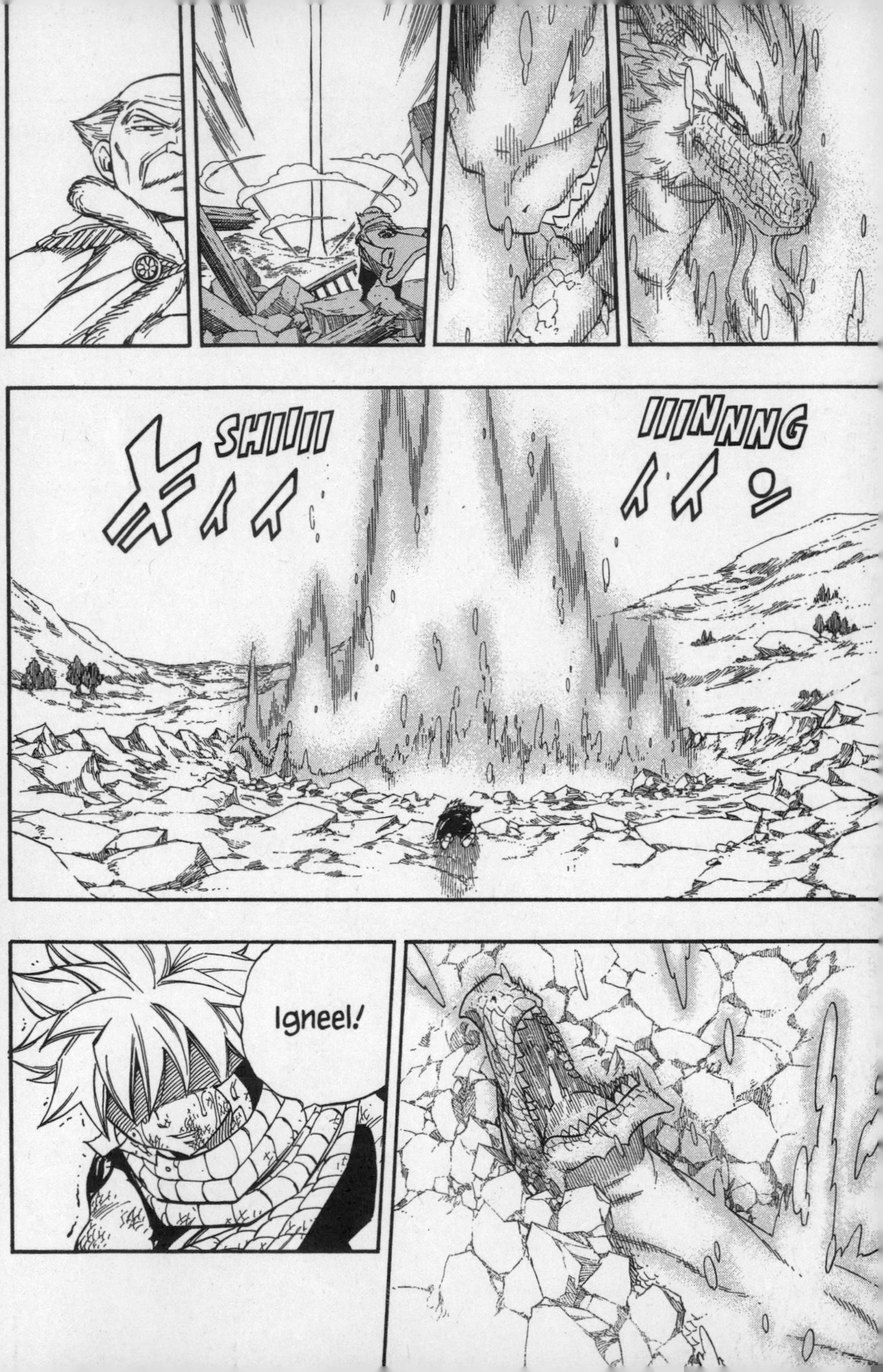
SHIIIII
IIINNNG
Igneel!

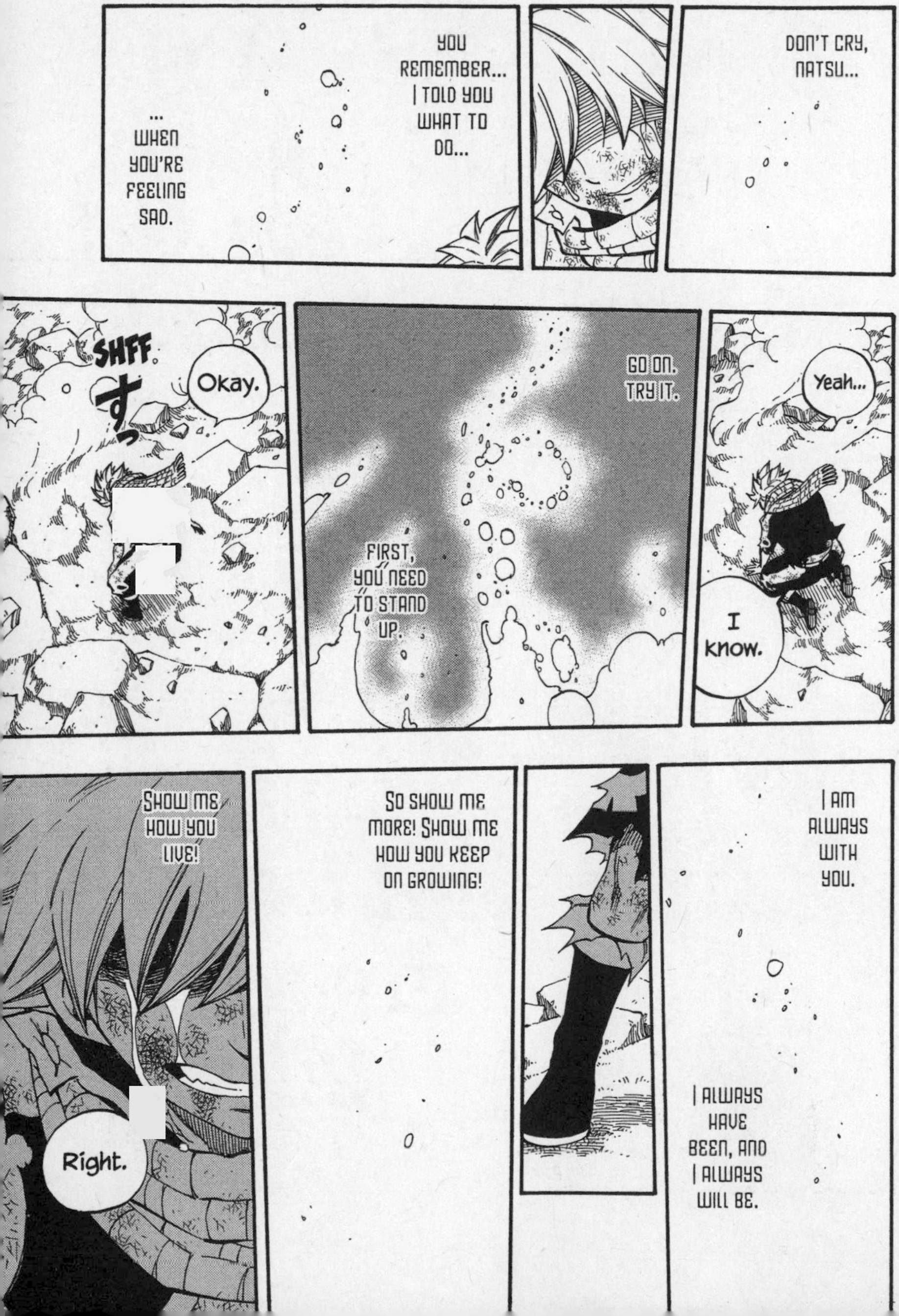
DON'T CRY, NATSU...
YOU REMEMBER... I TOLD YOU WHAT TO DO...
...WHEN YOU'RE FEELING SAD.
Yeah...
I know.
GO ON. TRY IT.
FIRST, YOU NEED TO STAND UP.
SHFF
すっ
Okay.
I AM ALWAYS WITH YOU.
I ALWAYS HAVE BEEN, AND I ALWAYS WILL BE.
SO SHOW ME MORE! SHOW ME HOW YOU KEEP ON GROWING!
SHOW ME HOW YOU LIVE!
Right.

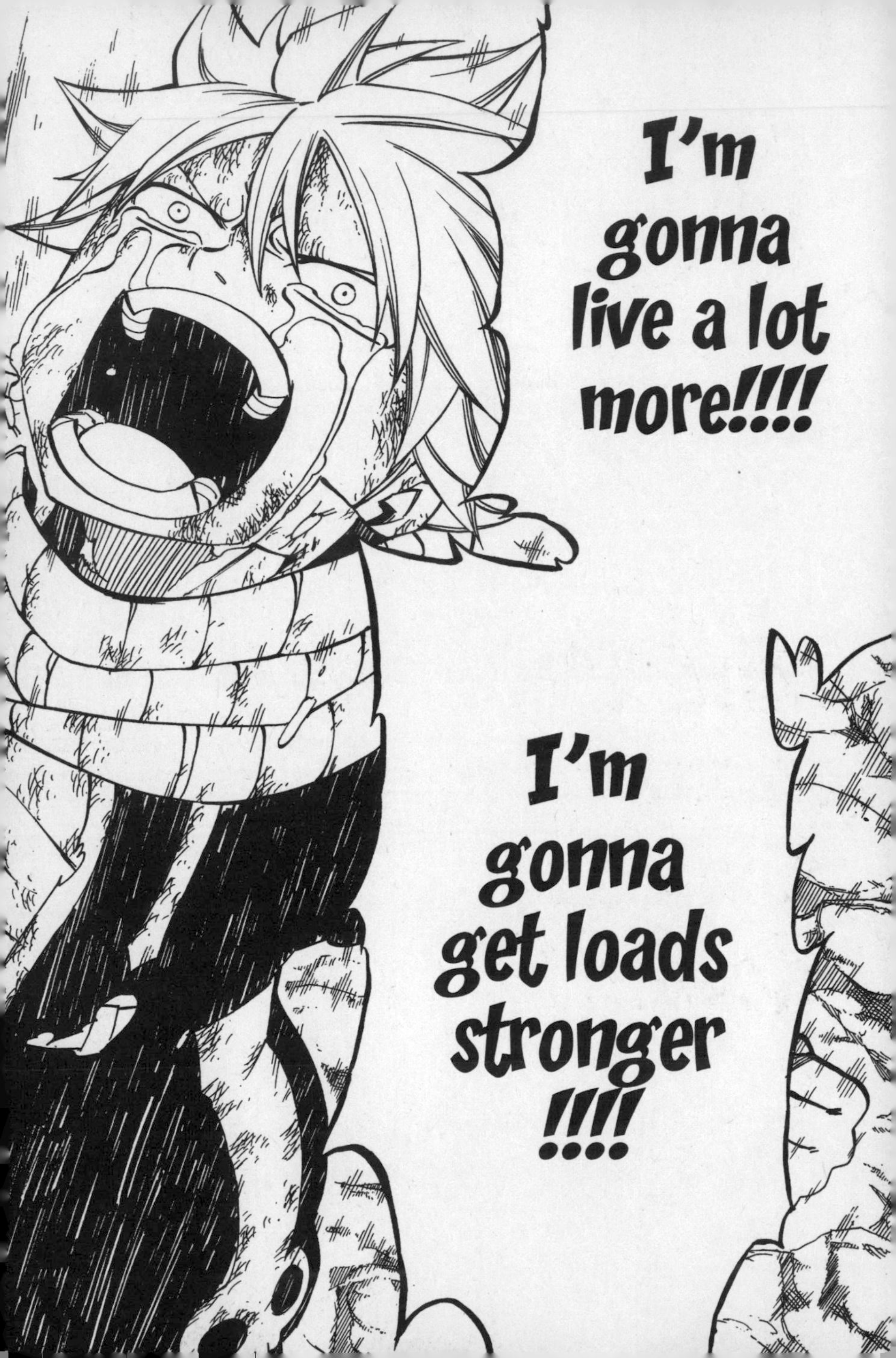
I'm gonna live a lot more!!!!
I'm gonna get loads stronger!!!!

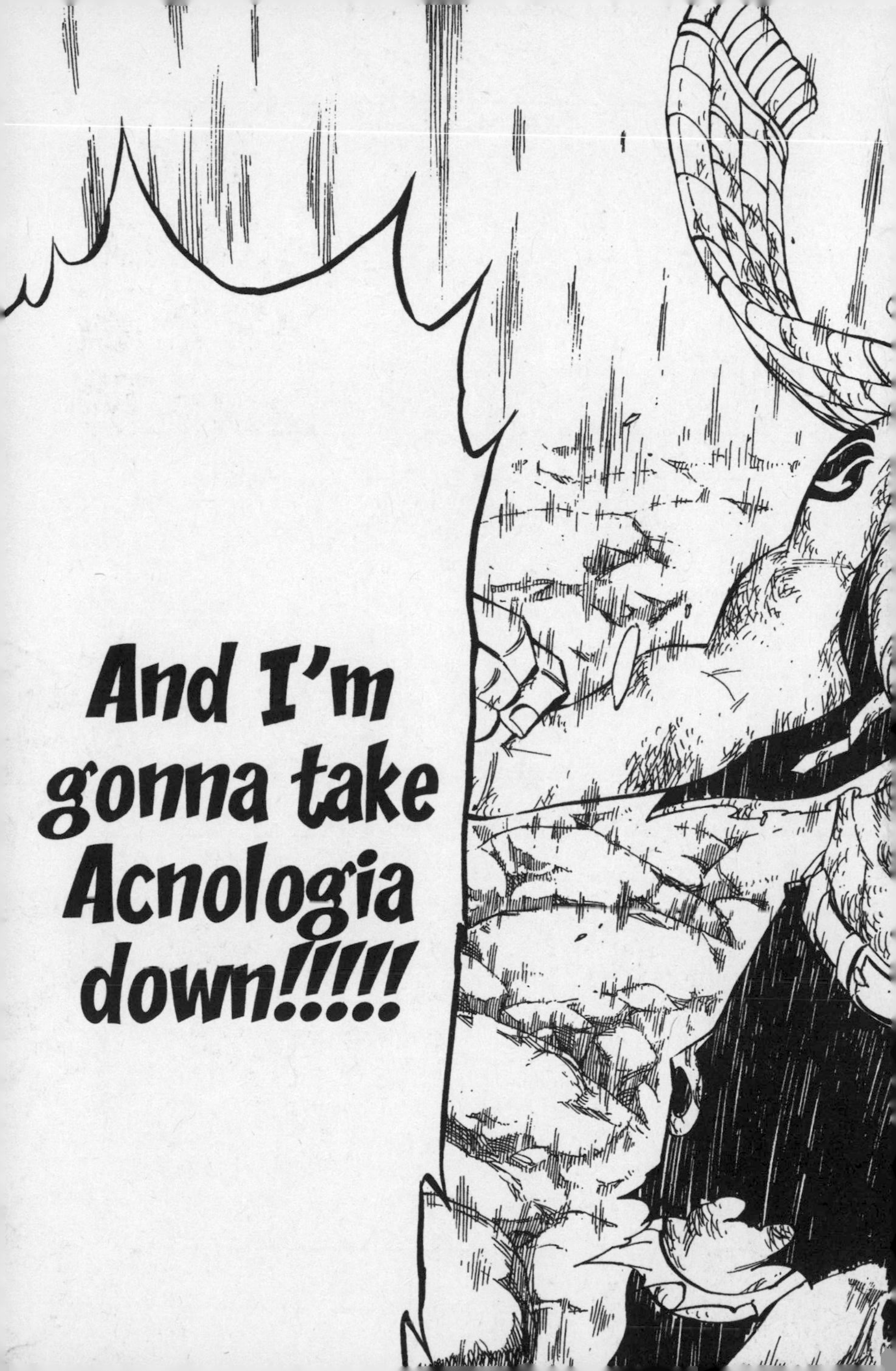
And I'm gonna take Acnologia down!!!!!

YES!

LOOK TO THE
FUTURE!

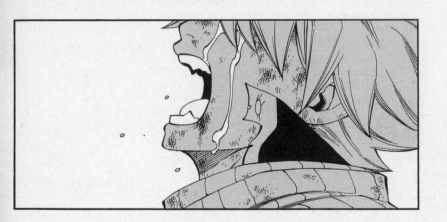

THAT IS THE
POWER OF LIFE!

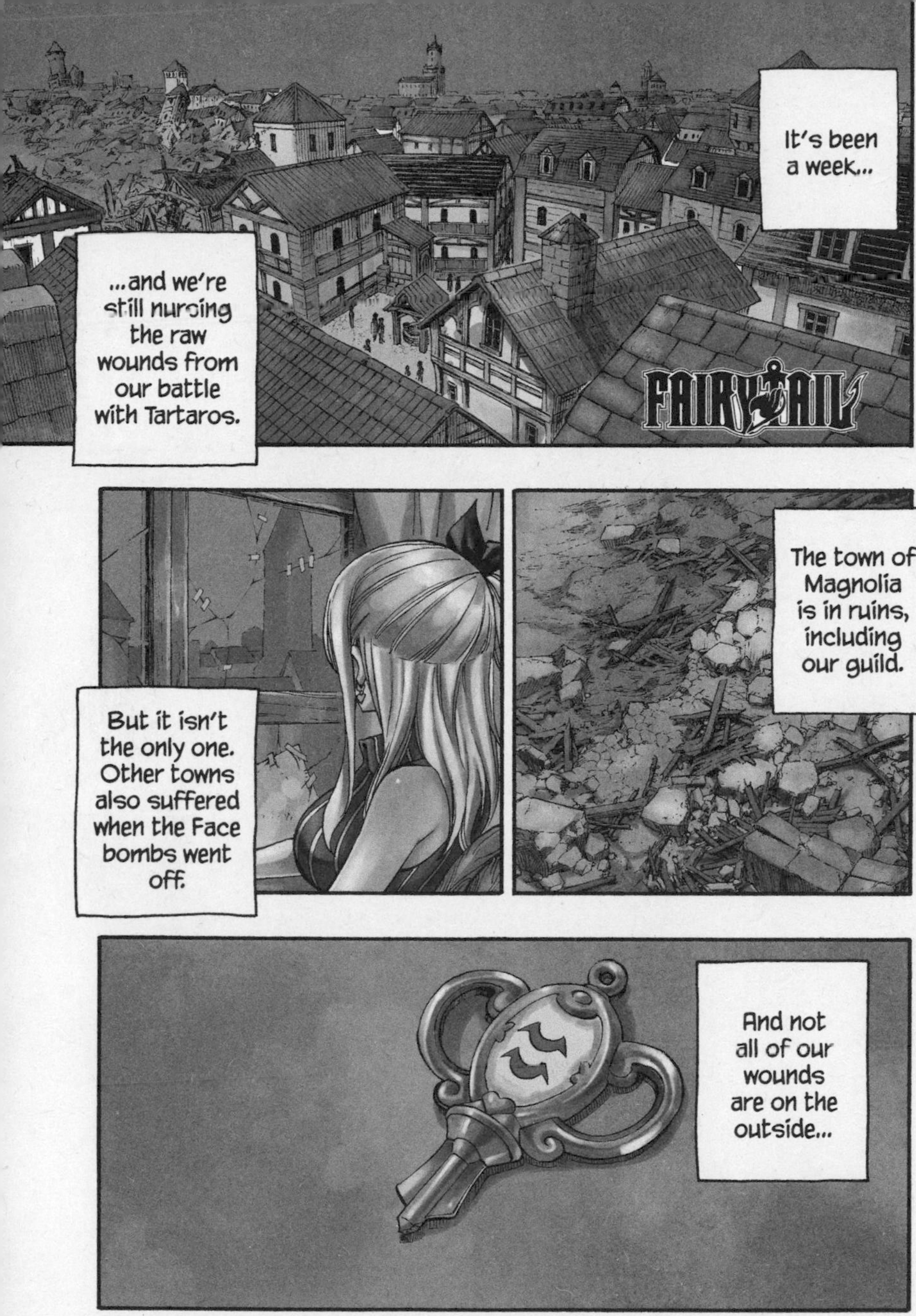
It's been a week...
...and we're still nursing the raw wounds from our battle with Tartaros.
FAIRY TAIL
The town of Magnolia is in ruins, including our guild.
But it isn't the only one. Other towns also suffered when the Face bombs went off.
And not all of our wounds are on the outside...

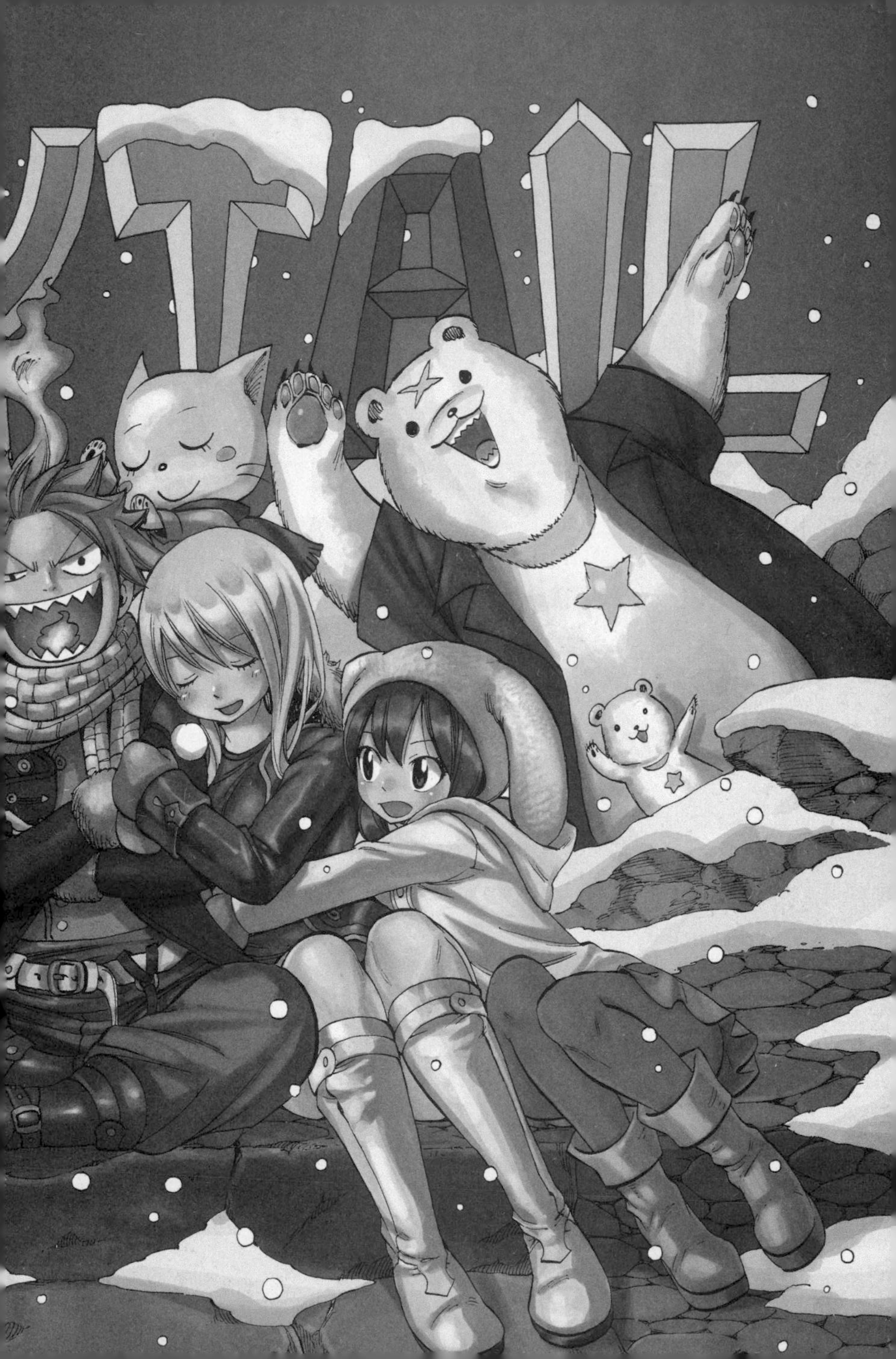

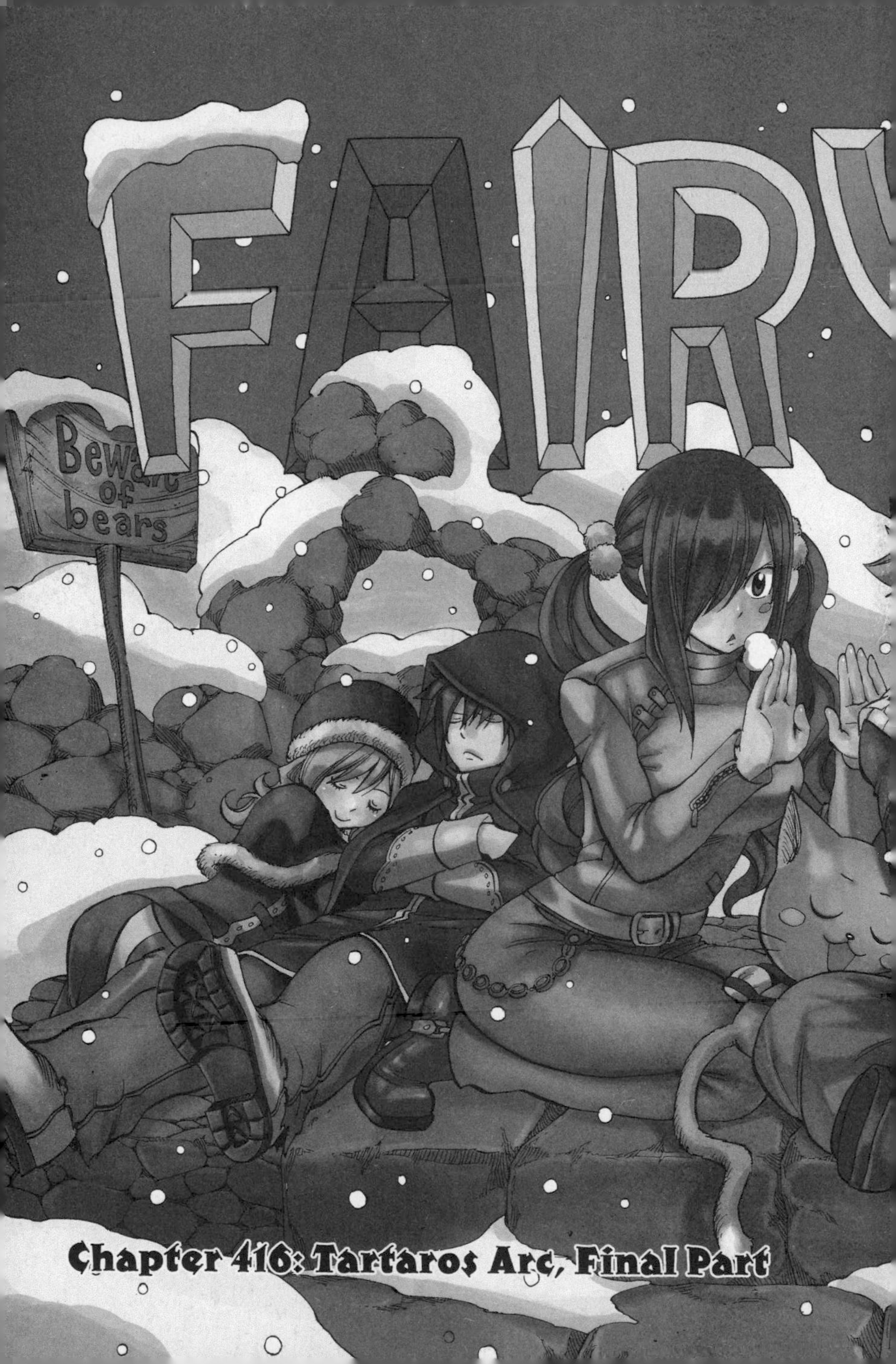
FAIRY
Beware of bears
Chapter 416: Tartaros Arc, Final Part

FAIRY TAIL
フェアリーテイル

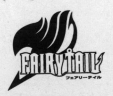

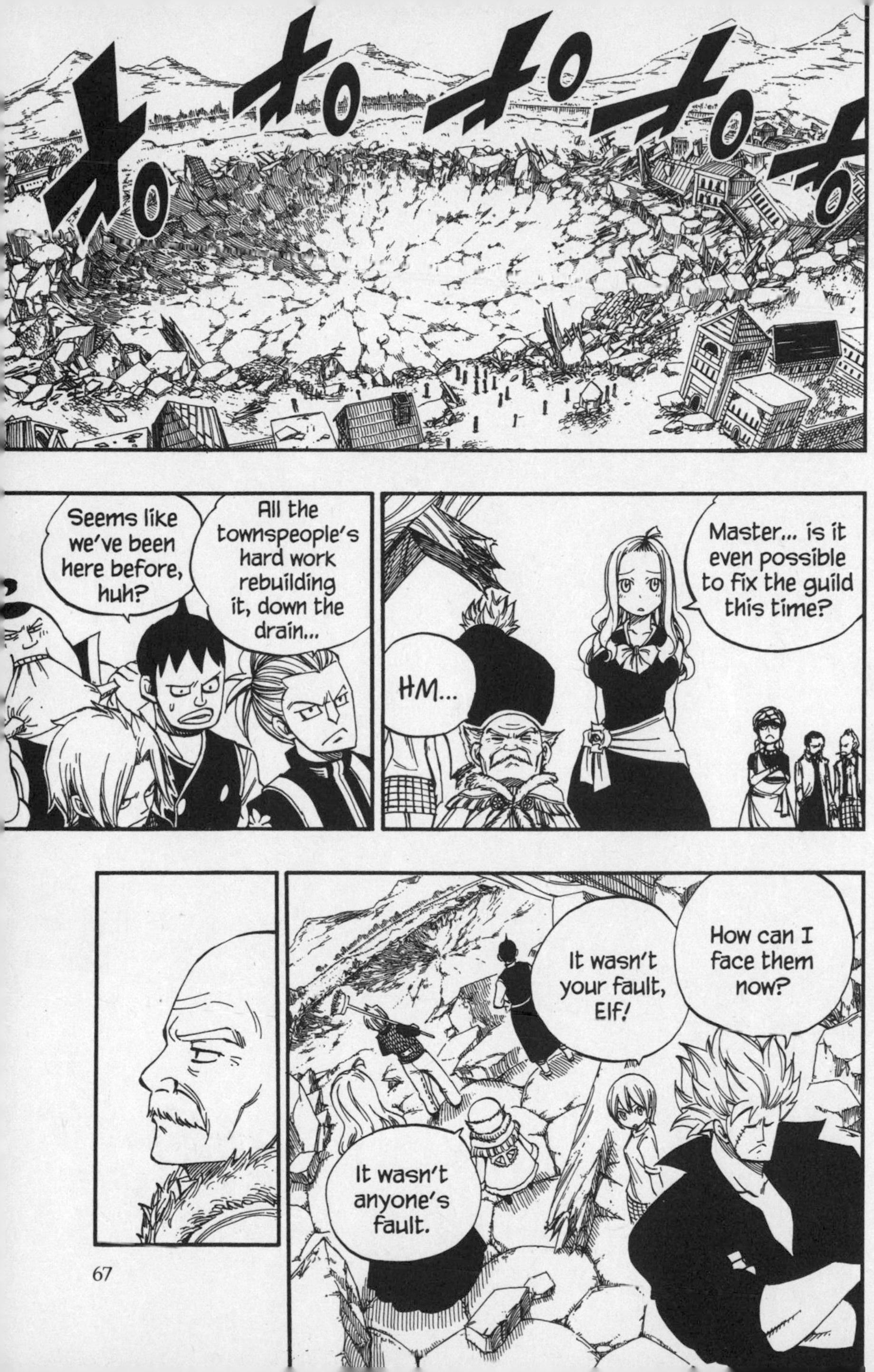
Master... is it even possible to fix the guild this time?
HM...
All the townspeople's hard work rebuilding it, down the drain...
Seems like we've been here before, huh?
How can I face them now?
It wasn't your fault, Elf!
It wasn't anyone's fault.

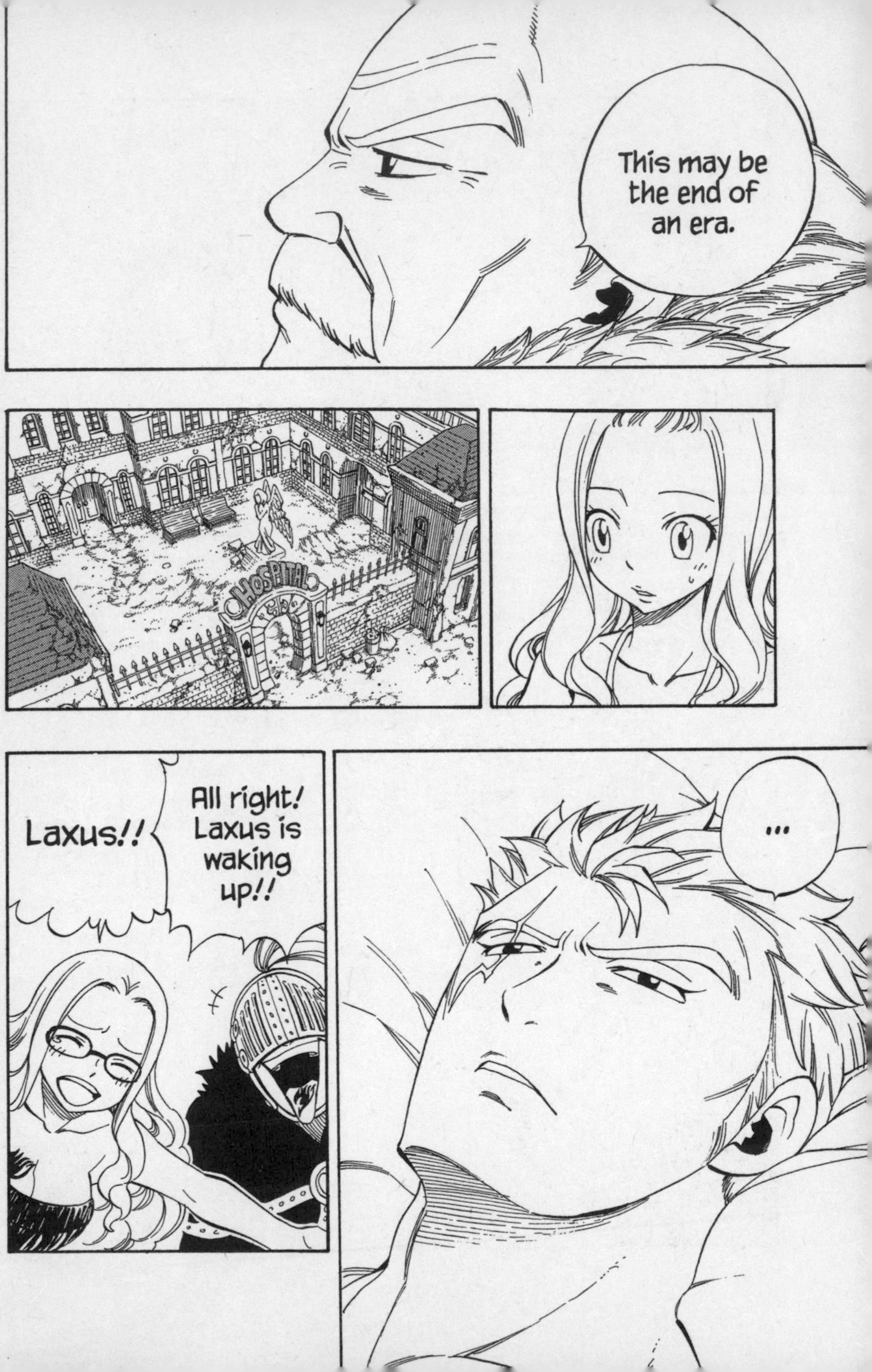
This may be the end of an era.
HOSPITAL
...
All right! Laxus is waking up!!
Laxus!!

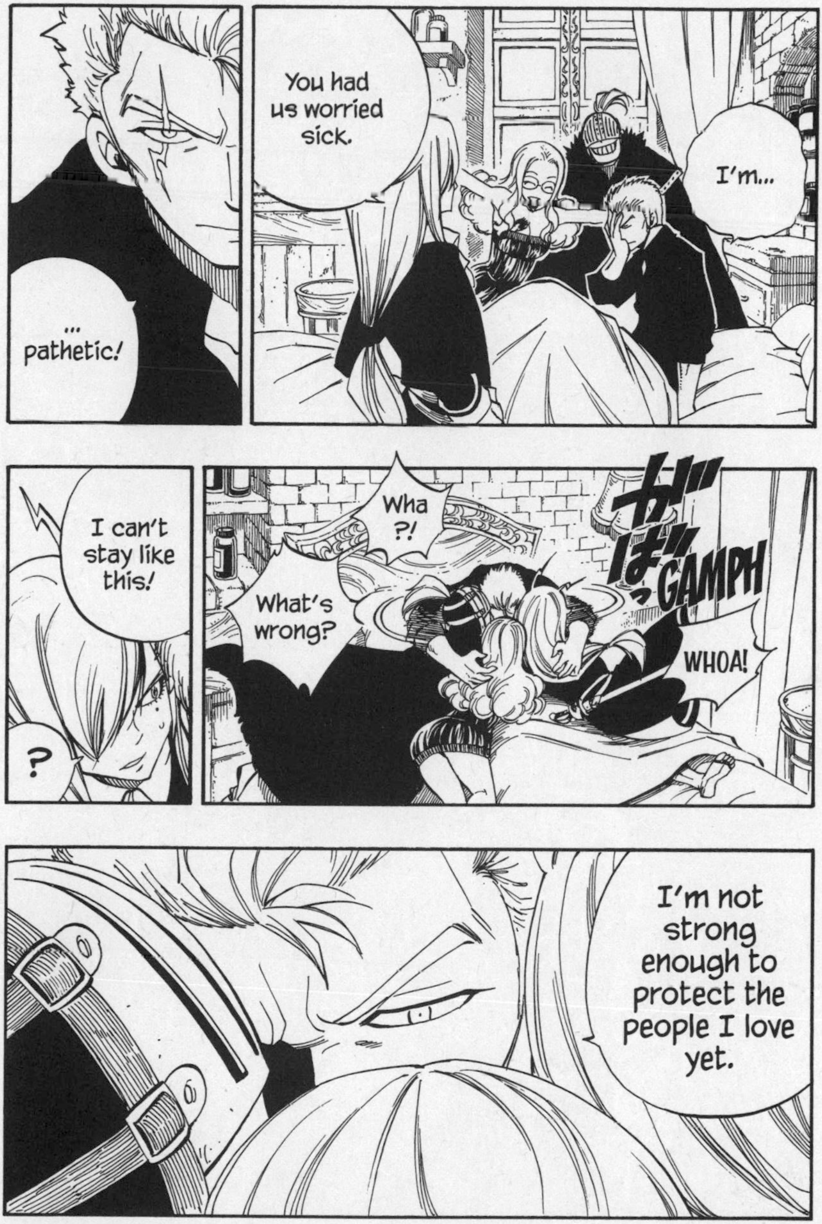
You had us worried sick.
I'm...
... pathetic!
GAMPH
WHOA!
Wha ?!
What's wrong?
I can't stay like this!
?
I'm not strong enough to protect the people I love yet.

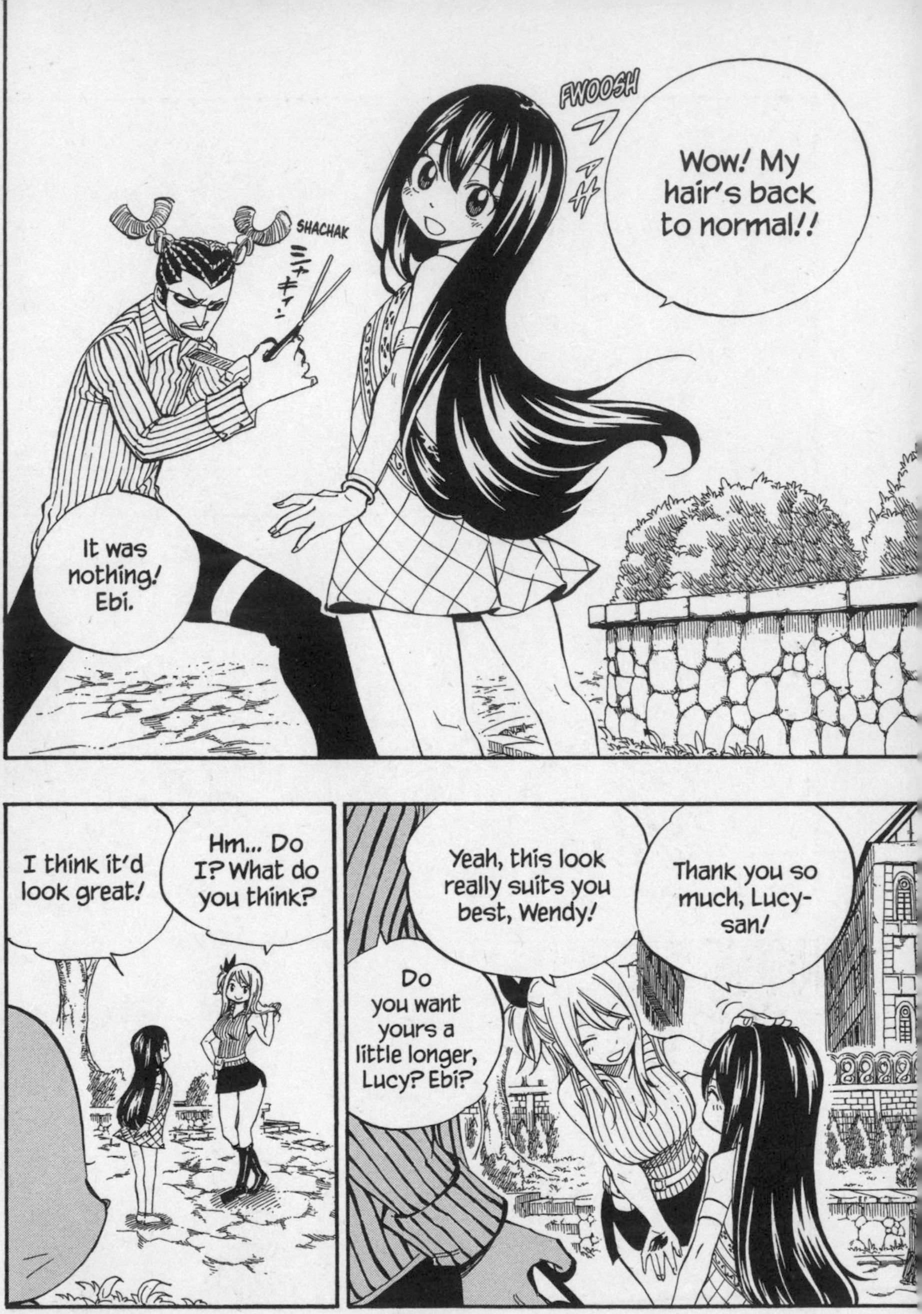
FWOOSH
Wow! My hair's back to normal!!
SHACHAK
It was nothing! Ebi.
Thank you so much, Lucy-san!
Yeah, this look really suits you best, Wendy!
Do you want yours a little longer, Lucy? Ebi?
Hm... Do I? What do you think?
I think it'd look great!

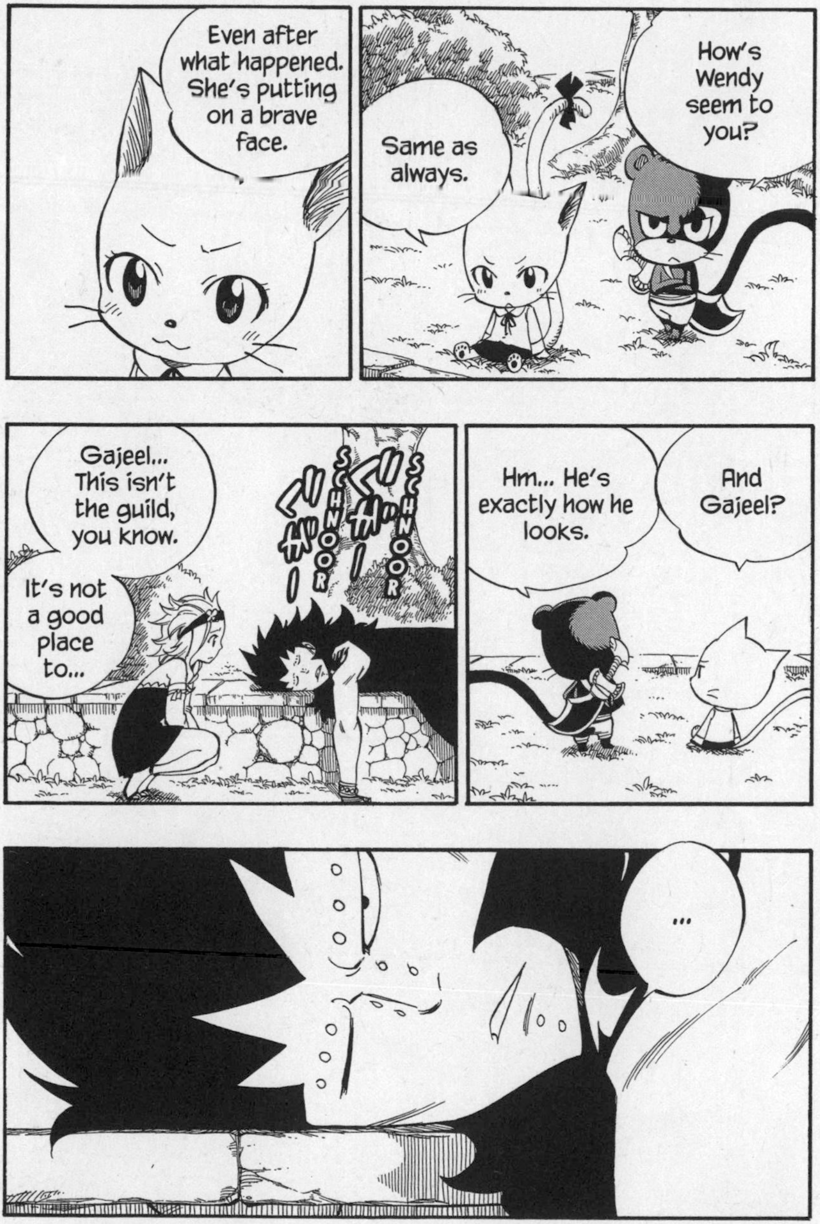
How's Wendy seem to you?
Same as always.
Even after what happened. She's putting on a brave face.
And Gajeel?
Hm... He's exactly how he looks.
SCHNOOR
SCHNOOR
Gajeel... This isn't the guild, you know.
It's not a good place to...
...

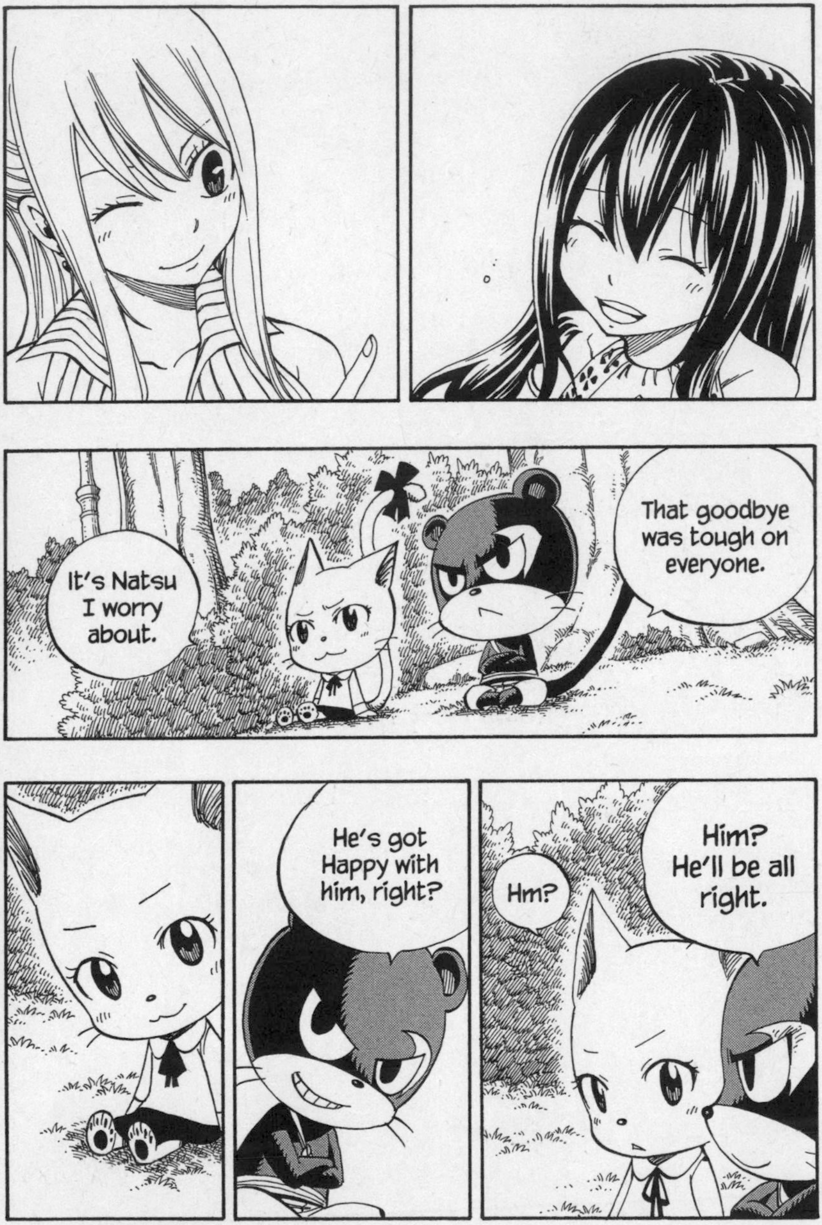

That goodbye was tough on everyone.
It's Natsu I worry about.
Him? He'll be all right.
Hm?
He's got Happy with him, right?

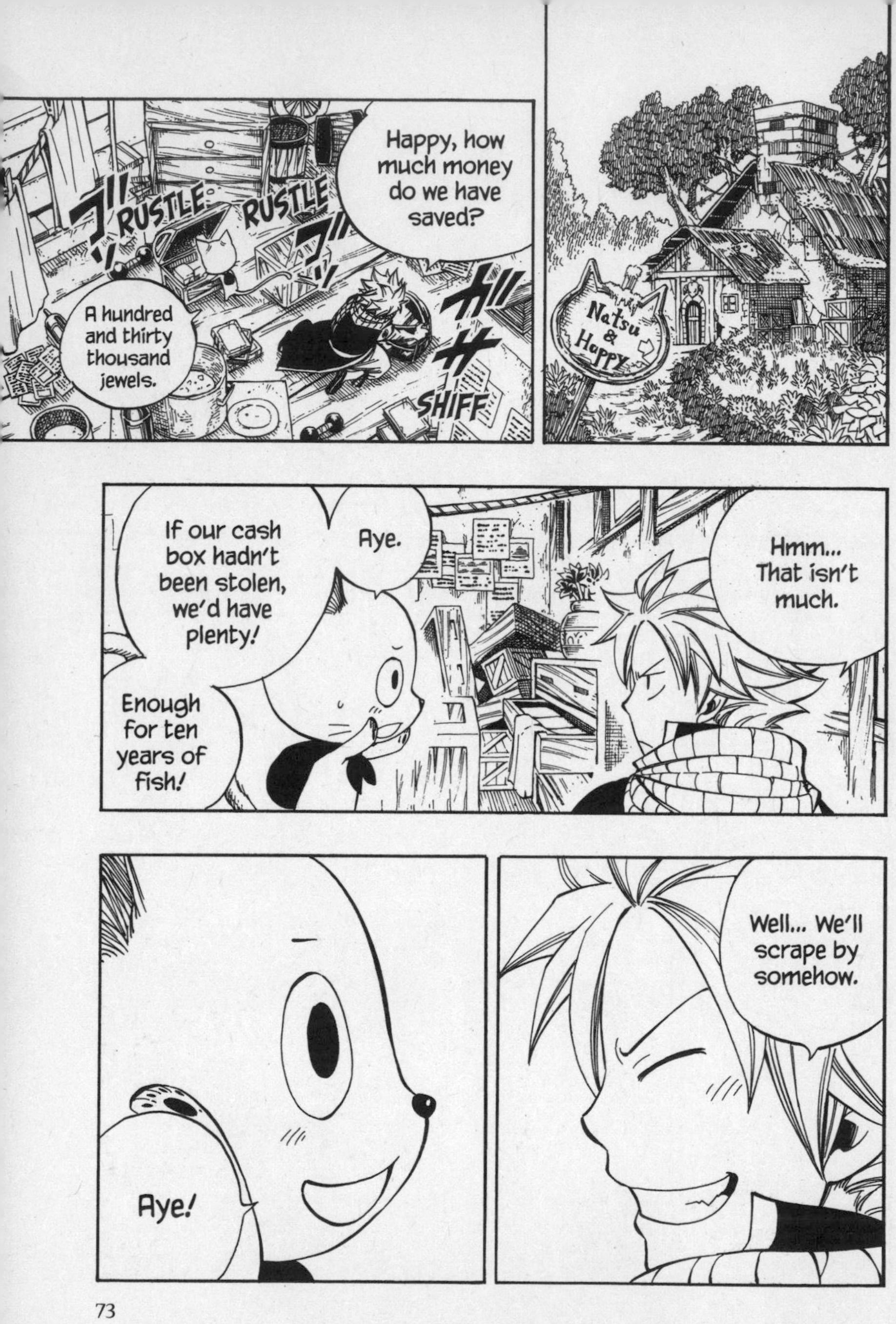

Natsu & Happy
Happy, how much money do we have saved?
RUSTLE
RUSTLE
SHIFF
A hundred and thirty thousand jewels.
Hmm... That isn't much.
Aye.
If our cash box hadn't been stolen, we'd have plenty!
Enough for ten years of fish!
Well... We'll scrape by somehow.
Aye!

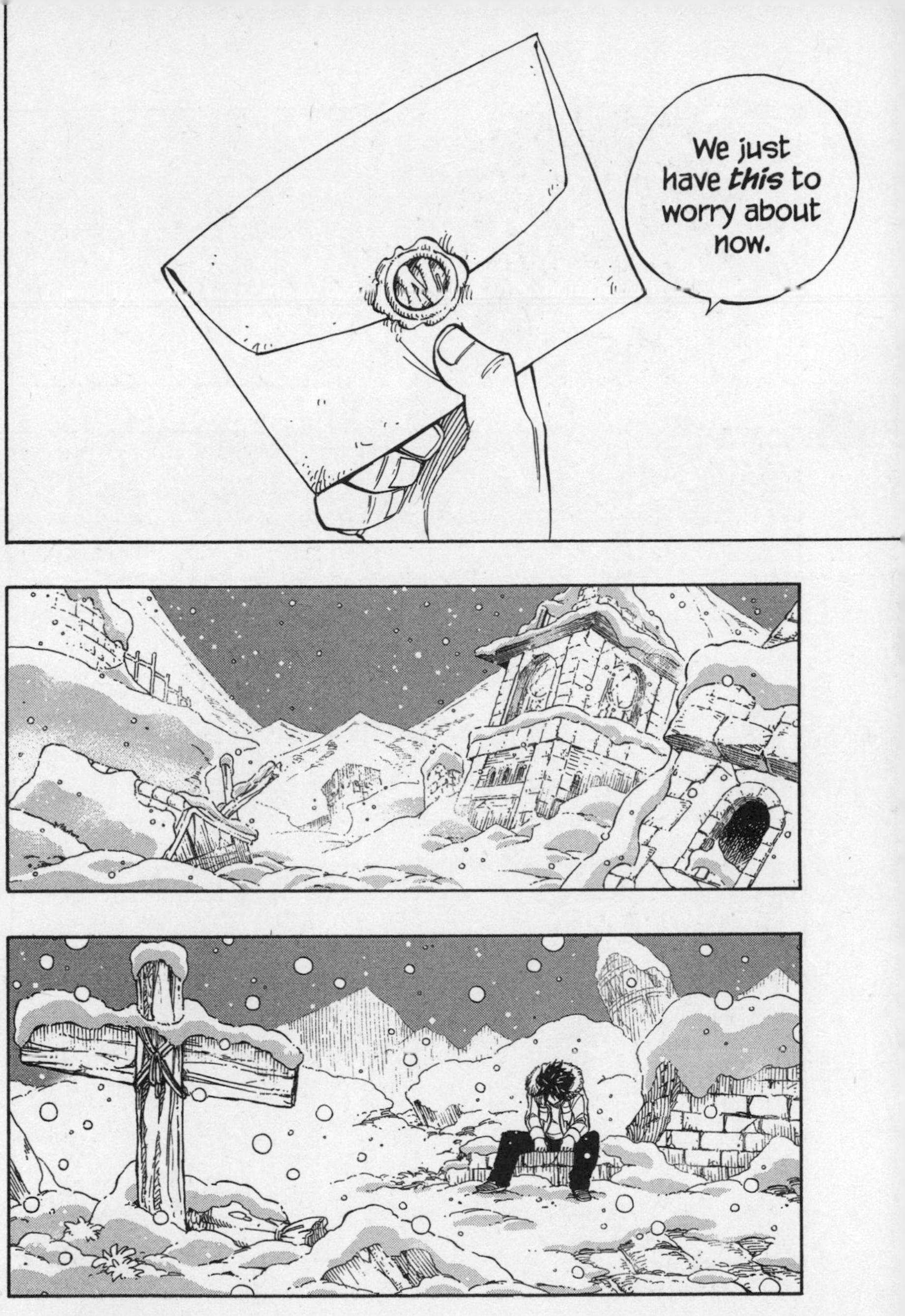
We just have *this* to worry about now.

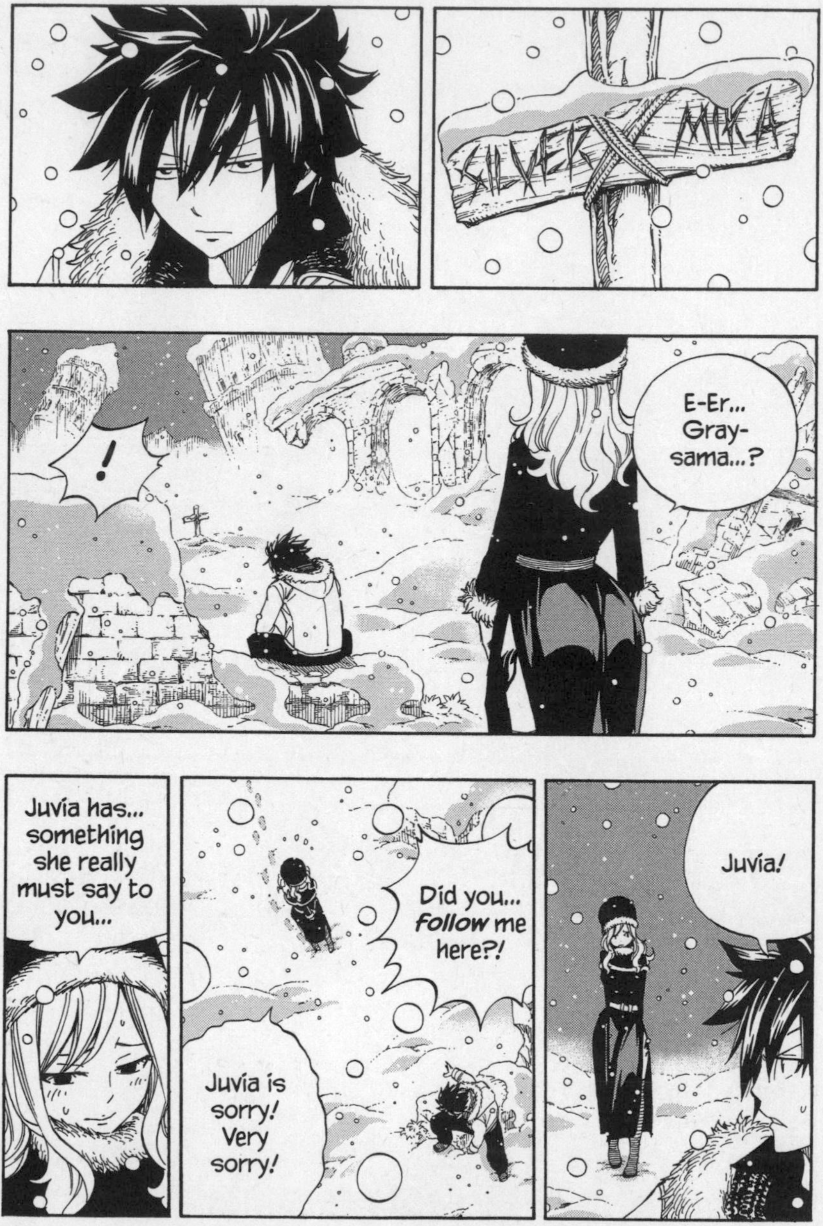
SILVER MIKA
E-Er... Gray-sama...?
!
Juvia!
Did you... *follow* me here?!
Juvia is sorry! Very sorry!
Juvia has... something she really must say to you...

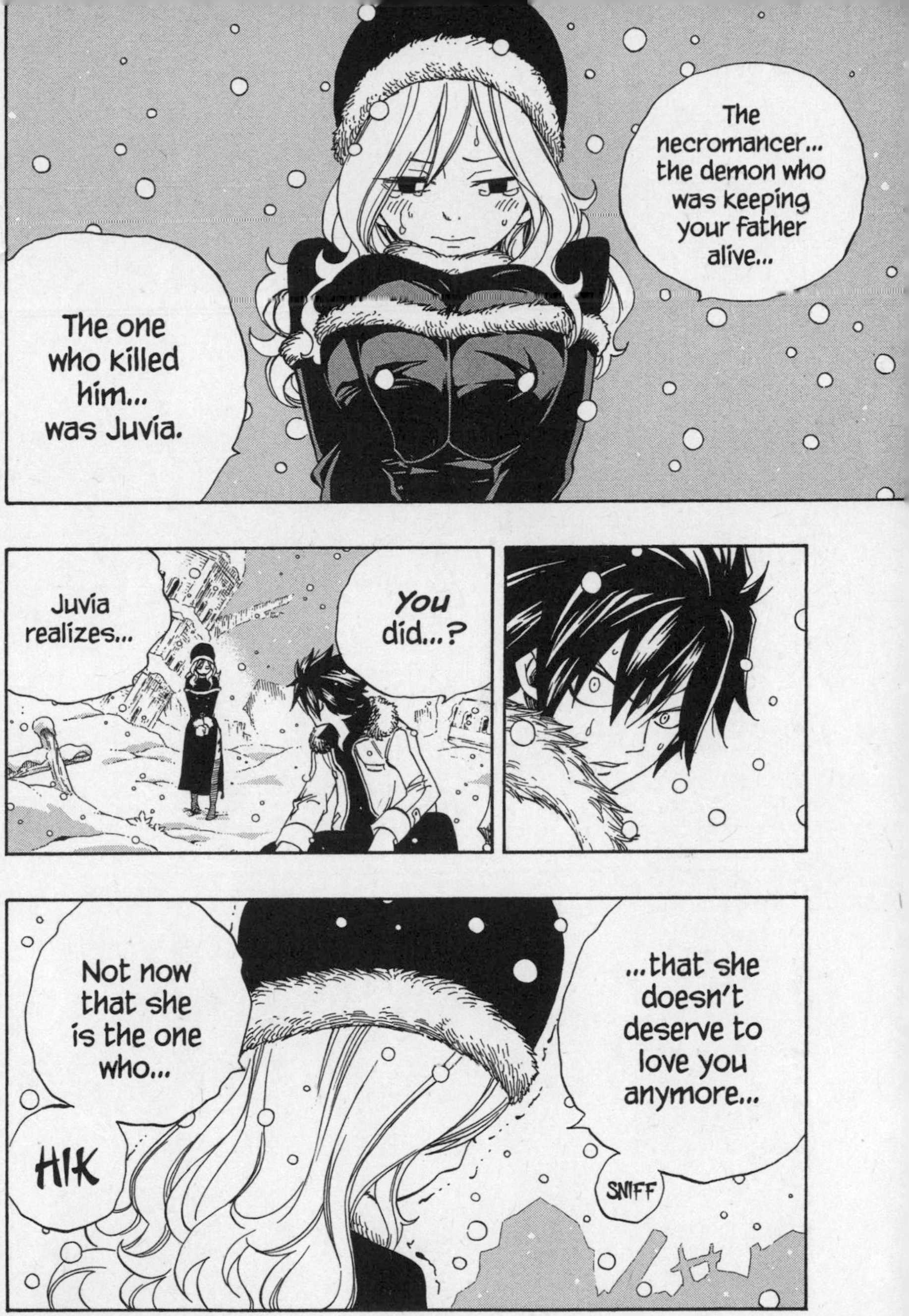
The necromancer... the demon who was keeping your father alive...
The one who killed him... was Juvia.
You did...?
Juvia realizes...
...that she doesn't deserve to love you anymore...
SNIFF
Not now that she is the one who...
HIK

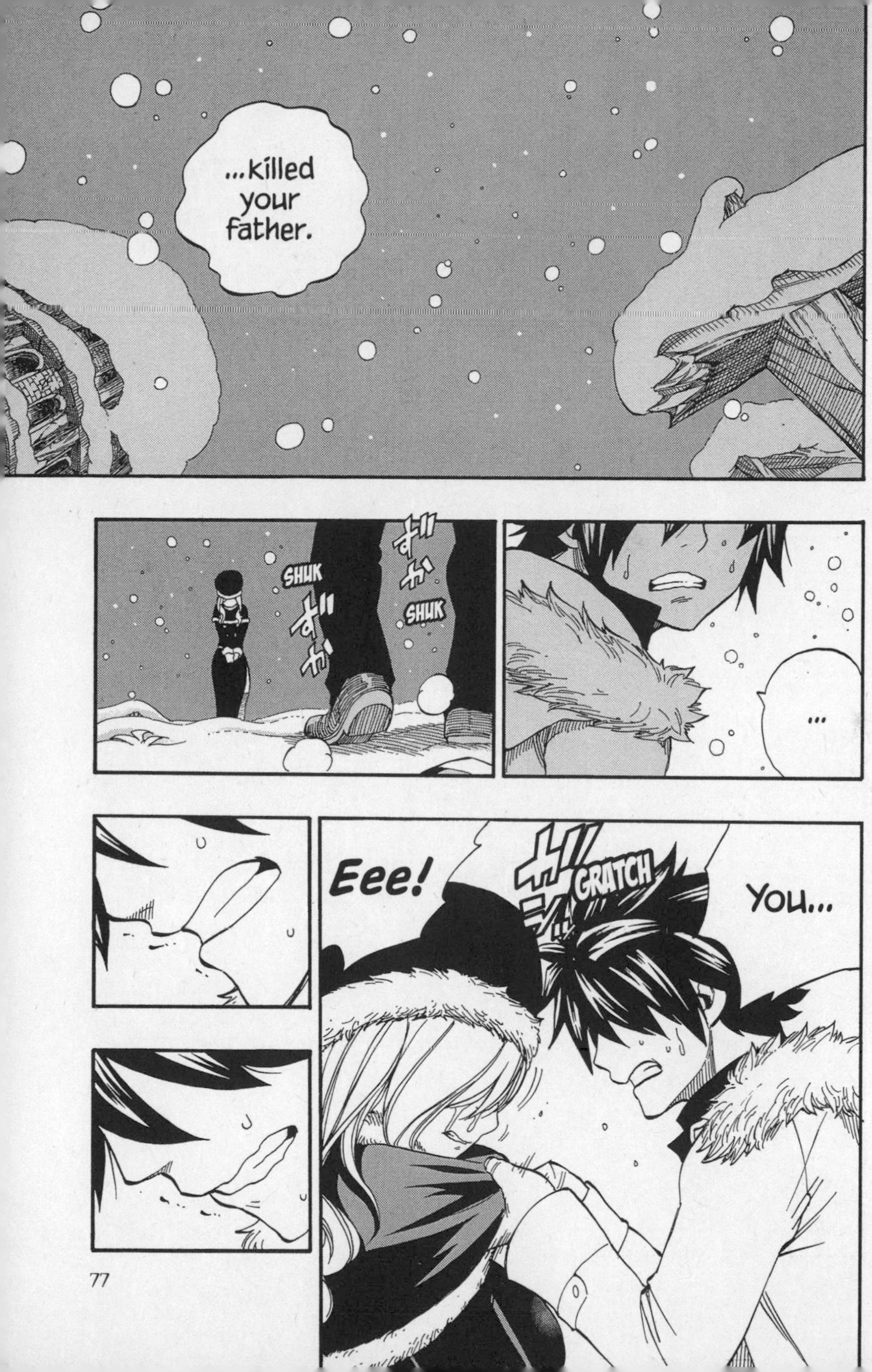
...killed your father.
...
SHUK
SHUK
You...
GRATCH
Eee!

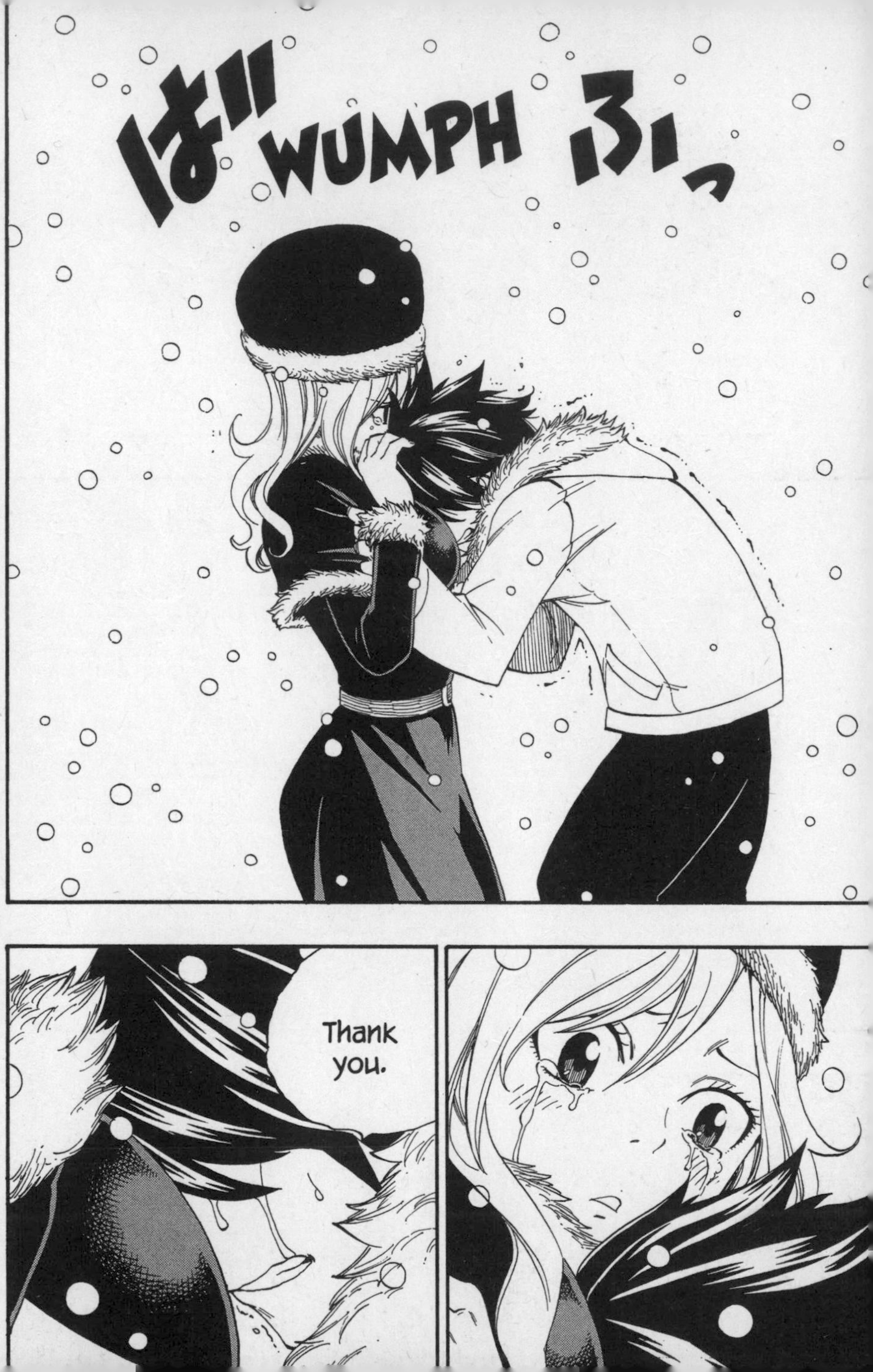
WUMPH
Thank you.

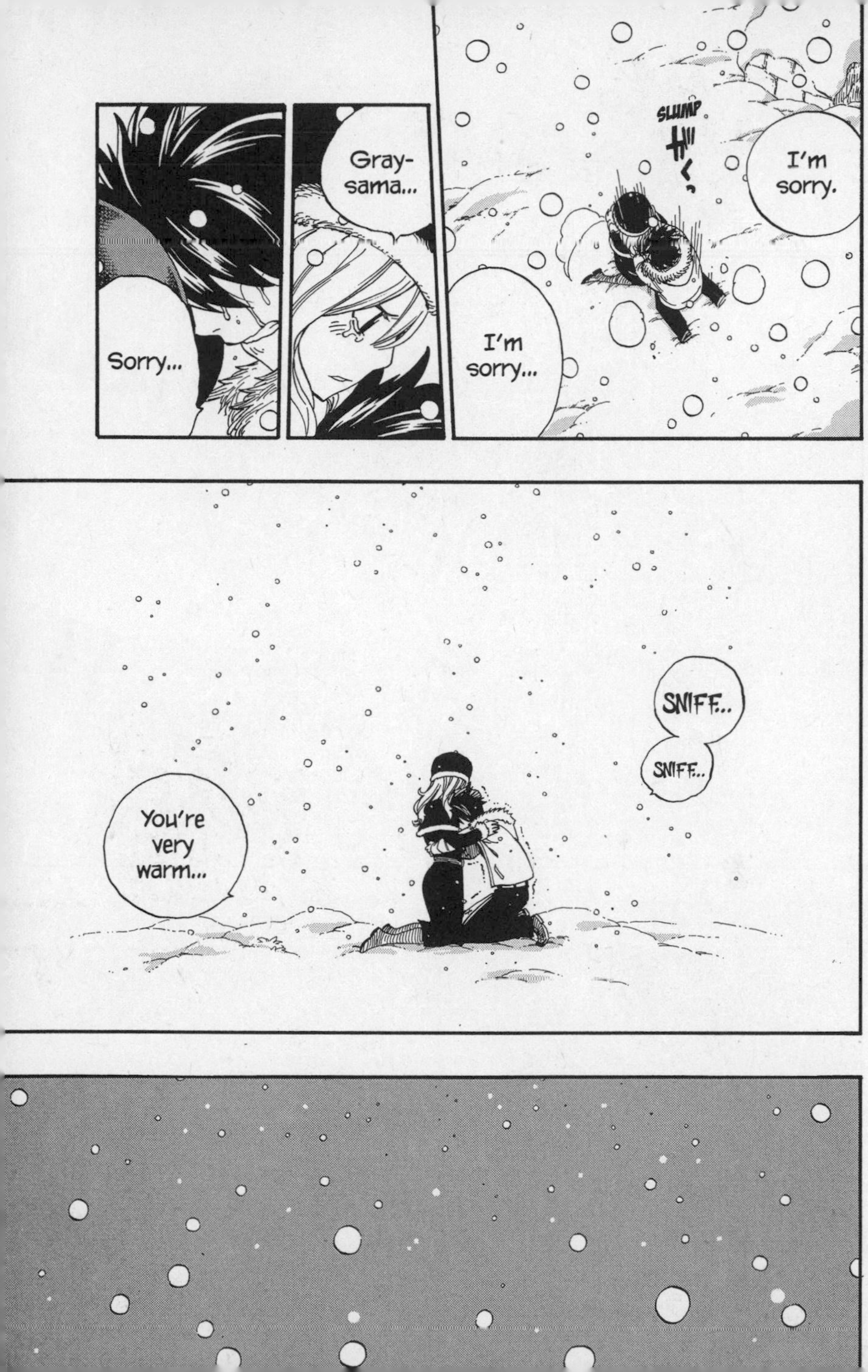
I'm sorry.
SLUMP
I'm sorry...
Gray-sama...
Sorry...
SNIFF..
SNIFF..
You're very warm...

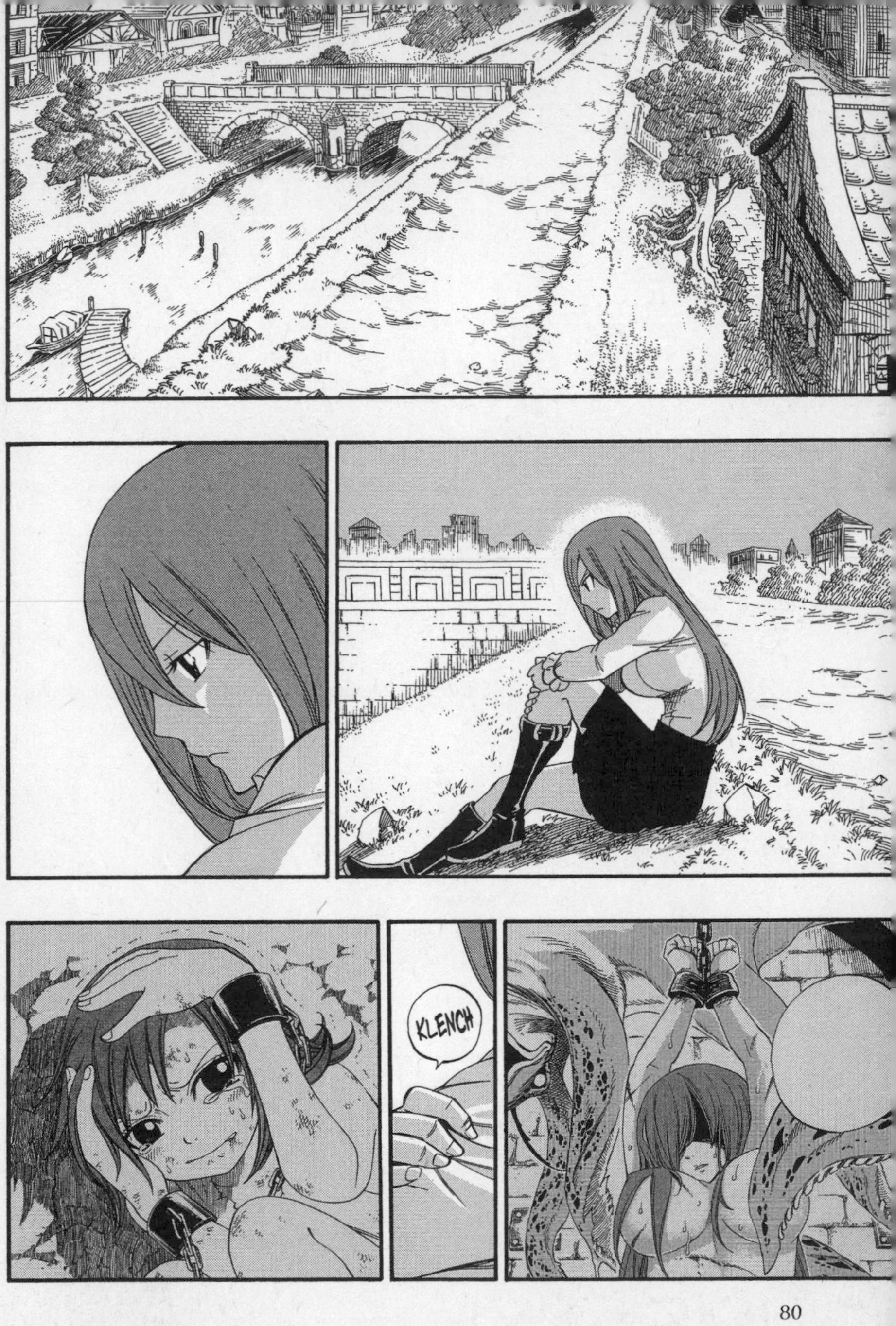
KLENCH

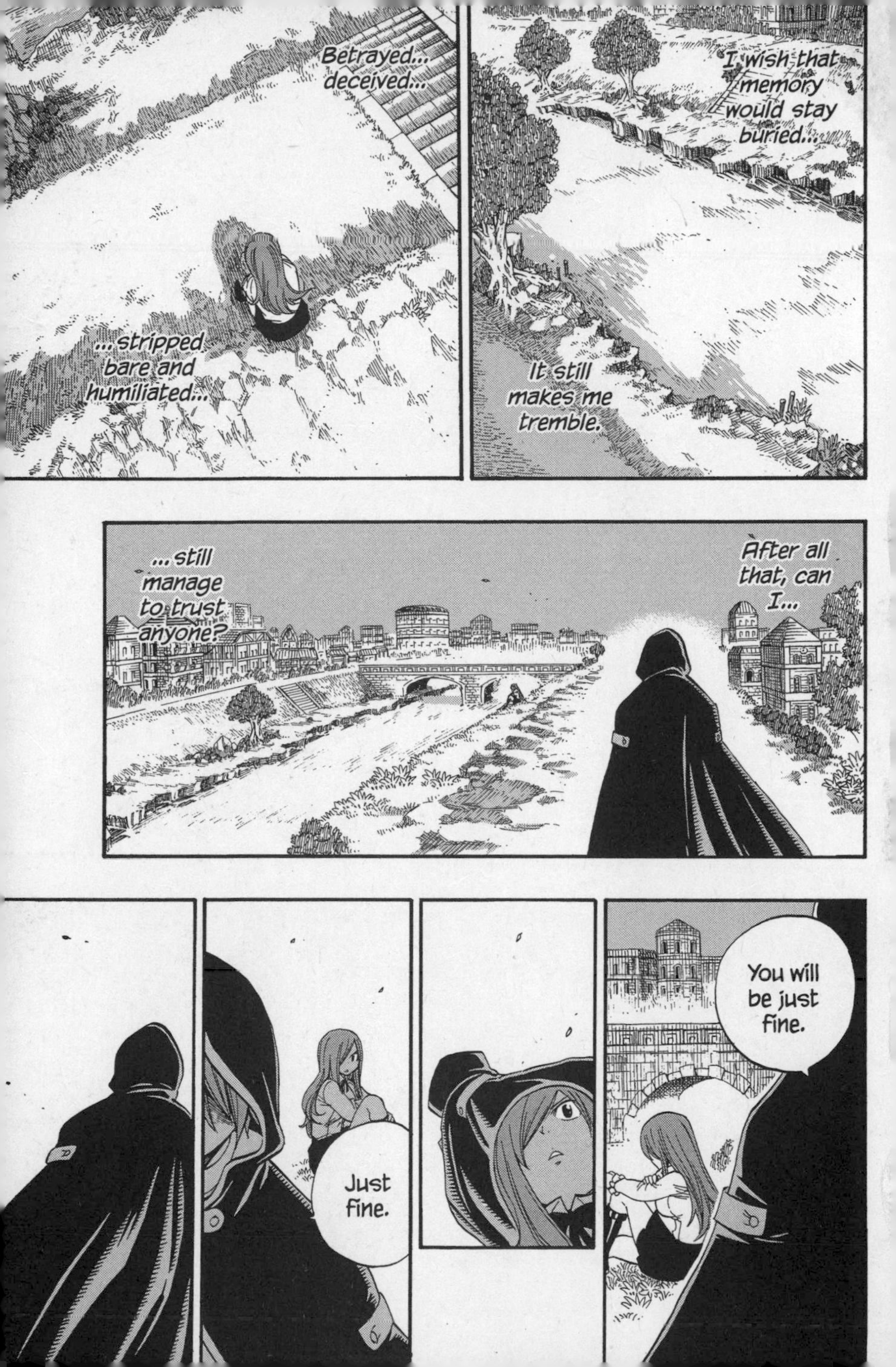
I wish that memory would stay buried...
It still makes me tremble.
Betrayed... deceived...
... stripped bare and humiliated...
After all that, can I...
... still manage to trust anyone?
You will be just fine.
Just fine.

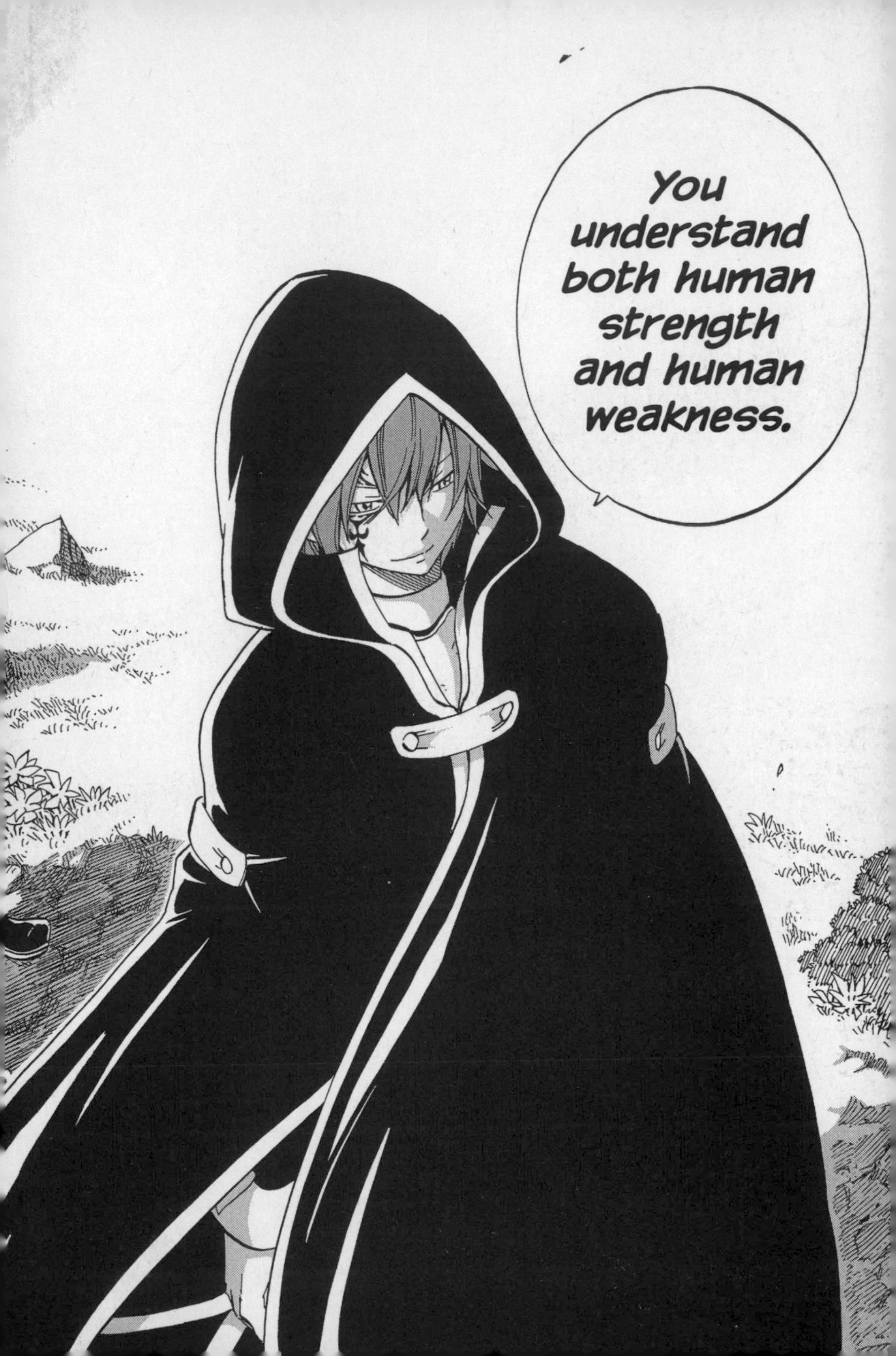
You understand both human strength and human weakness.

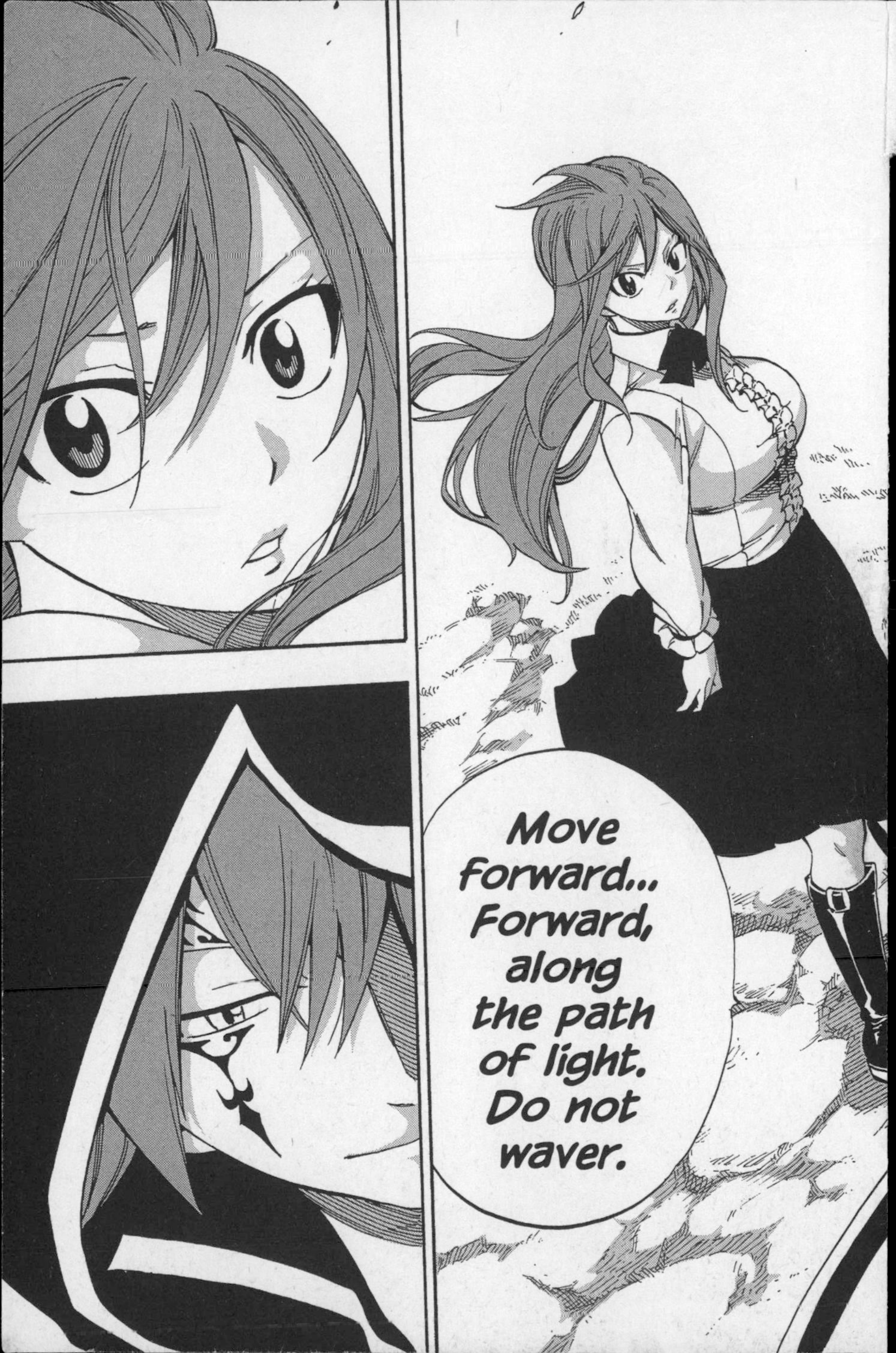
Move forward... Forward, along the path of light. Do not waver.

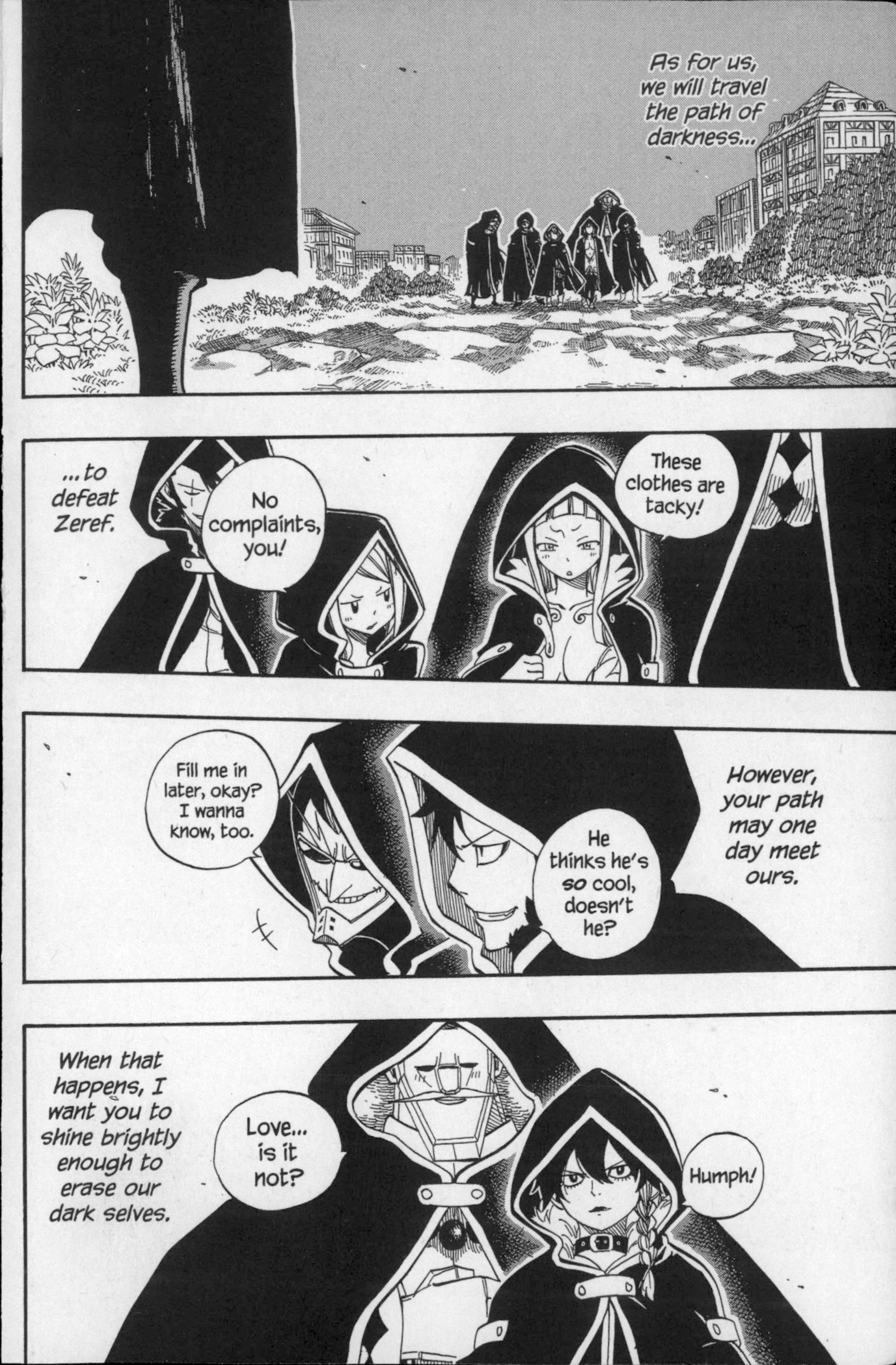
As for us, we will travel the path of darkness...
These clothes are tacky!
No complaints, you!
...to defeat Zeref.
However, your path may one day meet ours.
He thinks he's so cool, doesn't he?
Fill me in later, okay? I wanna know, too.
Humph!
Love... is it not?
When that happens, I want you to shine brightly enough to erase our dark selves.

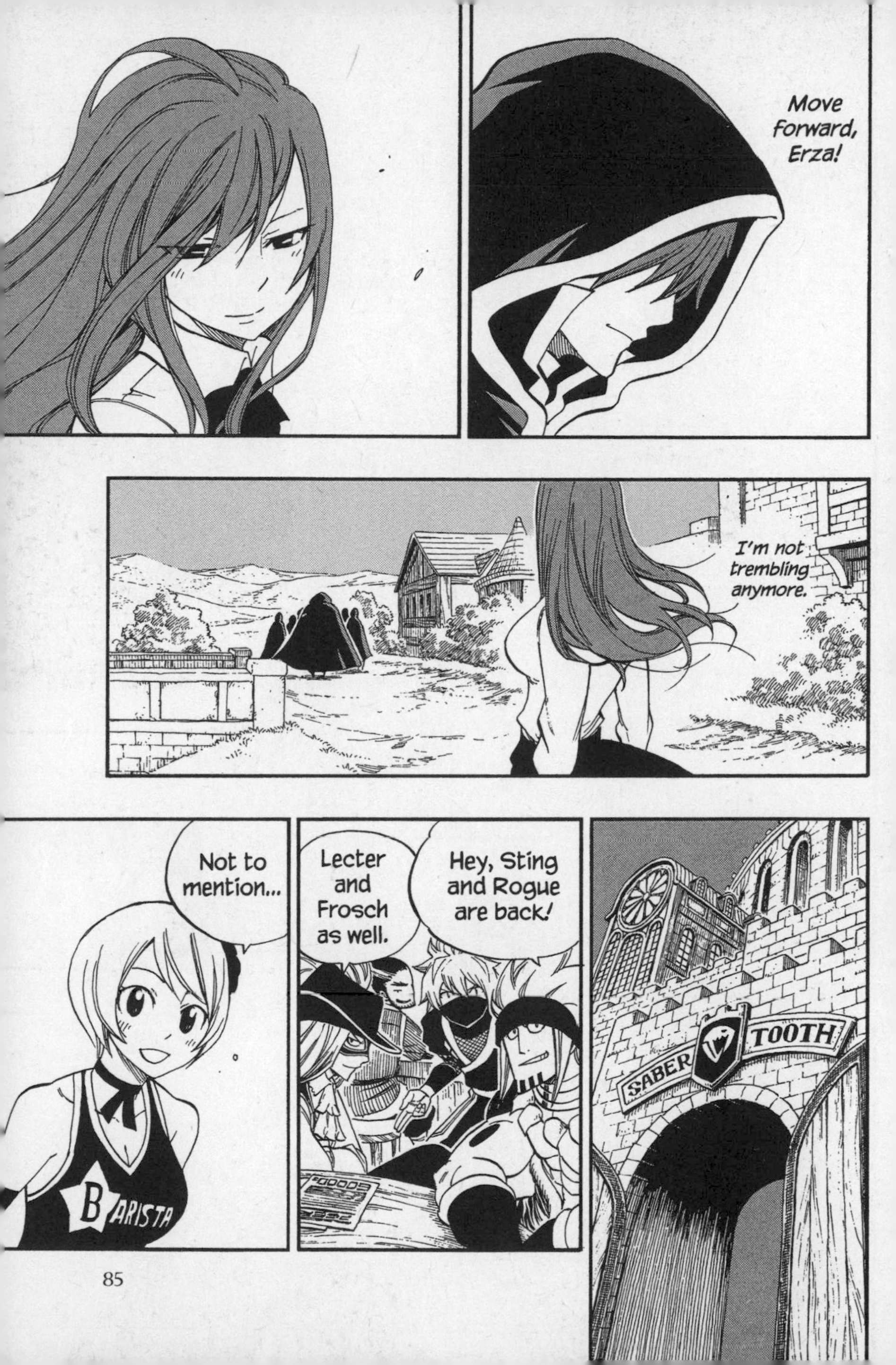
Move forward, Erza!
I'm not trembling anymore.
SABER TOOTH
Hey, Sting and Rogue are back!
Lecter and Frosch as well.
Not to mention...
BARISTA

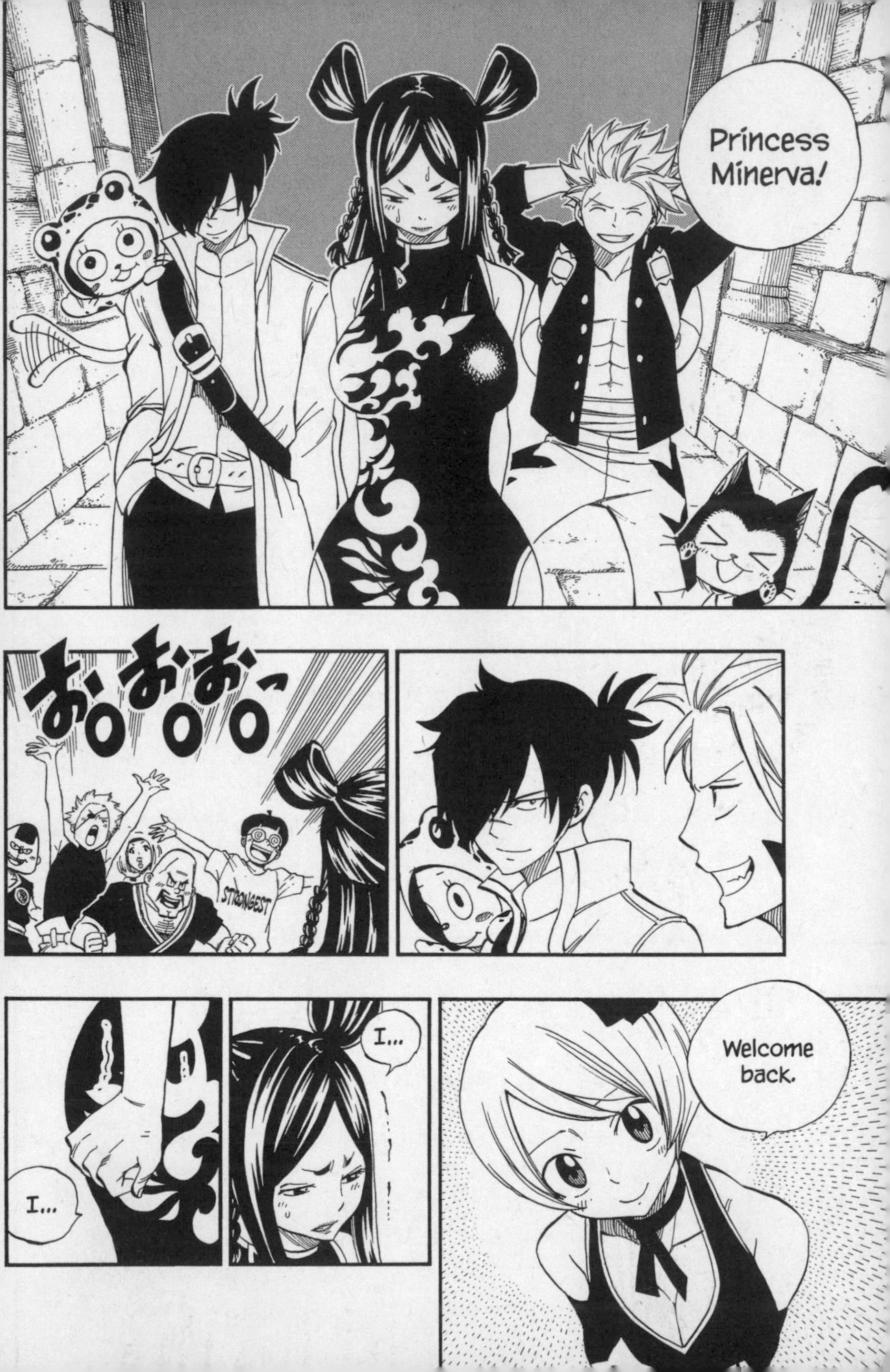
Princess Minerva!
Welcome back.
I...
I...

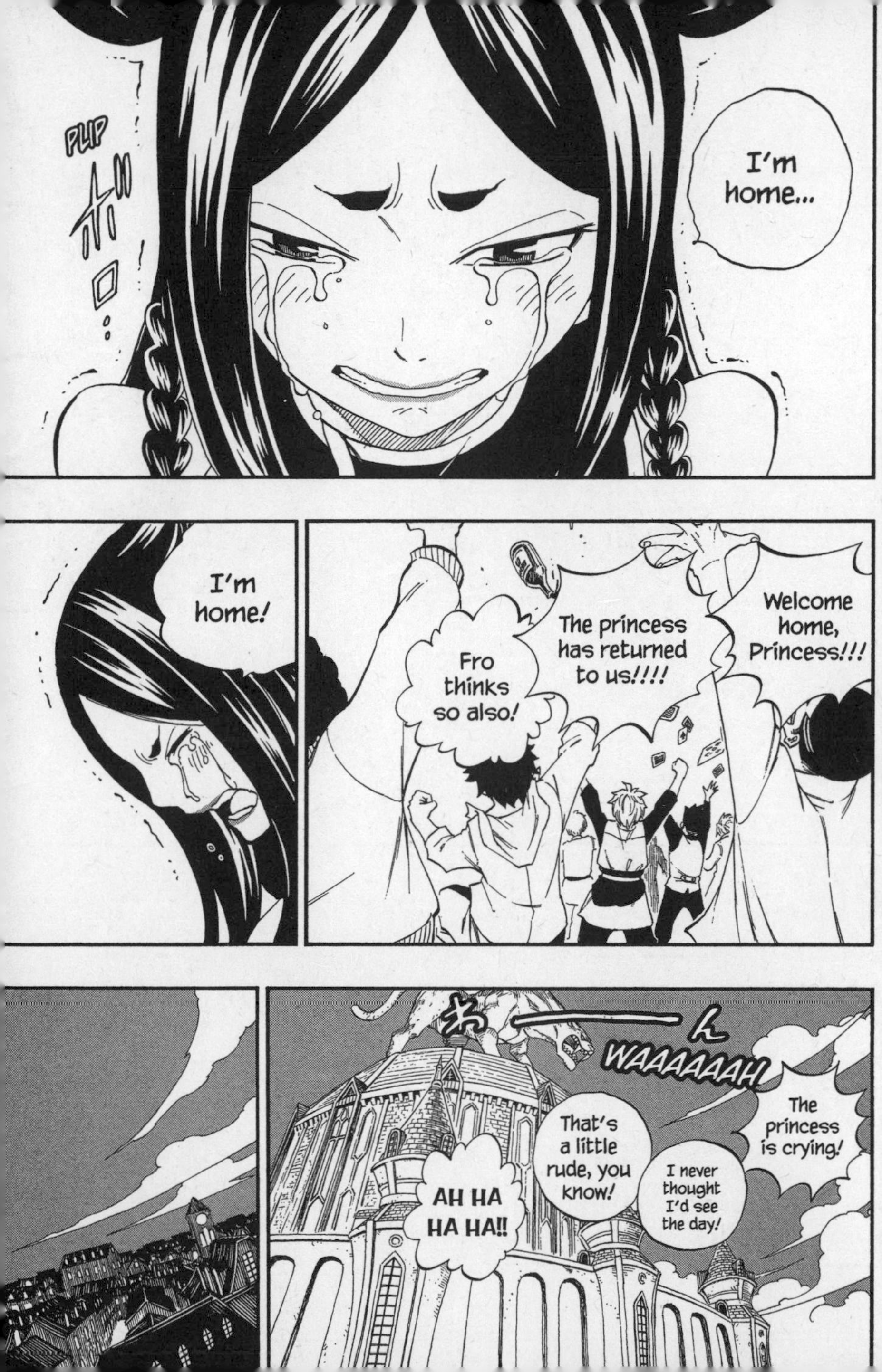
PLIP
I'm home...
Welcome home, Princess!!!
The princess has returned to us!!!!
Fro thinks so also!
I'm home!
WAAAAAAH
The princess is crying!
I never thought I'd see the day!
That's a little rude, you know!
AH HA HA HA!!

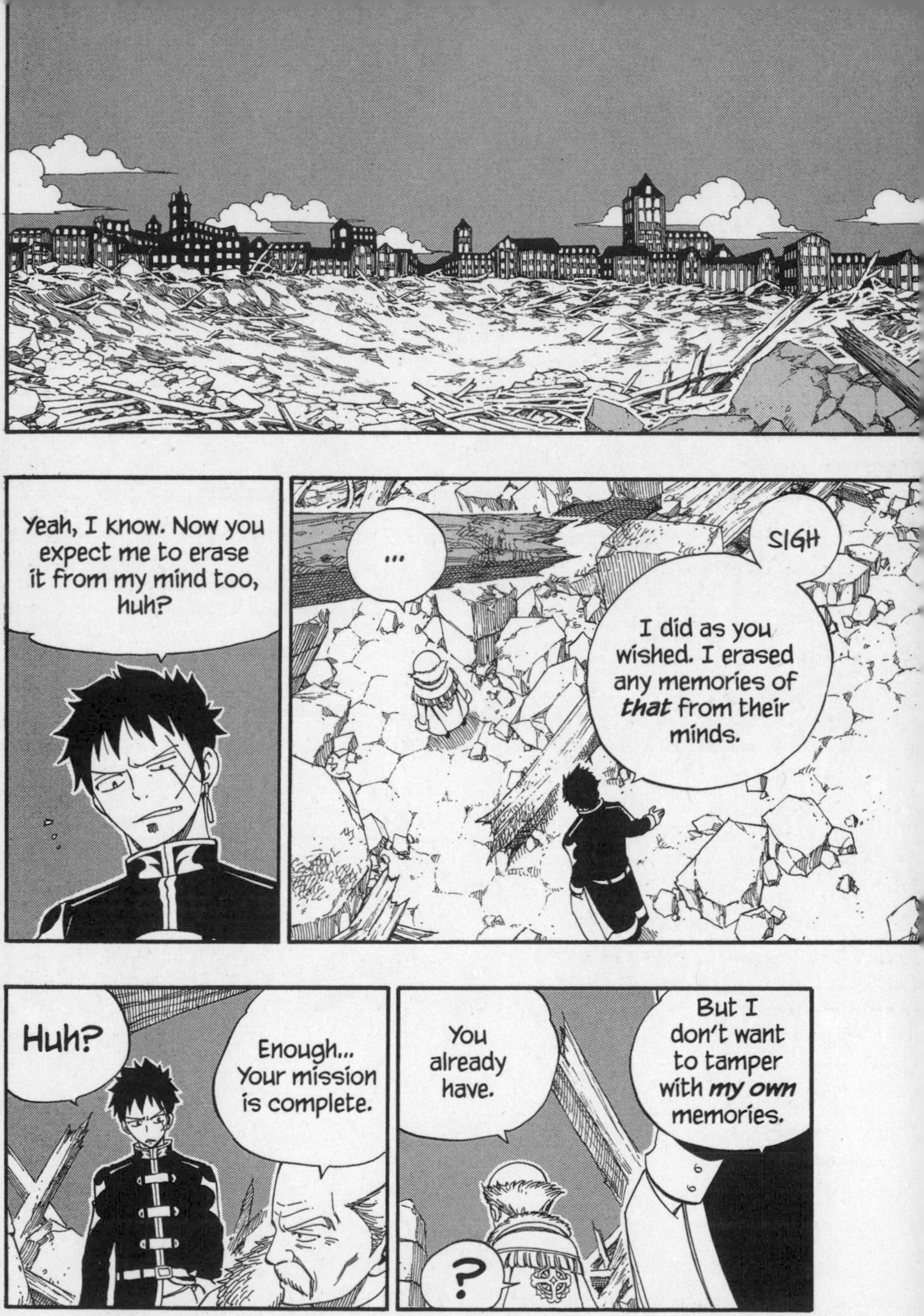
SIGH
I did as you wished. I erased any memories of *that* from their minds.
...
Yeah, I know. Now you expect me to erase it from my mind too, huh?
But I don't want to tamper with *my own* memories.
You already have.
?
Enough... Your mission is complete.
Huh?

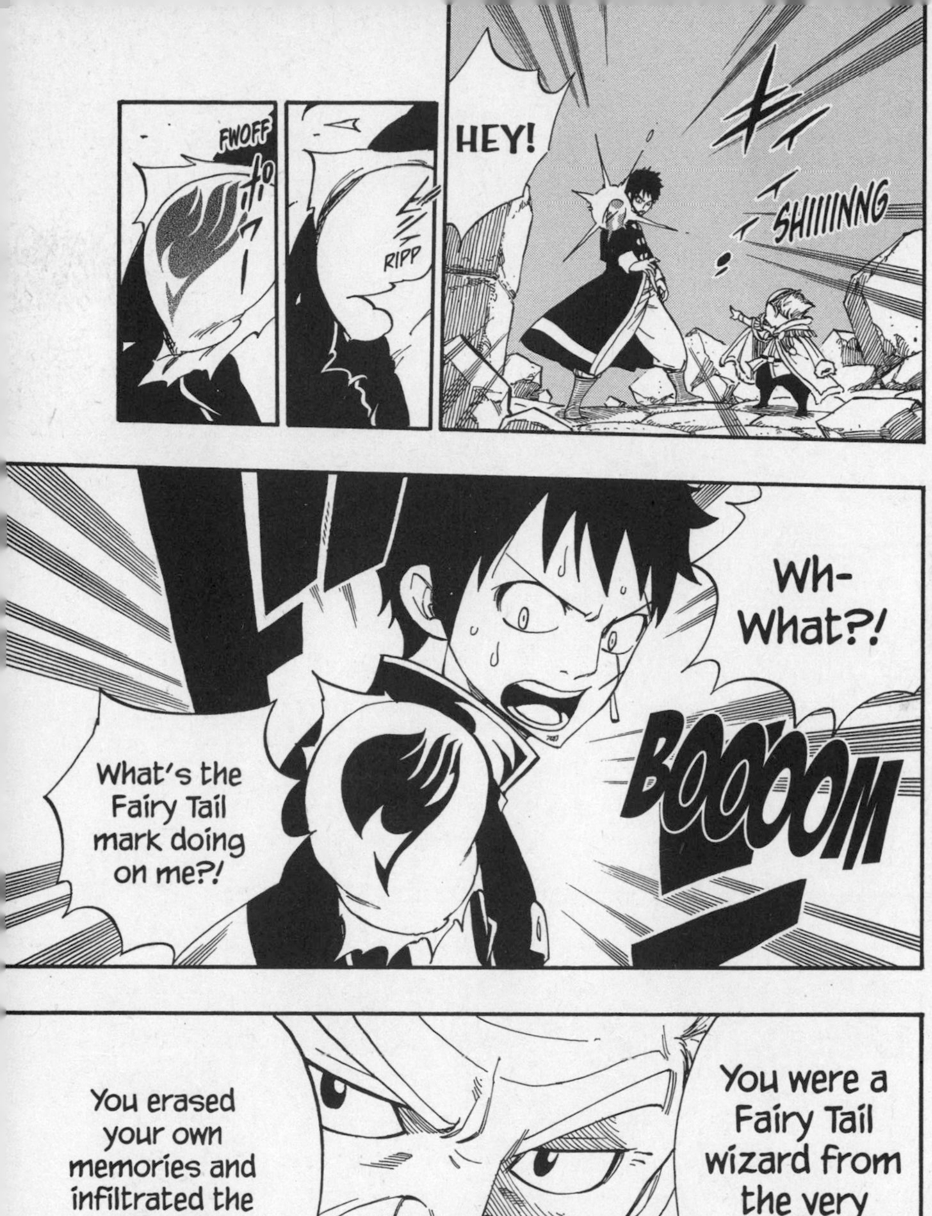
HEY!
SHIIIINNG
RIPP
FWOFF
Wh-What?!
BOOOOM
What's the Fairy Tail mark doing on me?!
You were a Fairy Tail wizard from the very start!
You erased your own memories and infiltrated the Council!

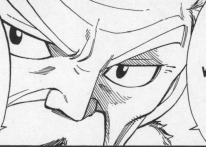

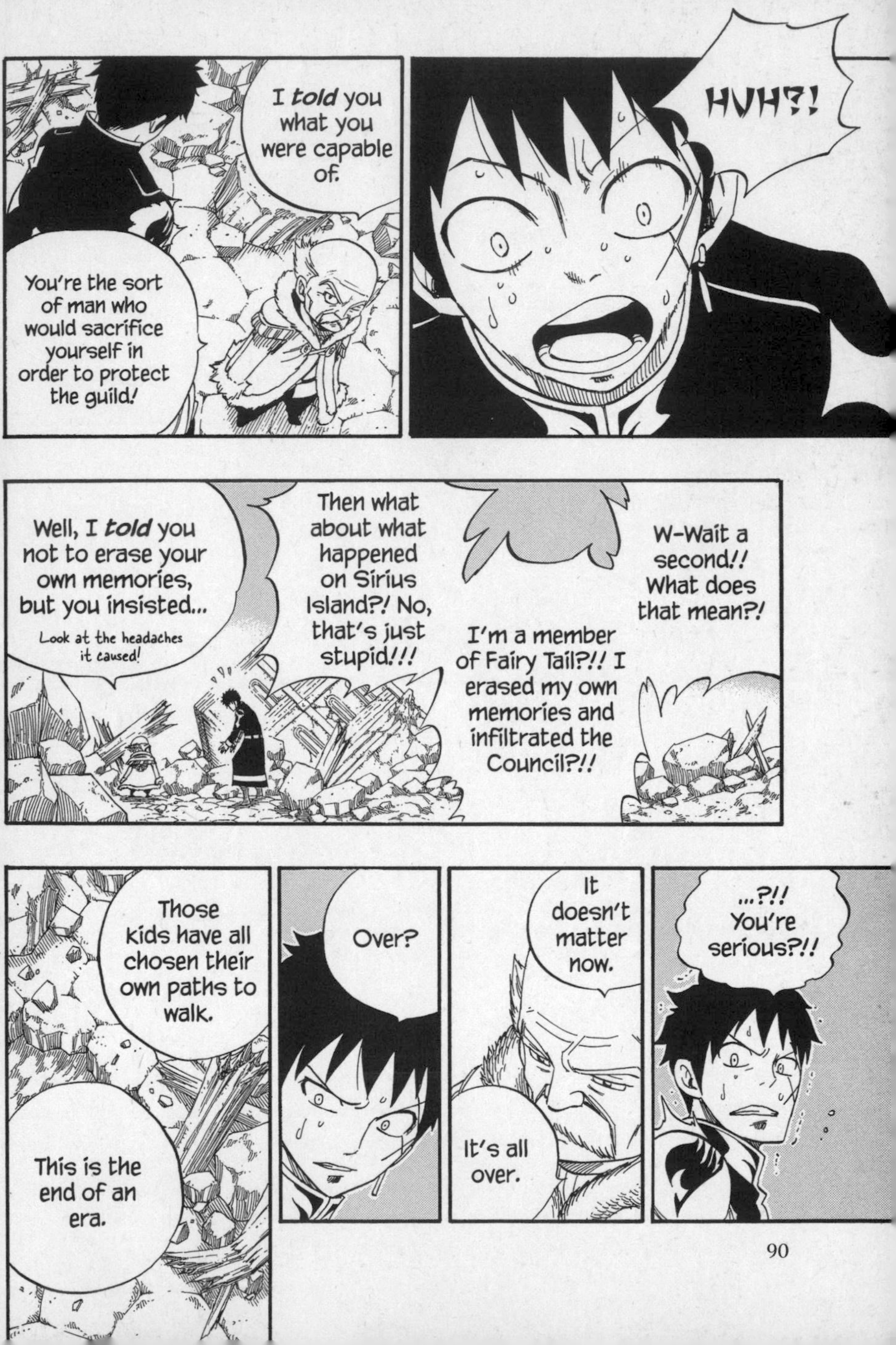
HUH?!
I *told* you what you were capable of.
You're the sort of man who would sacrifice yourself in order to protect the guild!
W-Wait a second!! What does that mean?!
I'm a member of Fairy Tail?!! I erased my own memories and infiltrated the Council?!!
Then what about what happened on Sirius Island?! No, that's just stupid!!!
Well, I *told* you not to erase your own memories, but you insisted...
Look at the headaches it caused!
...?!! You're serious?!!
It doesn't matter now.
It's all over.
Over?
Those kids have all chosen their own paths to walk.
This is the end of an era.

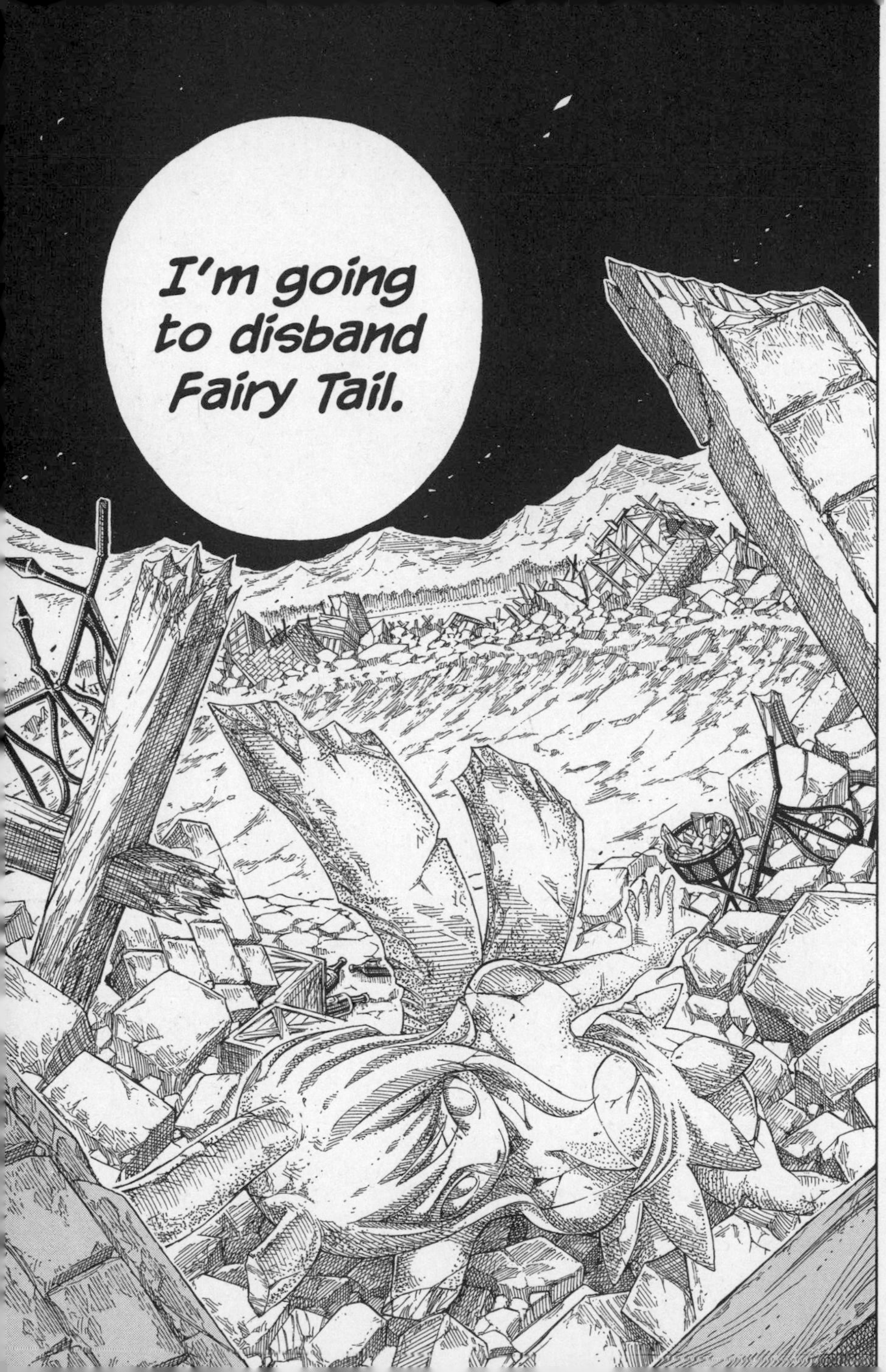
I'm going to disband Fairy Tail.

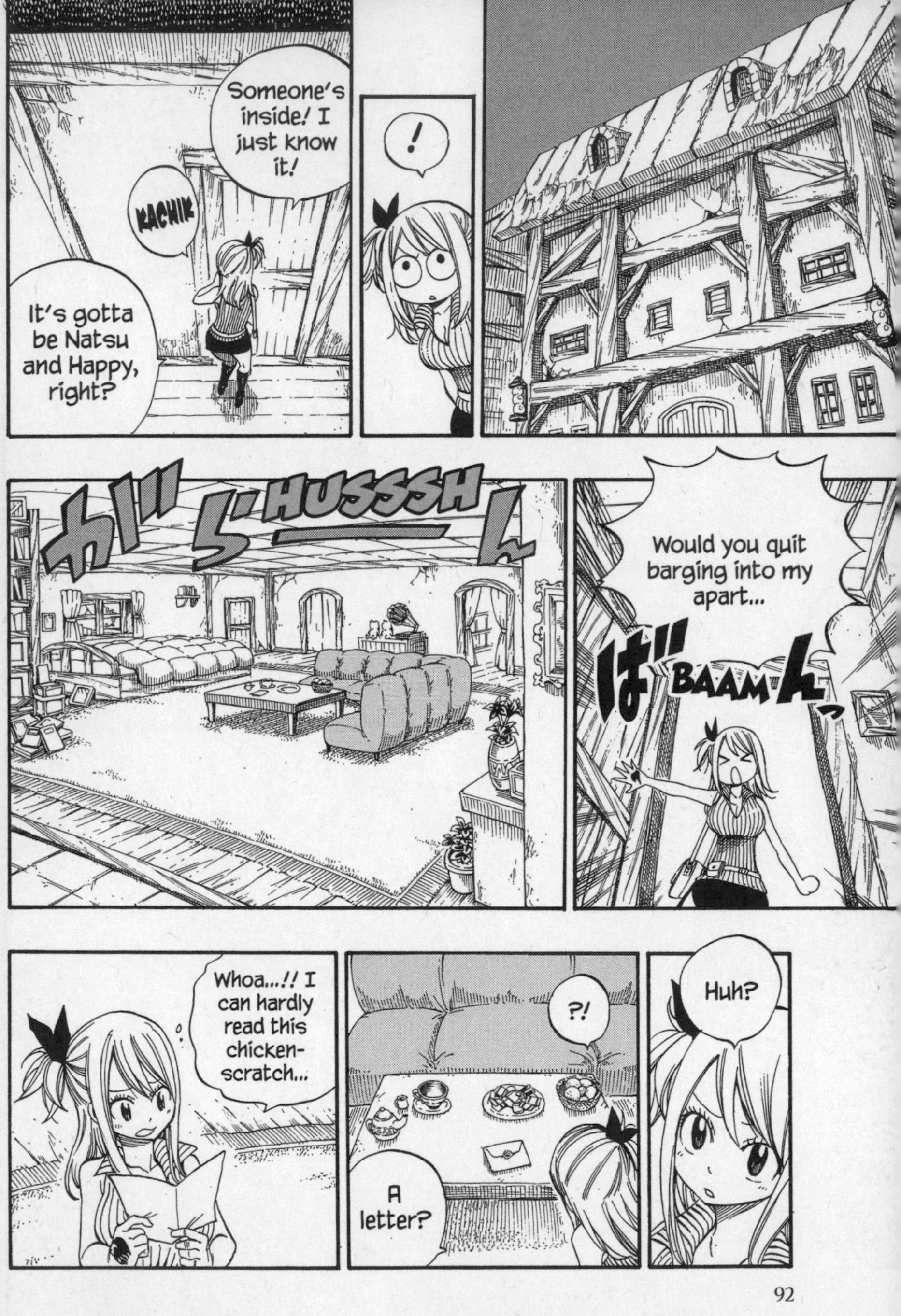
!
Someone's inside! I just know it!
KACHIK
It's gotta be Natsu and Happy, right?
Would you quit barging into my apart...
BAAM
HUSSSH
Huh?
?!
A letter?
Whoa...!! I can hardly read this chicken-scratch...

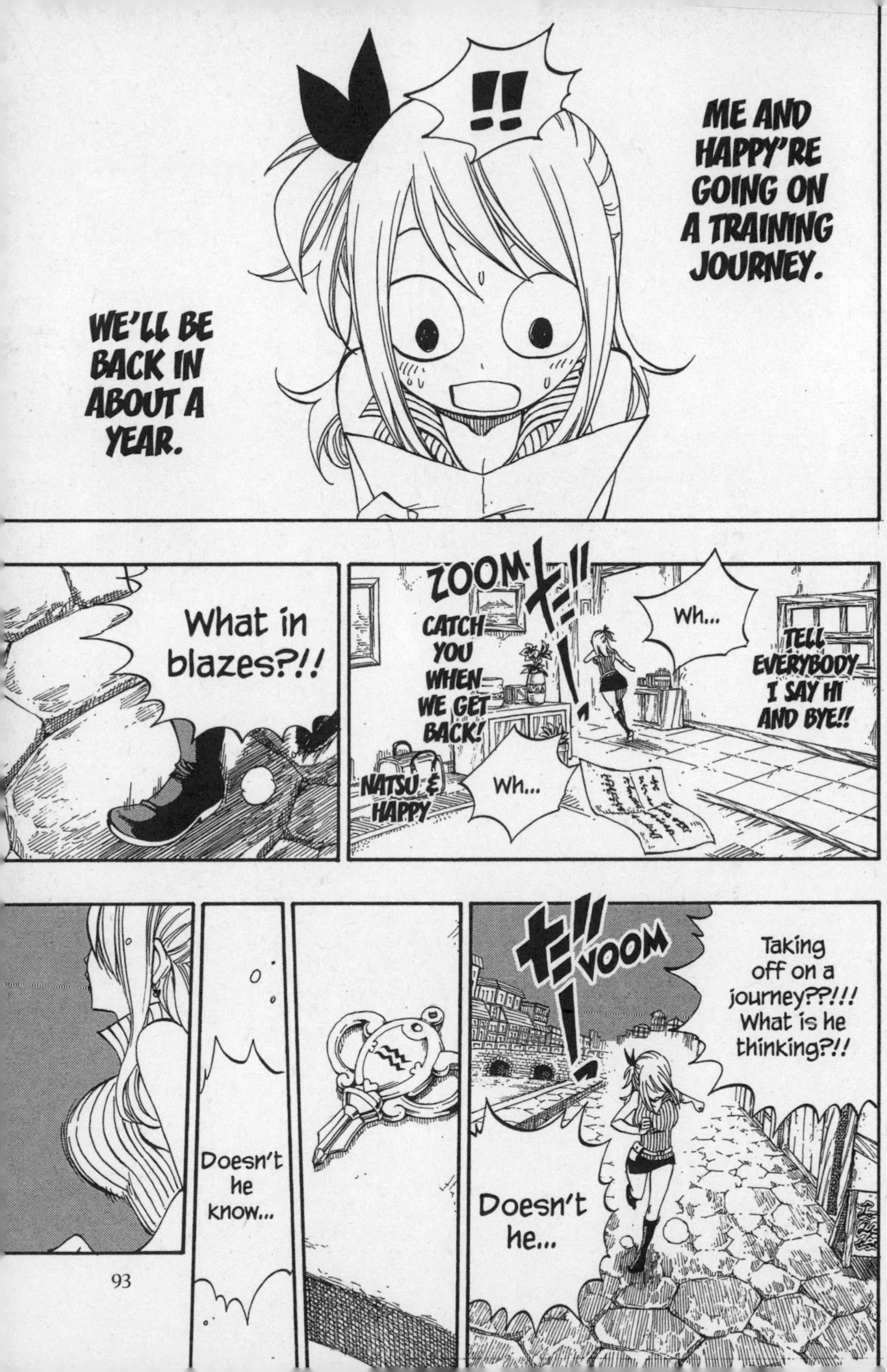
!!
ME AND HAPPY'RE GOING ON A TRAINING JOURNEY.
WE'LL BE BACK IN ABOUT A YEAR.
ZOOM
TELL EVERYBODY I SAY HI AND BYE!!
Wh...
CATCH YOU WHEN WE GET BACK!
NATSU & HAPPY
Wh...
What in blazes?!!
VOOM
Taking off on a journey??!!! What is he thinking?!!
Doesn't he...
Doesn't he know...

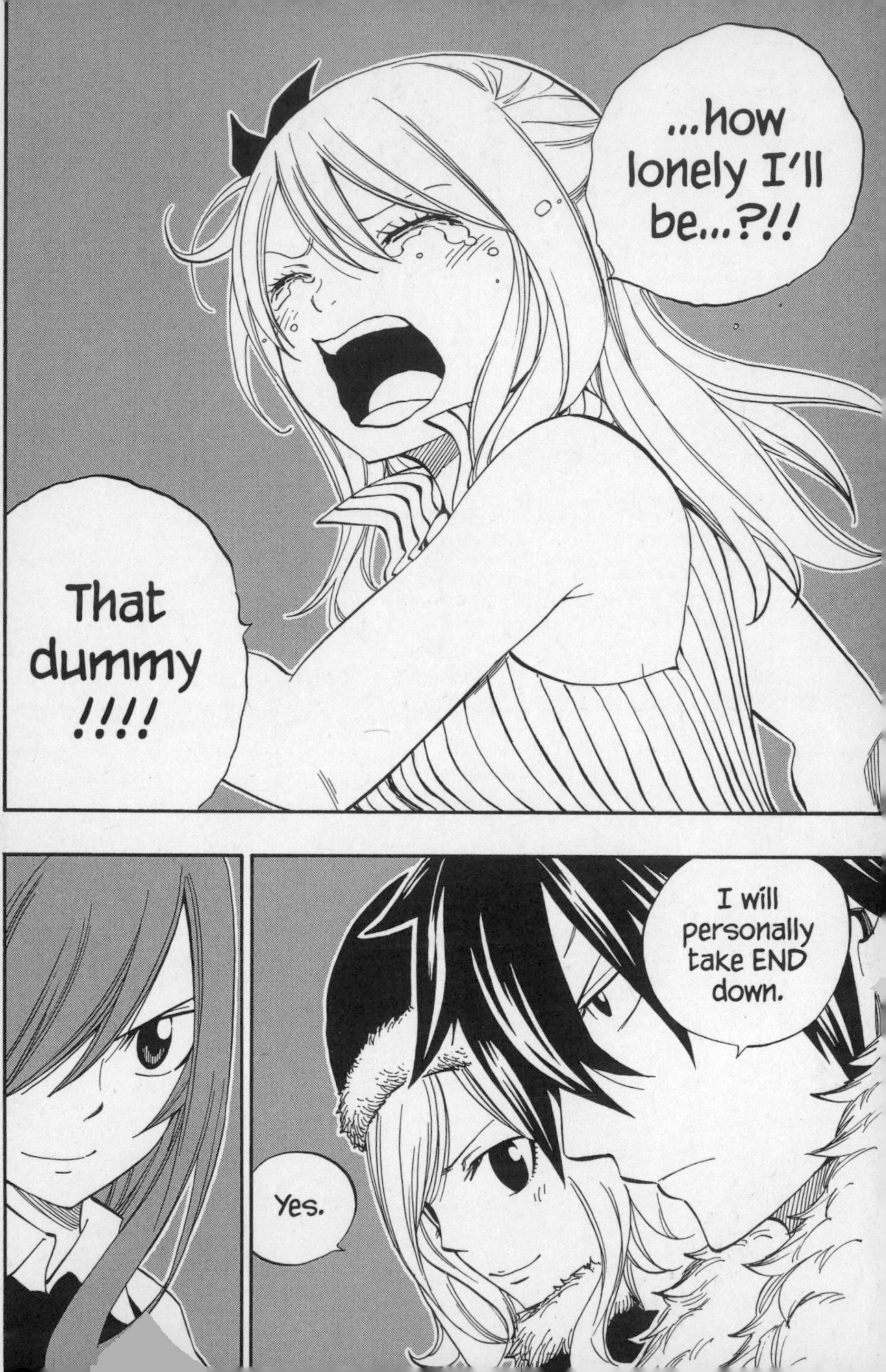
...how lonely I'll be...?!!
That dummy !!!!
I will personally take END down.
Yes.

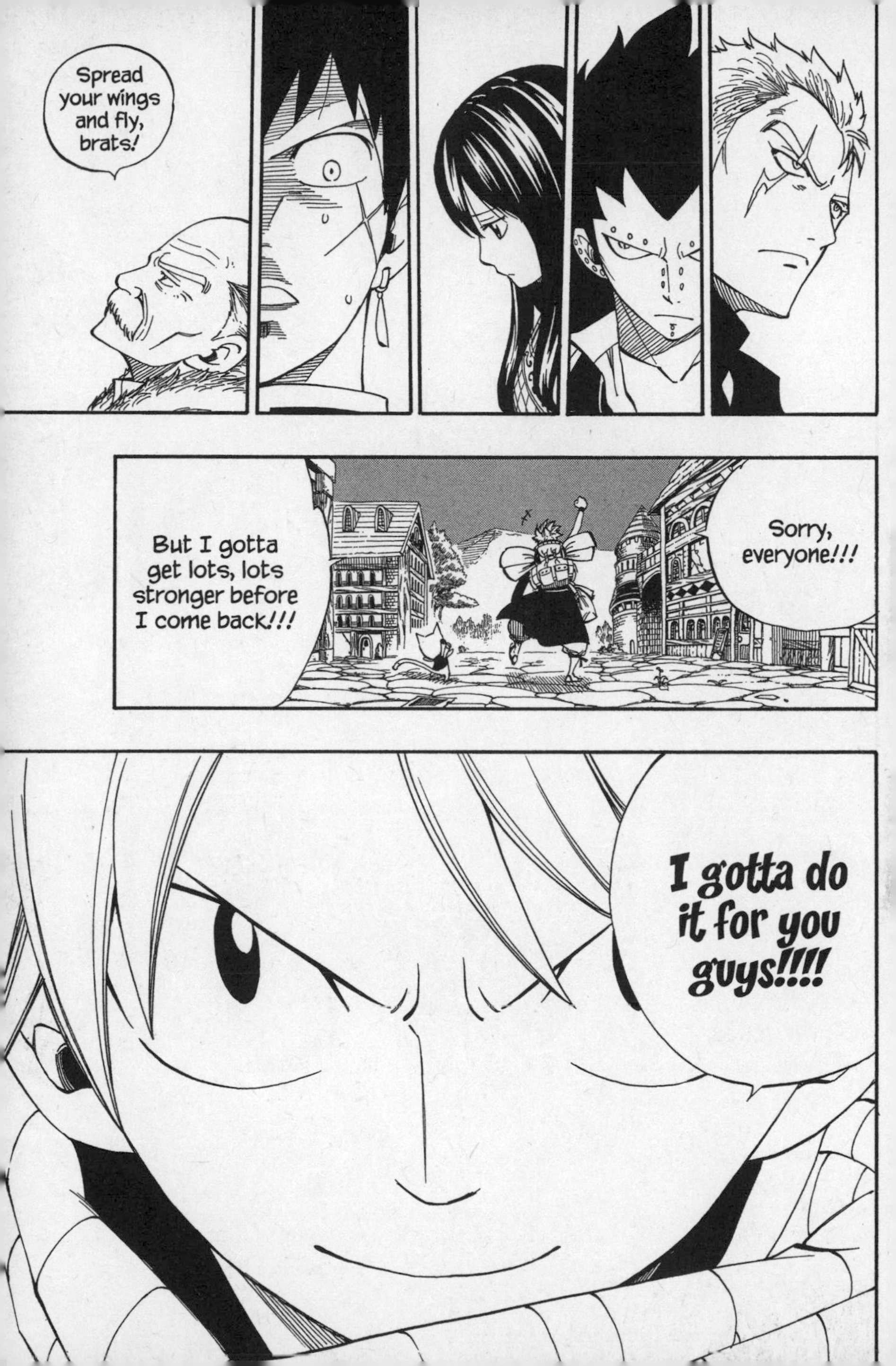
Spread your wings and fly, brats!
Sorry, everyone!!!
But I gotta get lots, lots stronger before I come back!!!
I gotta do it for you guys!!!!

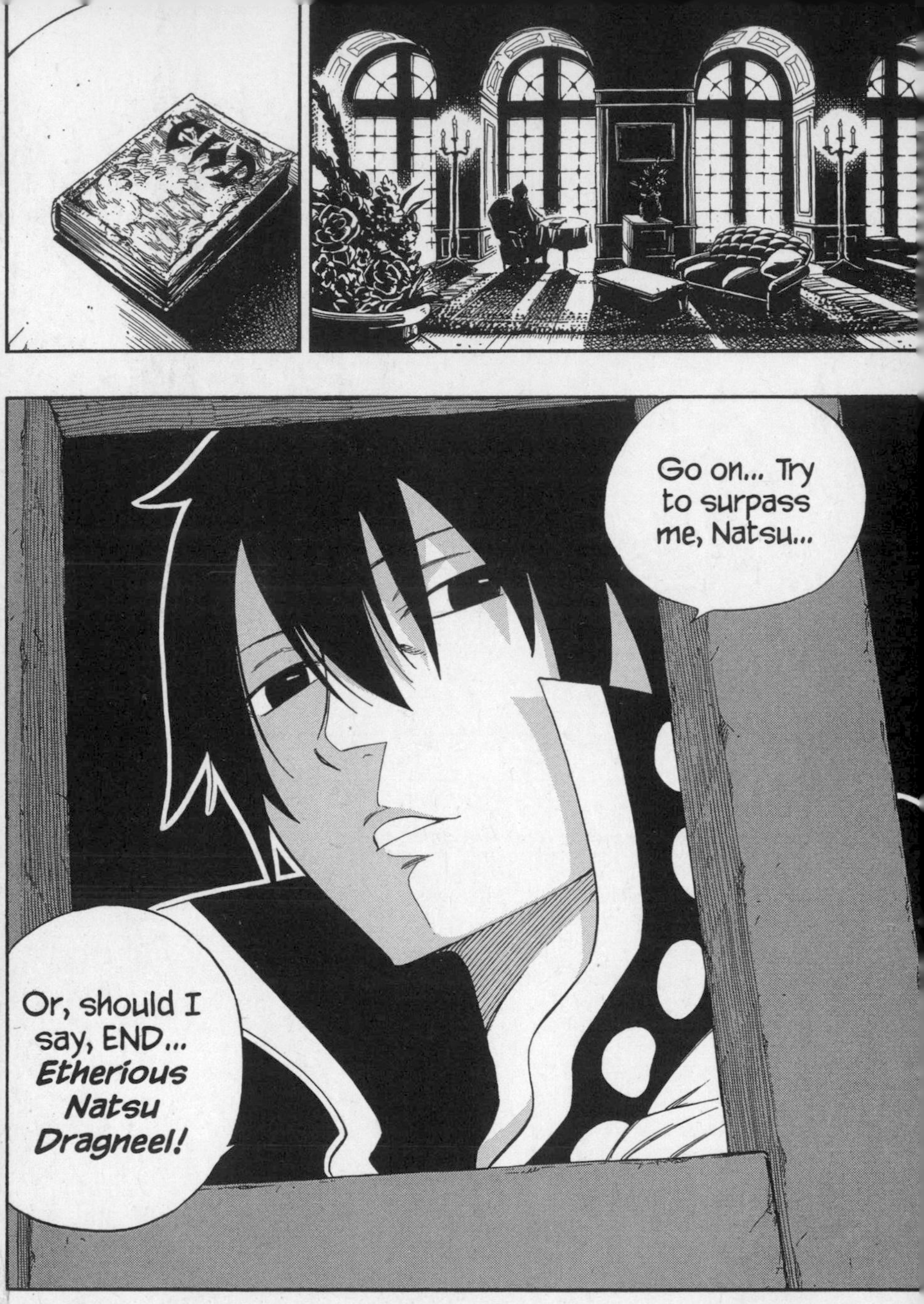
Go on... Try to surpass me, Natsu...
Or, should I say, END... *Etherious Natsu Dragneel!*

Chapter 417: Lone Journey II

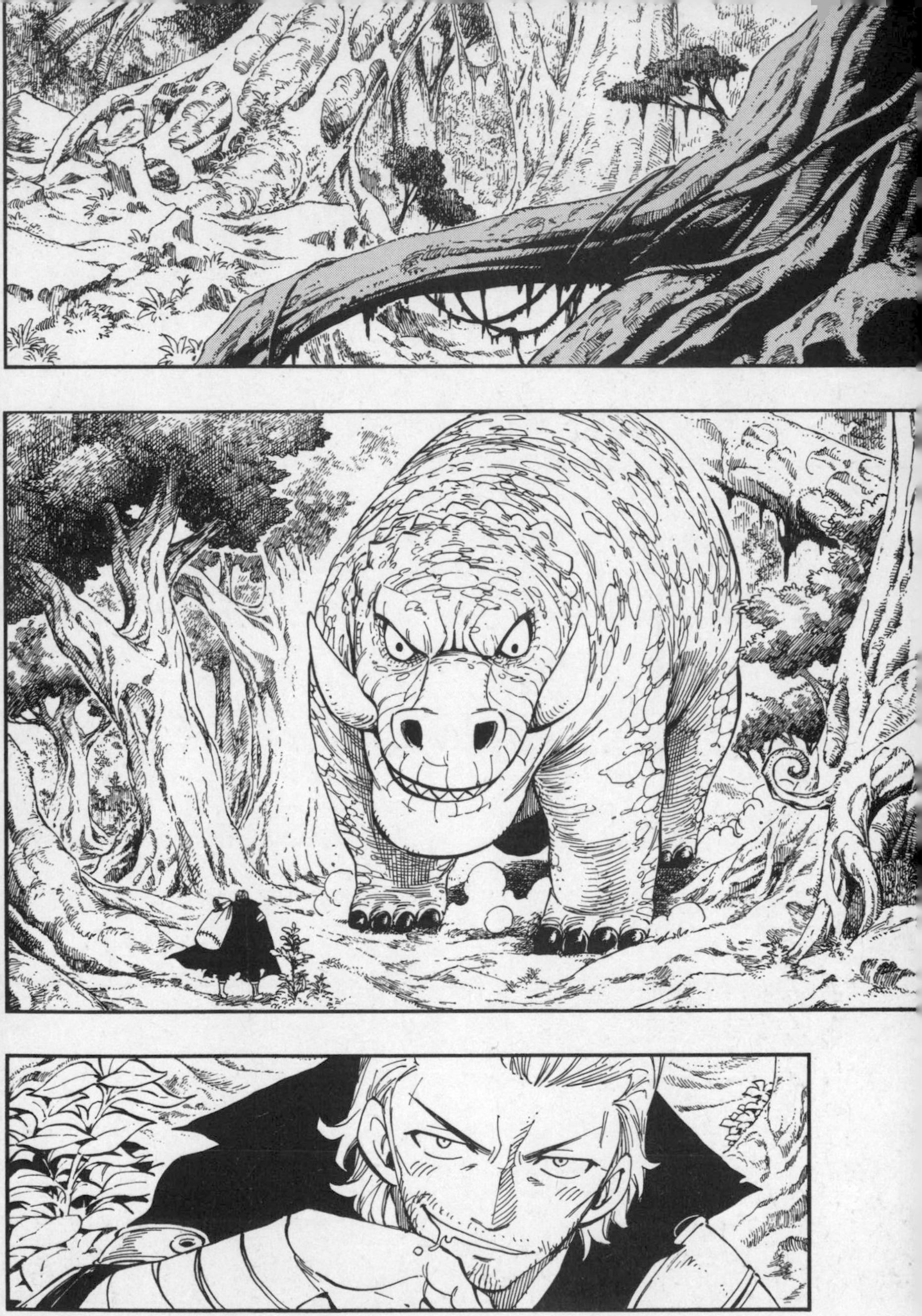

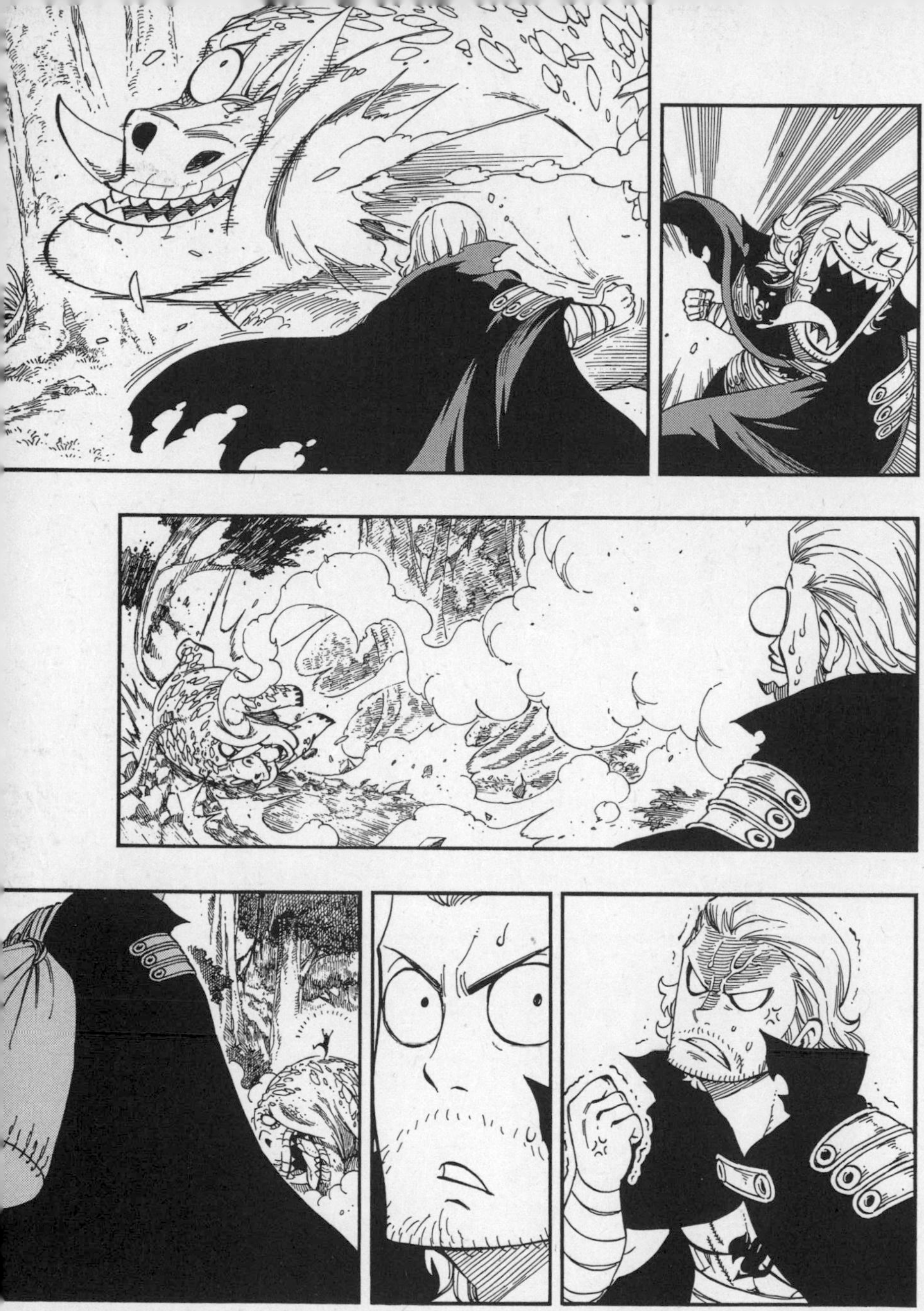

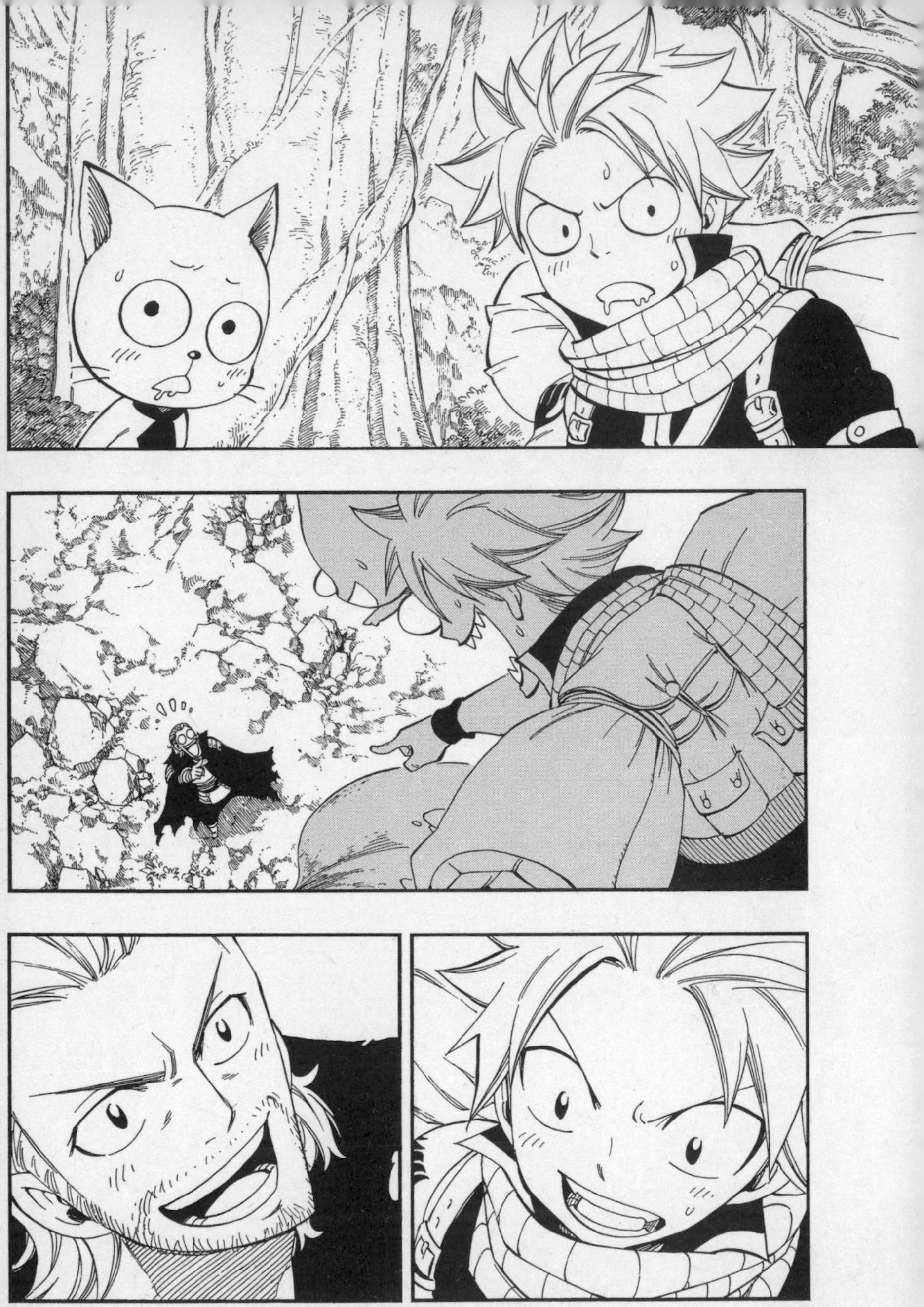

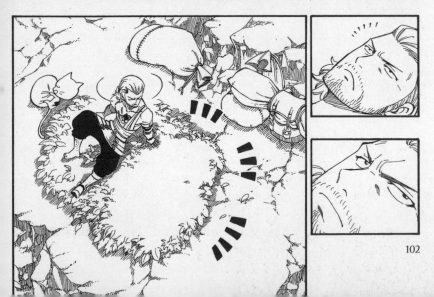

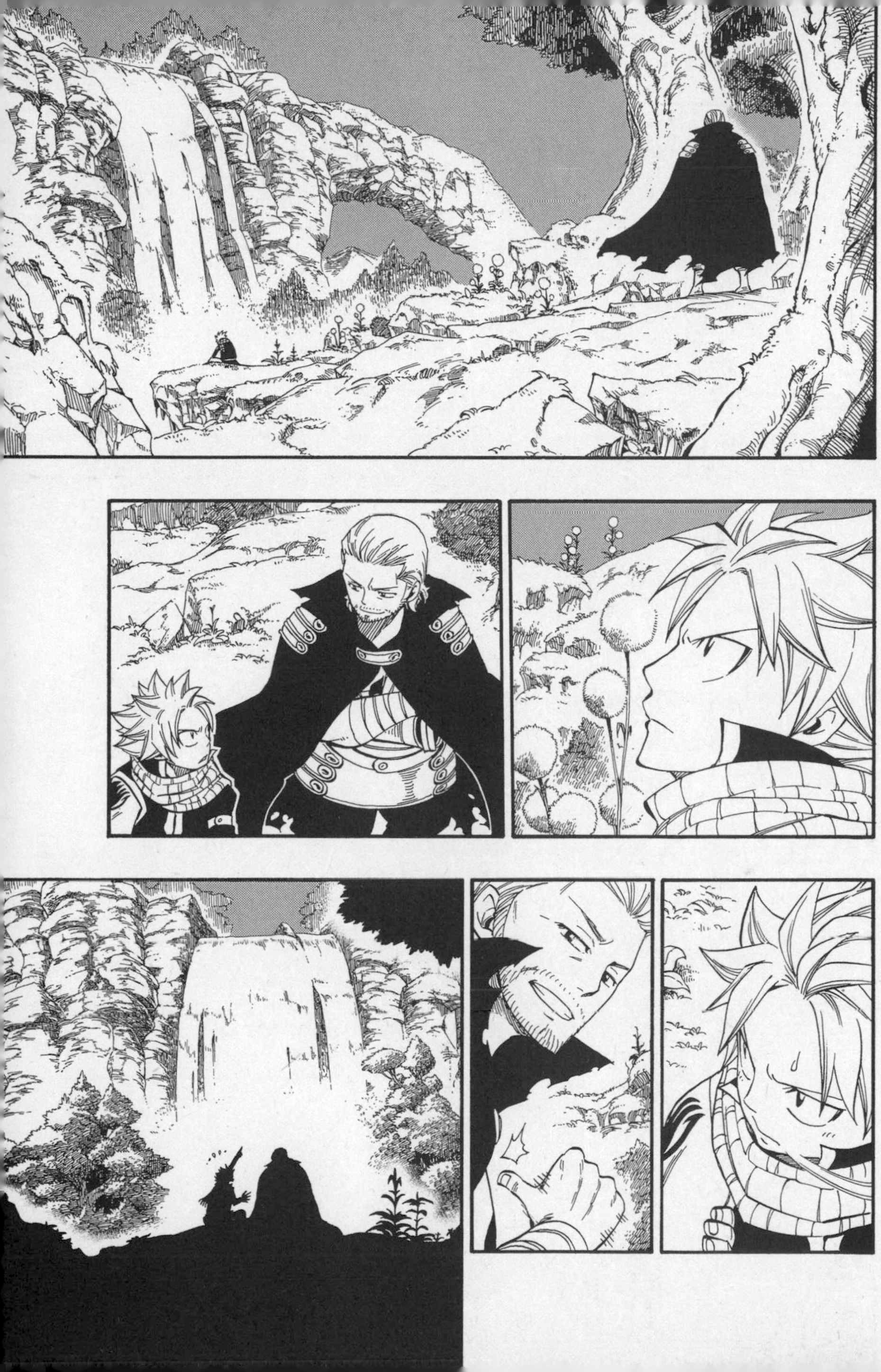

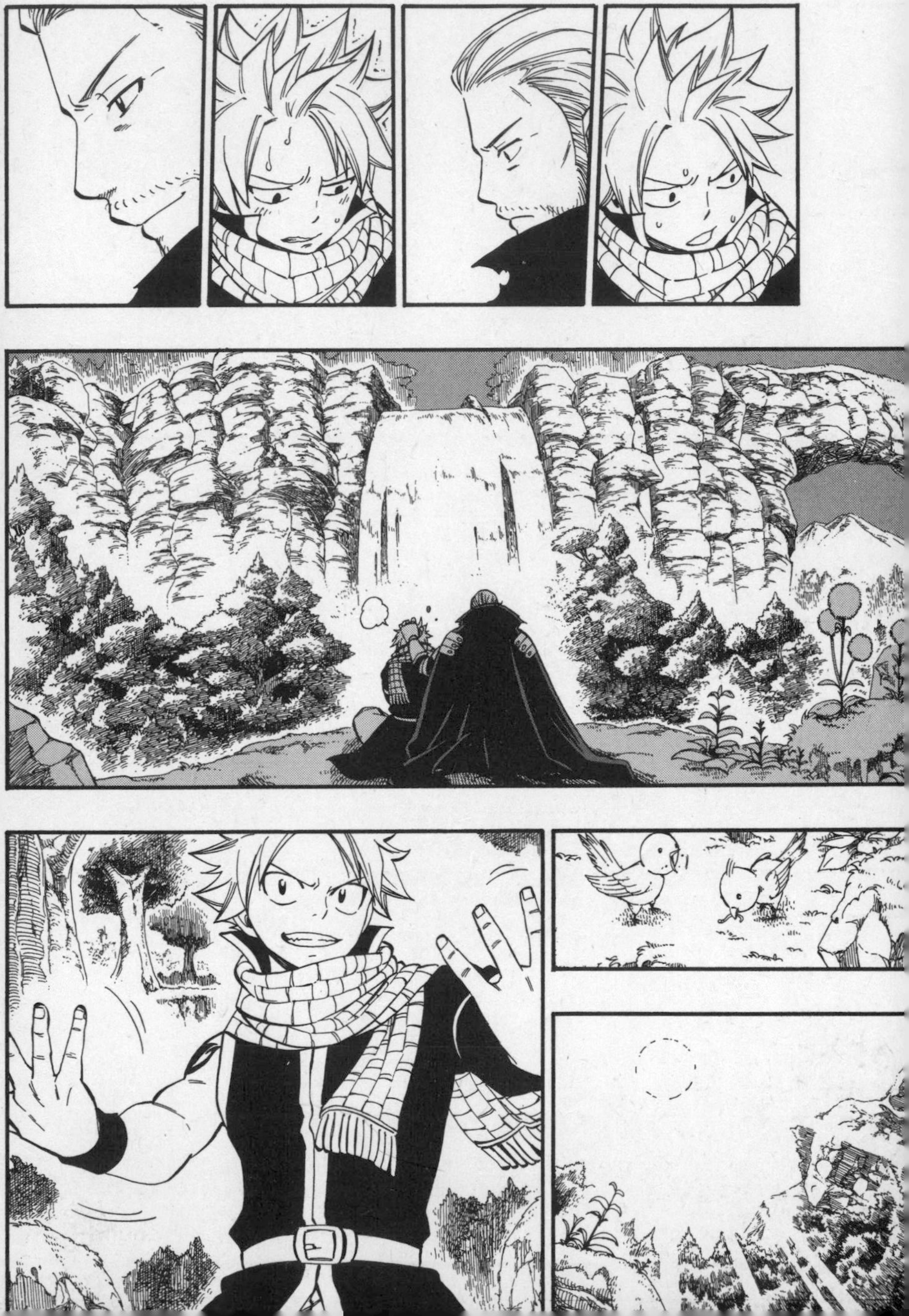

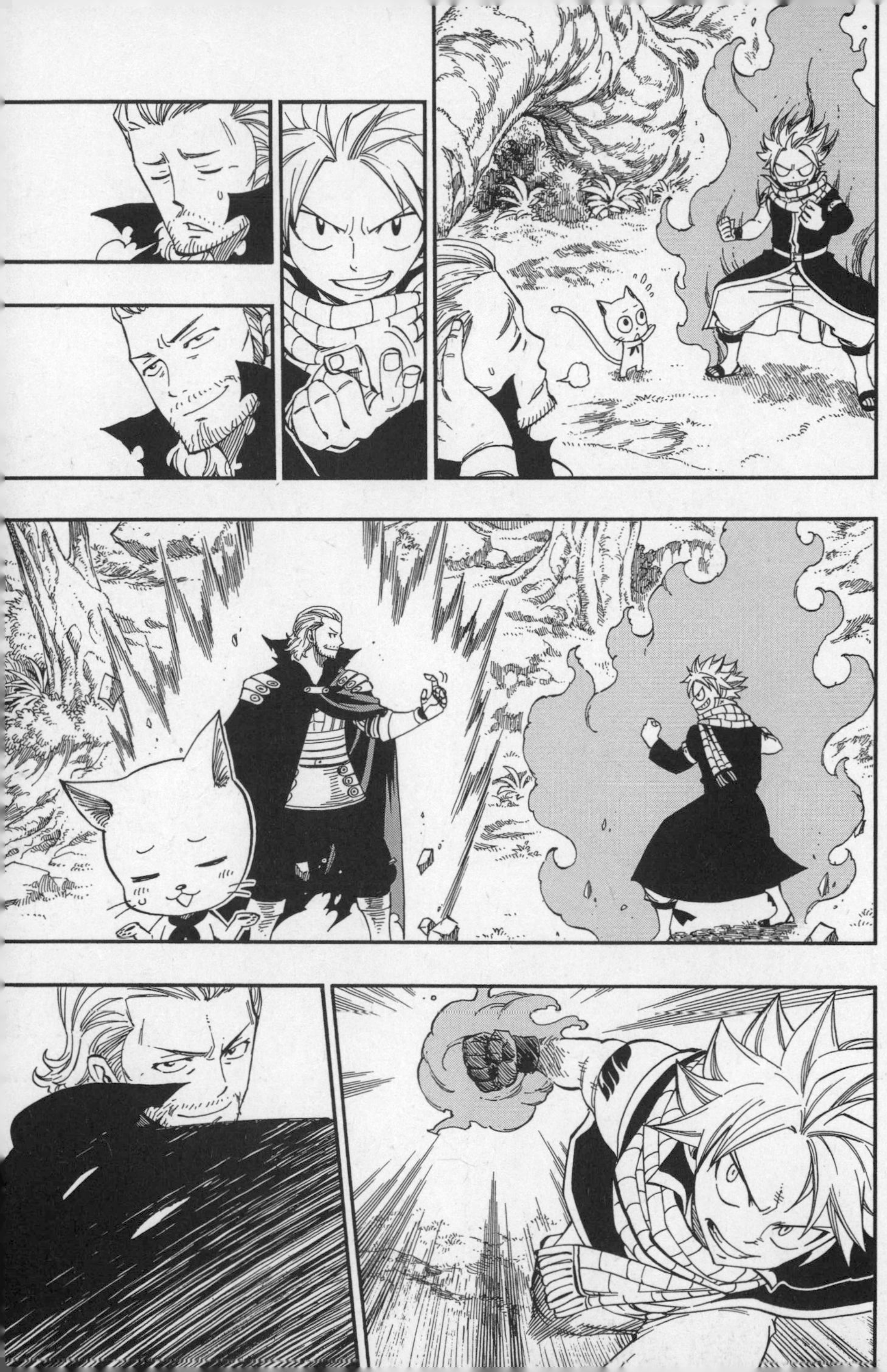

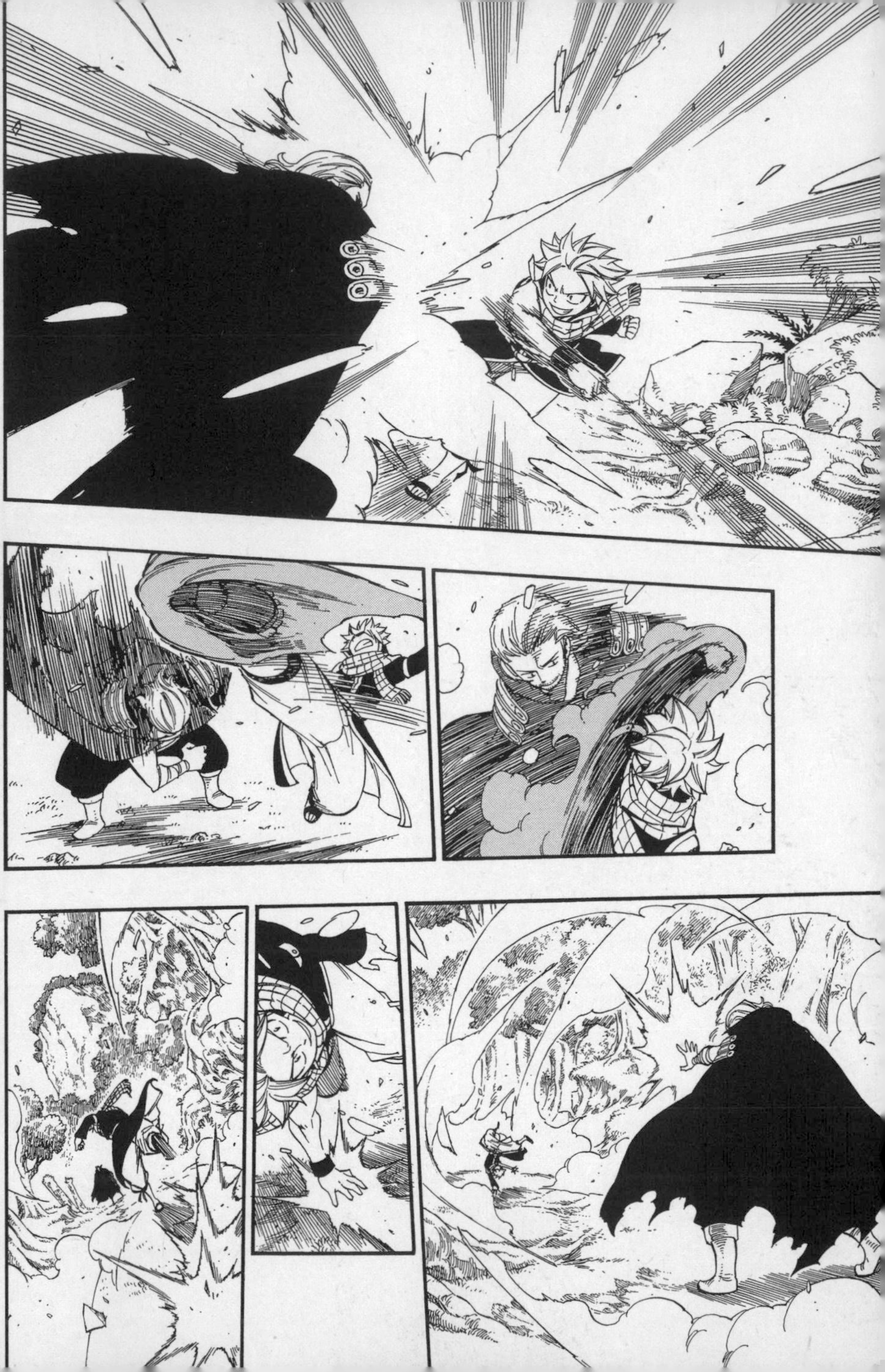

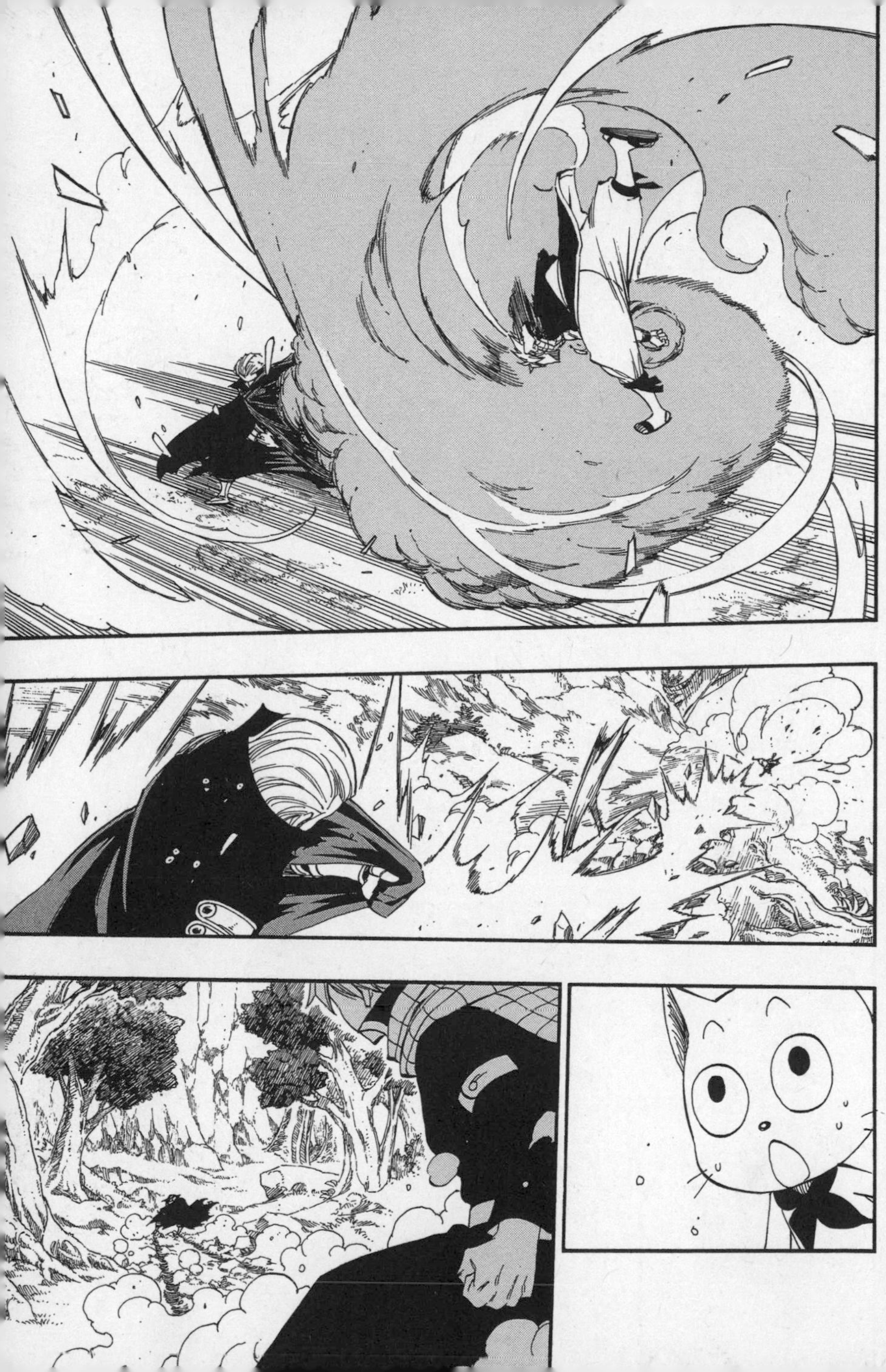

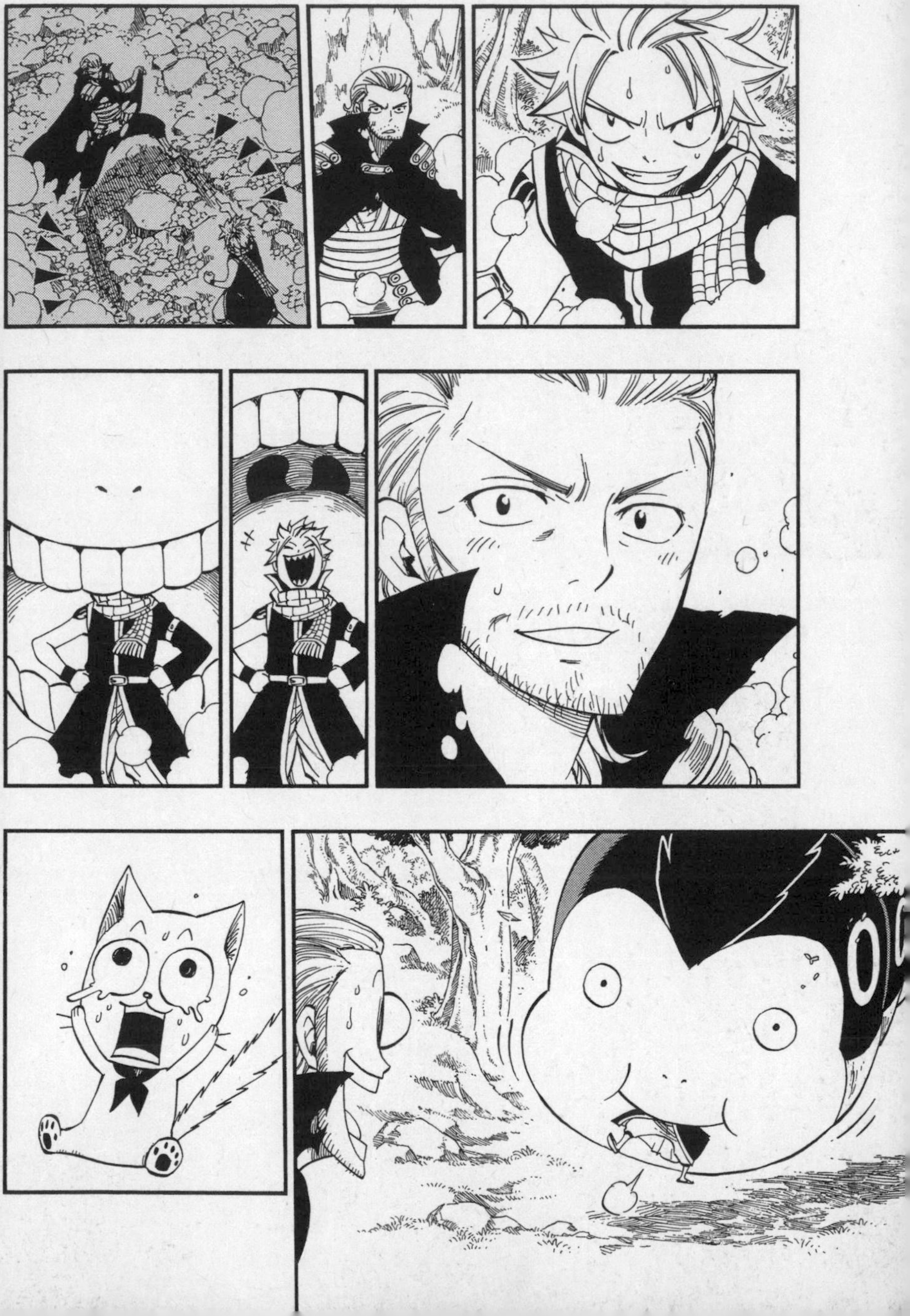

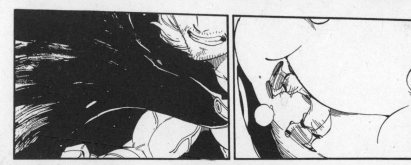

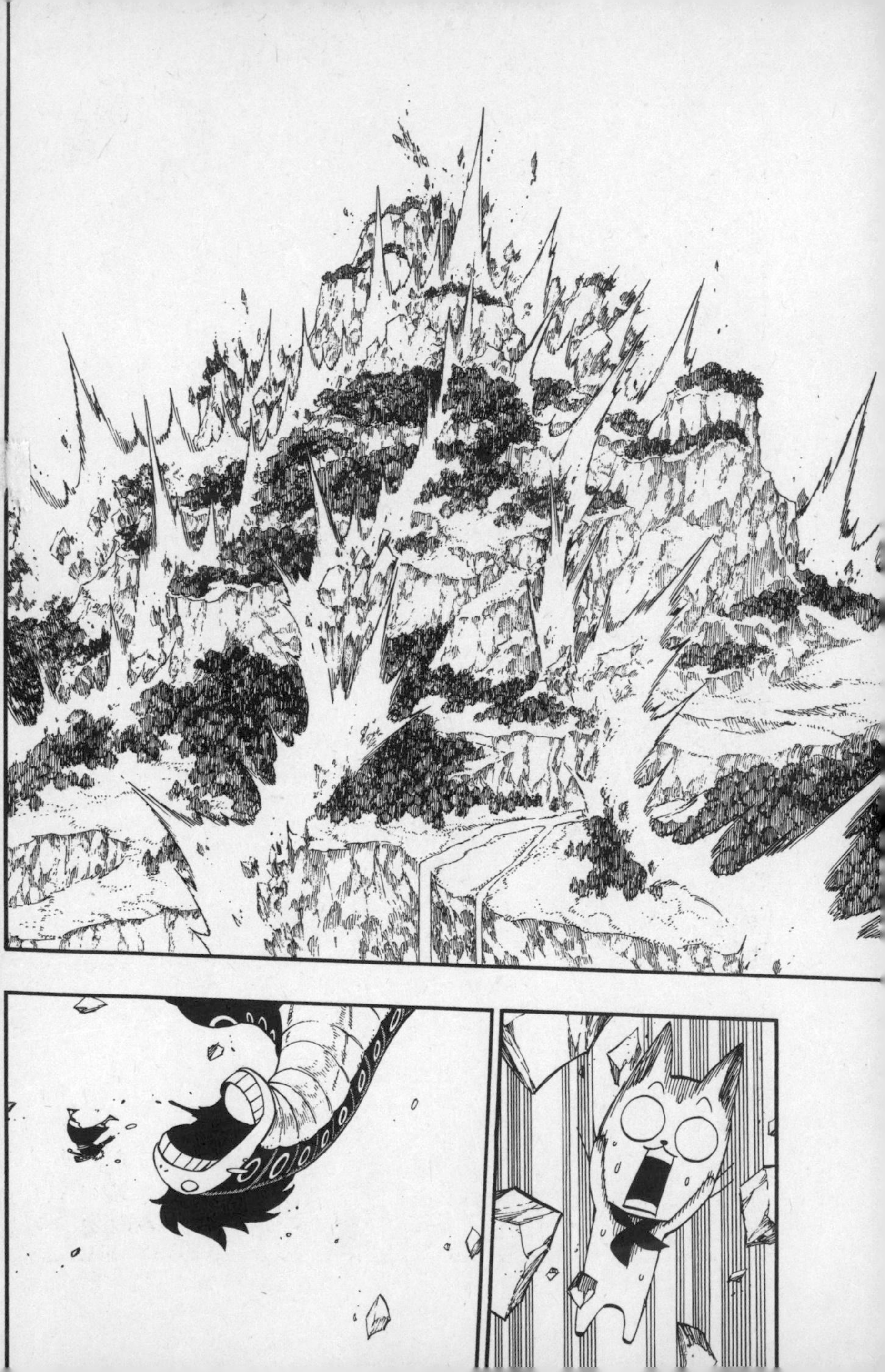

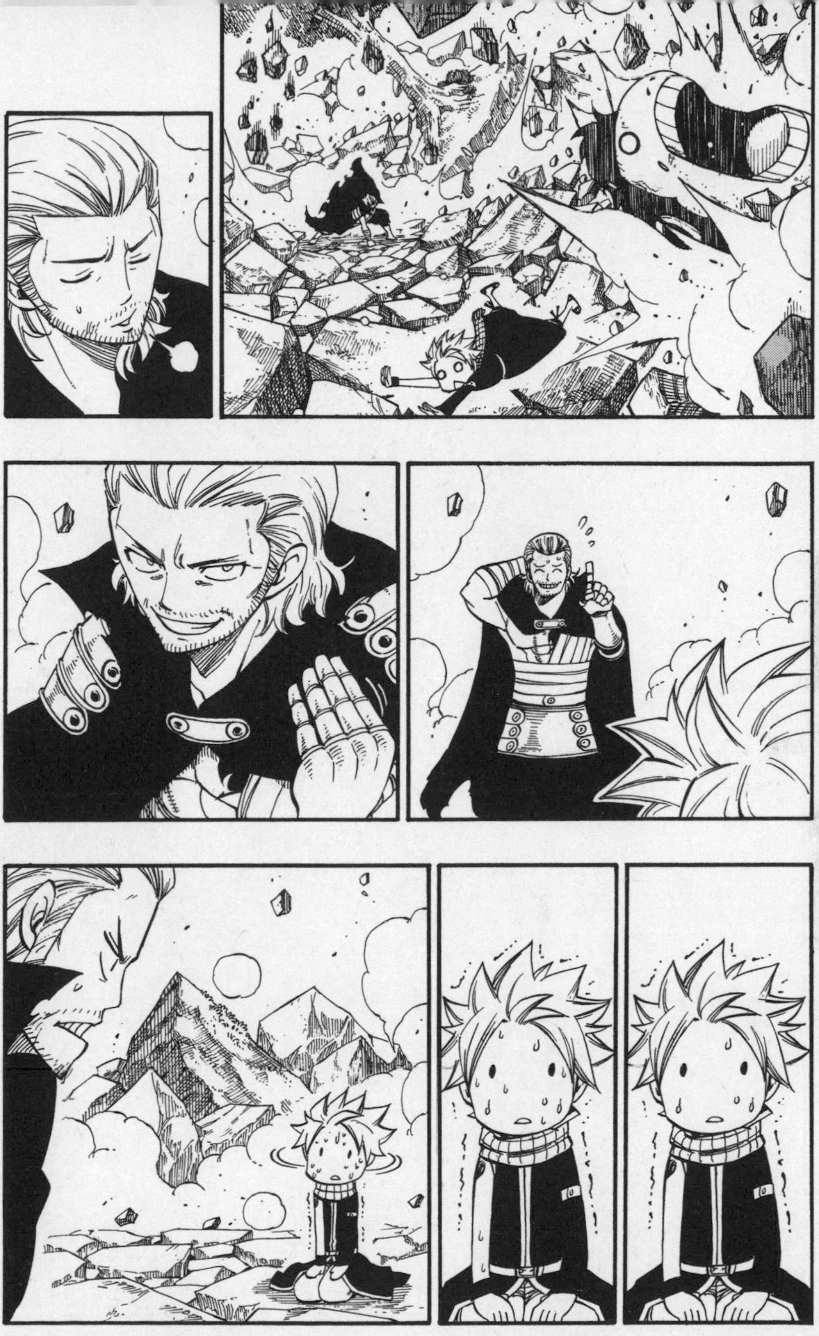

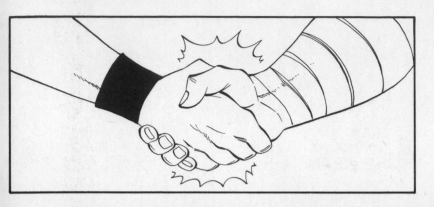

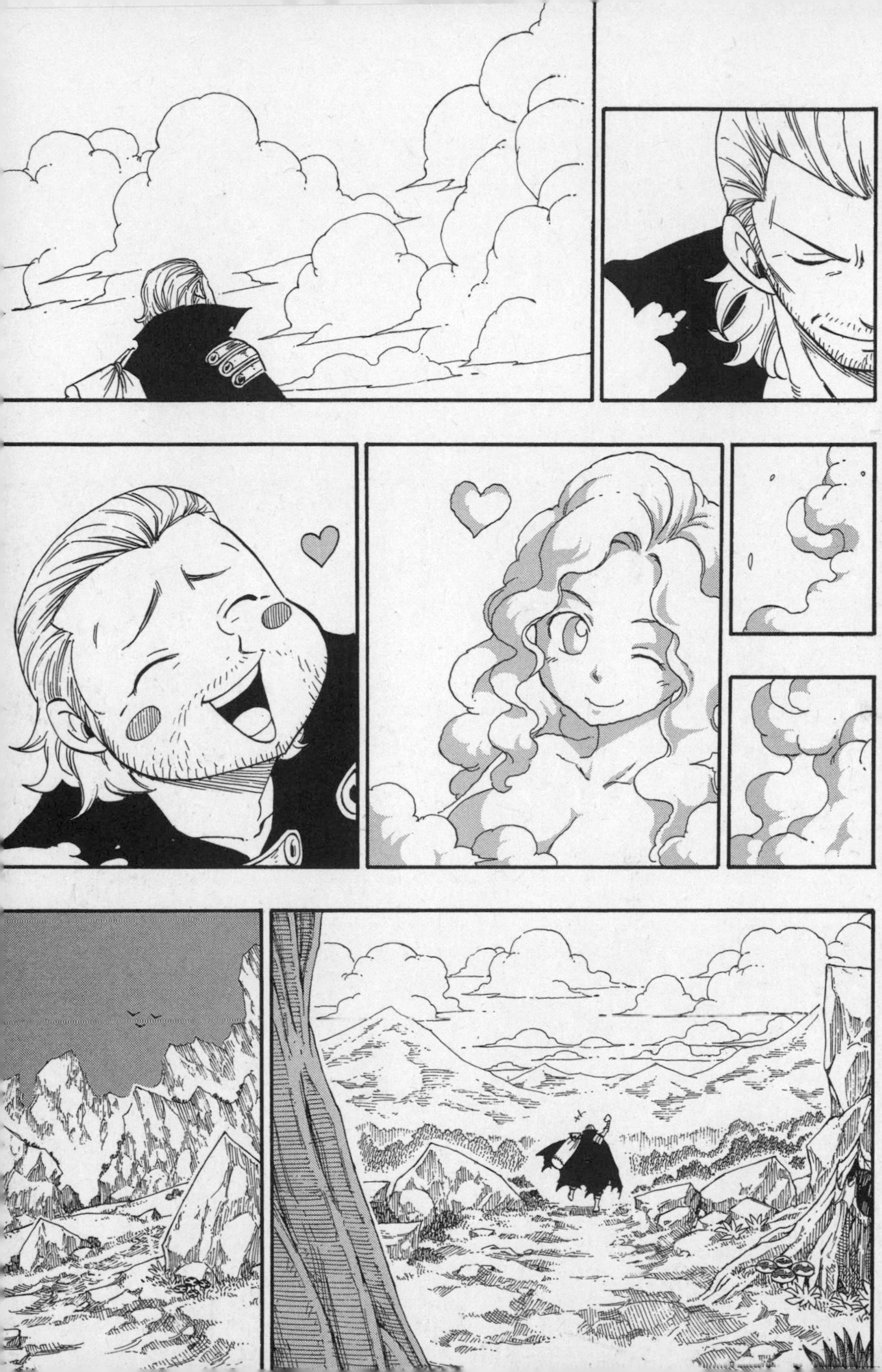

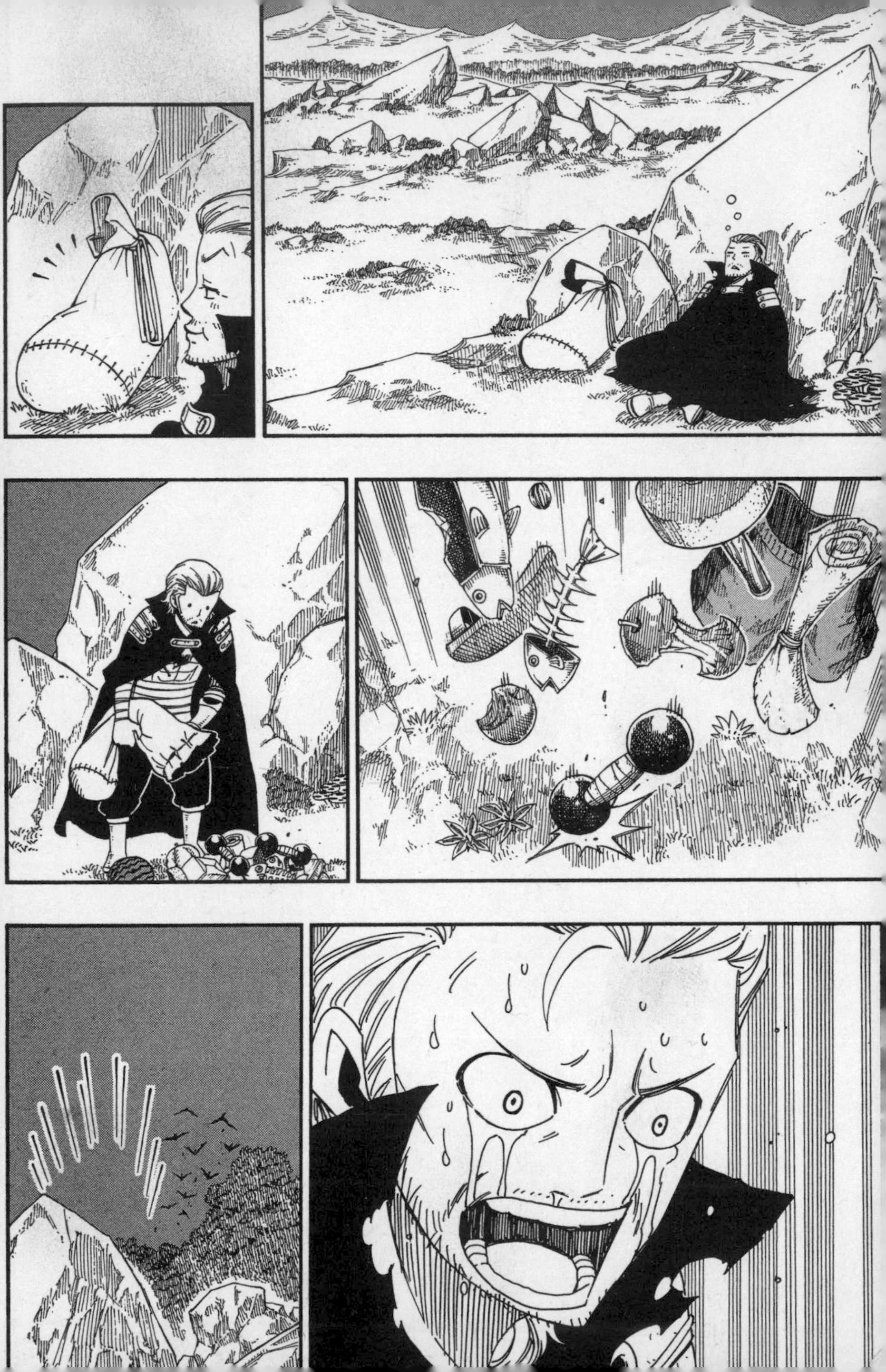

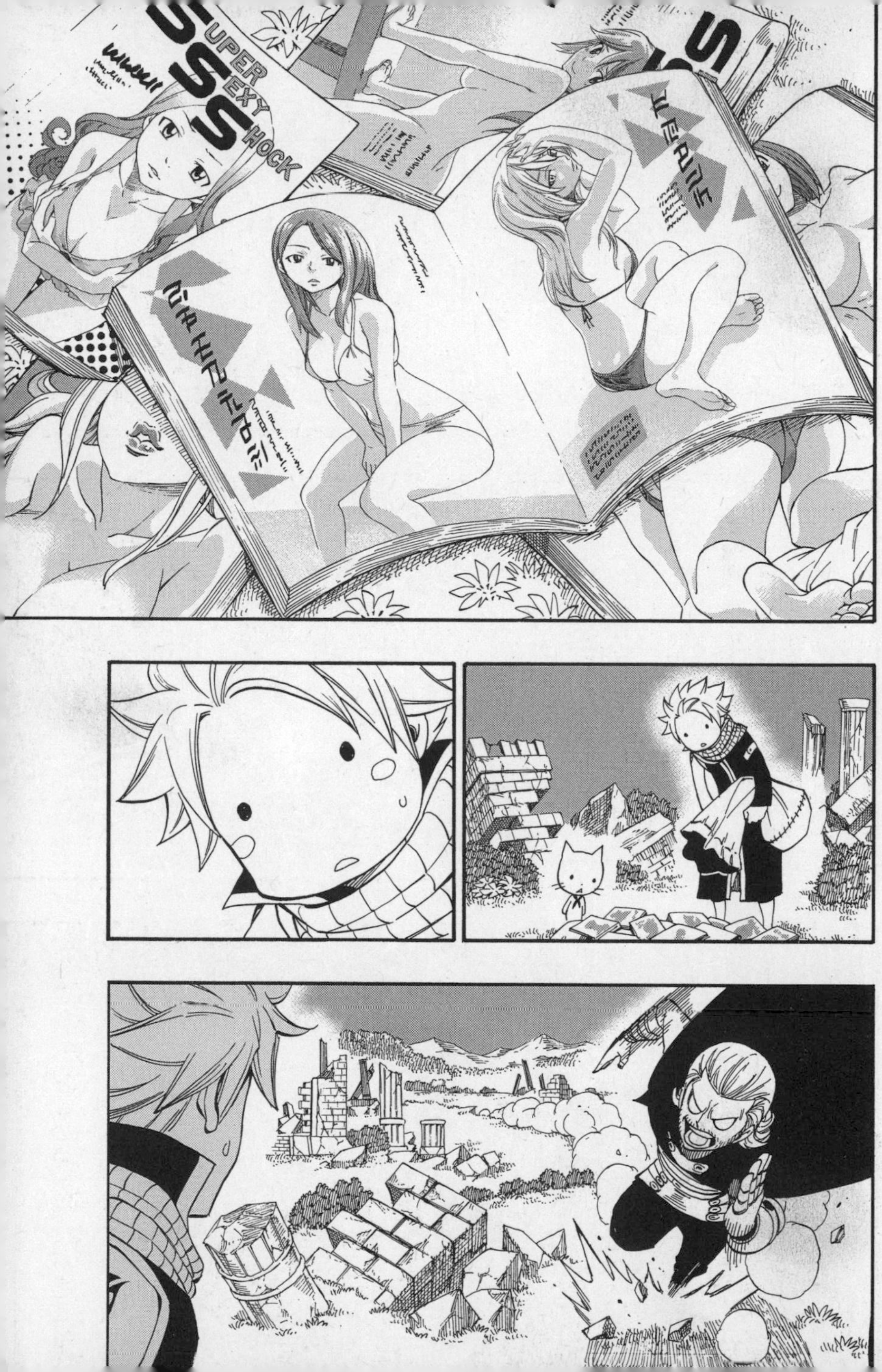
SUPER SEXY SHOCK

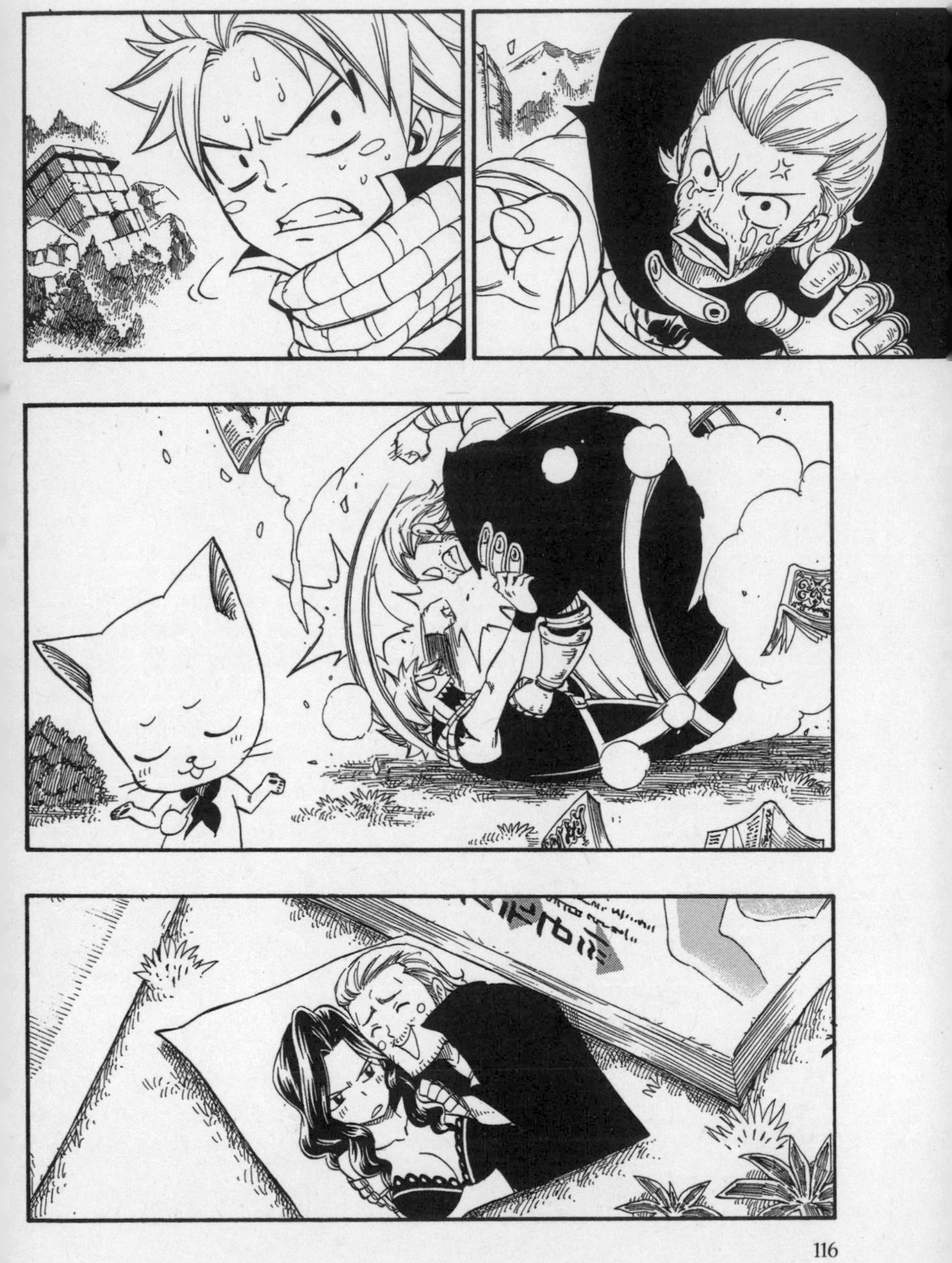

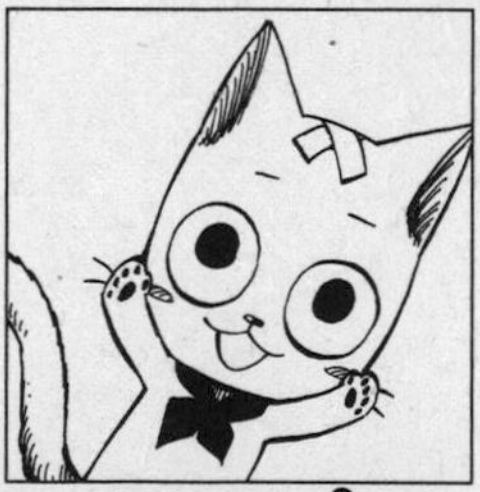

FAIRY TAIL

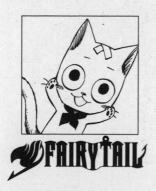

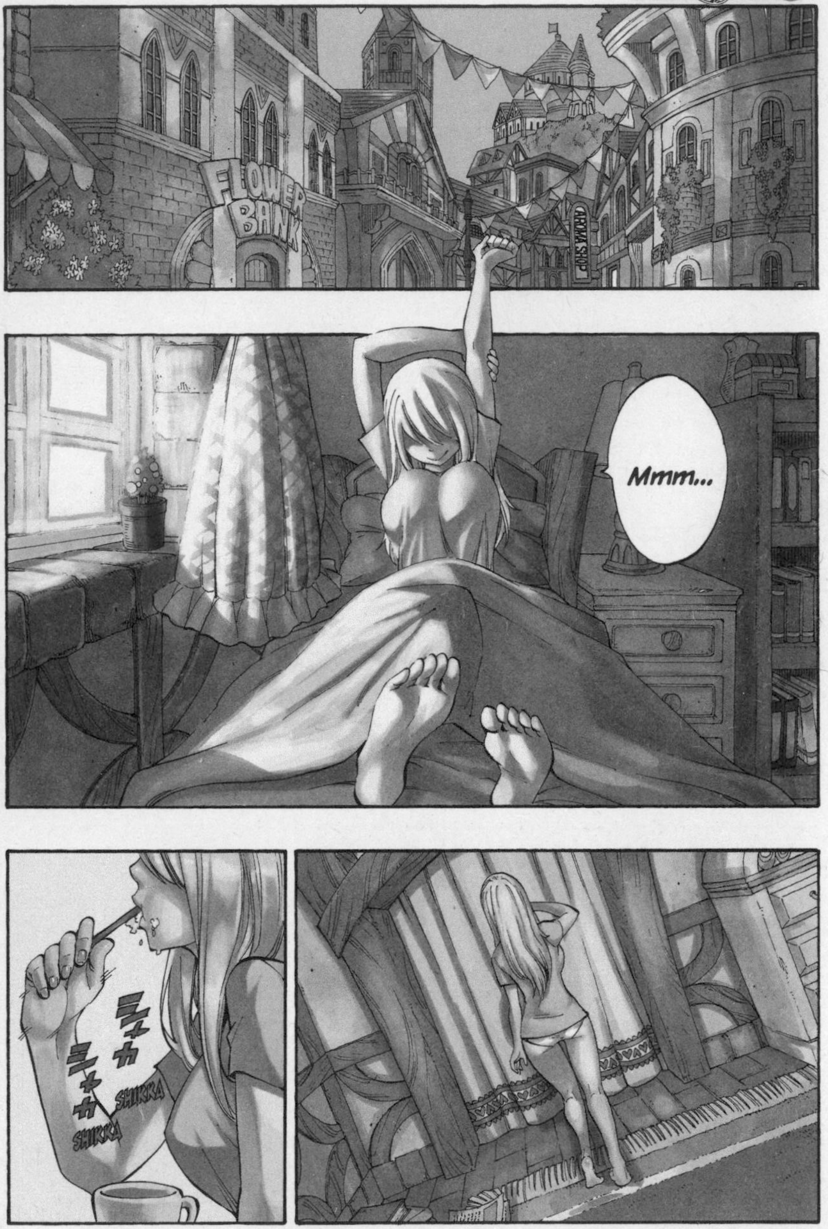
FLOWER BANK
AROMA SHOP
Mmm...
SHIKKA
SHIKKA

♪
SHHHHHH
CHIK
GWIMM
Right!!

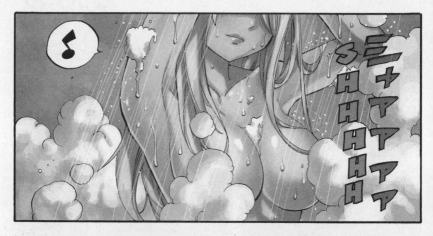

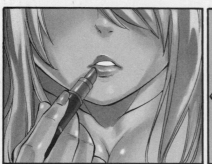

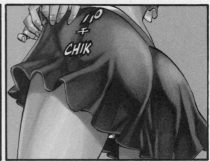

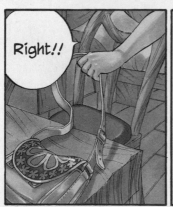

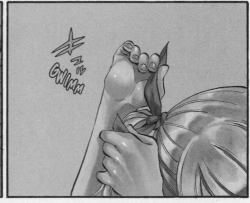

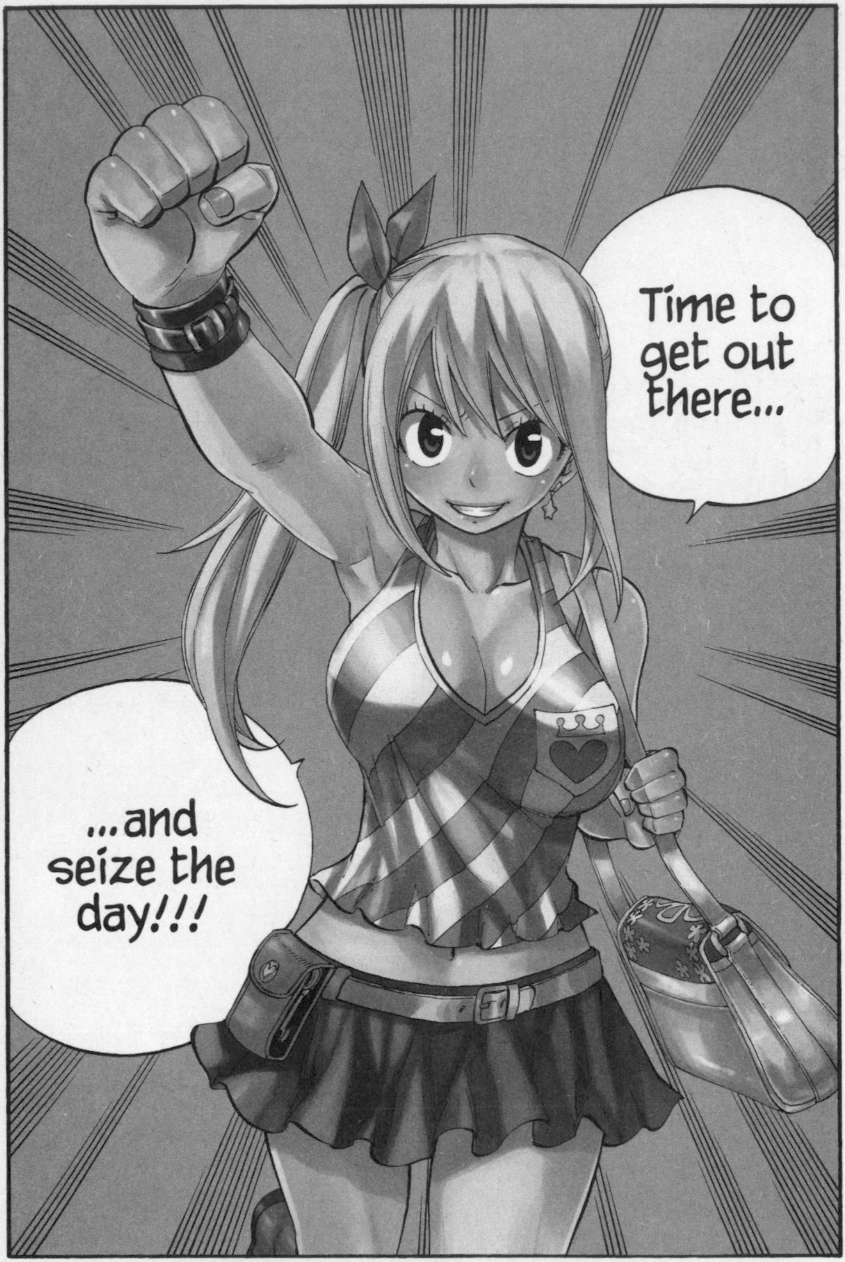
Time to get out there...
...and seize the day!!!

Chapter 418: Challenger

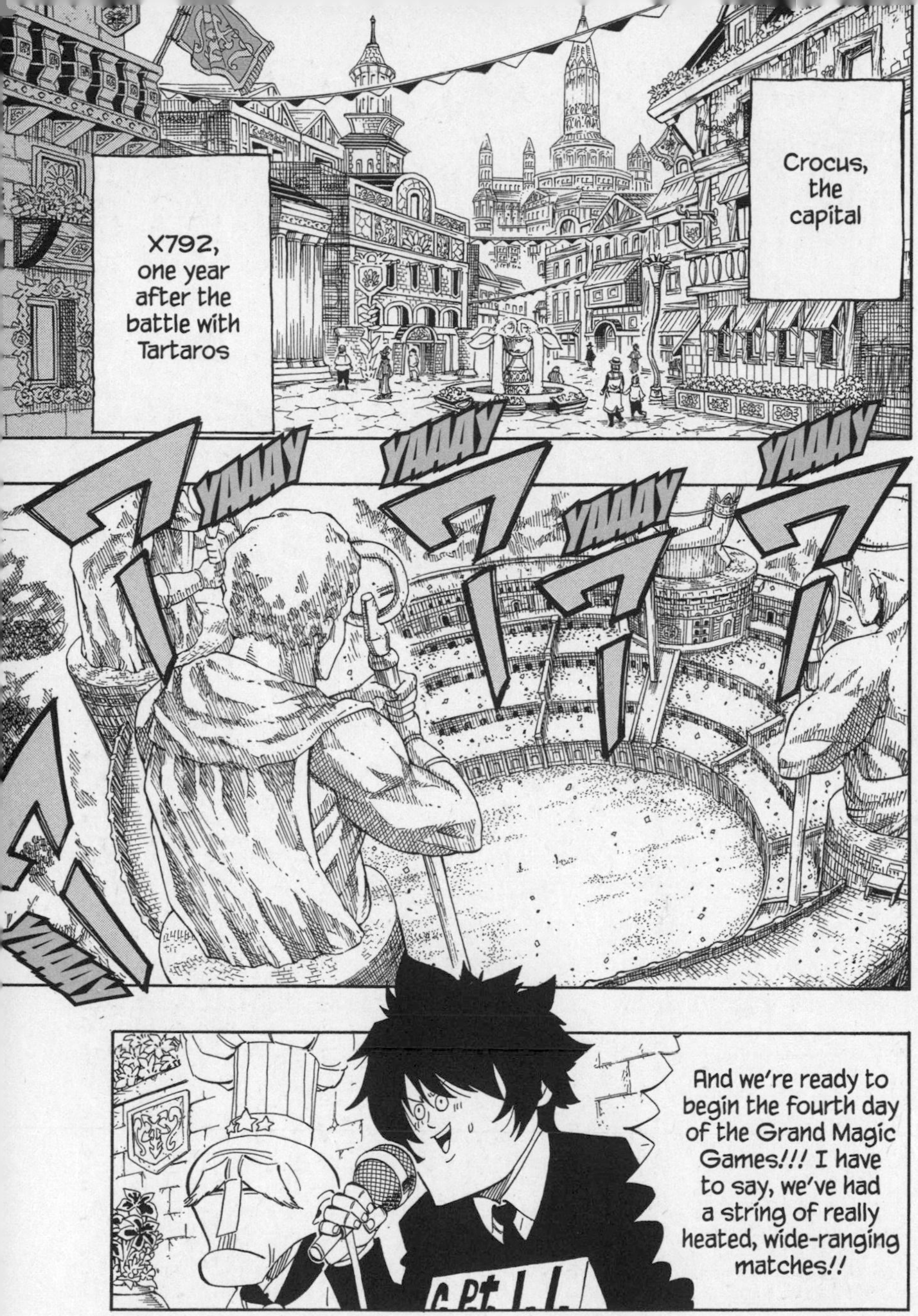
Crocus, the capital
X792, one year after the battle with Tartaros
YAAAY
YAAAY
YAAAY
YAAAY
YAAAY
And we're ready to begin the fourth day of the Grand Magic Games!!! I have to say, we've had a string of really heated, wide-ranging matches!!

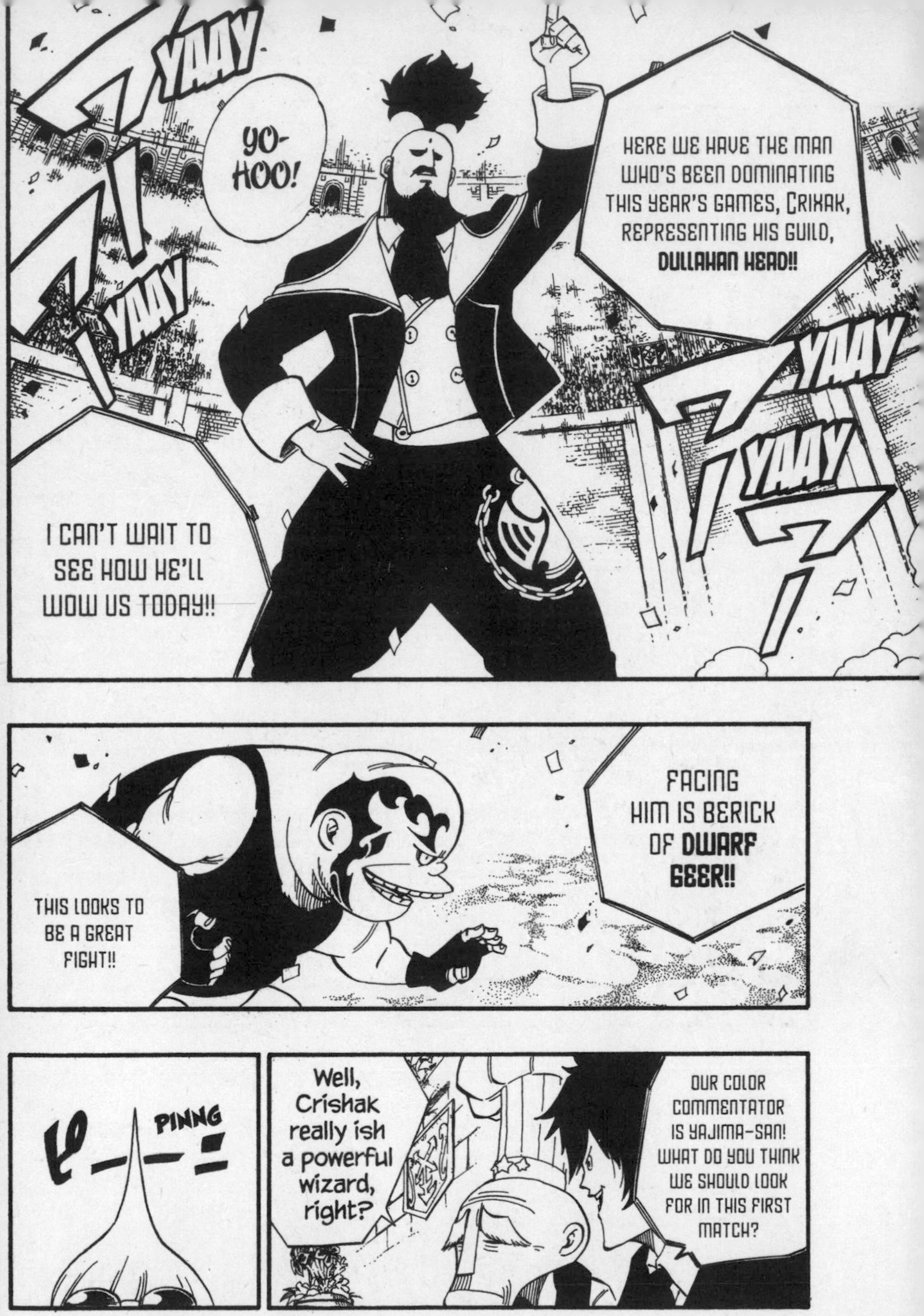
HERE WE HAVE THE MAN WHO'S BEEN DOMINATING THIS YEAR'S GAMES, CRIXAK, REPRESENTING HIS GUILD, **DULLAHAN HEAD!!**
YAAY
YAAY
YO-HOO!
YAAY
YAAY
I CAN'T WAIT TO SEE HOW HE'LL WOW US TODAY!!
FACING HIM IS BERICK OF **DWARF GEER!!**
THIS LOOKS TO BE A GREAT FIGHT!!
OUR COLOR COMMENTATOR IS YAJIMA-SAN! WHAT DO YOU THINK WE SHOULD LOOK FOR IN THIS FIRST MATCH?
Well, Crishak really ish a powerful wizard, right?
PINNG

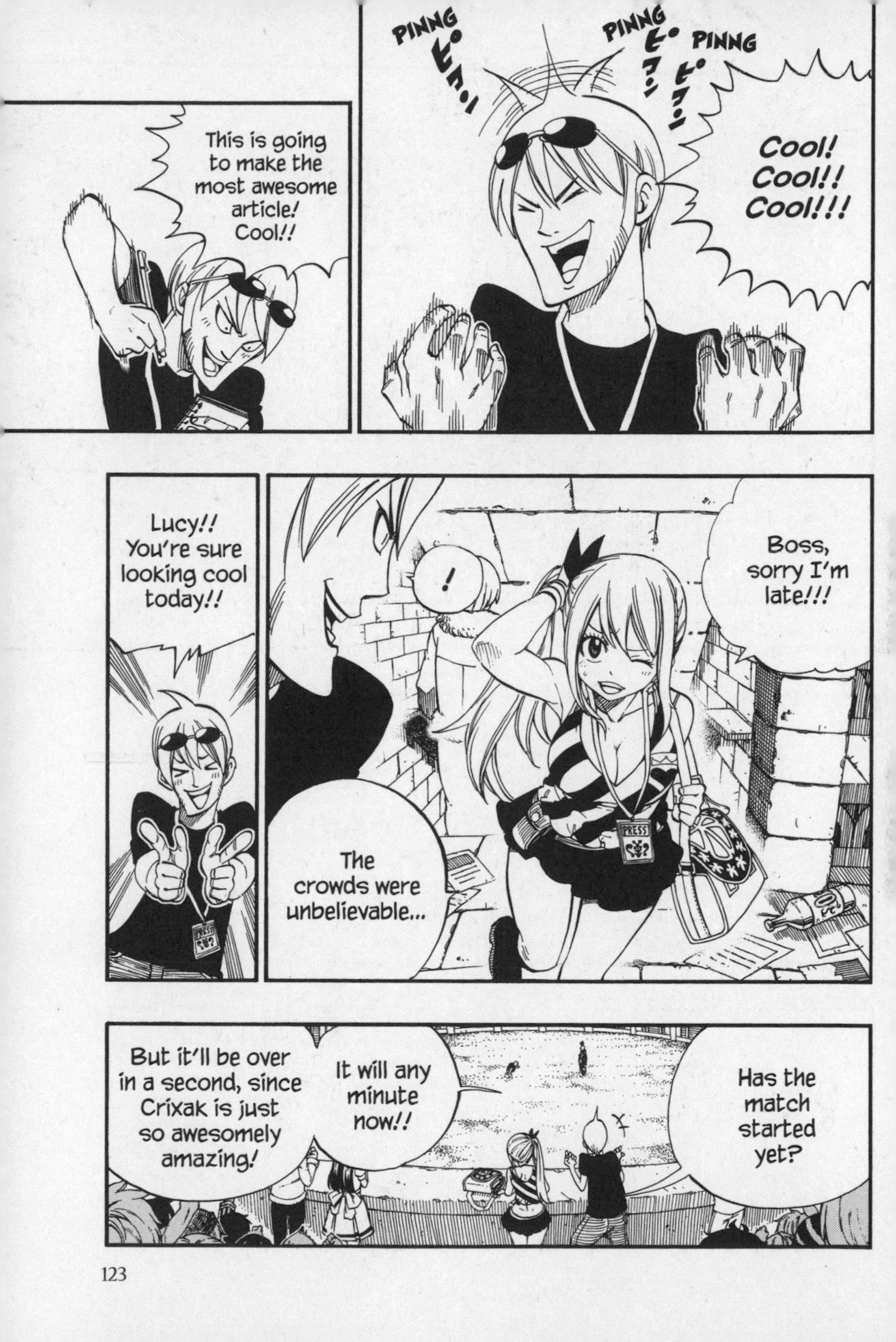
PINNG
PINNG
PINNG
Cool! Cool!! Cool!!!
This is going to make the most awesome article! Cool!!
Boss, sorry I'm late!!!
The crowds were unbelievable...
!
Lucy!! You're sure looking cool today!!
Has the match started yet?
It will any minute now!!
But it'll be over in a second, since Crixak is just so awesomely amazing!

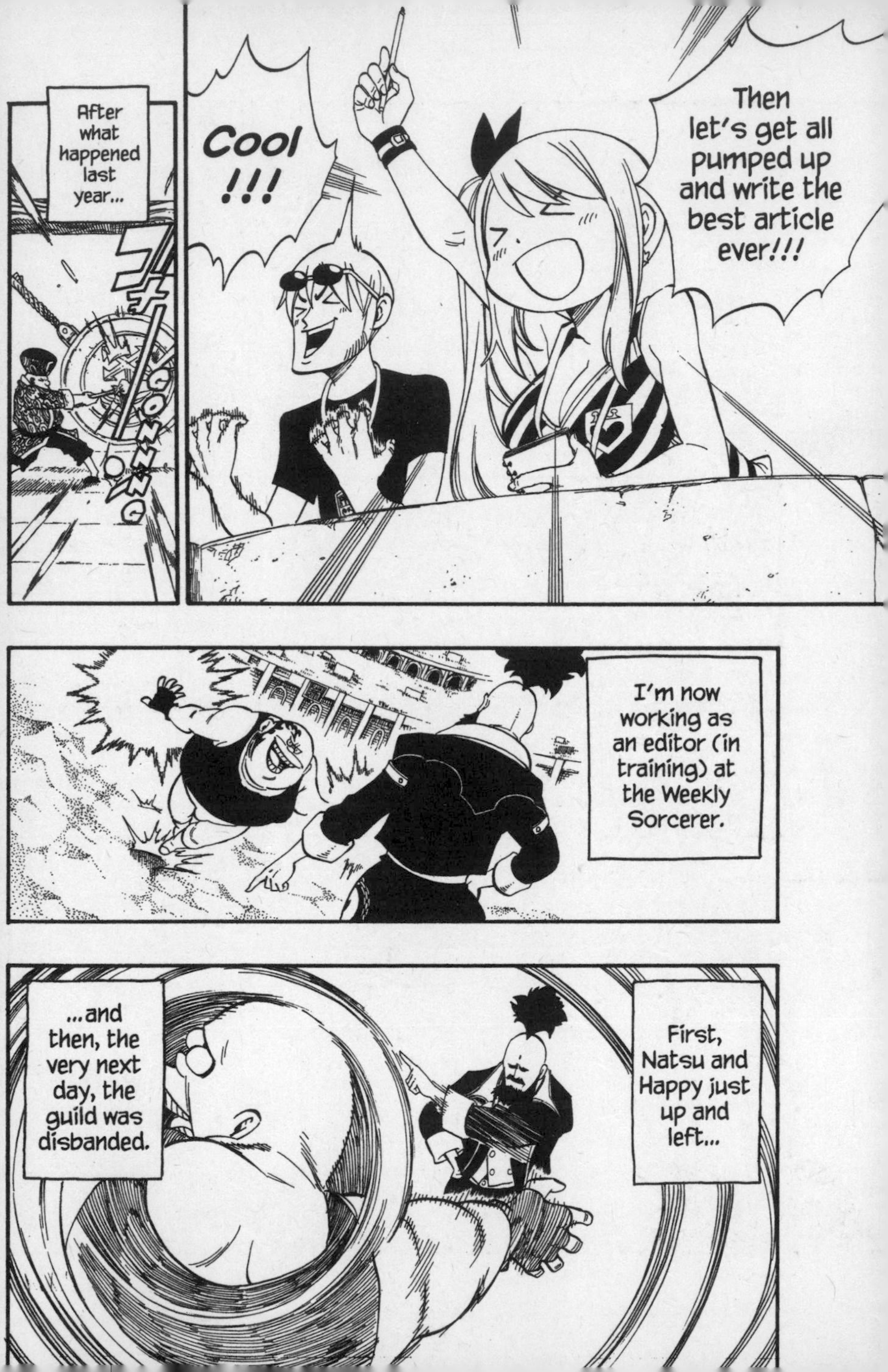
Then let's get all pumped up and write the best article ever!!!
Cool !!!
After what happened last year...
GONNNNG
I'm now working as an editor (in training) at the Weekly Sorcerer.
First, Natsu and Happy just up and left...
...and then, the very next day, the guild was disbanded.

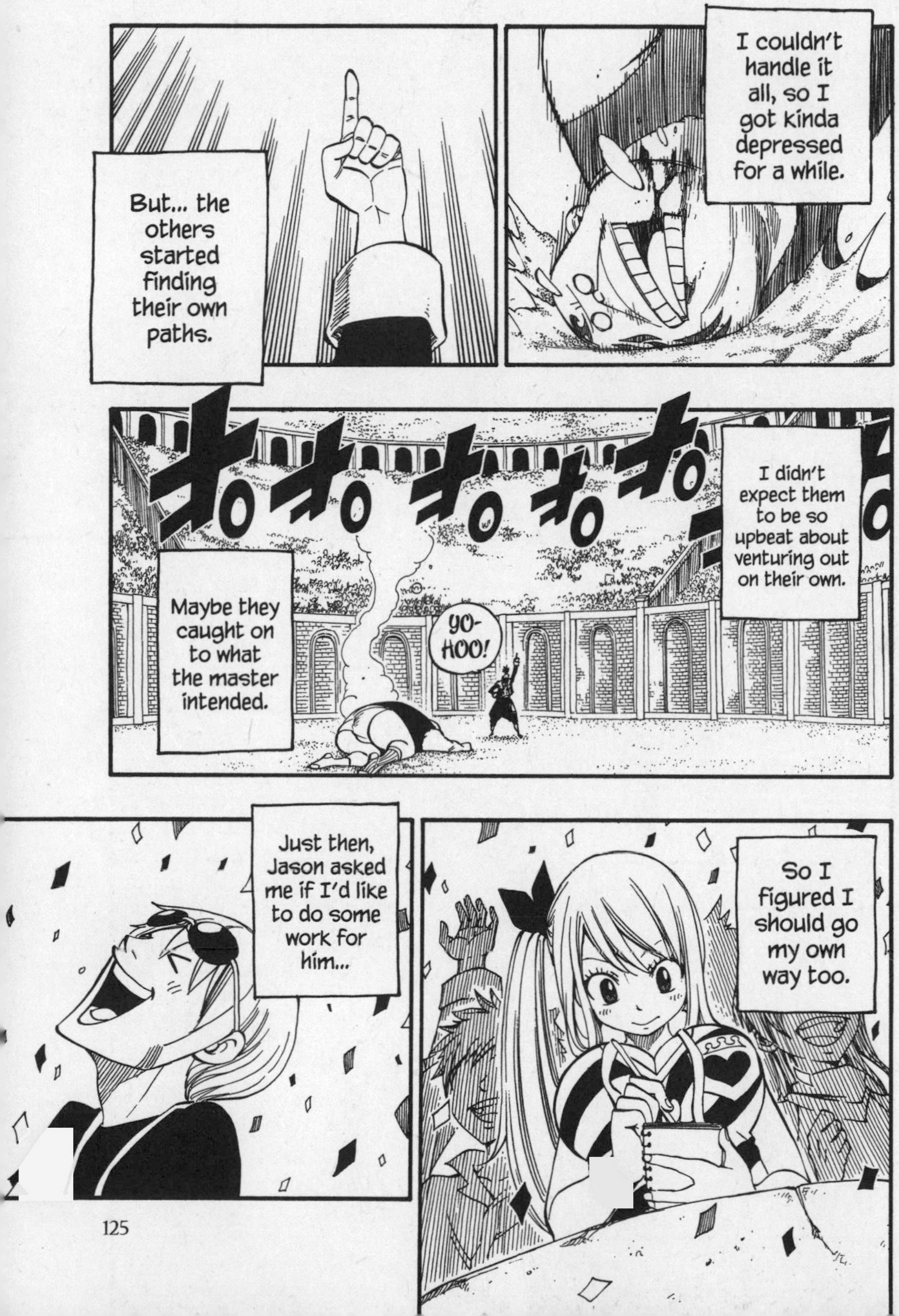
I couldn't handle it all, so I got kinda depressed for a while.
But... the others started finding their own paths.
I didn't expect them to be so upbeat about venturing out on their own.
YO-HOO!
Maybe they caught on to what the master intended.
So I figured I should go my own way too.
Just then, Jason asked me if I'd like to do some work for him...

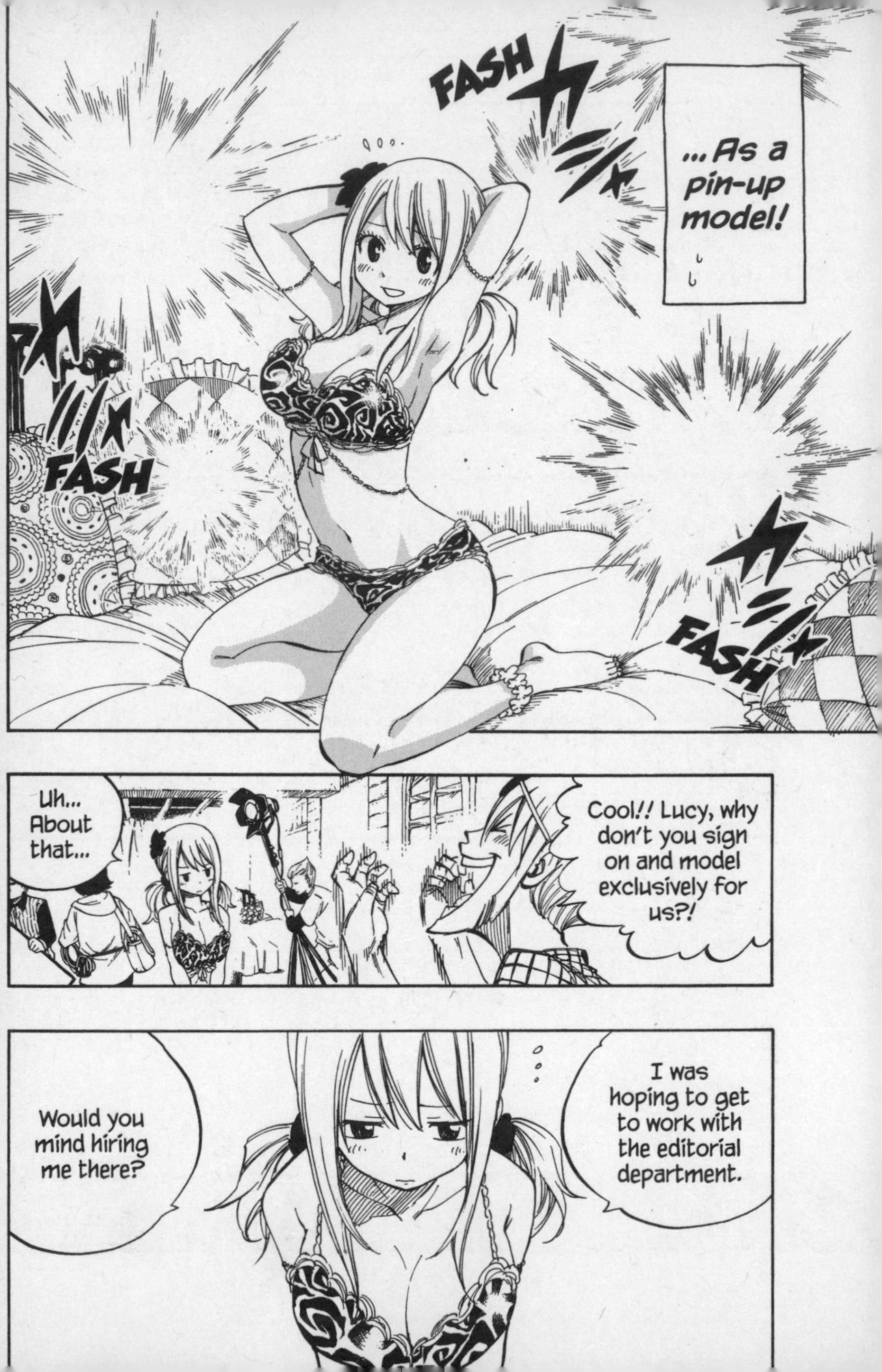

...As a pin-up model!
FASH
FASH
FASH
Cool!! Lucy, why don't you sign on and model exclusively for us?!
Uh... About that...
I was hoping to get to work with the editorial department.
Would you mind hiring me there?

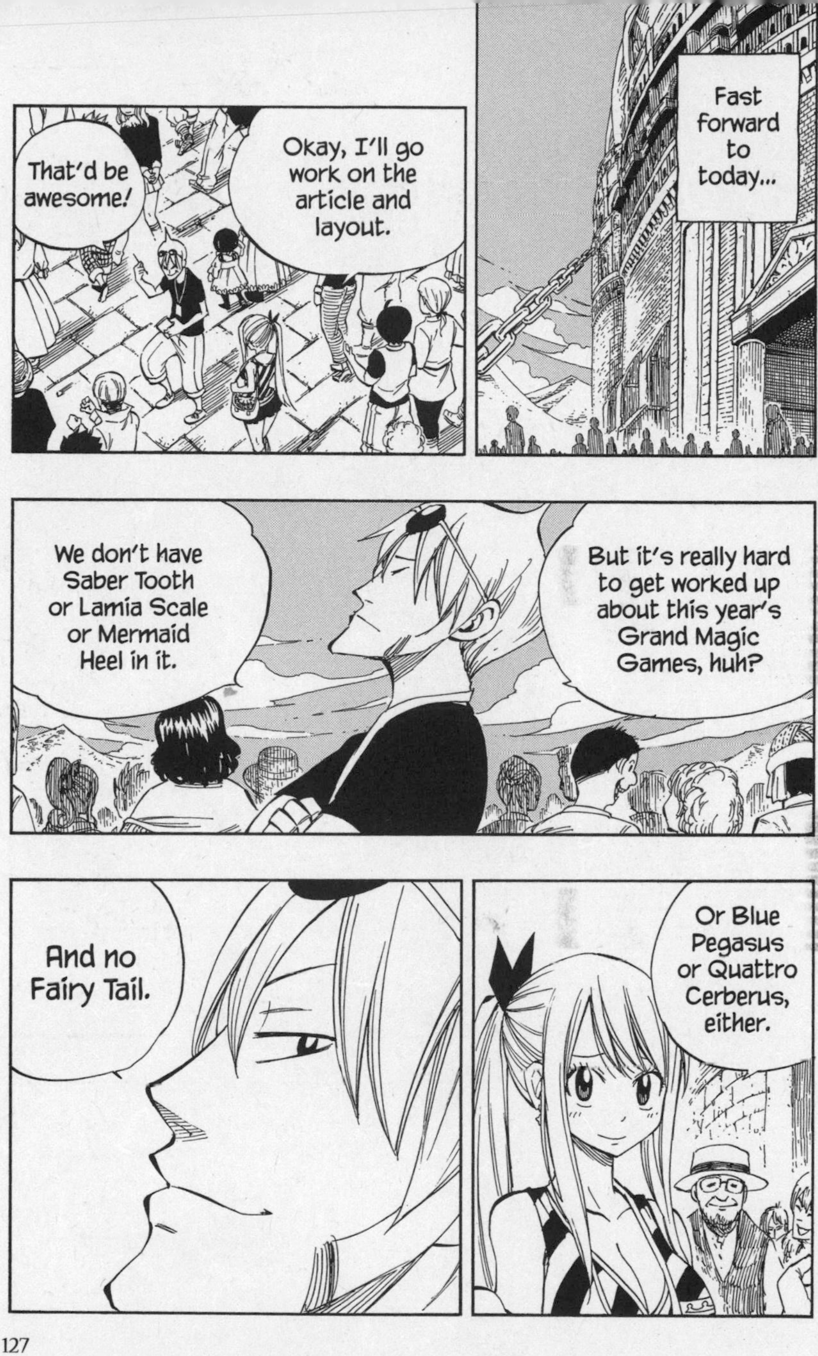
Fast forward to today...
Okay, I'll go work on the article and layout.
That'd be awesome!
But it's really hard to get worked up about this year's Grand Magic Games, huh?
We don't have Saber Tooth or Lamia Scale or Mermaid Heel in it.
Or Blue Pegasus or Quattro Cerberus, either.
And no Fairy Tail.

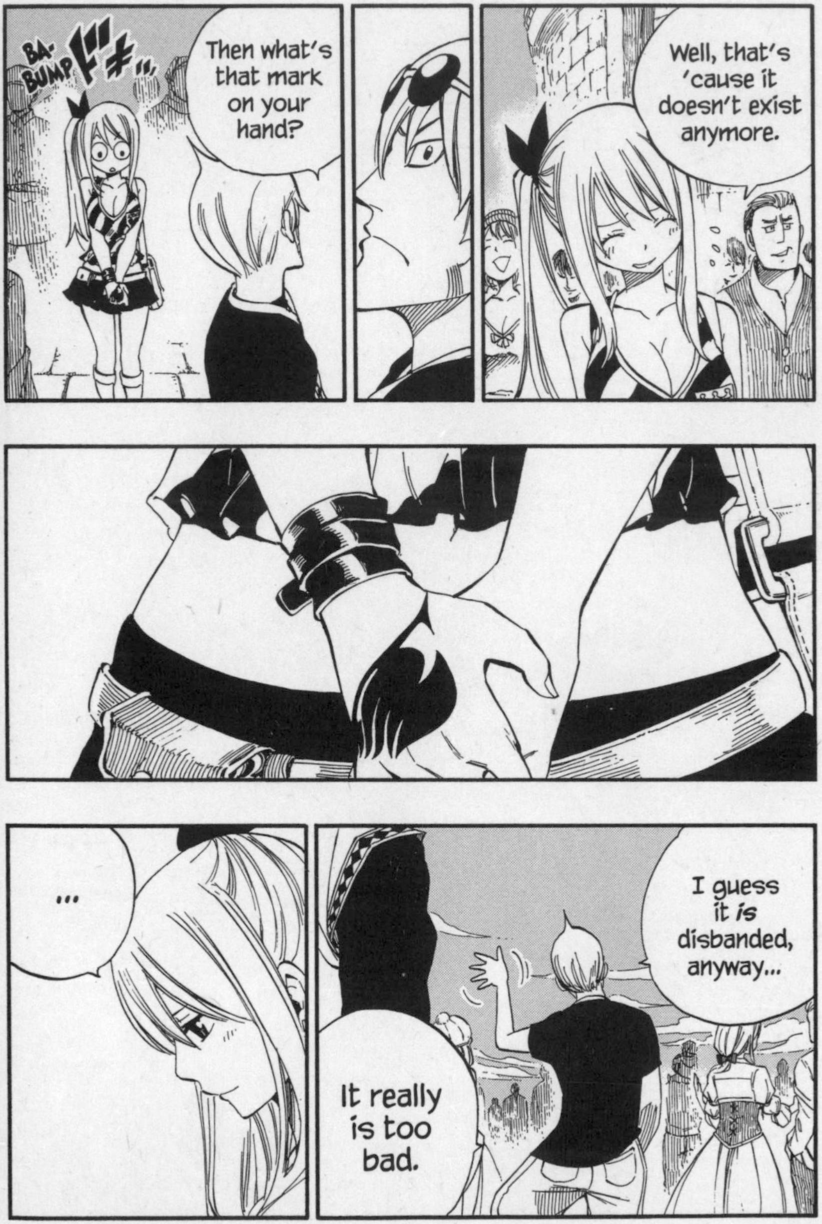
Well, that's 'cause it doesn't exist anymore.
Then what's that mark on your hand?
BA-BUMP
I guess it *is* disbanded, anyway...
It really is too bad.
...

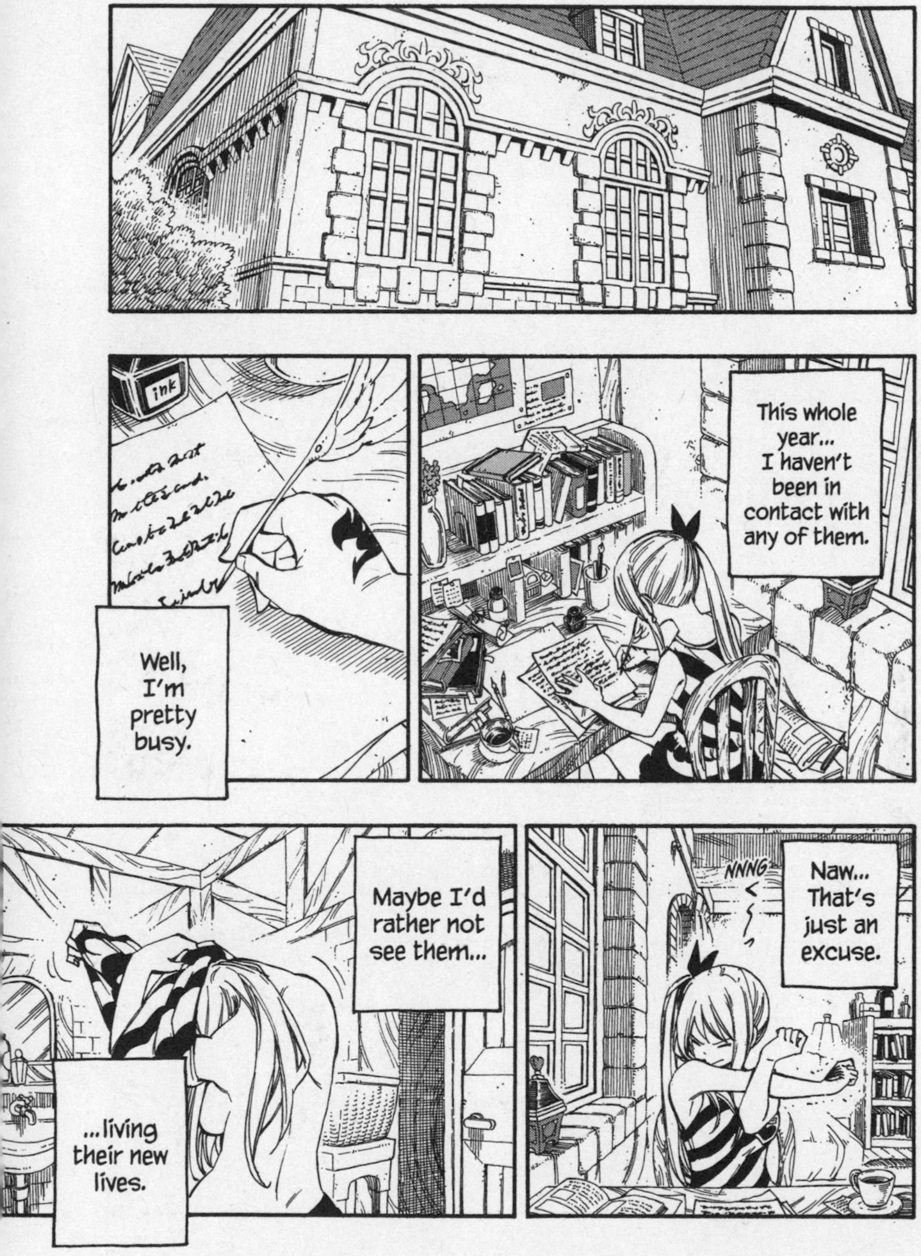
This whole year... I haven't been in contact with any of them.
ink
Well, I'm pretty busy.
NNNG
Naw... That's just an excuse.
Maybe I'd rather not see them...
...living their new lives.

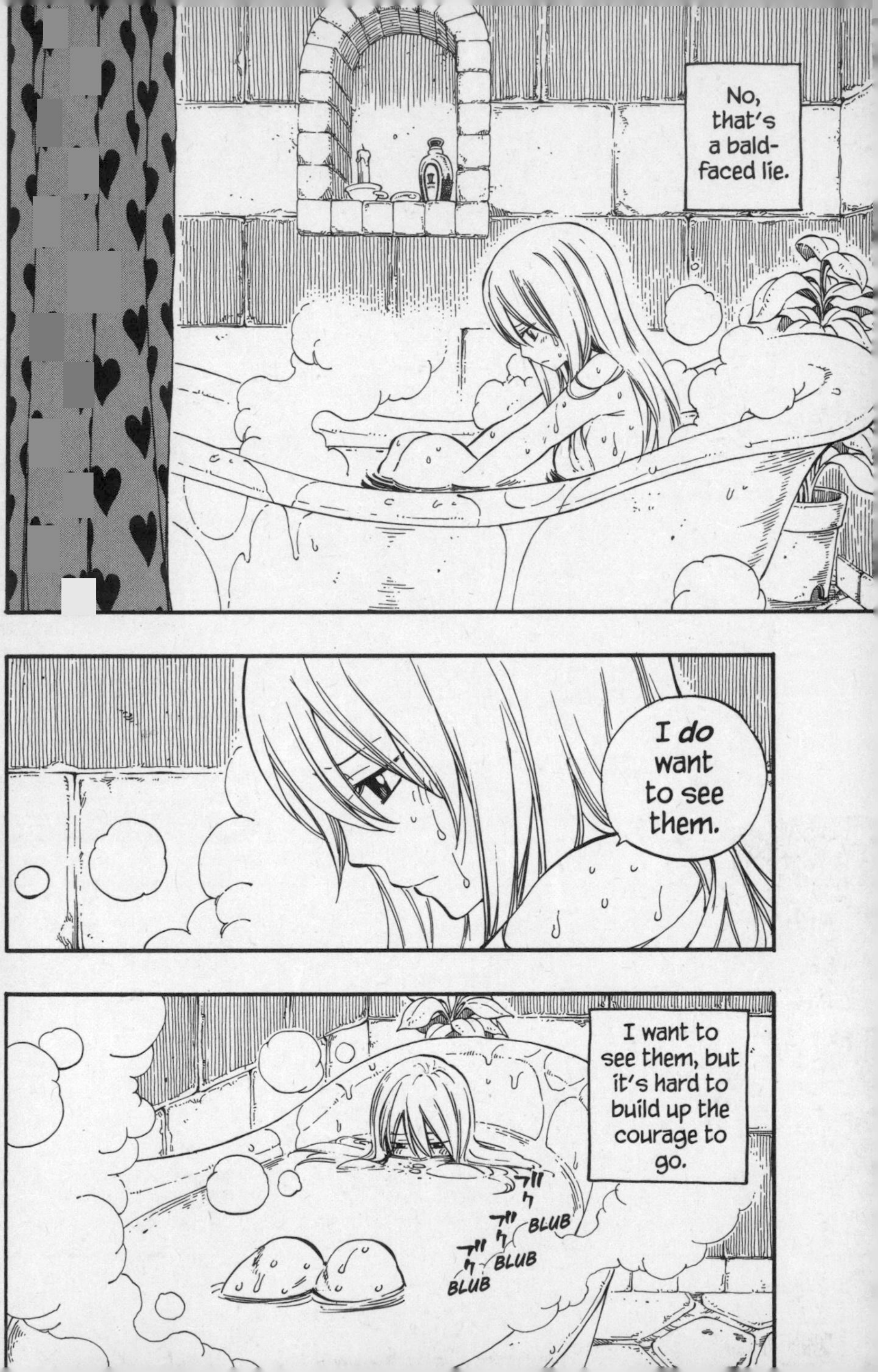
No, that's a bald-faced lie.
I *do* want to see them.
I want to see them, but it's hard to build up the courage to go.
ブク
ブク BLUB
ブク BLUB
BLUB

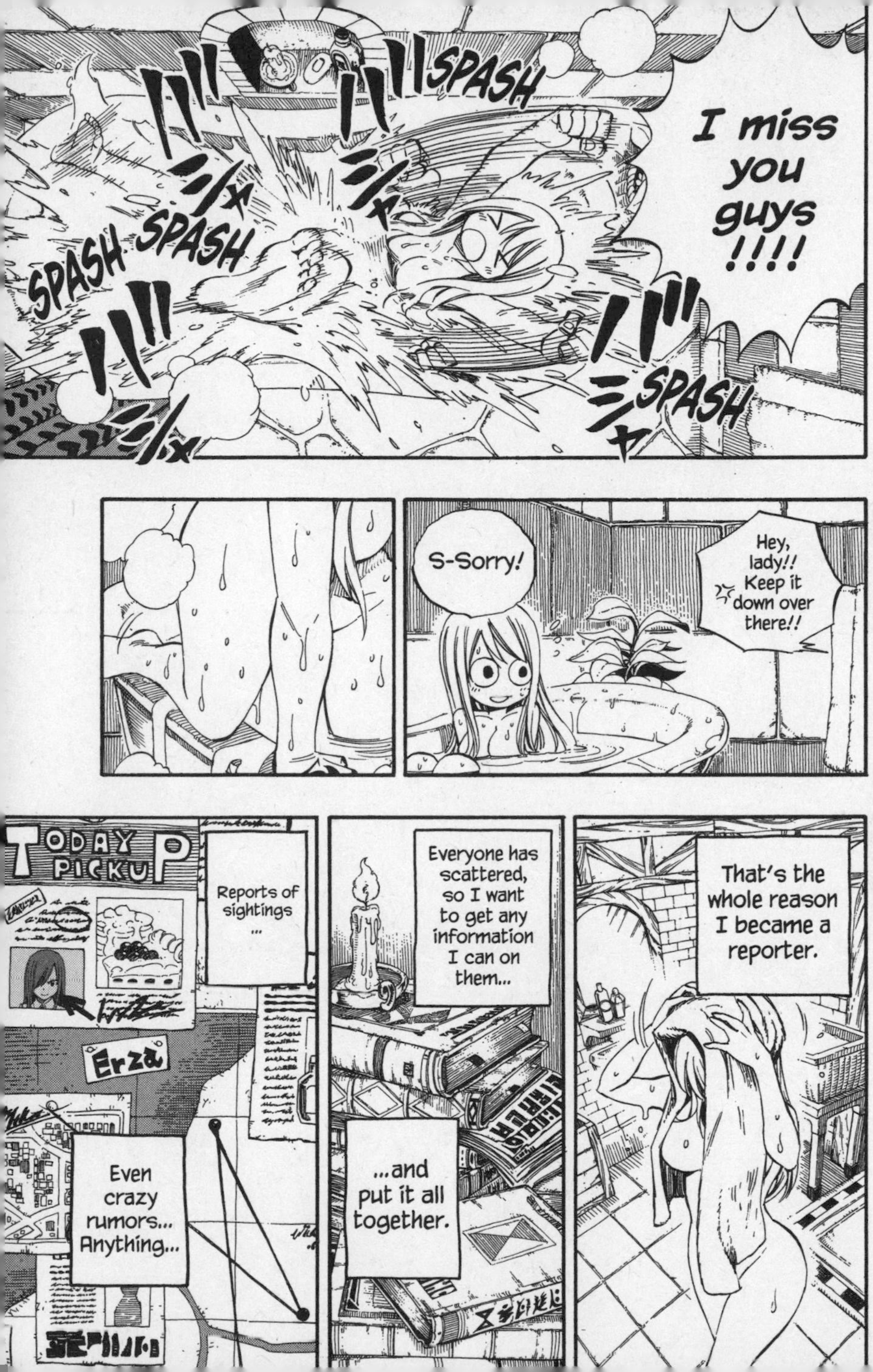
I miss you guys !!!!
SPASH
SPASH
SPASH
SPASH
Hey, lady!! Keep it down over there!!
S-Sorry!
That's the whole reason I became a reporter.
Everyone has scattered, so I want to get any information I can on them...
...and put it all together.
TODAY PICKUP
Reports of sightings ...
Erza
Even crazy rumors... Anything...

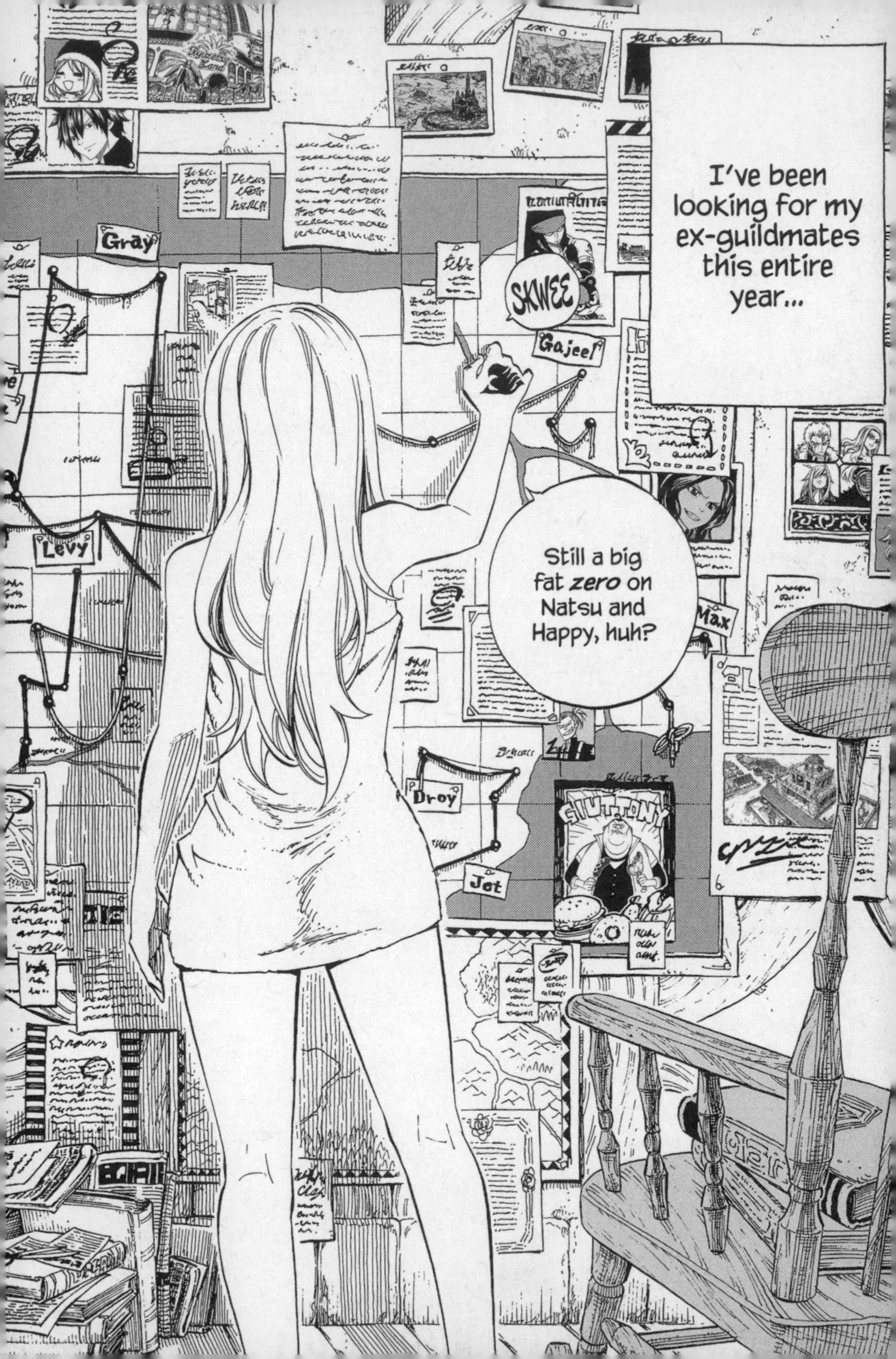
I've been looking for my ex-guildmates this entire year...
SKWEE
Still a big fat *zero* on Natsu and Happy, huh?
Gajeel
Gray
Levy
Max
Droy
Jet
GLUTTONY

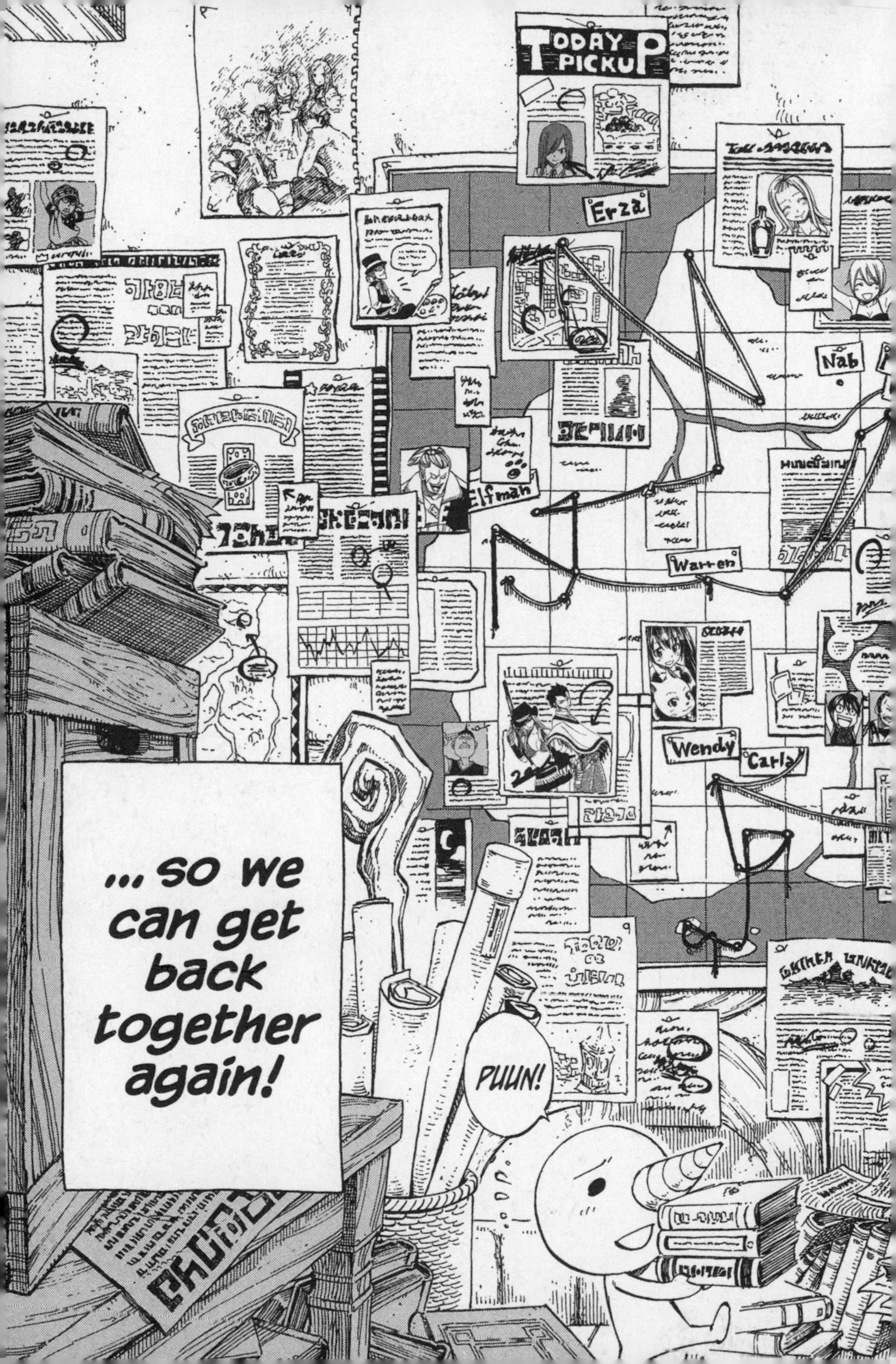
TODAY PICKUP
Erza
Nab
Elfman
Warren
Wendy
Carla
... so we can get back together again!
PUUN!

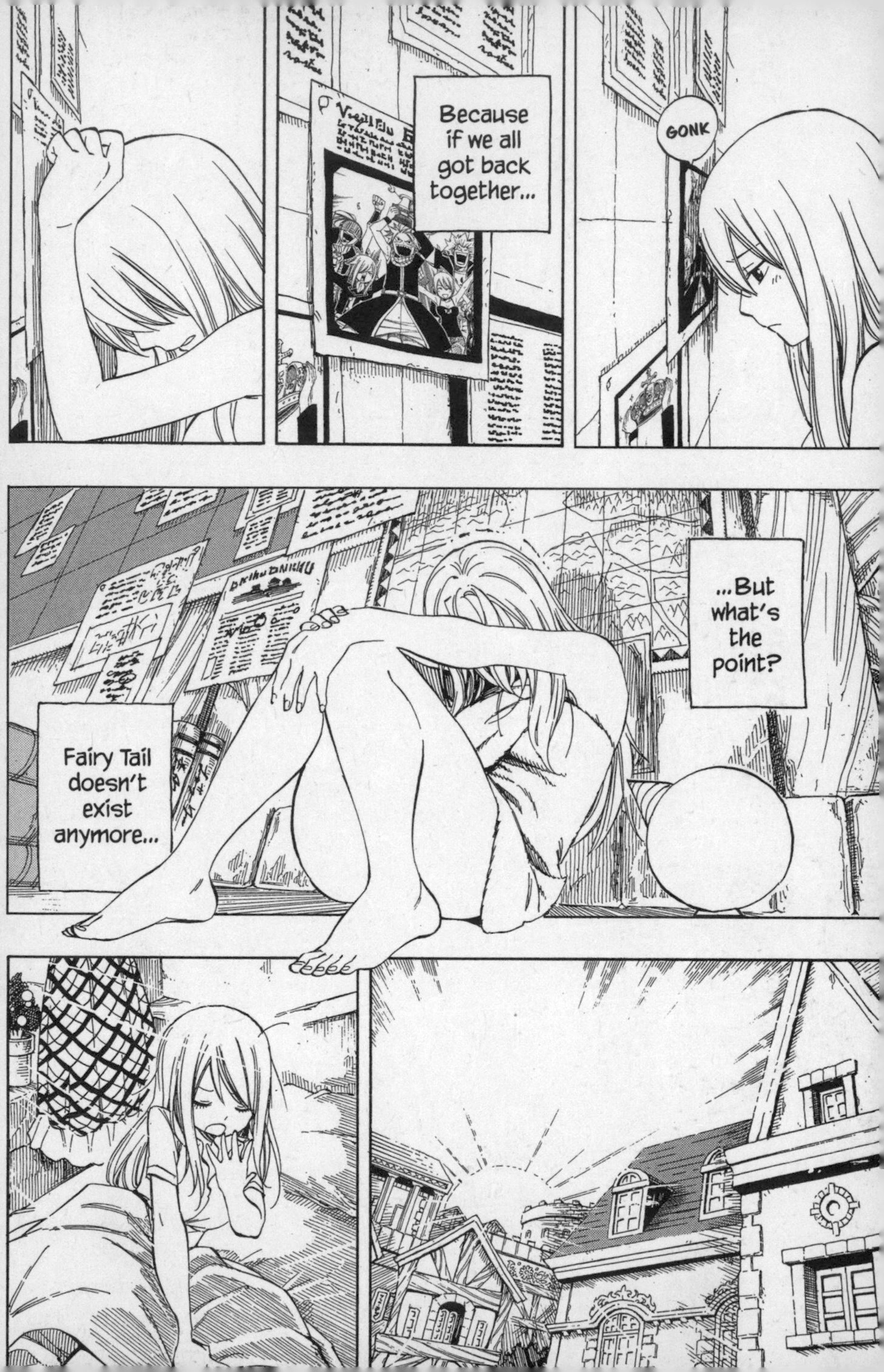
GONK
Because if we all got back together...
...But what's the point?
Fairy Tail doesn't exist anymore...

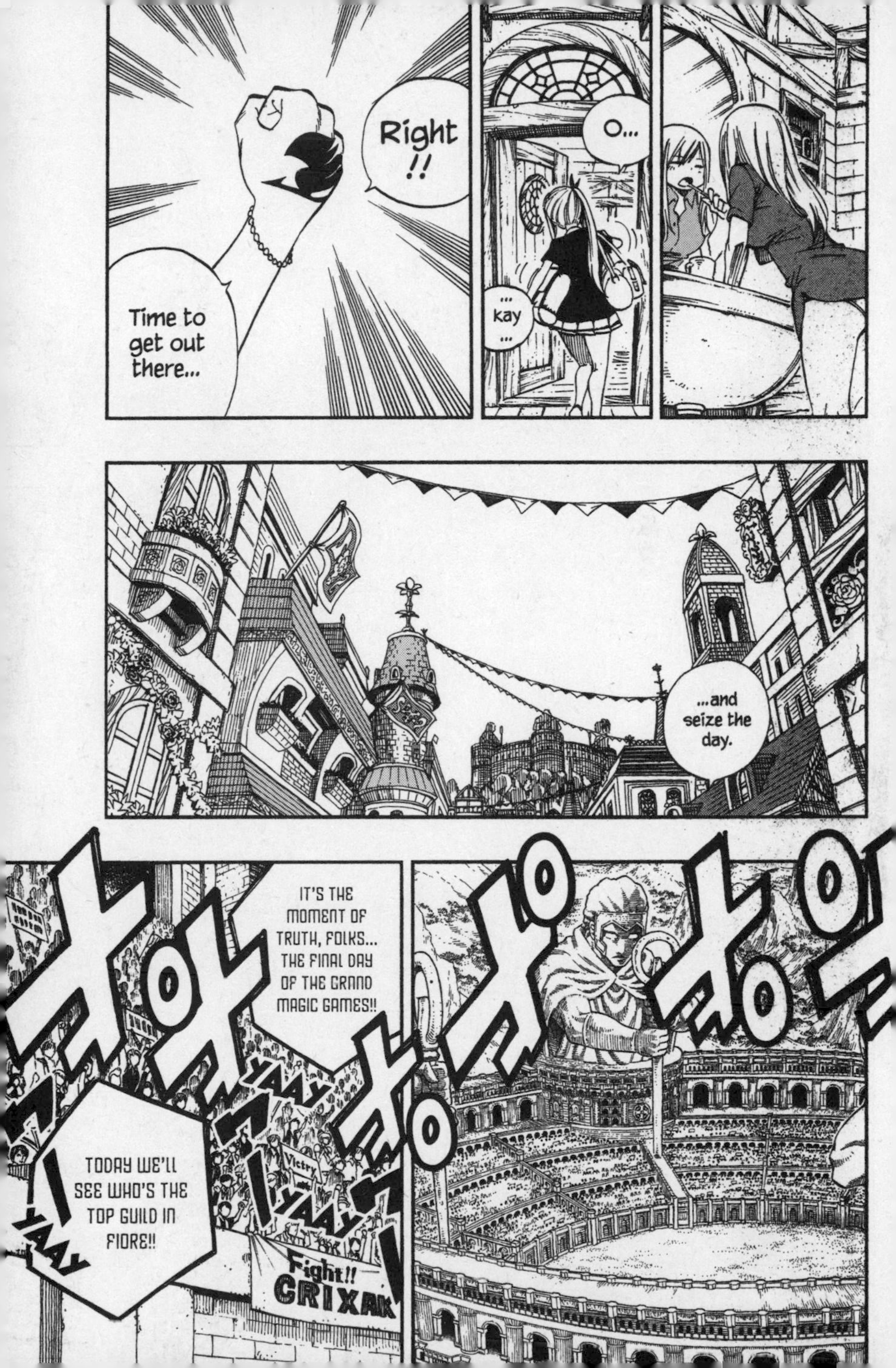
O...
...kay...
Right!!
Time to get out there...
...and seize the day.
IT'S THE MOMENT OF TRUTH, FOLKS... THE FINAL DAY OF THE GRAND MAGIC GAMES!!
TODAY WE'LL SEE WHO'S THE TOP GUILD IN FIORE!!
YAAY
YAAY
YAAY
Victry
Fight!! CRIXAK

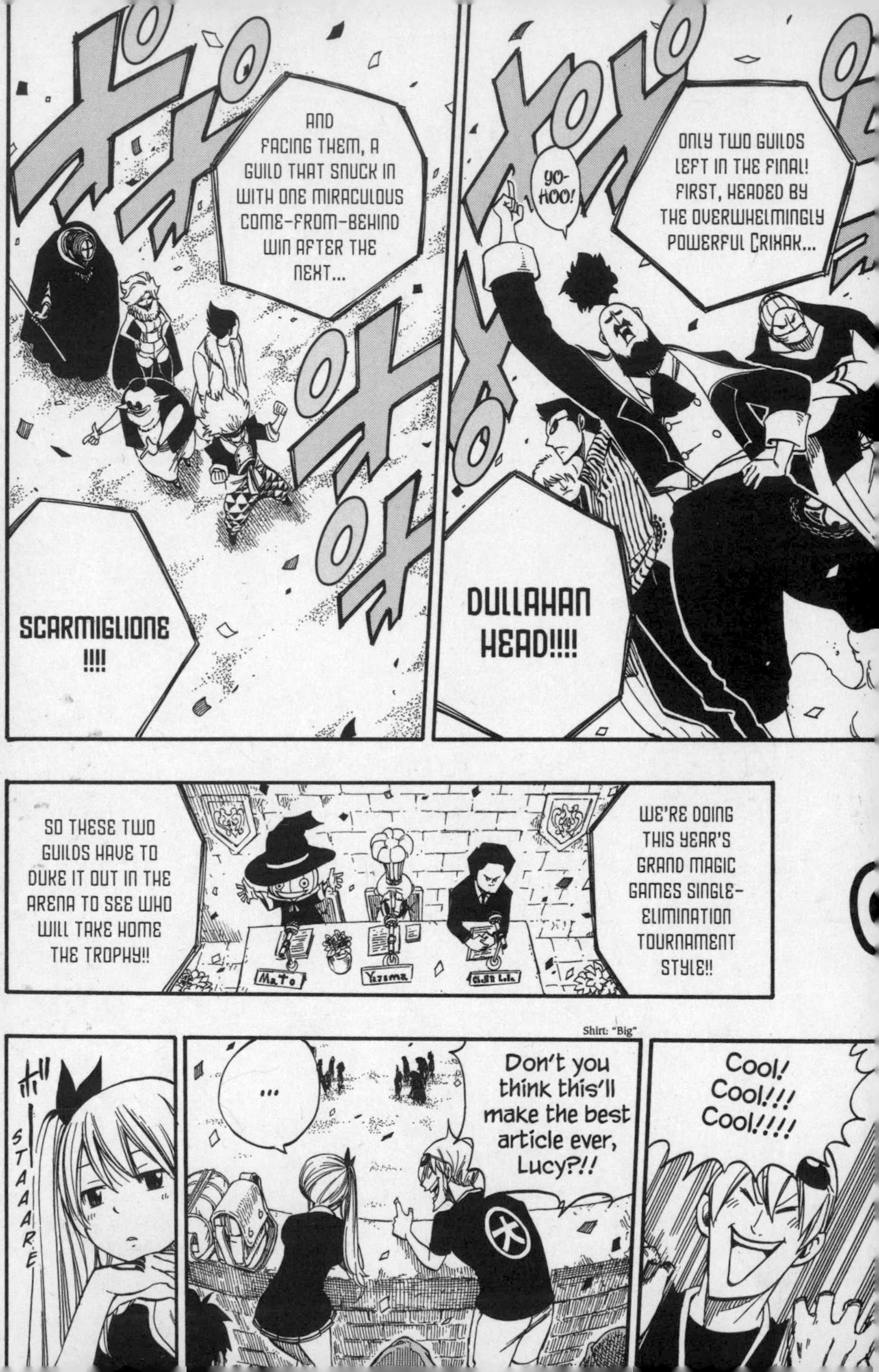
ONLY TWO GUILDS LEFT IN THE FINAL! FIRST, HEADED BY THE OVERWHELMINGLY POWERFUL CRIXAK...
YO-HOO!
DULLAHAN HEAD!!!!
AND FACING THEM, A GUILD THAT SNUCK IN WITH ONE MIRACULOUS COME-FROM-BEHIND WIN AFTER THE NEXT...
SCARMIGLIONE !!!!
WE'RE DOING THIS YEAR'S GRAND MAGIC GAMES SINGLE-ELIMINATION TOURNAMENT STYLE!!
SO THESE TWO GUILDS HAVE TO DUKE IT OUT IN THE ARENA TO SEE WHO WILL TAKE HOME THE TROPHY!!
Cool! Cool!!! Cool!!!!
Shirt: "Big"
Don't you think this'll make the best article ever, Lucy?!!
...
STAAARE

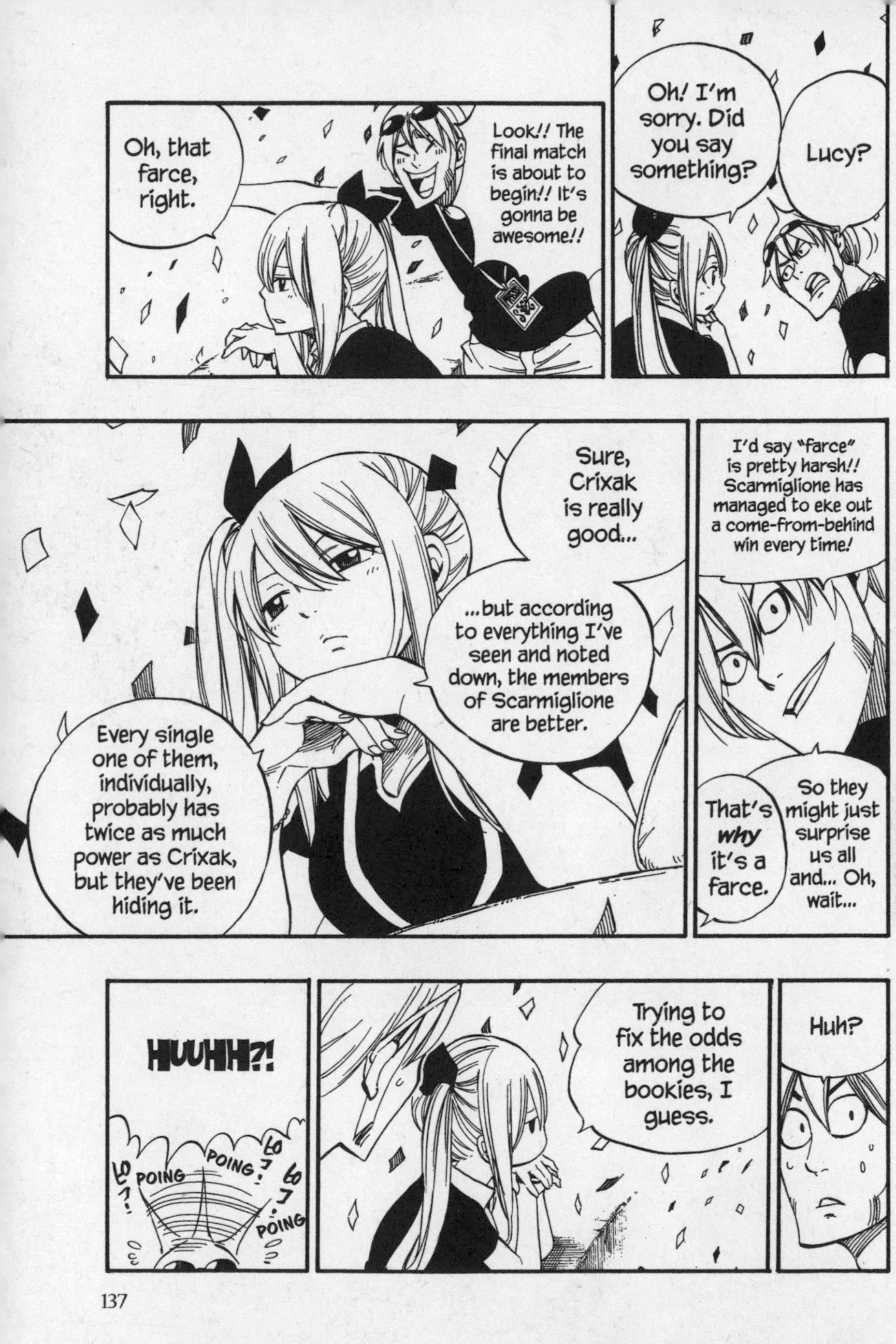
Lucy?
Oh! I'm sorry. Did you say something?
Look!! The final match is about to begin!! It's gonna be awesome!!
Oh, that farce, right.
I'd say "farce" is pretty harsh!! Scarmiglione has managed to eke out a come-from-behind win every time!
So they might just surprise us all and... Oh, wait...
That's *why* it's a farce.
Sure, Crixak is really good...
...but according to everything I've seen and noted down, the members of Scarmiglione are better.
Every single one of them, individually, probably has twice as much power as Crixak, but they've been hiding it.
Huh?
Trying to fix the odds among the bookies, I guess.
HUUHH?!
POING
POING
POING

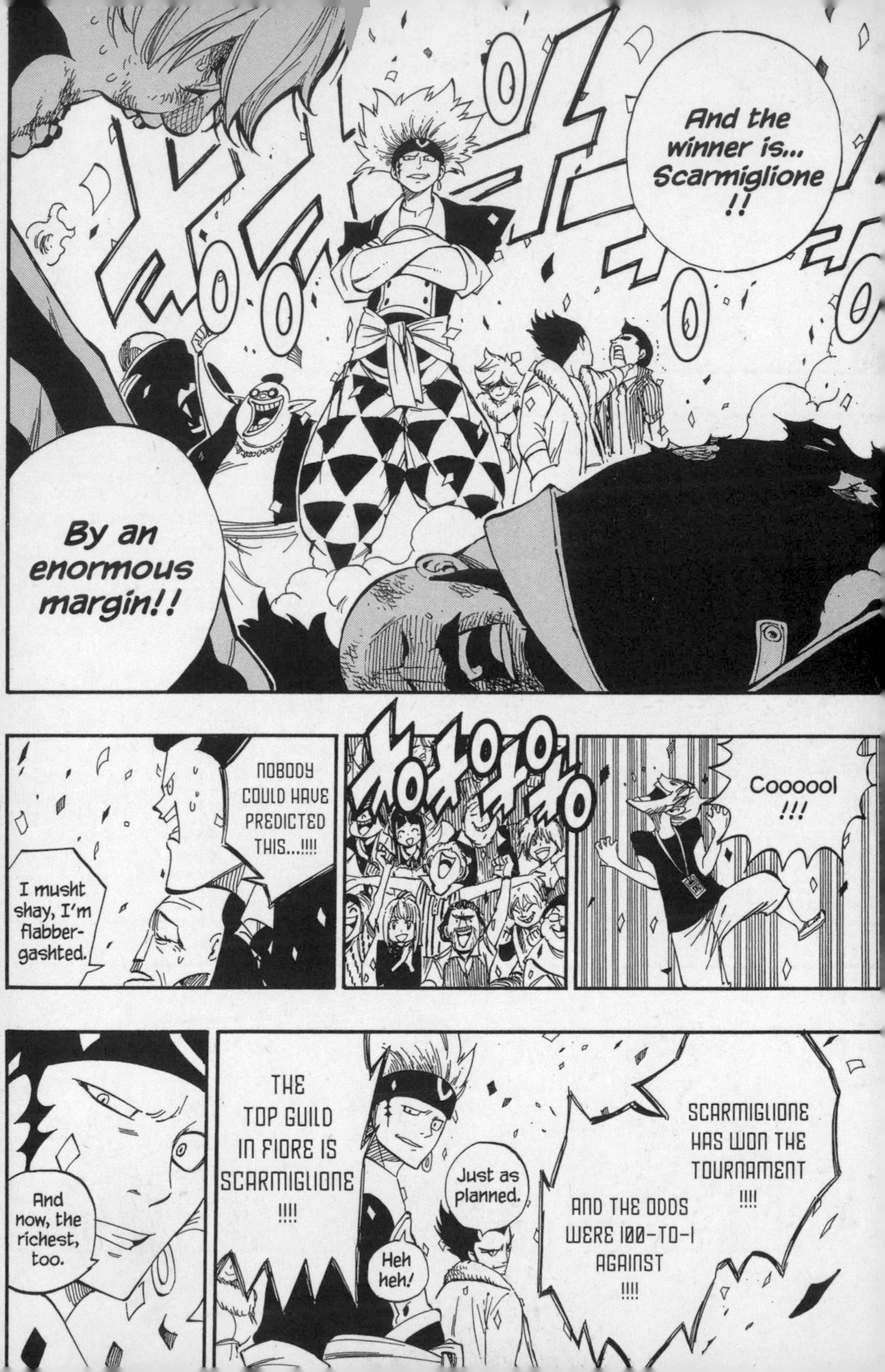
And the winner is... Scarmiglione !!
By an enormous margin!!
Cooooool !!!
NOBODY COULD HAVE PREDICTED THIS...!!!!
I musht shay, I'm flabber-gashted.
SCARMIGLIONE HAS WON THE TOURNAMENT !!!!
AND THE ODDS WERE 100-TO-1 AGAINST !!!!
Just as planned.
Heh heh!
THE TOP GUILD IN FIORE IS SCARMIGLIONE !!!!
And now, the richest, too.

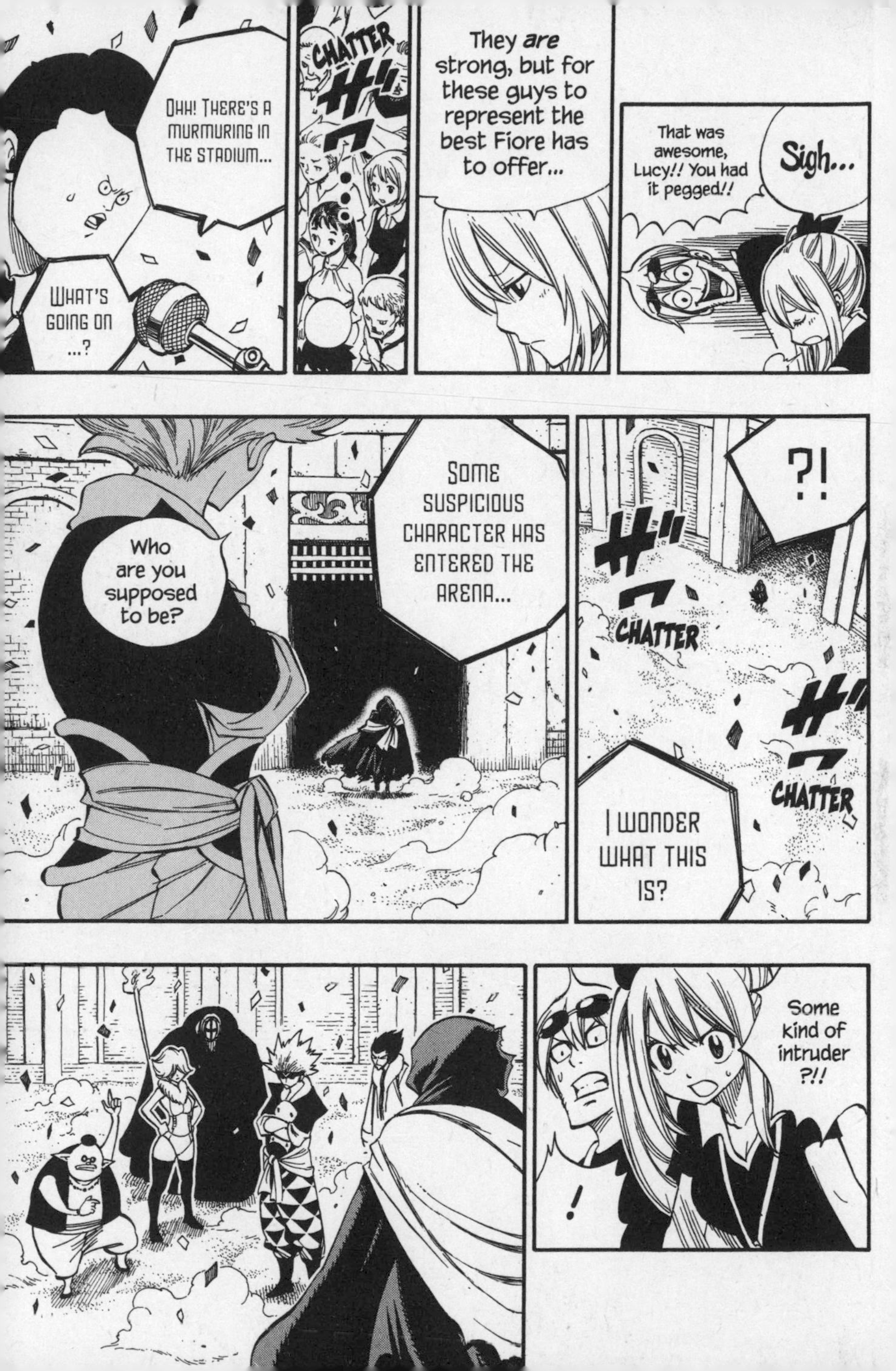

Sigh...
That was awesome, Lucy!! You had it pegged!!
They *are* strong, but for these guys to represent the best Fiore has to offer...
CHATTER
OHH! THERE'S A MURMURING IN THE STADIUM...
WHAT'S GOING ON ...?
?!
CHATTER
CHATTER
I WONDER WHAT THIS IS?
SOME SUSPICIOUS CHARACTER HAS ENTERED THE ARENA...
Who are you supposed to be?
Some kind of intruder?!!
!

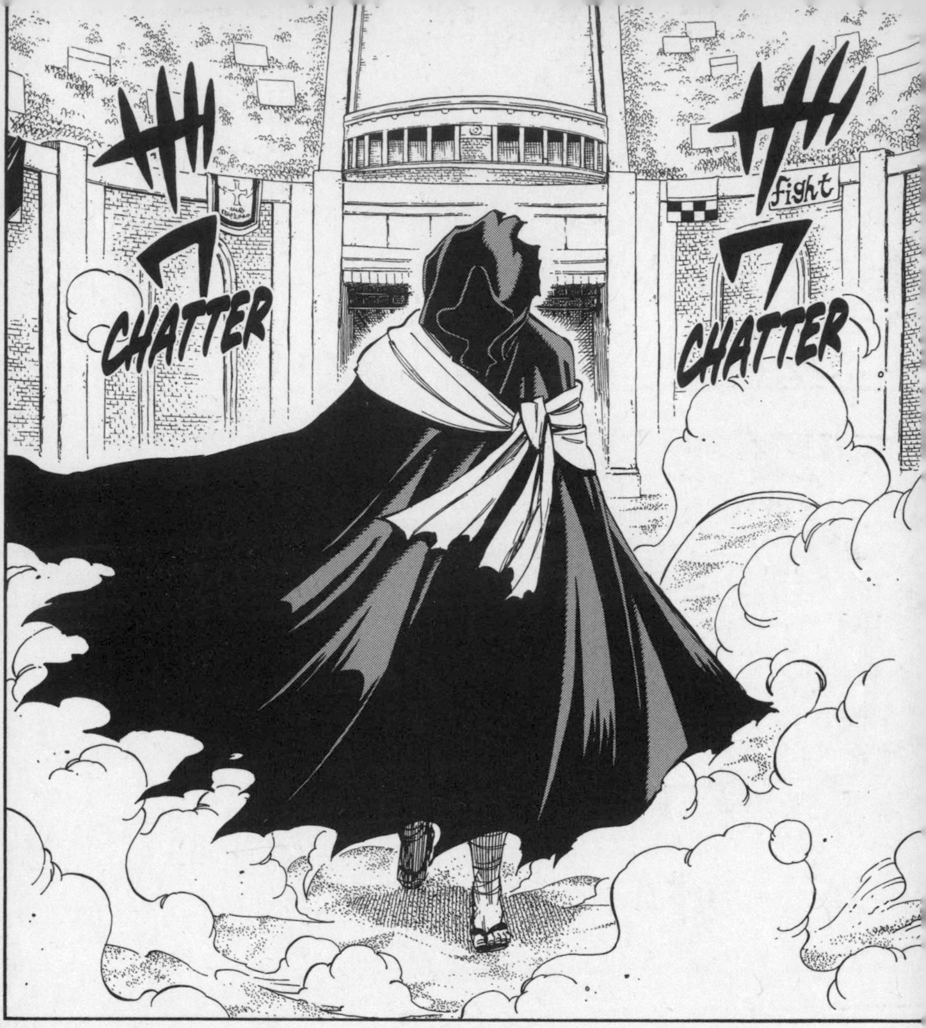
CHATTER
fight
CHATTER

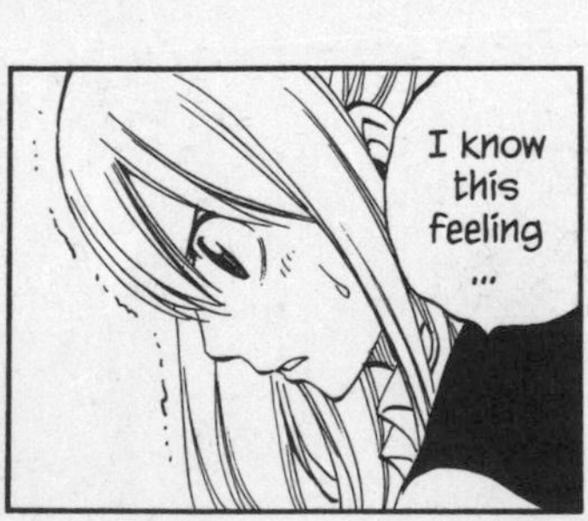
I know this feeling ...

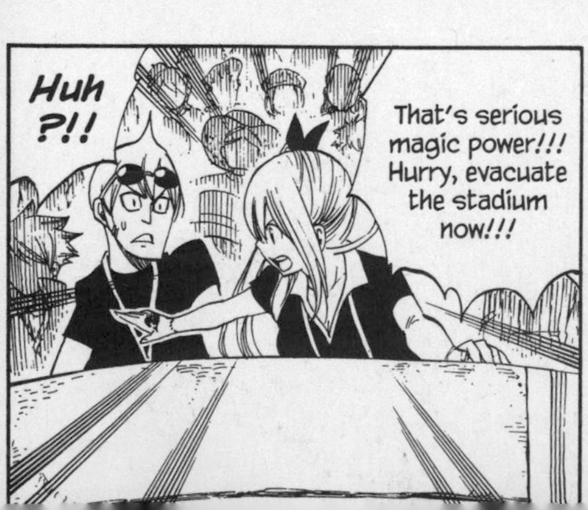
Huh ?!!
That's serious magic power!!! Hurry, evacuate the stadium now!!!

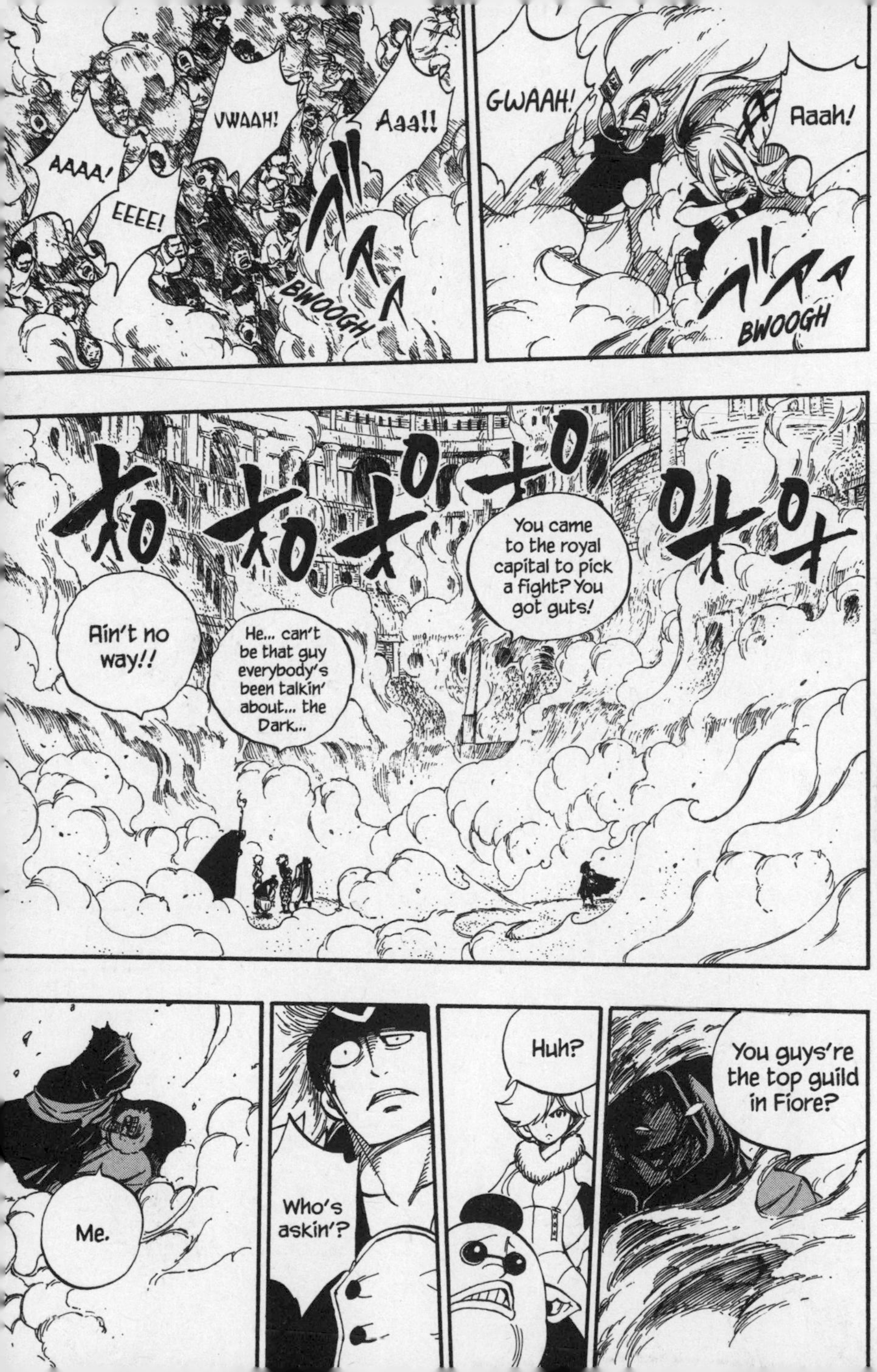
Aaah!
GWAAH!
BWOOGH
Aaa!!
VWAAH!
AAAA!
EEEE!
BWOOGH
You came to the royal capital to pick a fight? You got guts!
He... can't be that guy everybody's been talkin' about... the Dark...
Ain't no way!!
You guys're the top guild in Fiore?
Huh?
Who's askin'?
Me.

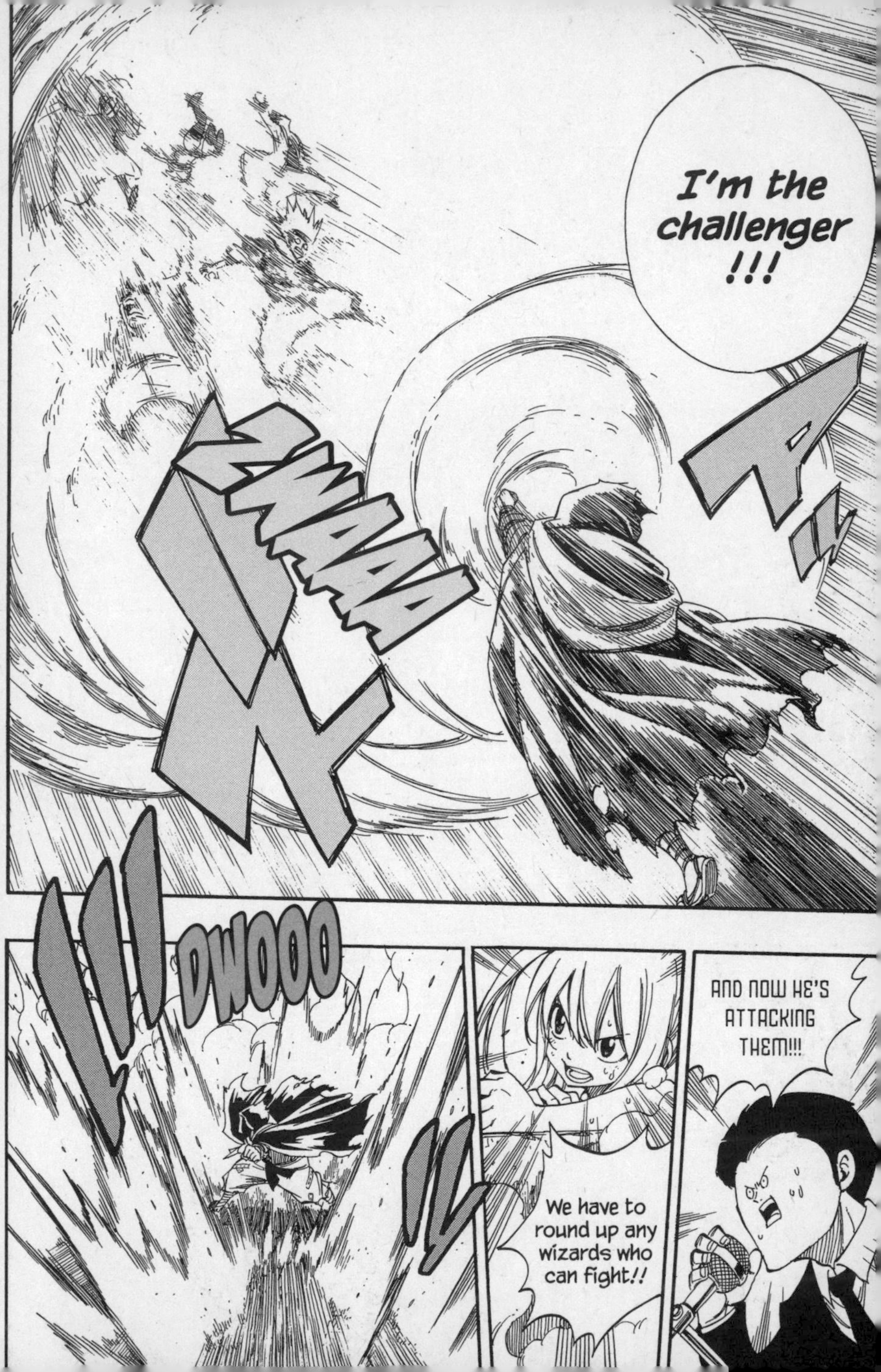
I'm the challenger!!!
AND NOW HE'S ATTACKING THEM!!!
We have to round up any wizards who can fight!!
DWOOO

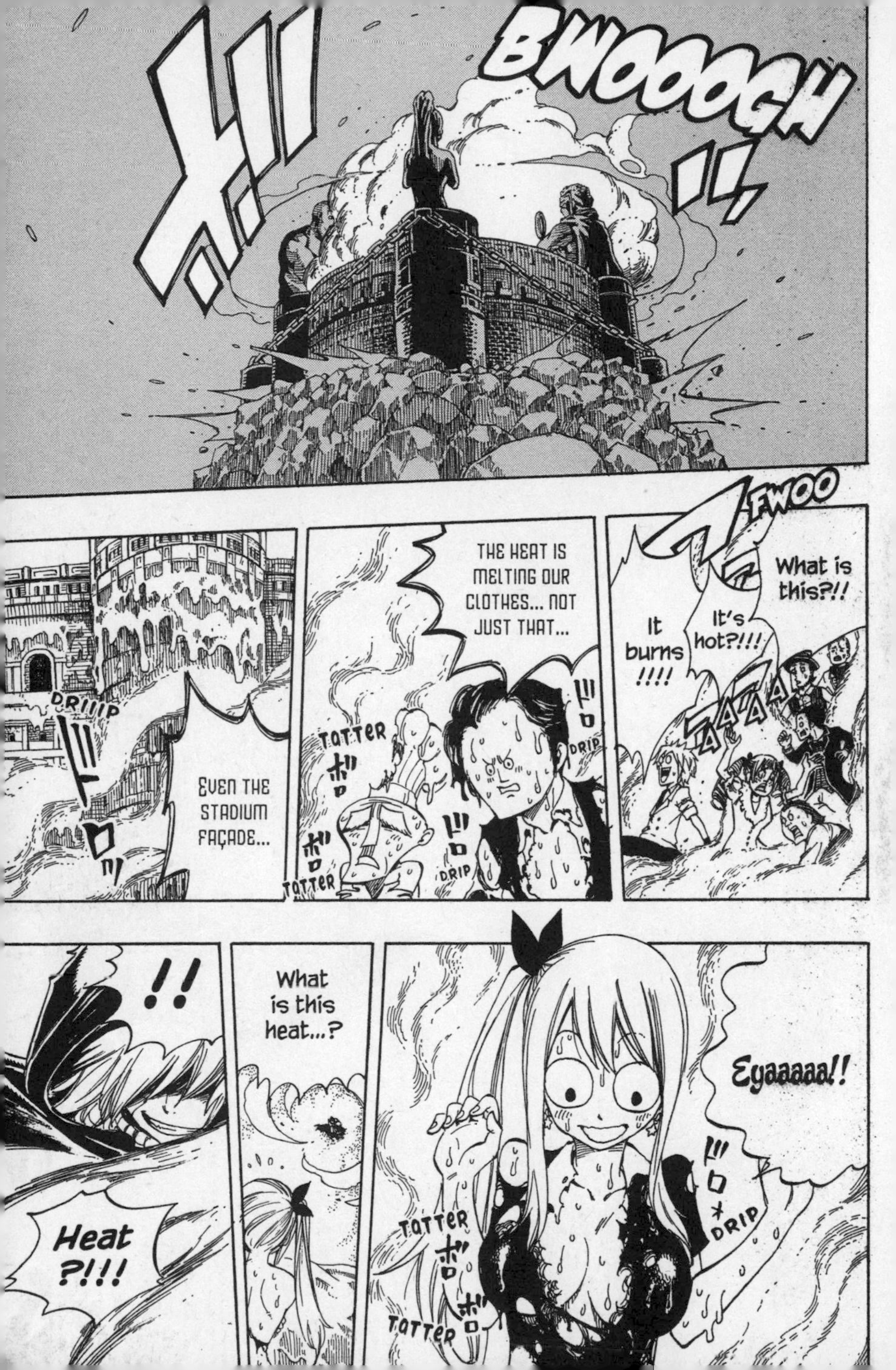
BWOOOCH
FWOO
What is this?!!
It's hot?!!!
It burns !!!!
THE HEAT IS MELTING OUR CLOTHES... NOT JUST THAT...
ドロ DRIP
ボロ TATTER
ドロ DRIP
ボロ TATTER
EVEN THE STADIUM FAÇADE...
DRIIIP
Eyaaaaa!!
ドロ* DRIP
ボロ TATTER
ボロ TATTER
What is this heat...?
!!
Heat ?!!!

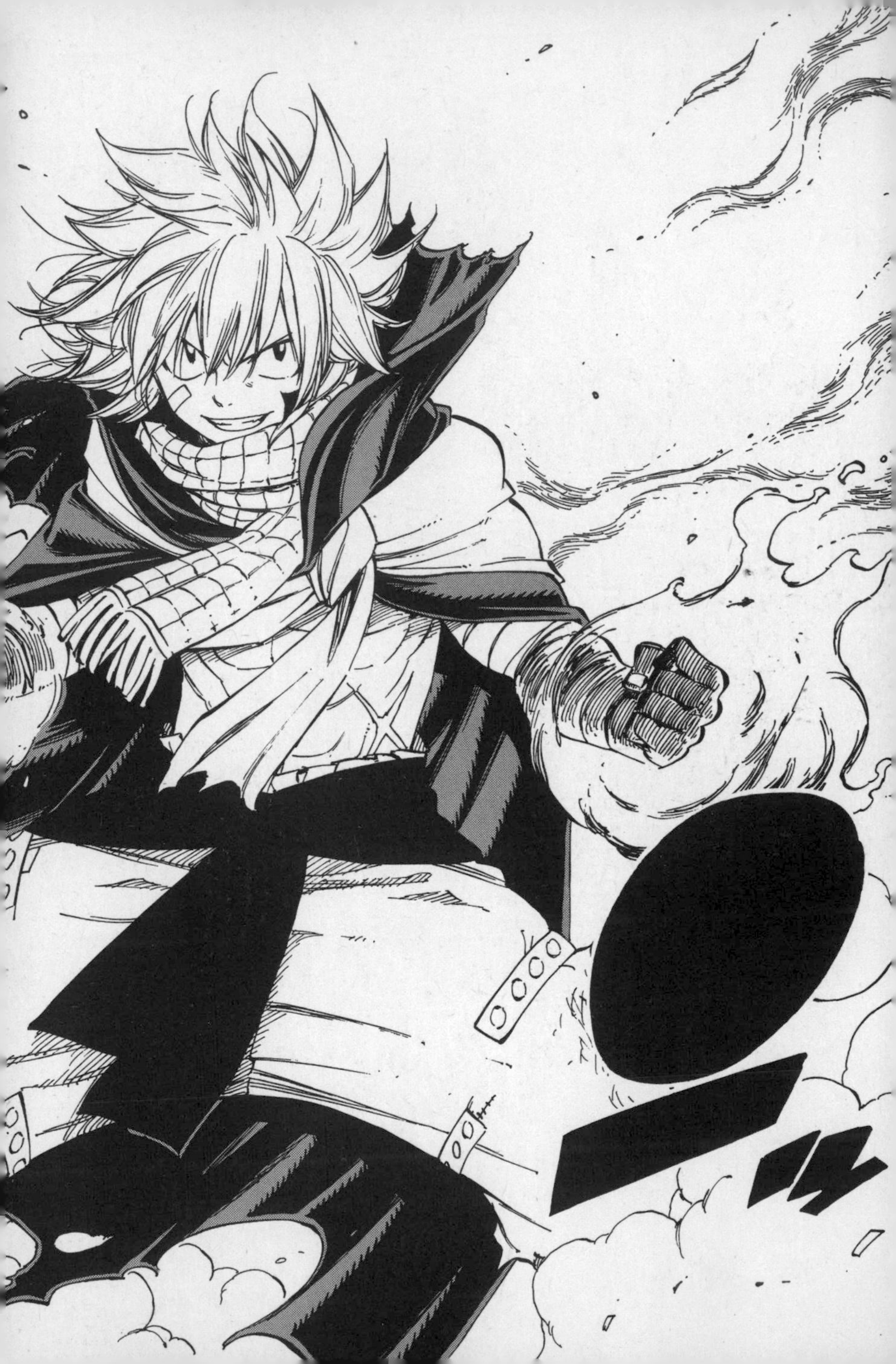

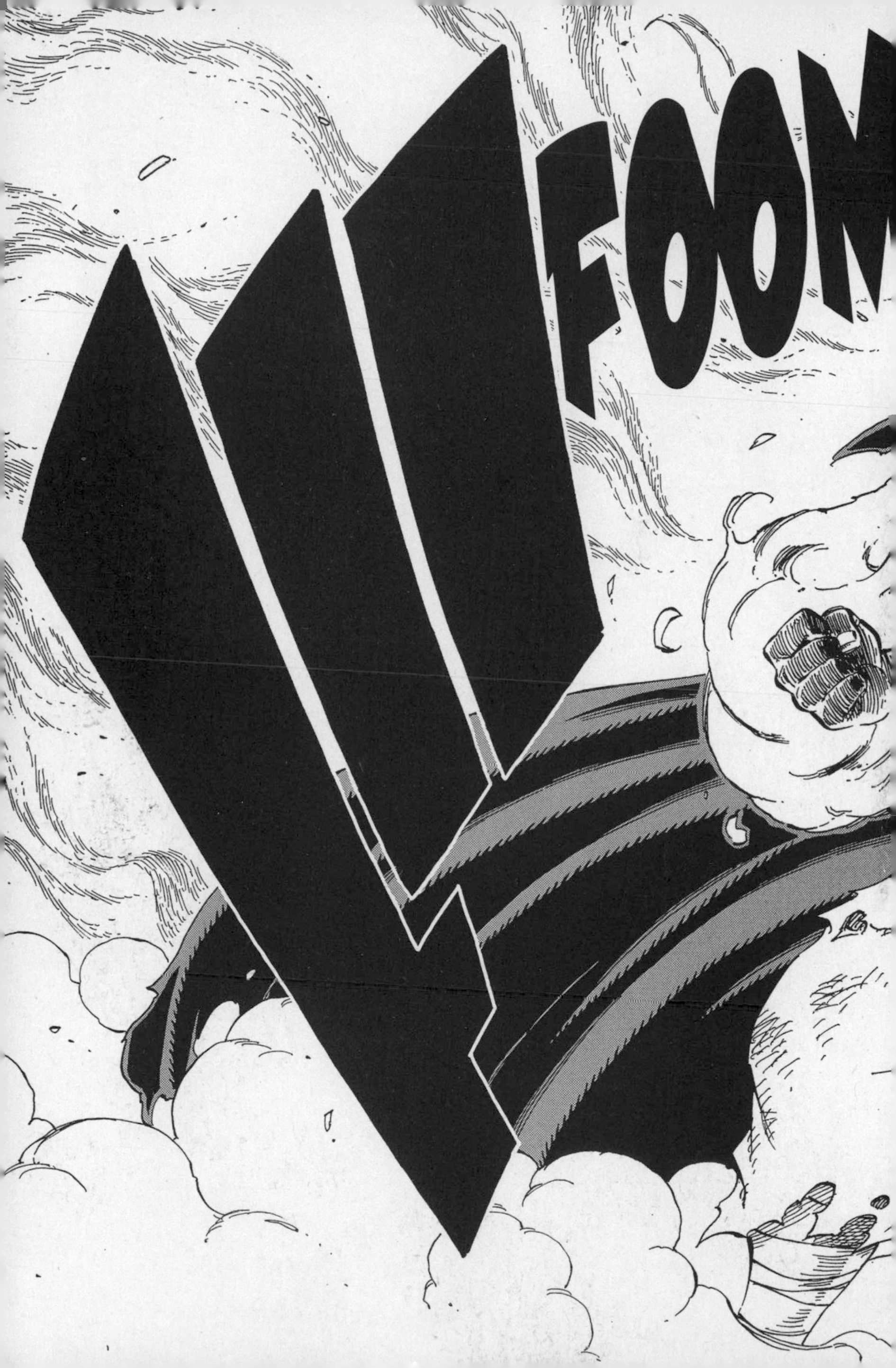
FOOM

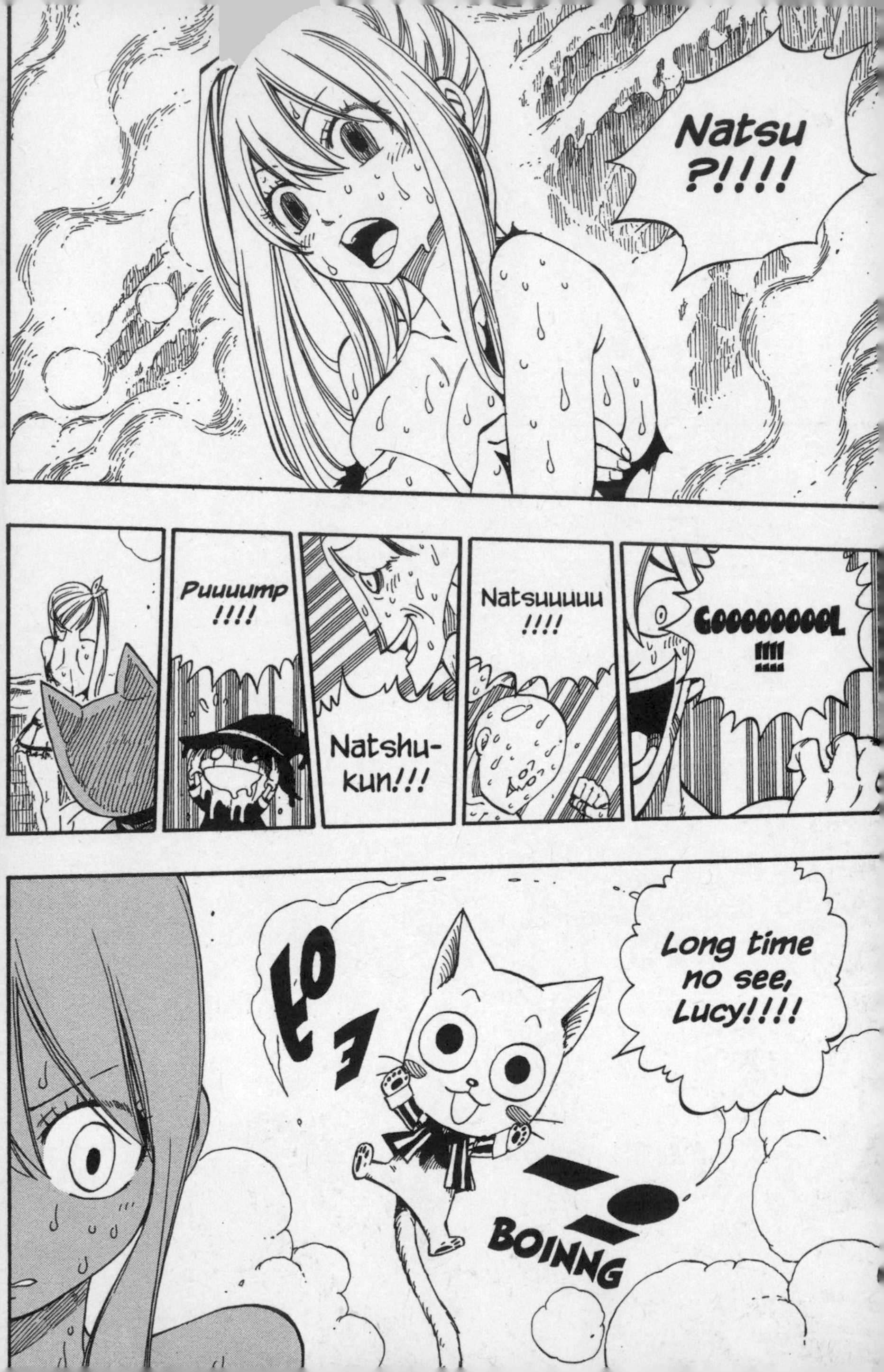

Natsu ?!!!!
GOOOOOOOOOL !!!!
Natsuuuuu !!!!
Natshu-kun!!!
Puuuump !!!!
Long time no see, Lucy!!!!
BOINNG

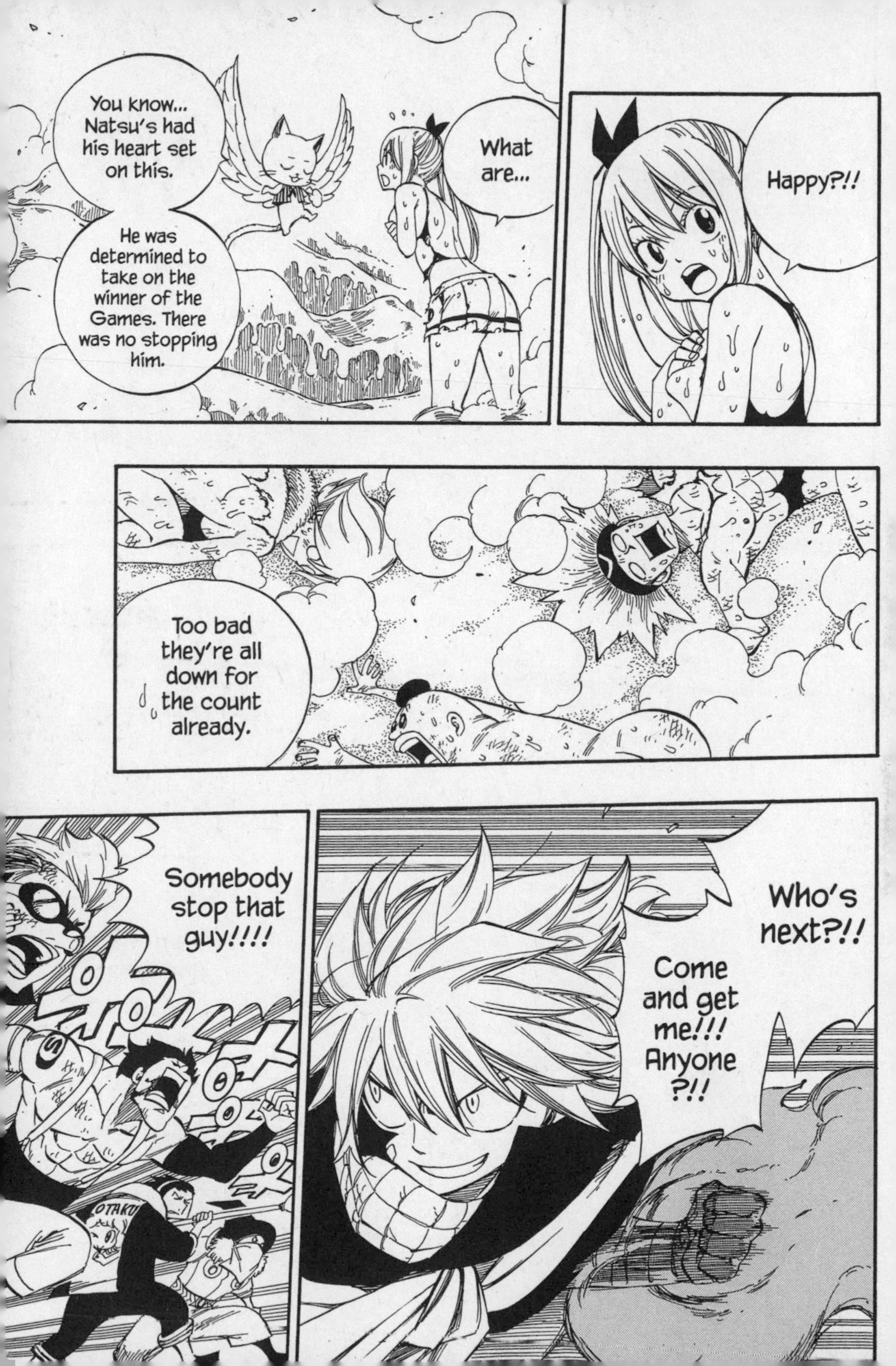
Happy?!!
What are...
You know... Natsu's had his heart set on this.
He was determined to take on the winner of the Games. There was no stopping him.
Too bad they're all down for the count already.
Who's next?!!
Come and get me!!! Anyone ?!!
Somebody stop that guy!!!!
OTAKU

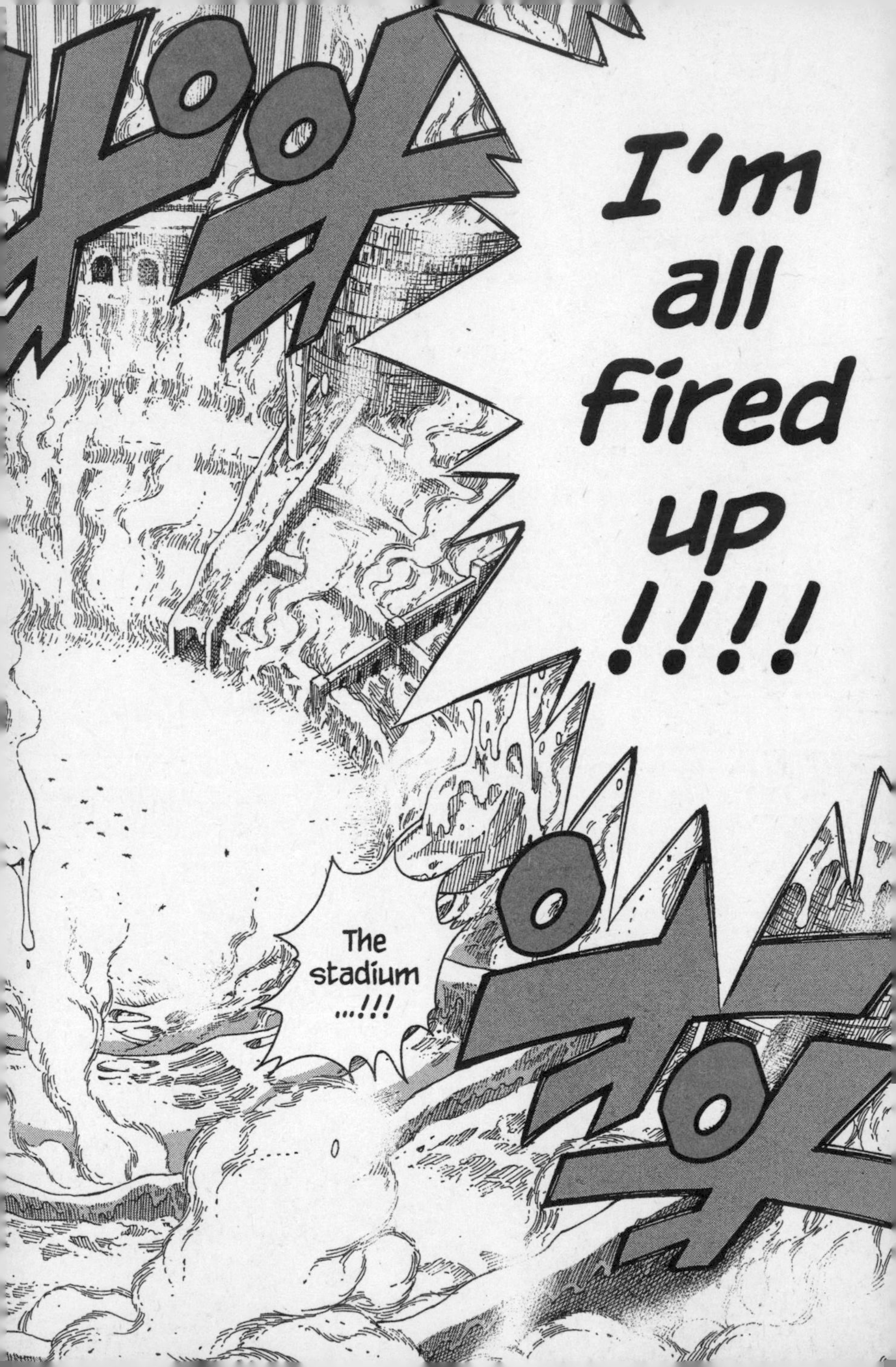
I'm all fired up!!!!
The stadium ...!!!

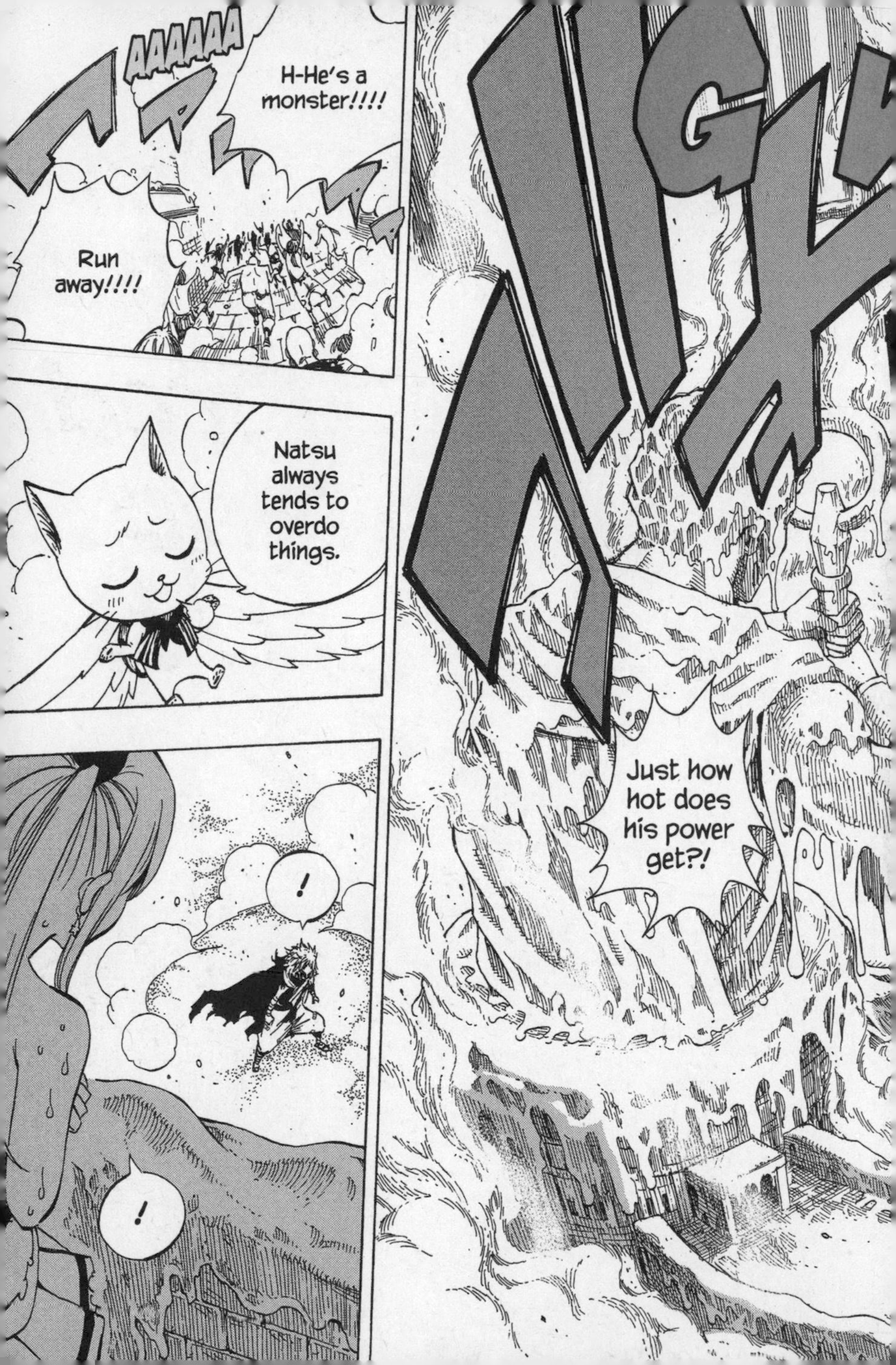
Just how hot does his power get?!
AAAAAA
H-He's a monster!!!!
Run away!!!!
Natsu always tends to overdo things.
!
!

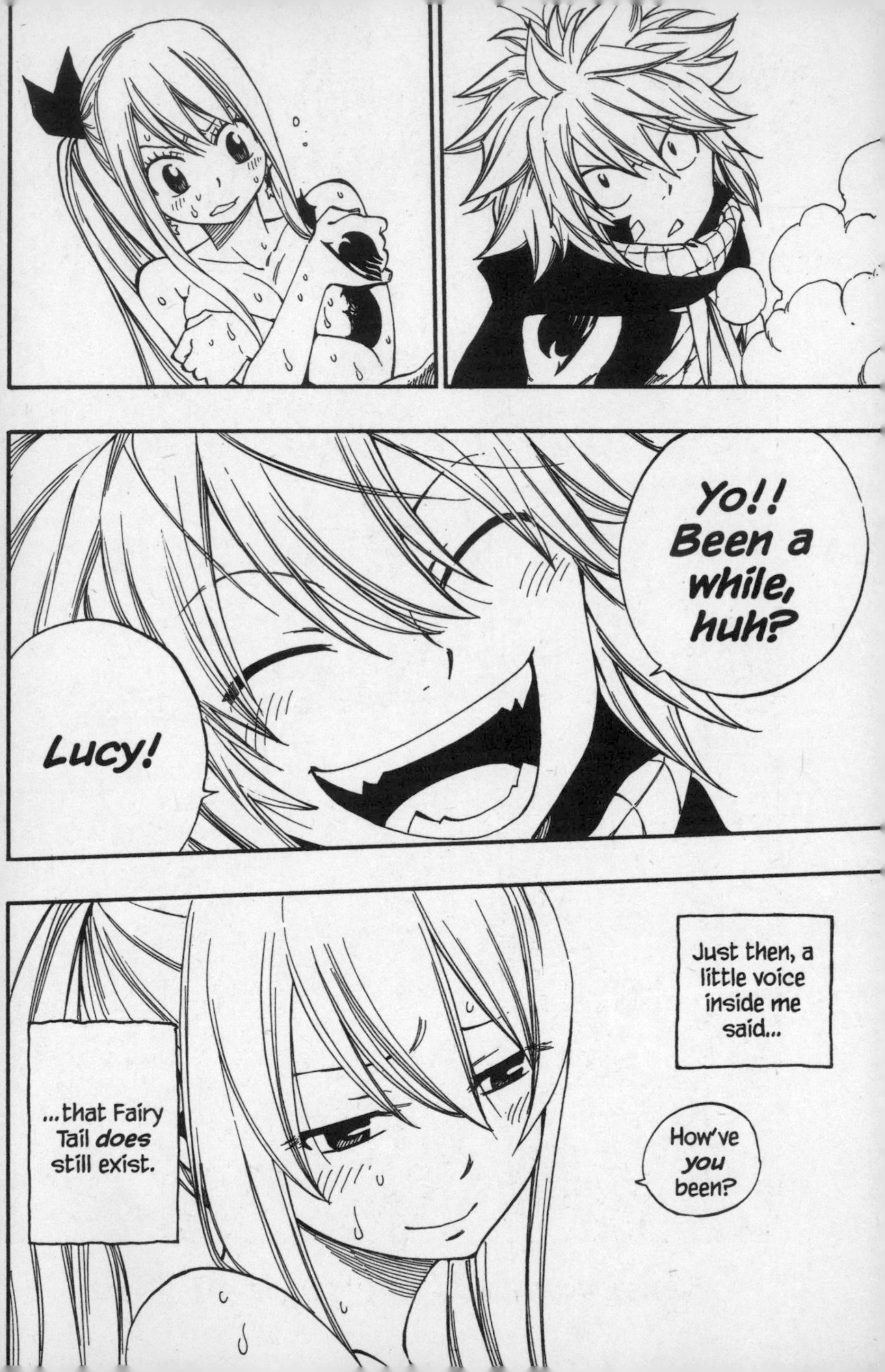
Yo!! Been a while, huh?
Lucy!
Just then, a little voice inside me said...
...that Fairy Tail *does* still exist.
How've *you* been?

FAIRY TAIL

フェアリーテイル

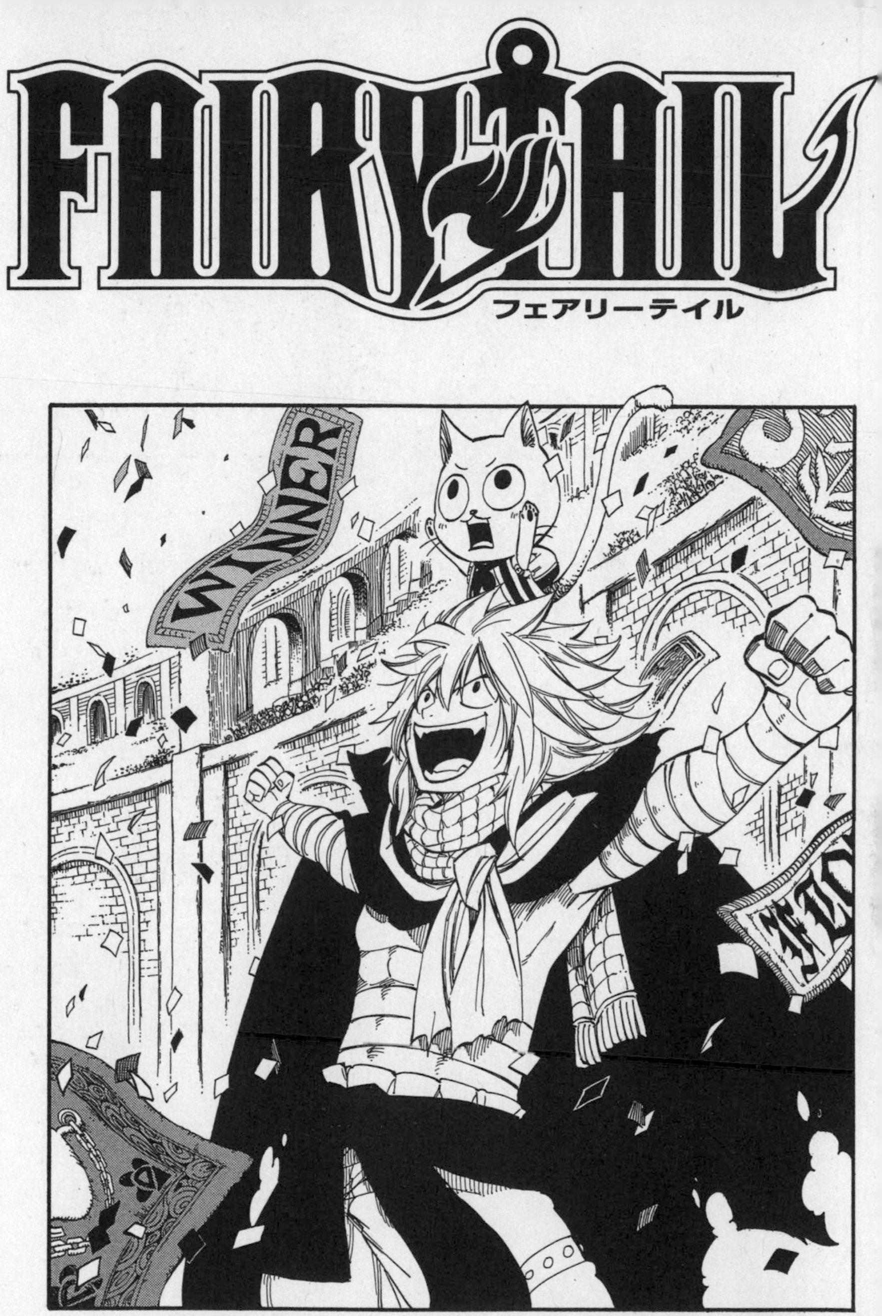
WINNER

Chapter 419: Message of Fire

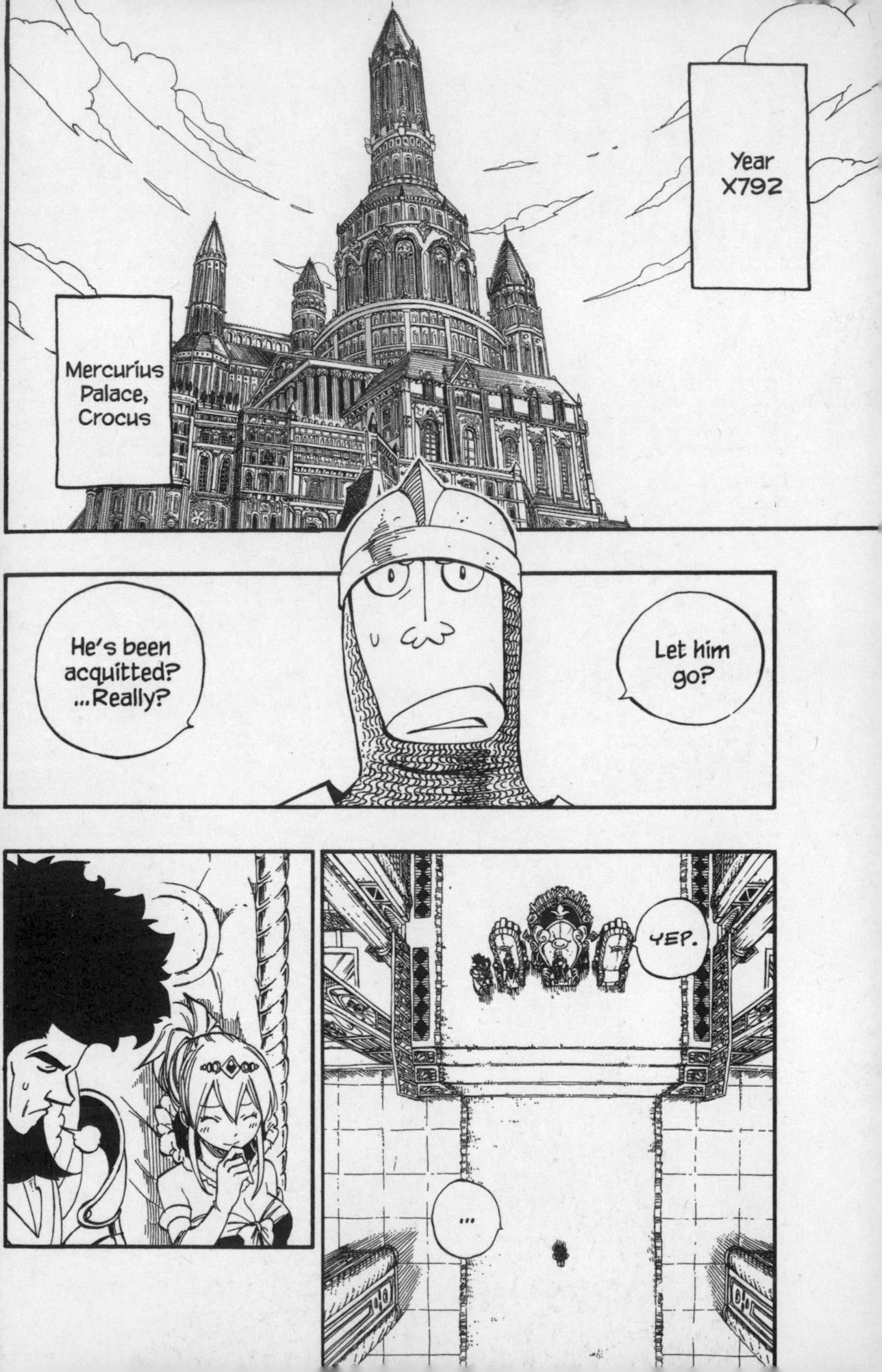
Year X792
Mercurius Palace, Crocus
Let him go?
He's been acquitted? ...Really?
YEP.
...

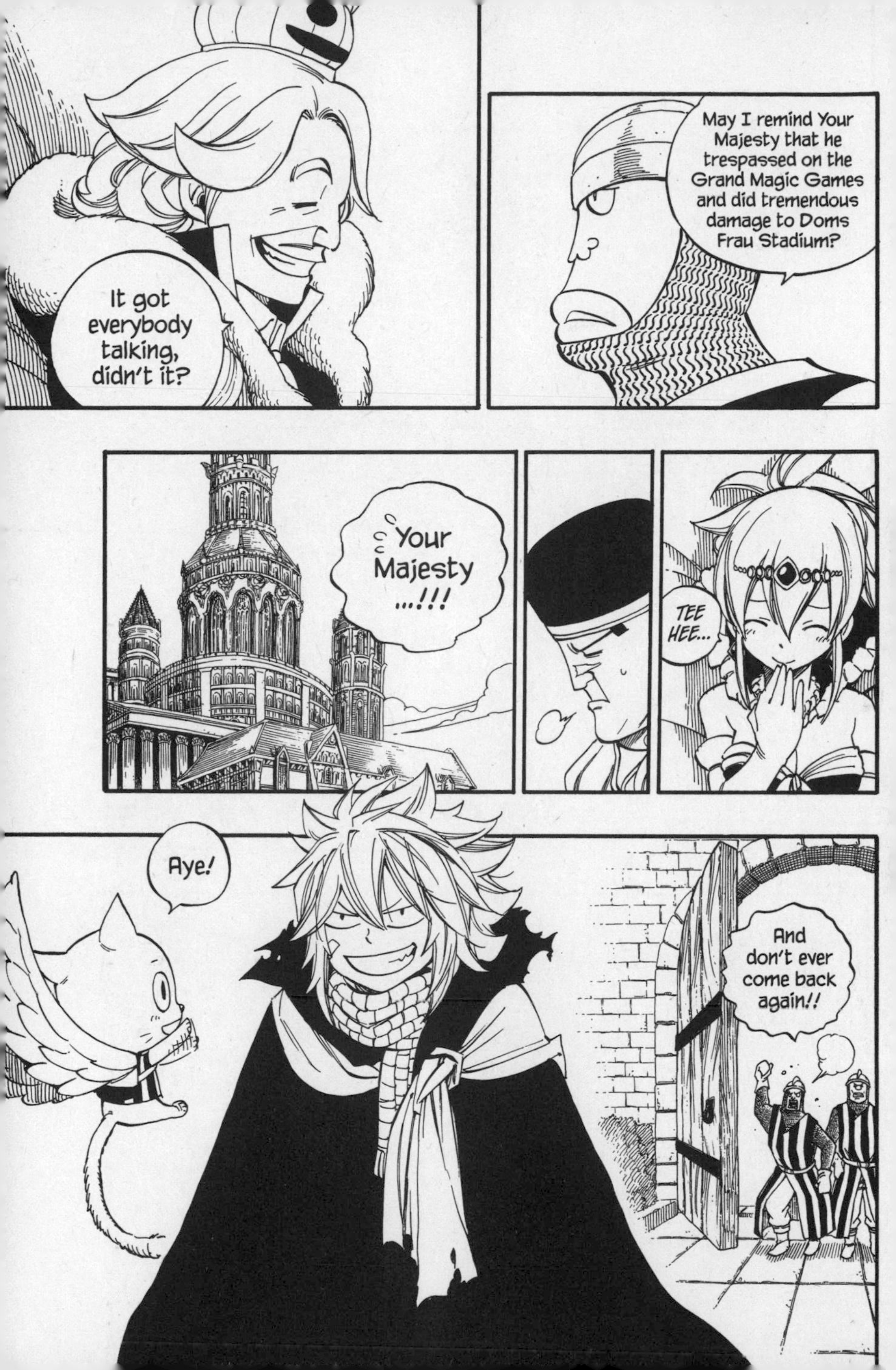
May I remind Your Majesty that he trespassed on the Grand Magic Games and did tremendous damage to Doms Frau Stadium?
It got everybody talking, didn't it?
TEE HEE...
Your Majesty ...!!!
And don't ever come back again!!
Aye!

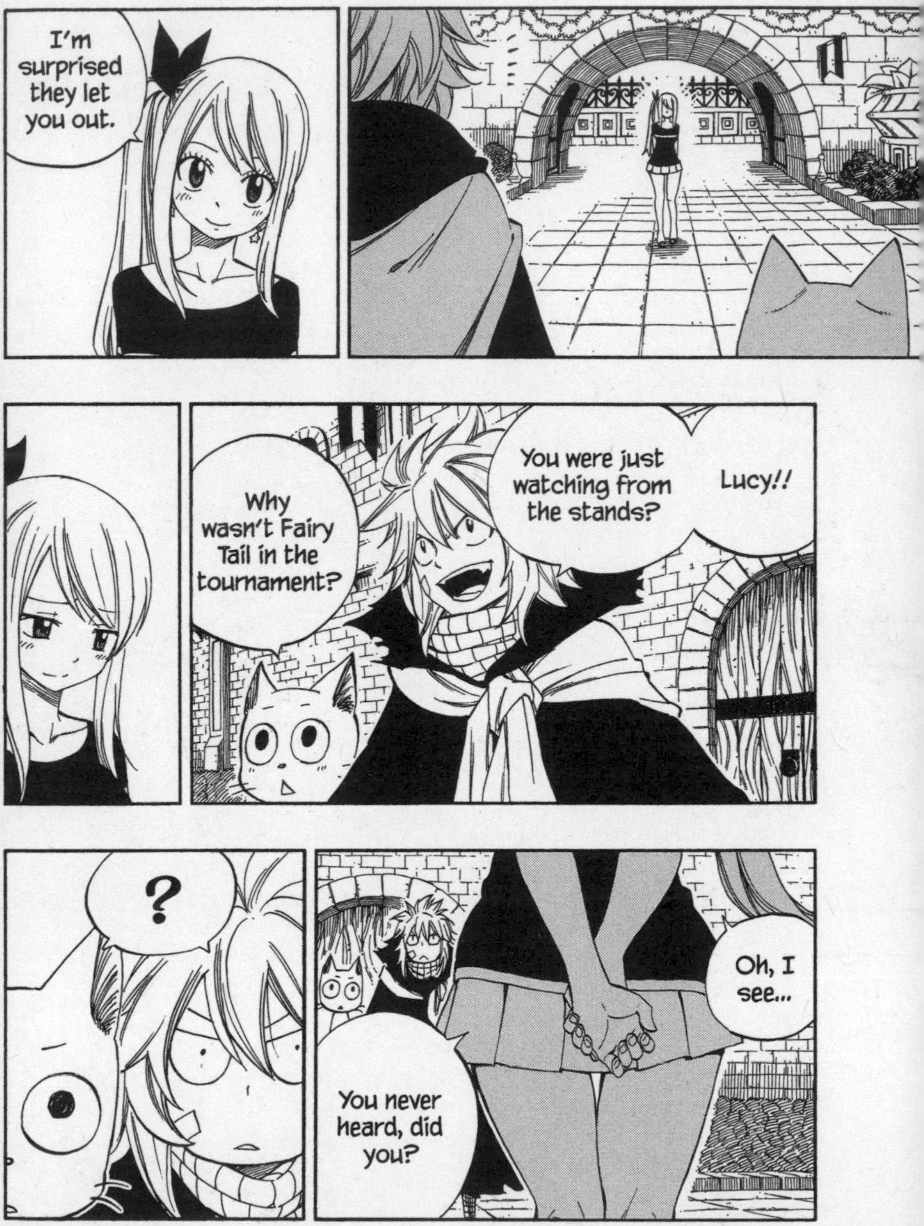
I'm surprised they let you out.
Lucy!!
You were just watching from the stands?
Why wasn't Fairy Tail in the tournament?
Oh, I see...
You never heard, did you?
?

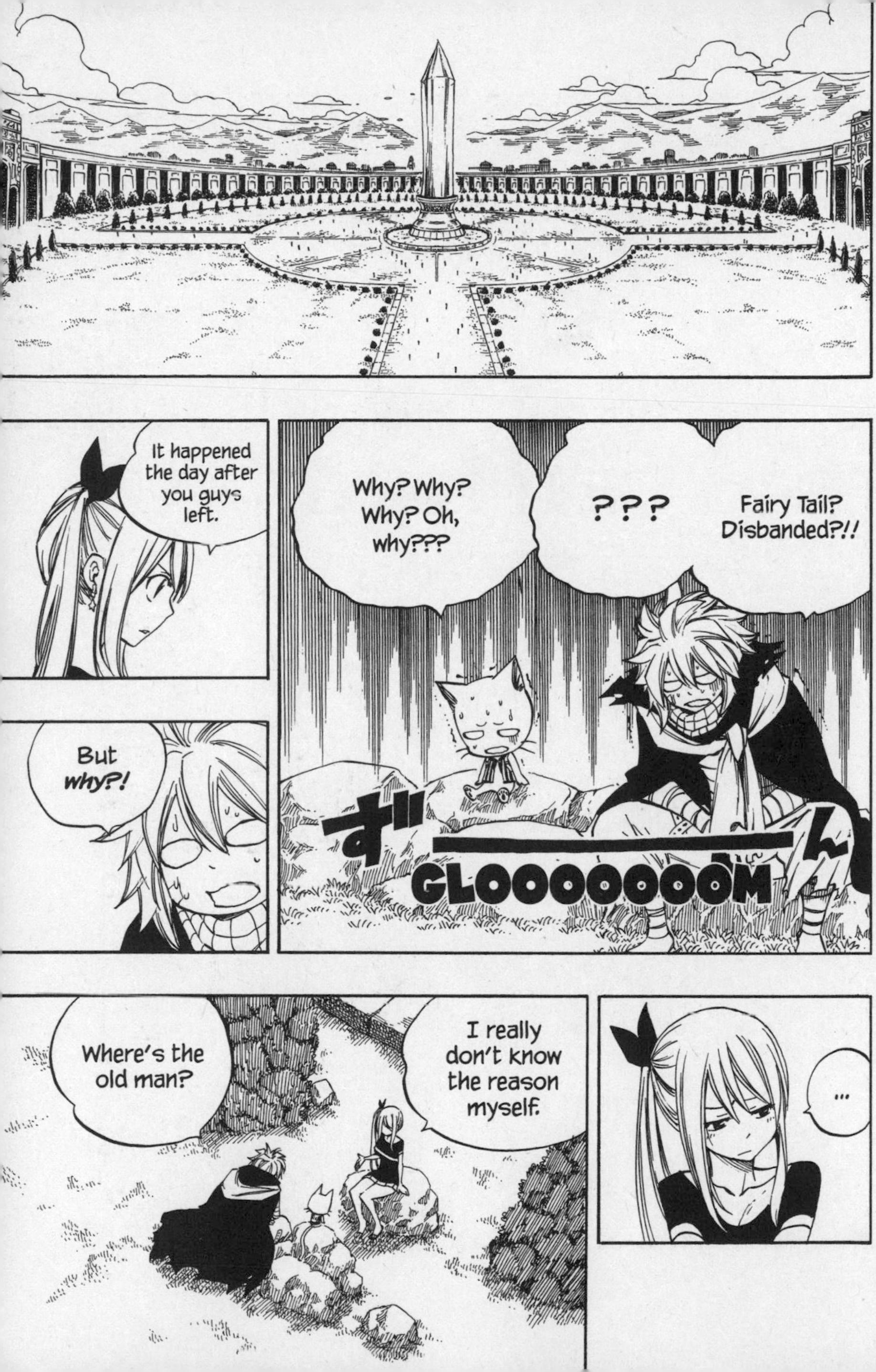
Fairy Tail? Disbanded?!!
???
Why? Why? Why? Oh, why???
GLOOOOOOOM
It happened the day after you guys left.
But *why?!*
...
I really don't know the reason myself.
Where's the old man?

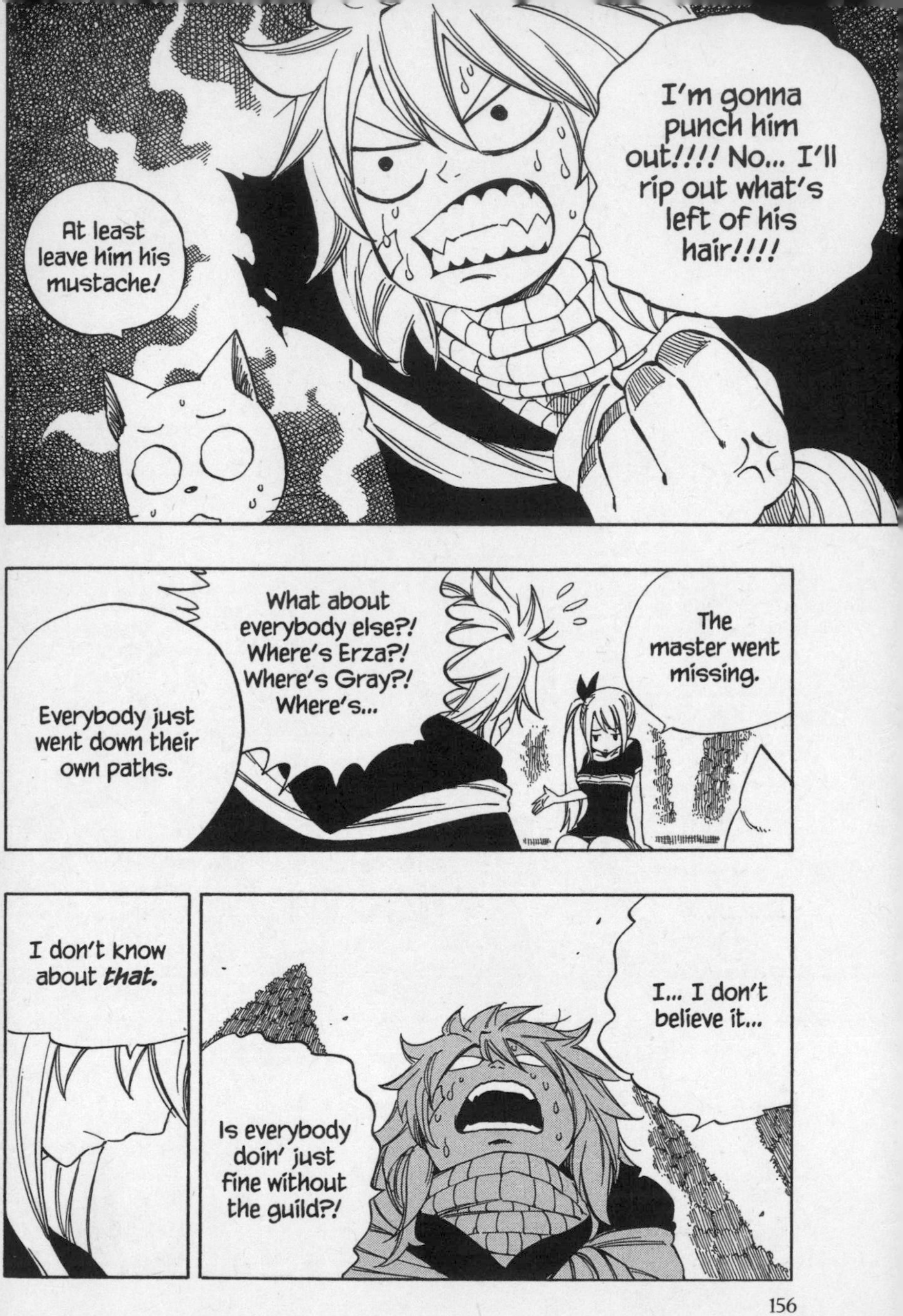
I'm gonna punch him out!!!! No... I'll rip out what's left of his hair!!!!
At least leave him his mustache!
The master went missing.
What about everybody else?! Where's Erza?! Where's Gray?! Where's...
Everybody just went down their own paths.
I... I don't believe it...
Is everybody doin' just fine without the guild?!
I don't know about *that.*

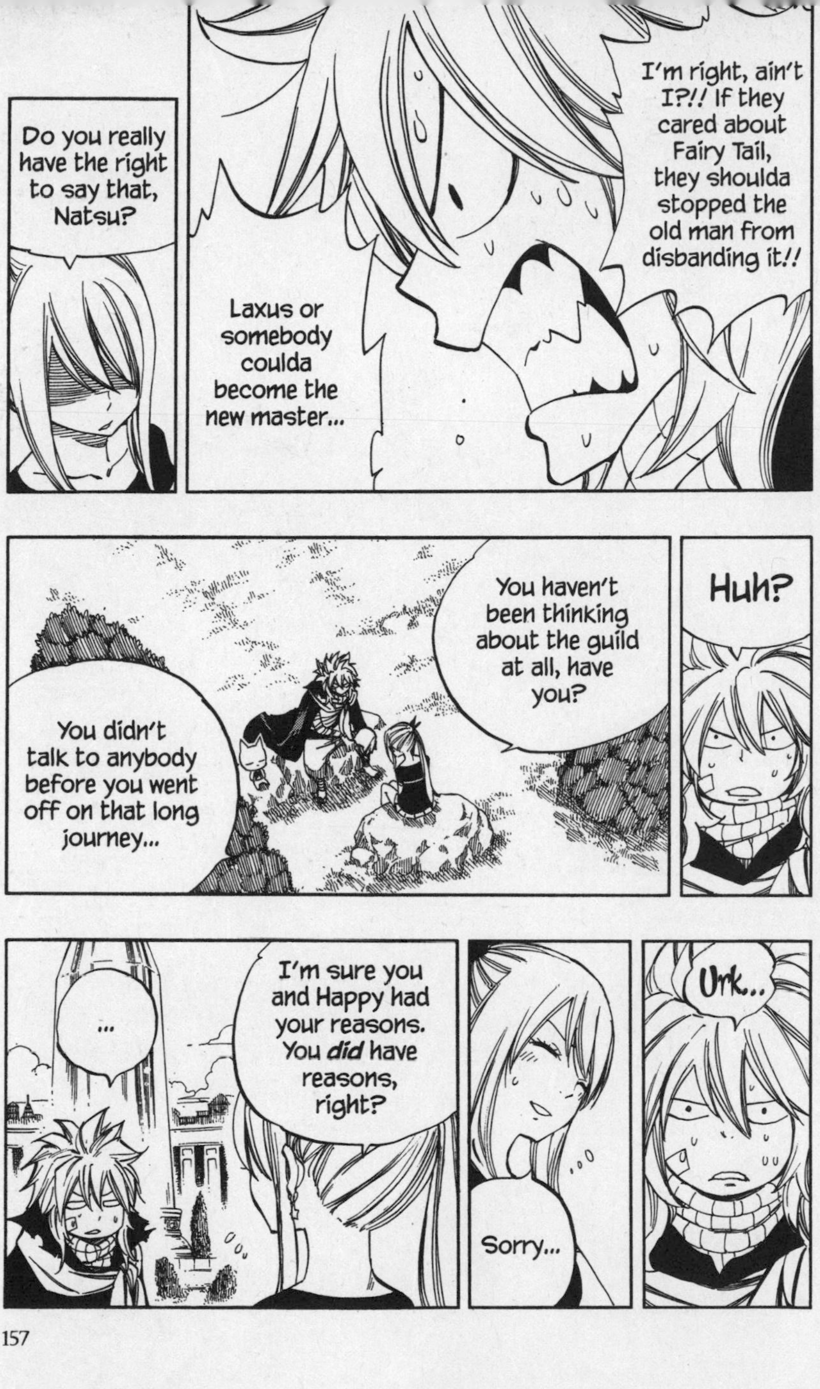
I'm right, ain't I?!! If they cared about Fairy Tail, they shoulda stopped the old man from disbanding it!!
Laxus or somebody coulda become the new master...
Do you really have the right to say that, Natsu?
Huh?
You haven't been thinking about the guild at all, have you?
You didn't talk to anybody before you went off on that long journey...
Urk...
Sorry...
I'm sure you and Happy had your reasons. You *did* have reasons, right?
...

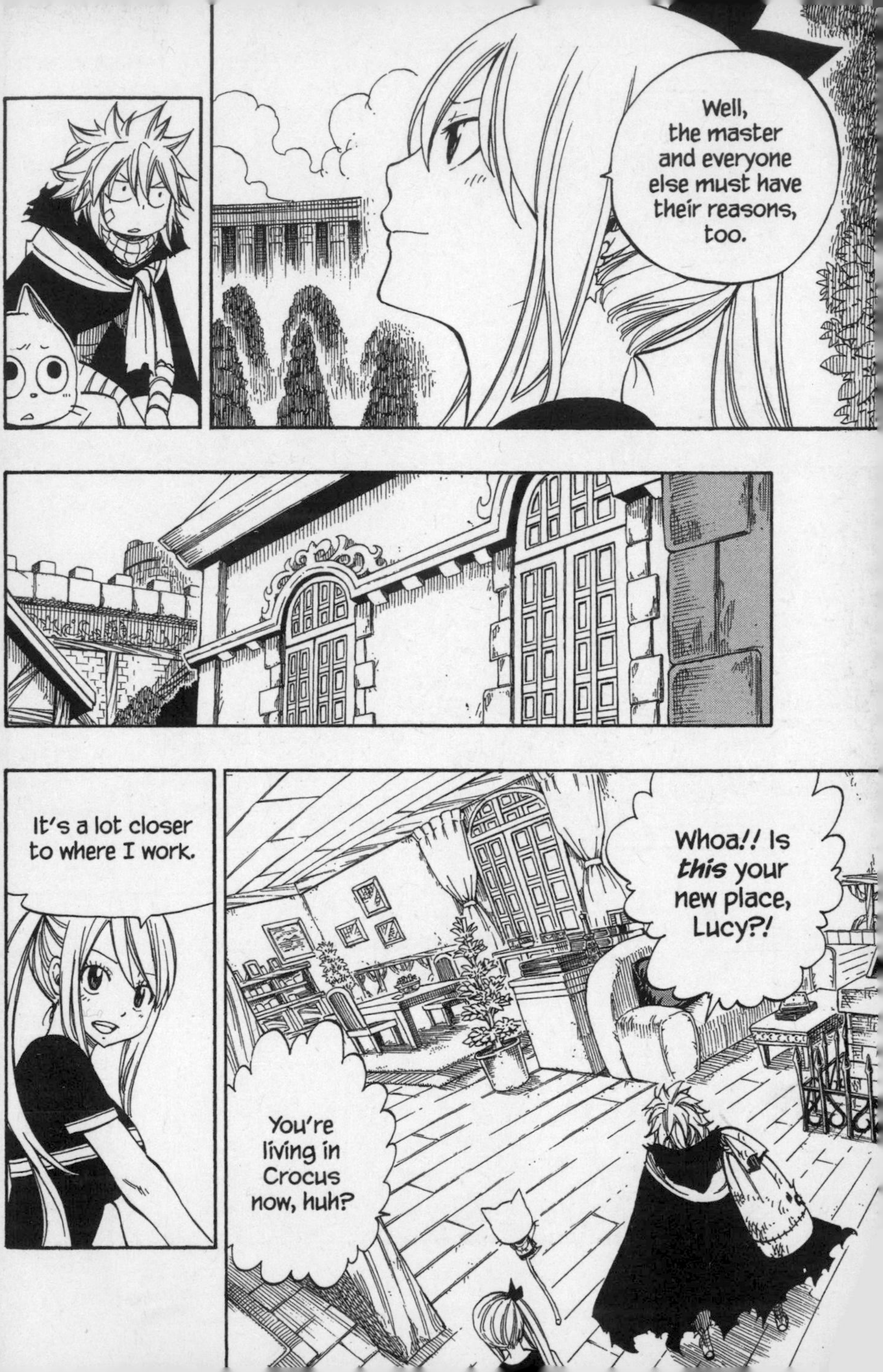
Well, the master and everyone else must have their reasons, too.
Whoa!! Is *this* your new place, Lucy?!
You're living in Crocus now, huh?
It's a lot closer to where I work.

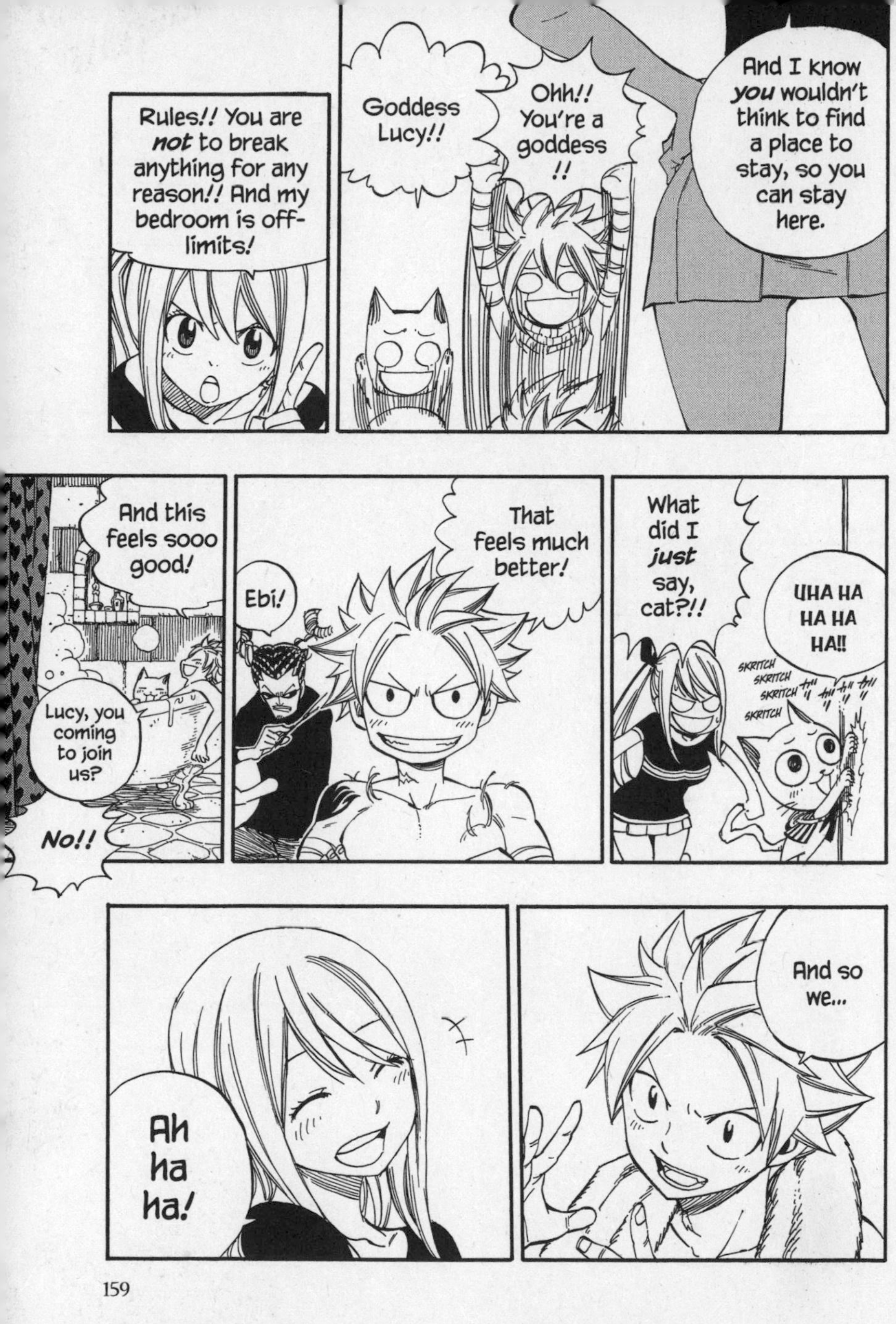
And I know *you* wouldn't think to find a place to stay, so you can stay here.
Ohh!! You're a goddess!!
Goddess Lucy!!
Rules!! You are *not* to break anything for any reason!! And my bedroom is off-limits!
What did I *just* say, cat?!!
UHA HA HA HA HA!!
SKRITCH
SKRITCH
SKRITCH
SKRITCH
That feels much better!
Ebi!
And this feels sooo good!
Lucy, you coming to join us?
No!!
And so we...
Ah ha ha!

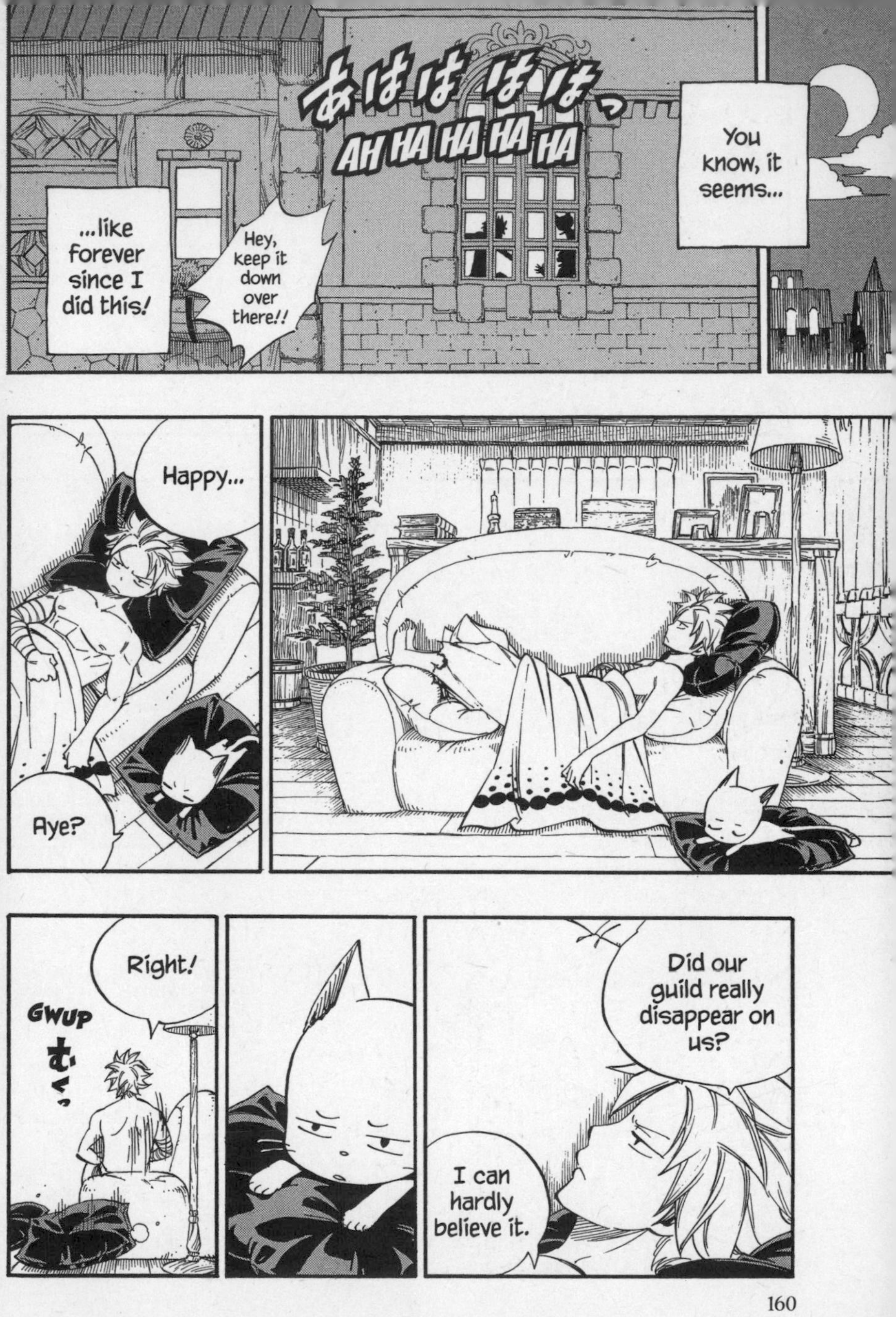
You know, it seems...
あははははっ
AH HA HA HA HA
Hey, keep it down over there!!
...like forever since I did this!
Happy...
Aye?
Did our guild really disappear on us?
I can hardly believe it.
Right!
GWUP
むくっ

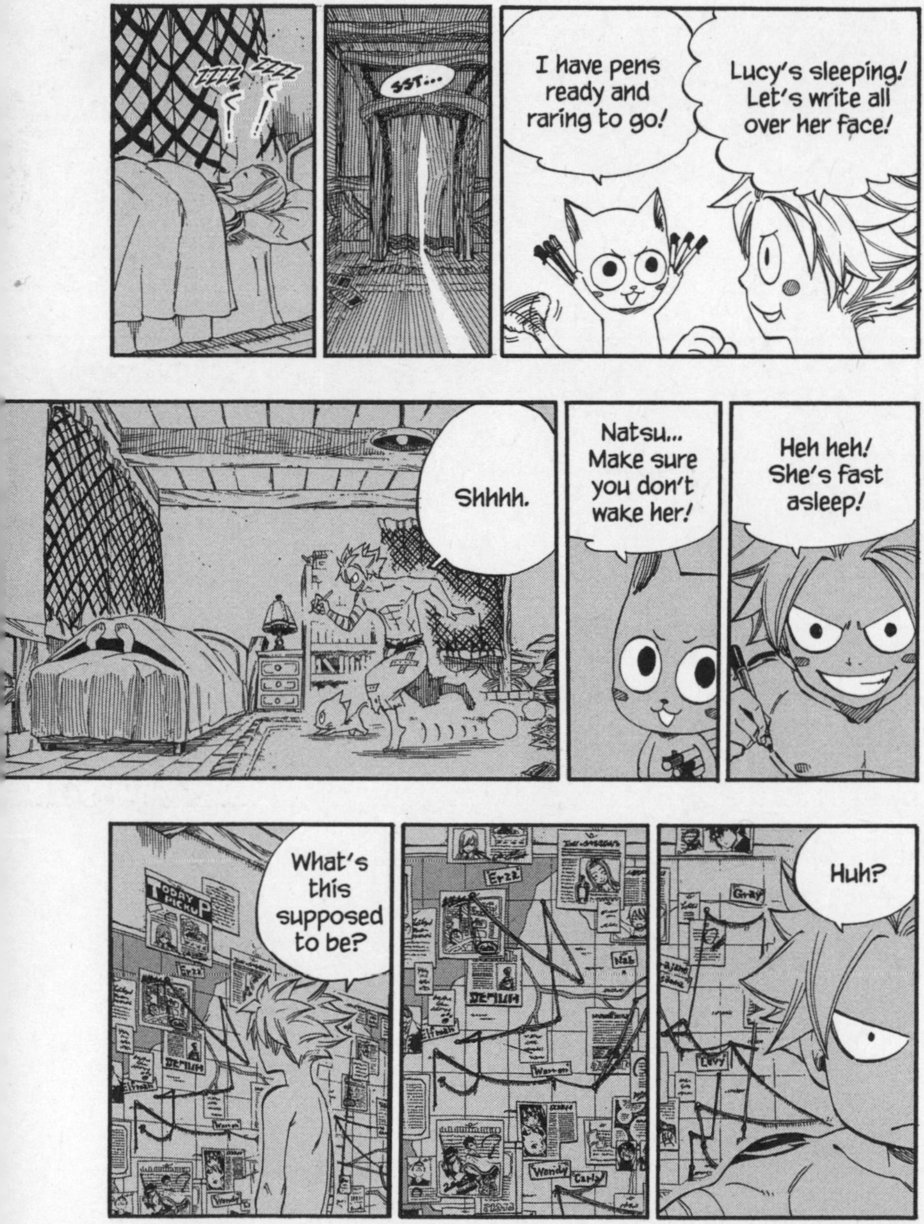
Lucy's sleeping! Let's write all over her face!
I have pens ready and raring to go!
SST...
ZZZZ
ZZZZ
Heh heh! She's fast asleep!
Natsu... Make sure you don't wake her!
Shhhh.
Huh?
What's this supposed to be?

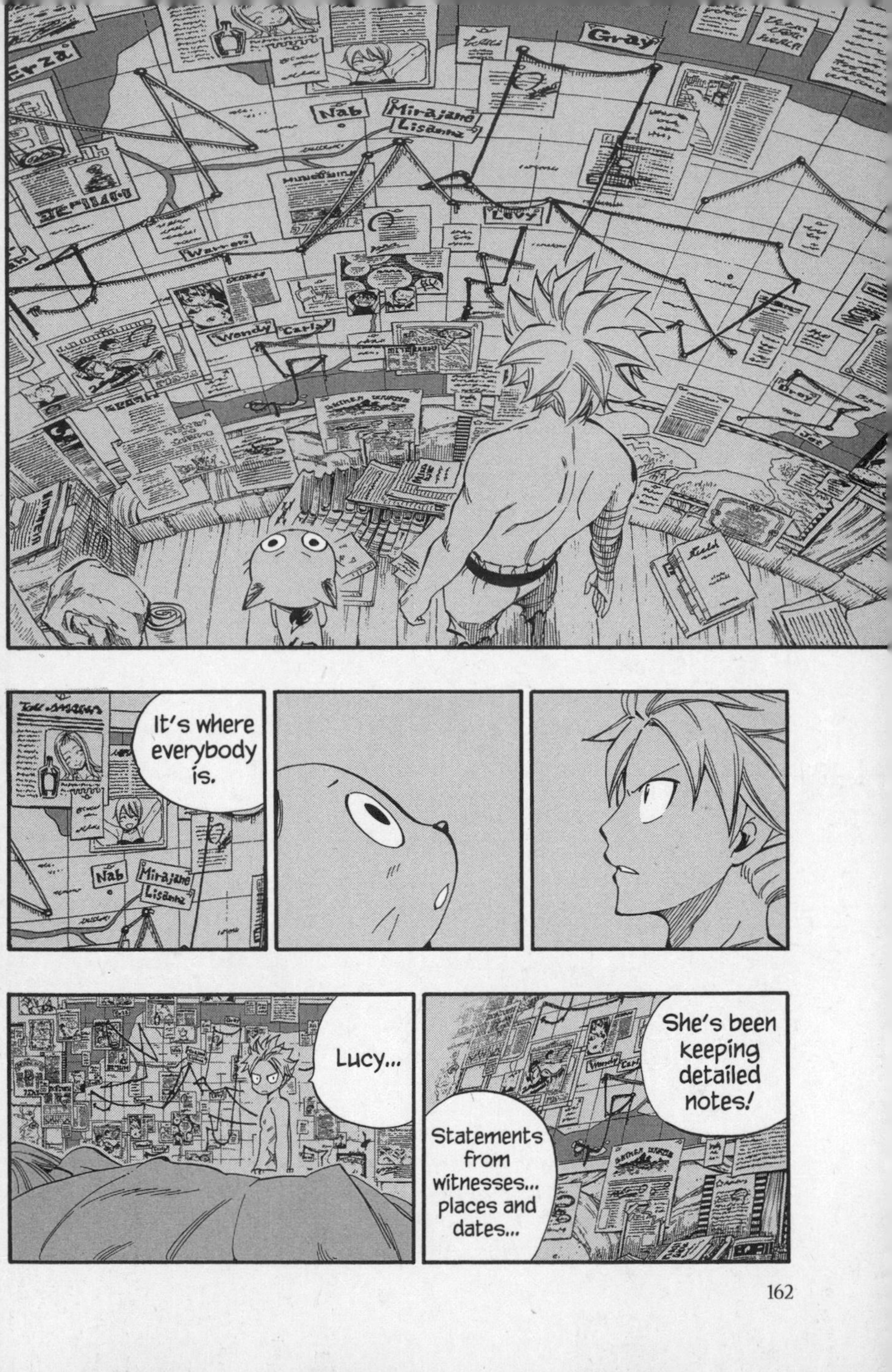
Gray
Erza
Nab
Mirajane
Lisanna
Levy
Wendy
Carla
It's where everybody is.
She's been keeping detailed notes!
Statements from witnesses... places and dates...
Lucy...

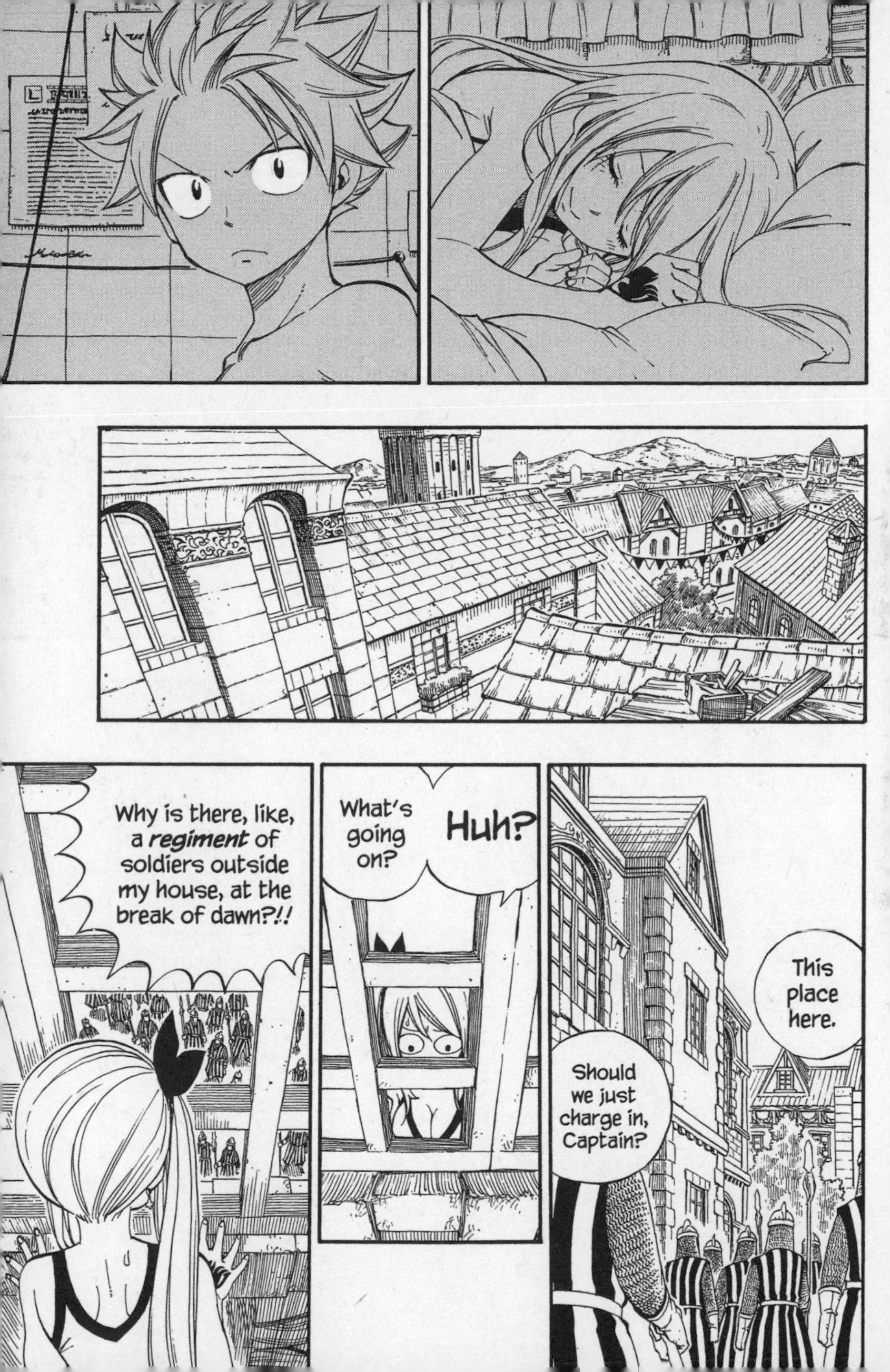

This place here.
Should we just charge in, Captain?
Huh?
What's going on?
Why is there, like, a *regiment* of soldiers outside my house, at the break of dawn?!!

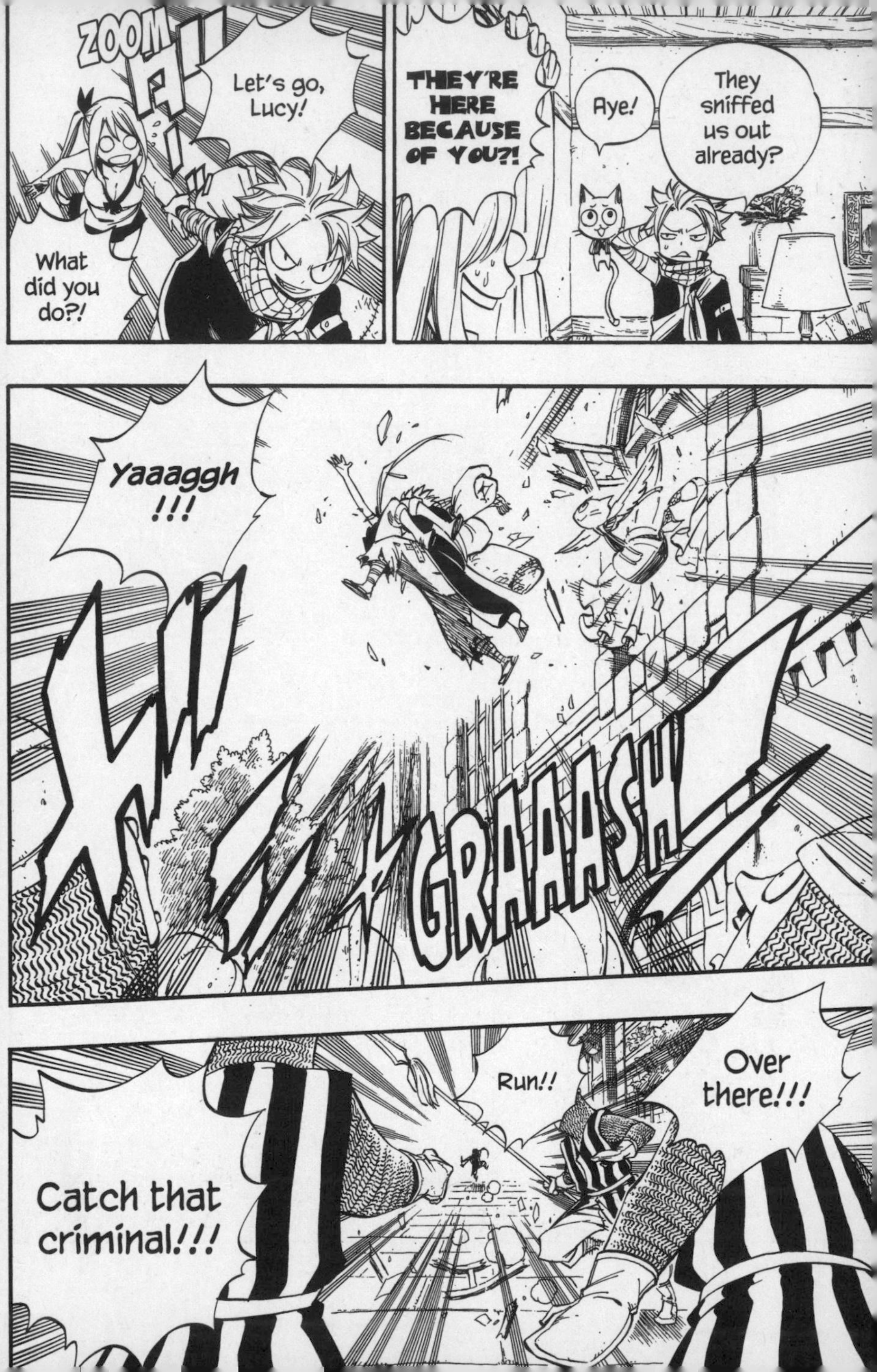
They sniffed us out already?
Aye!
THEY'RE HERE BECAUSE OF YOU?!
Let's go, Lucy!
ZOOM
What did you do?!
Yaaaggh!!!
GRAAASH
Over there!!!
Run!!
Catch that criminal!!!

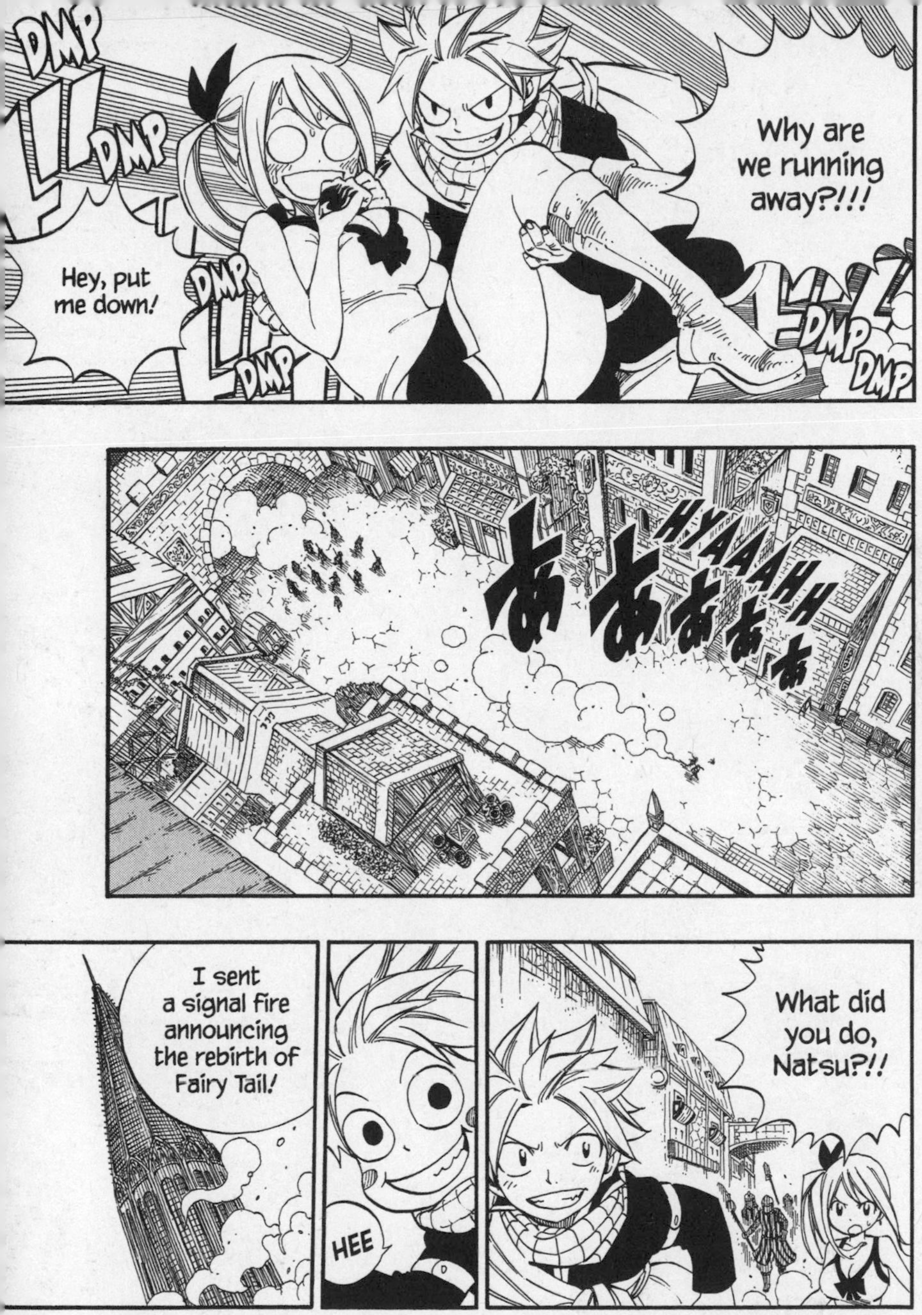

DMP
DMP
Why are we running away?!!!
Hey, put me down!
DMP
DMP
DMP
DMP
DMP
HYAAAHH
あああああ
What did you do, Natsu?!!
HEE
I sent a signal fire announcing the rebirth of Fairy Tail!

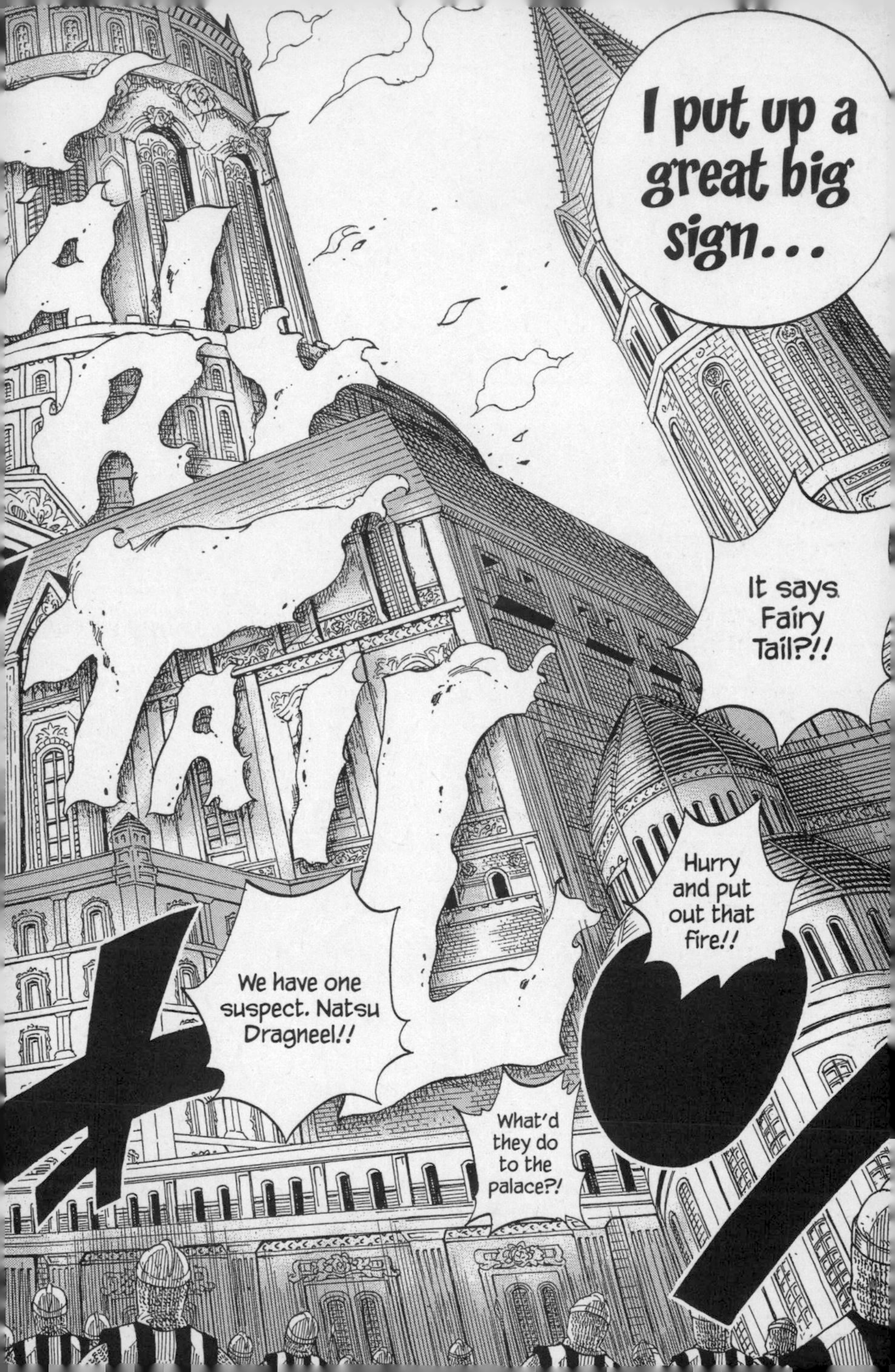
I put up a great big sign...
It says Fairy Tail?!!
Hurry and put out that fire!!
What'd they do to the palace?!
We have one suspect. Natsu Dragneel!!

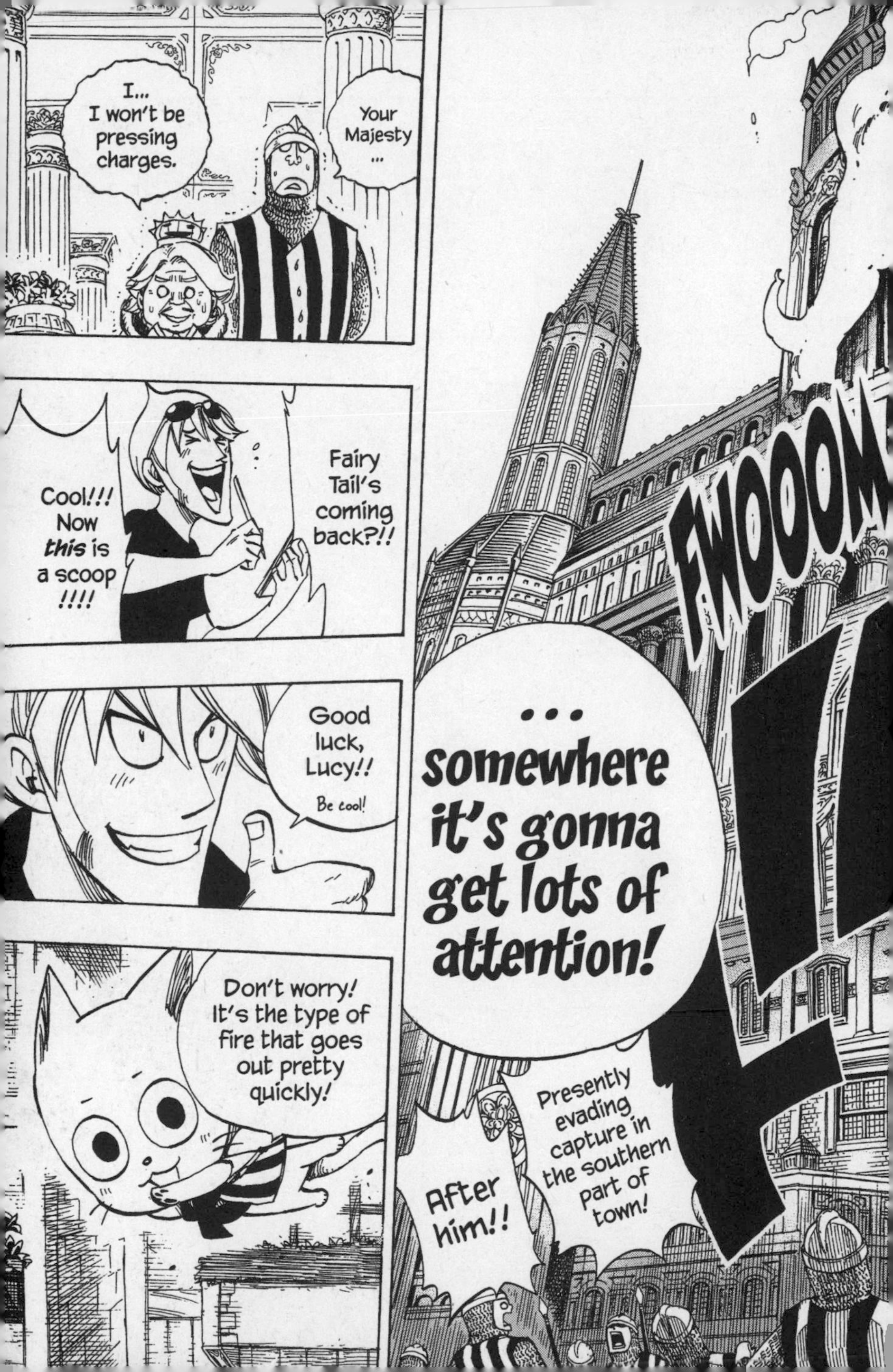

FWOOM
... somewhere it's gonna get lots of attention!
Presently evading capture in the southern part of town!
After him!!
Your Majesty ...
I... I won't be pressing charges.
Fairy Tail's coming back?!!
Cool!!! Now this is a scoop !!!!
Good luck, Lucy!!
Be cool!
Don't worry! It's the type of fire that goes out pretty quickly!

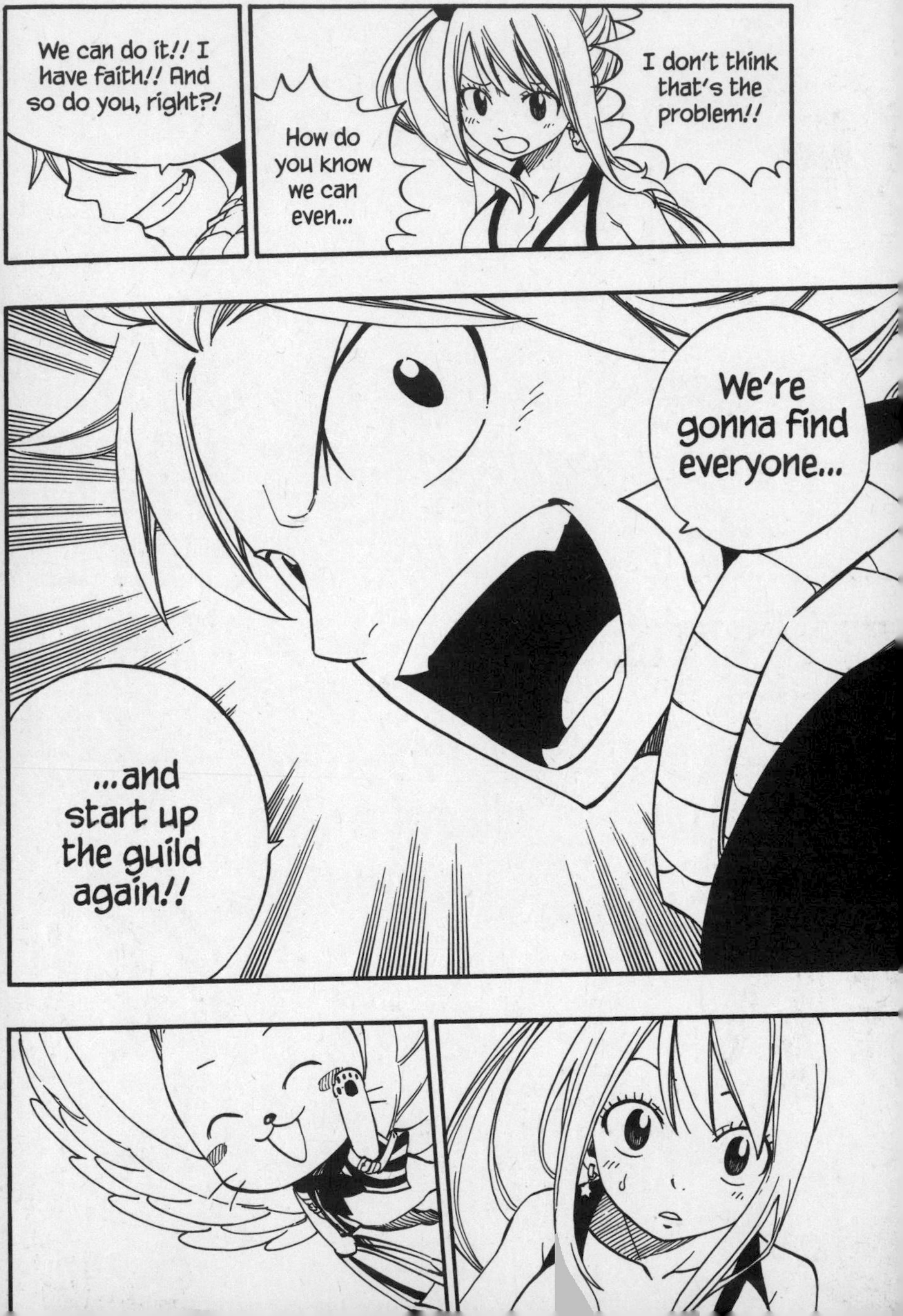
I don't think that's the problem!!
How do you know we can even...
We can do it!! I have faith!! And so do you, right?!
We're gonna find everyone...
...and start up the guild again!!

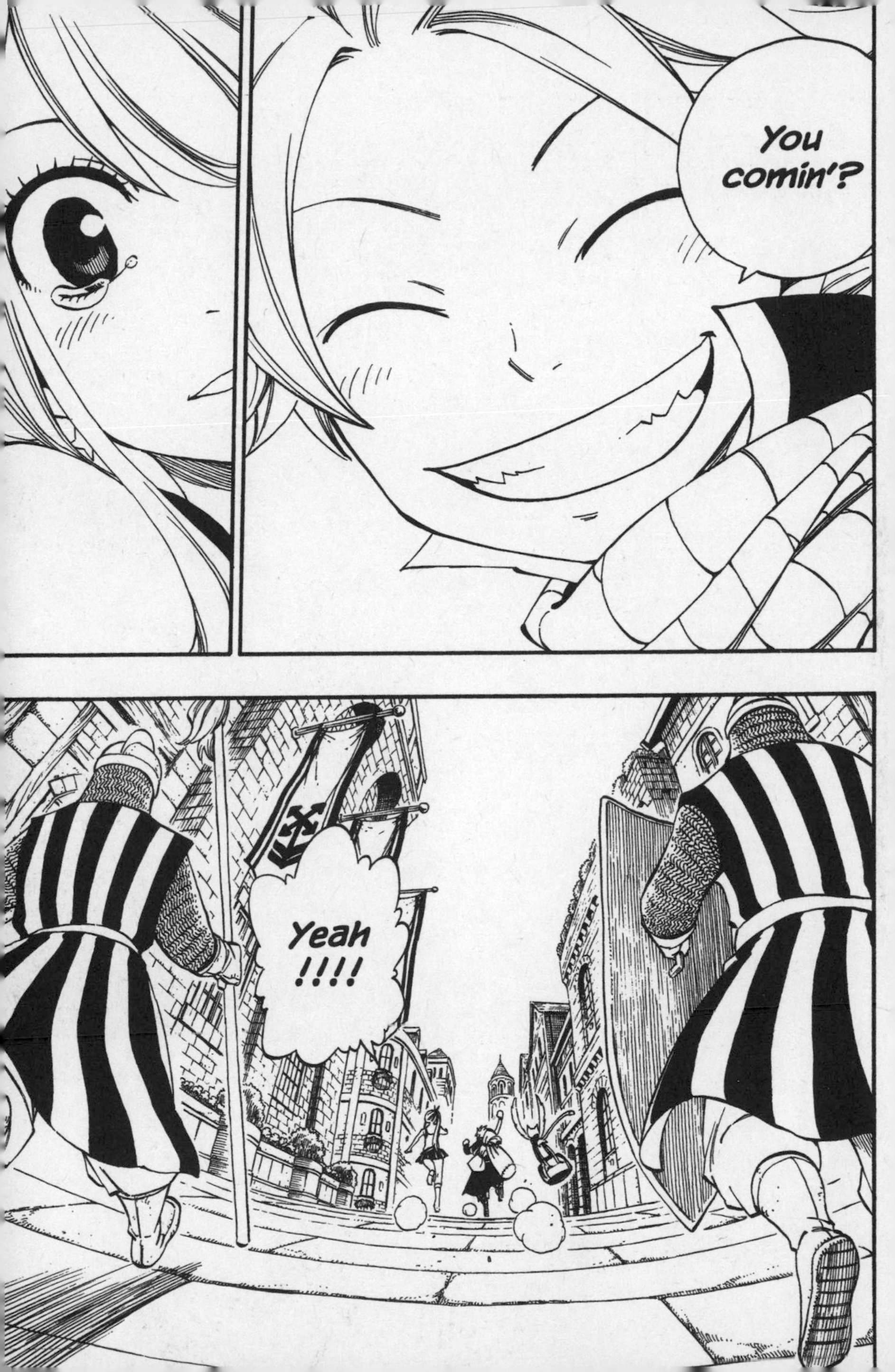
You comin'?
Yeah !!!!

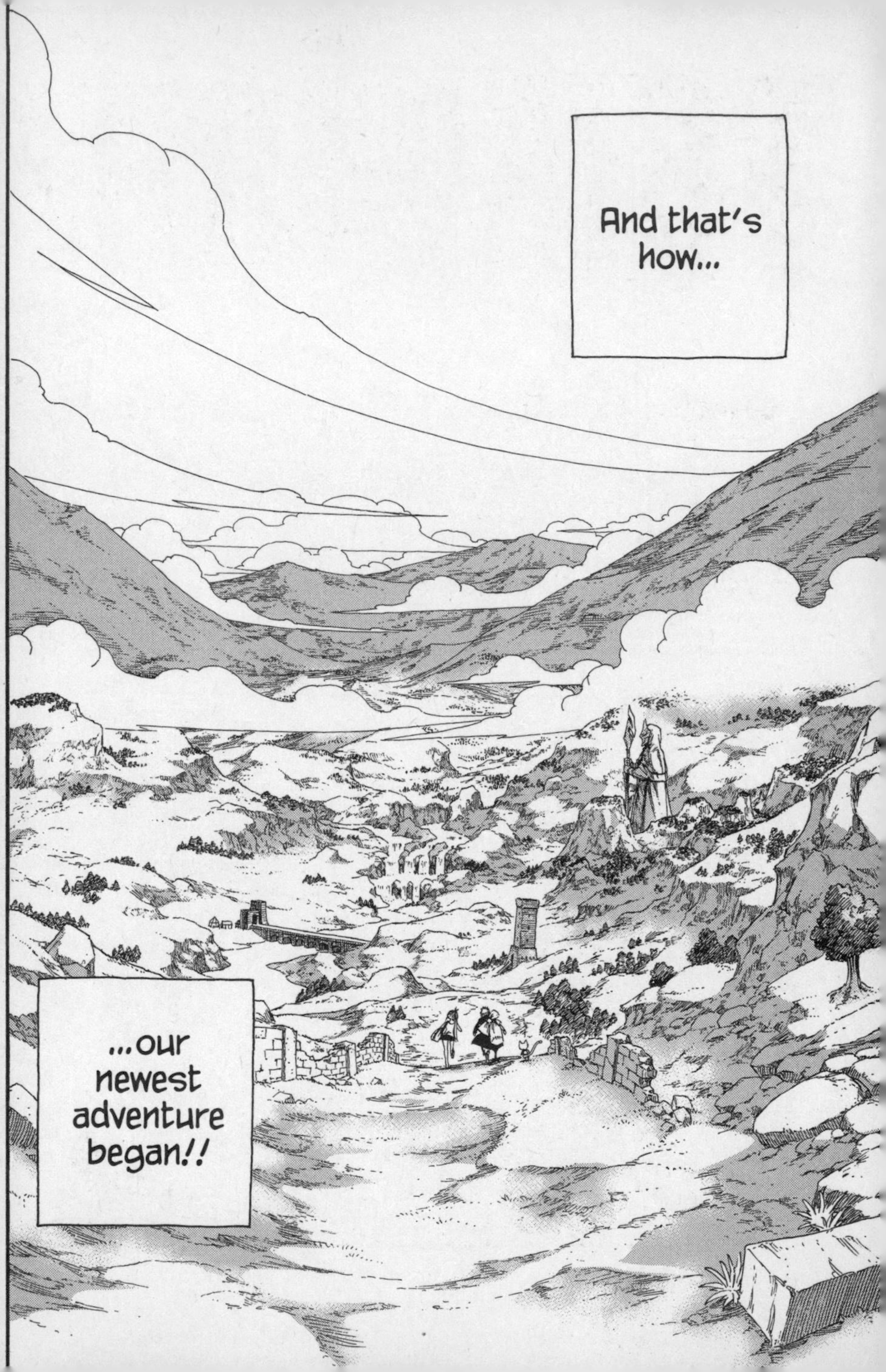
And that's how...
...our newest adventure began!!

Chapter 420: Lamia Scale's Thanksgiving Day

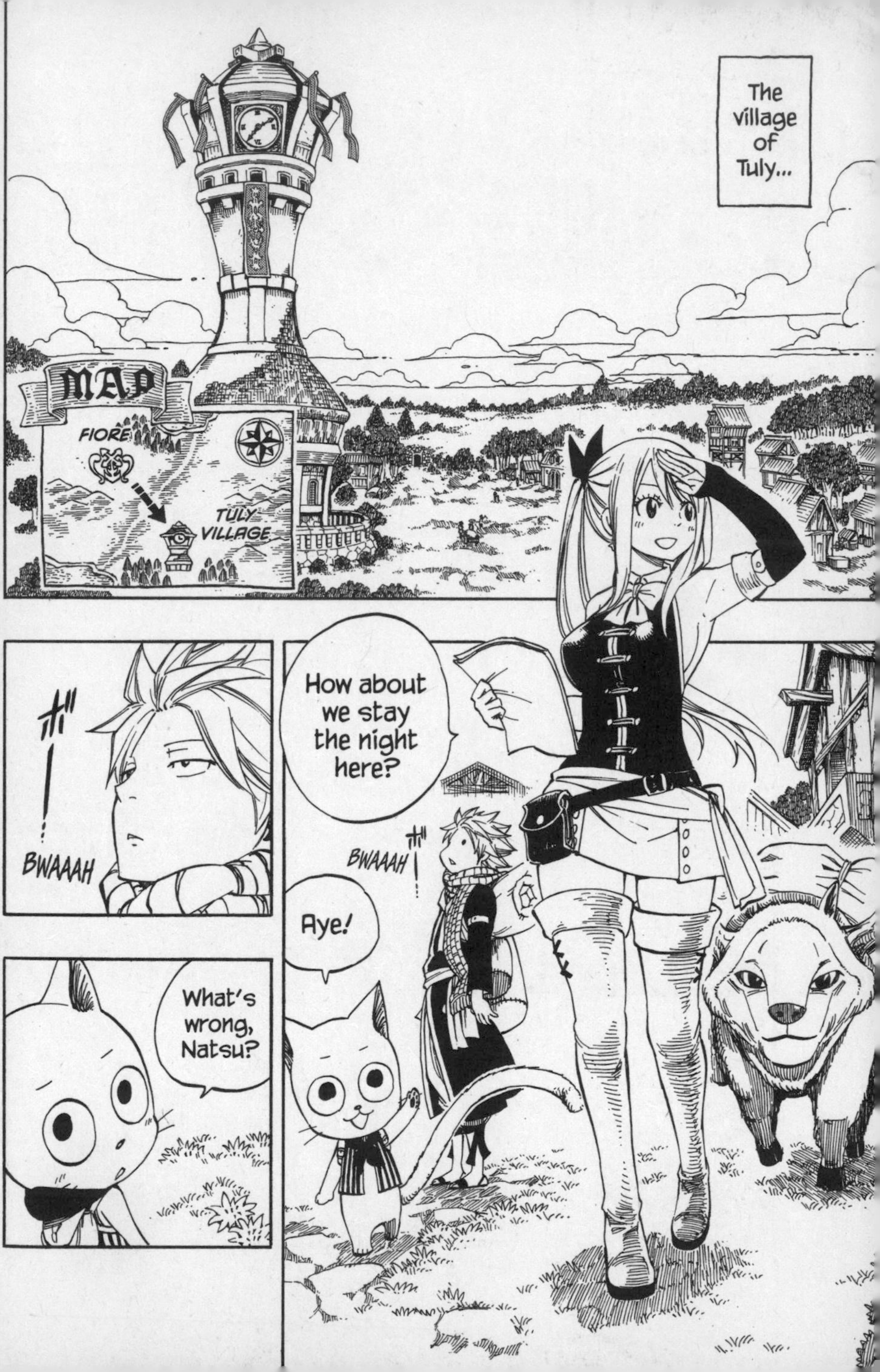
The village of Tuly...
MAP
FIORE
TULY VILLAGE
How about we stay the night here?
BWAAAH
Aye!
BWAAAH
What's wrong, Natsu?

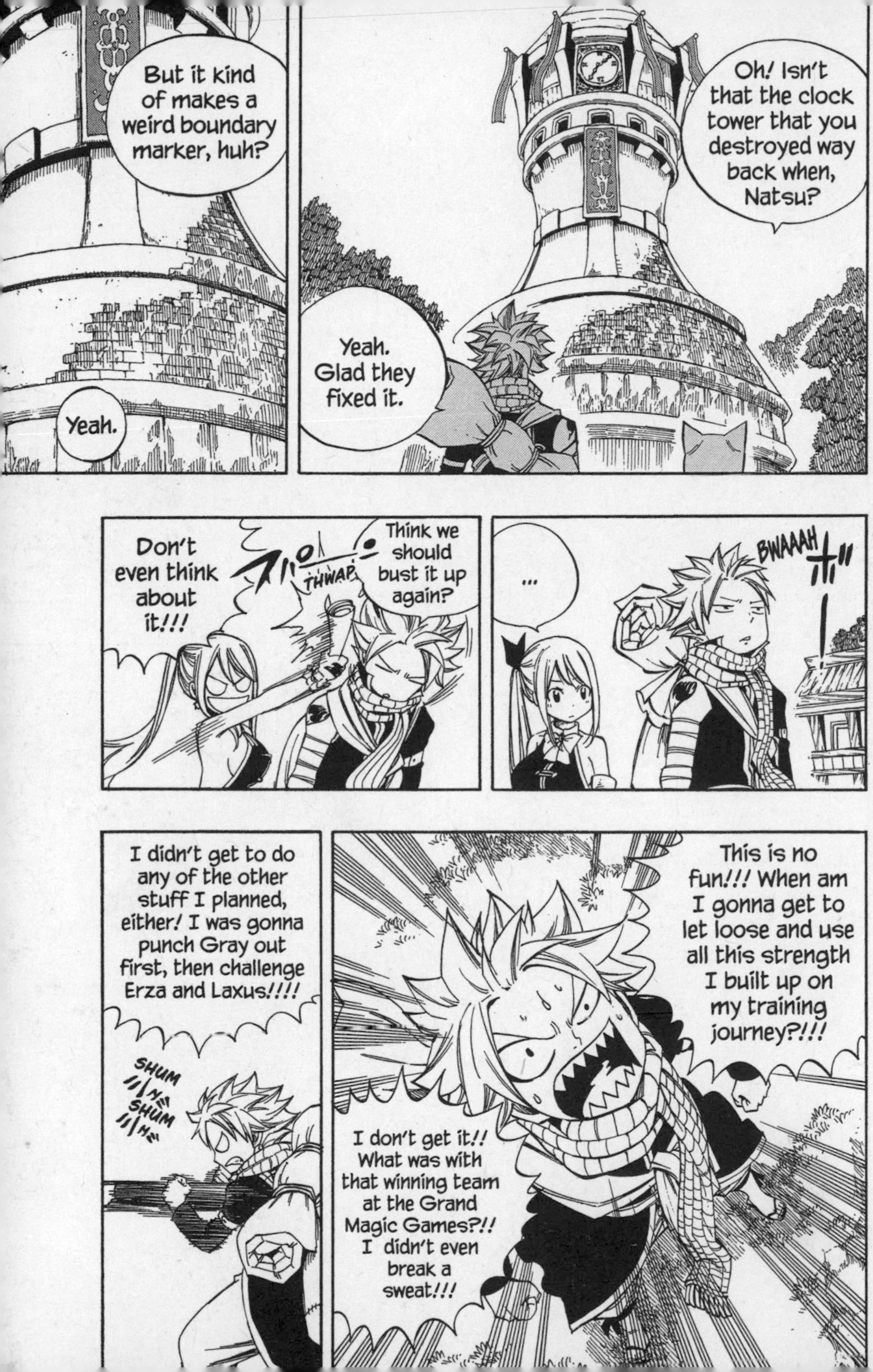
Oh! Isn't that the clock tower that you destroyed way back when, Natsu?
Yeah. Glad they fixed it.
But it kind of makes a weird boundary marker, huh?
Yeah.
BWAAAH
...
Think we should bust it up again?
THWAP
Don't even think about it!!!
This is no fun!!! When am I gonna get to let loose and use all this strength I built up on my training journey?!!!
I don't get it!! What was with that winning team at the Grand Magic Games?!! I didn't even break a sweat!!!
I didn't get to do any of the other stuff I planned, either! I was gonna punch Gray out first, then challenge Erza and Laxus!!!!
SHUM
SHUM

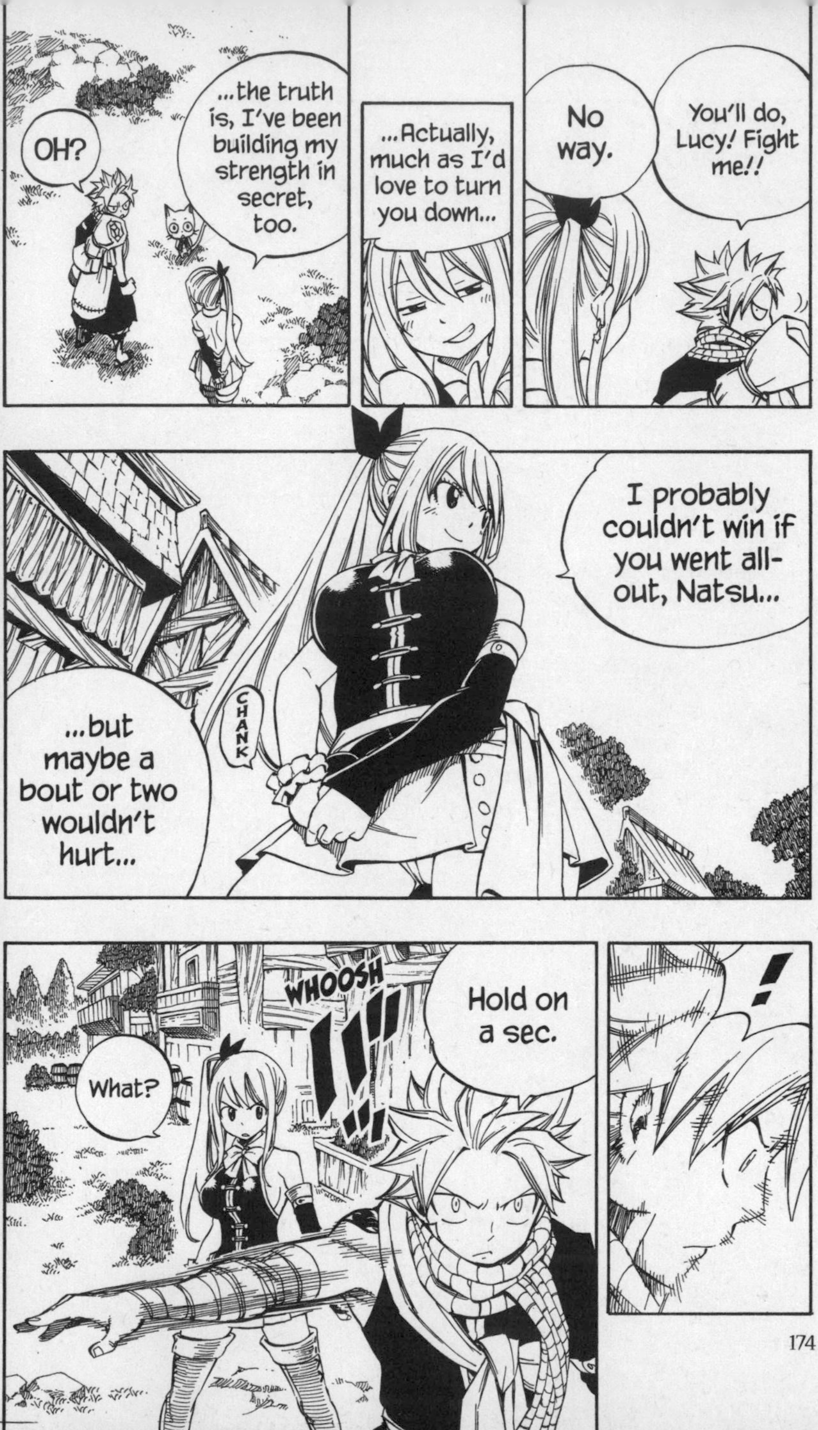
You'll do, Lucy! Fight me!!
No way.
...Actually, much as I'd love to turn you down...
...the truth is, I've been building my strength in secret, too.
OH?
I probably couldn't win if you went all-out, Natsu...
CHANK
...but maybe a bout or two wouldn't hurt...
!
Hold on a sec.
WHOOSH
What?

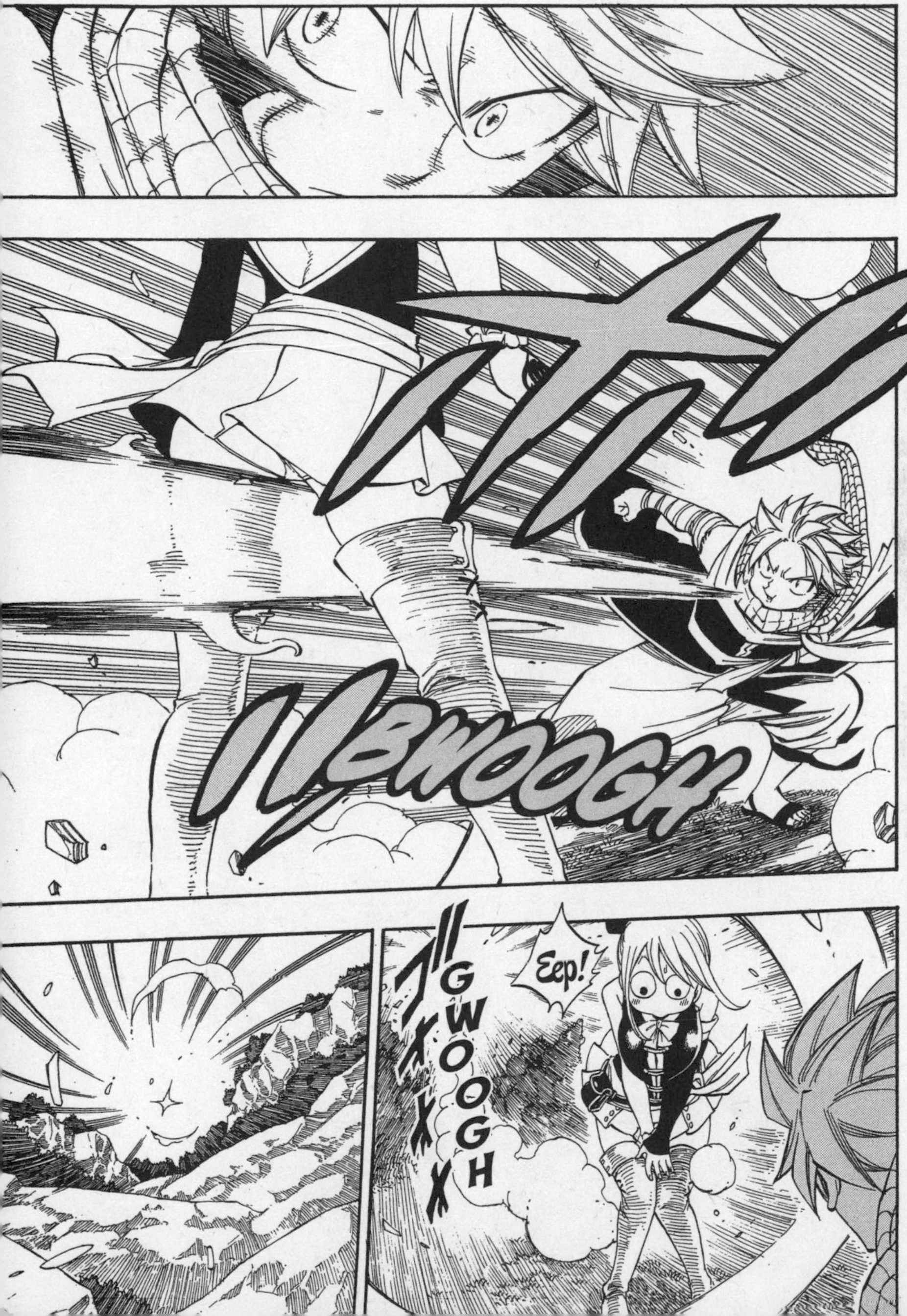
BWOOGH
Eep!
GWOOGH

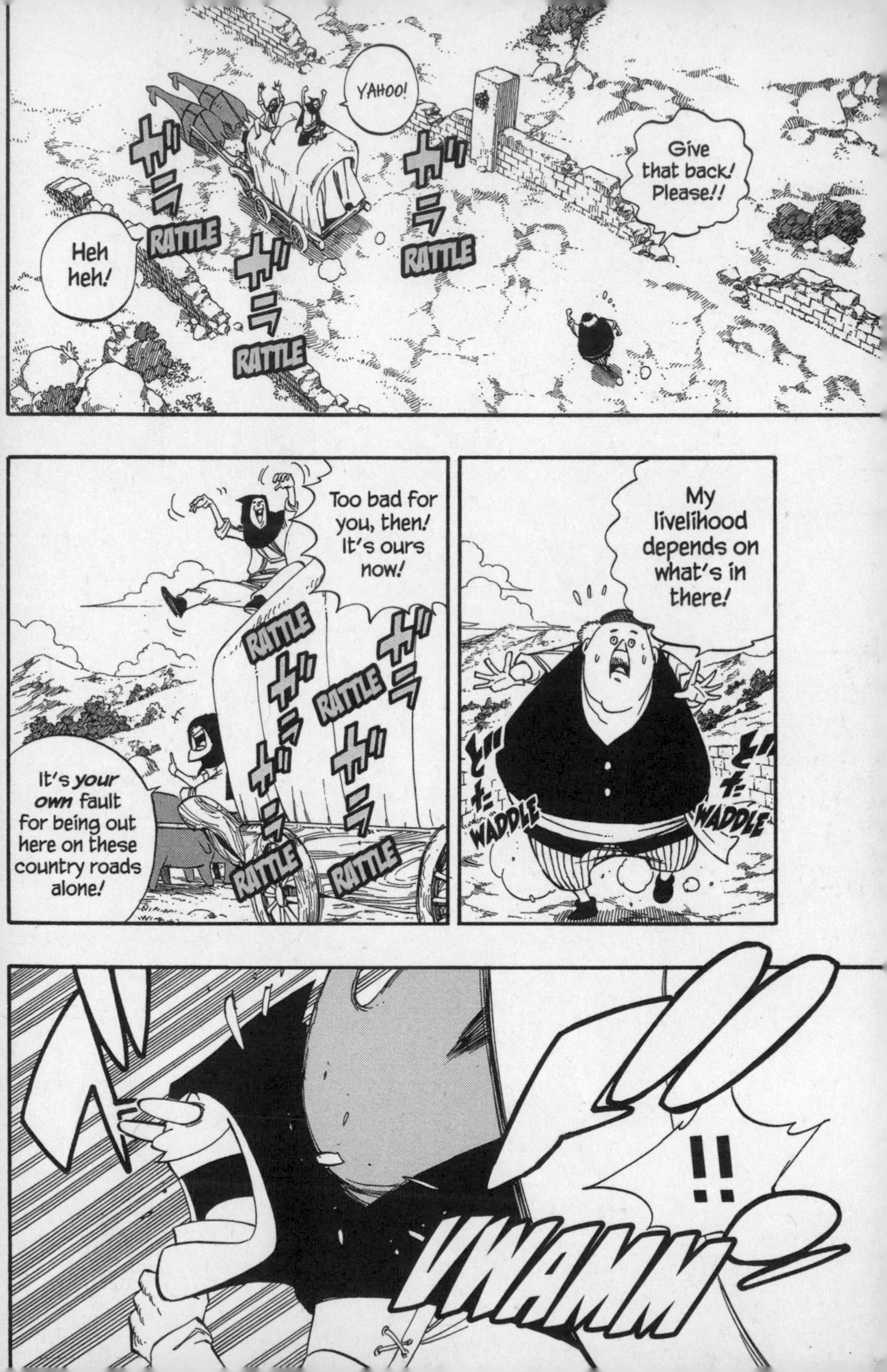

Give that back! Please!!
YAHOO!
RATTLE
RATTLE
RATTLE
Heh heh!
My livelihood depends on what's in there!
WADDLE
WADDLE
Too bad for you, then! It's ours now!
RATTLE
RATTLE
RATTLE
RATTLE
It's *your own* fault for being out here on these country roads alone!
!!
WHAMM

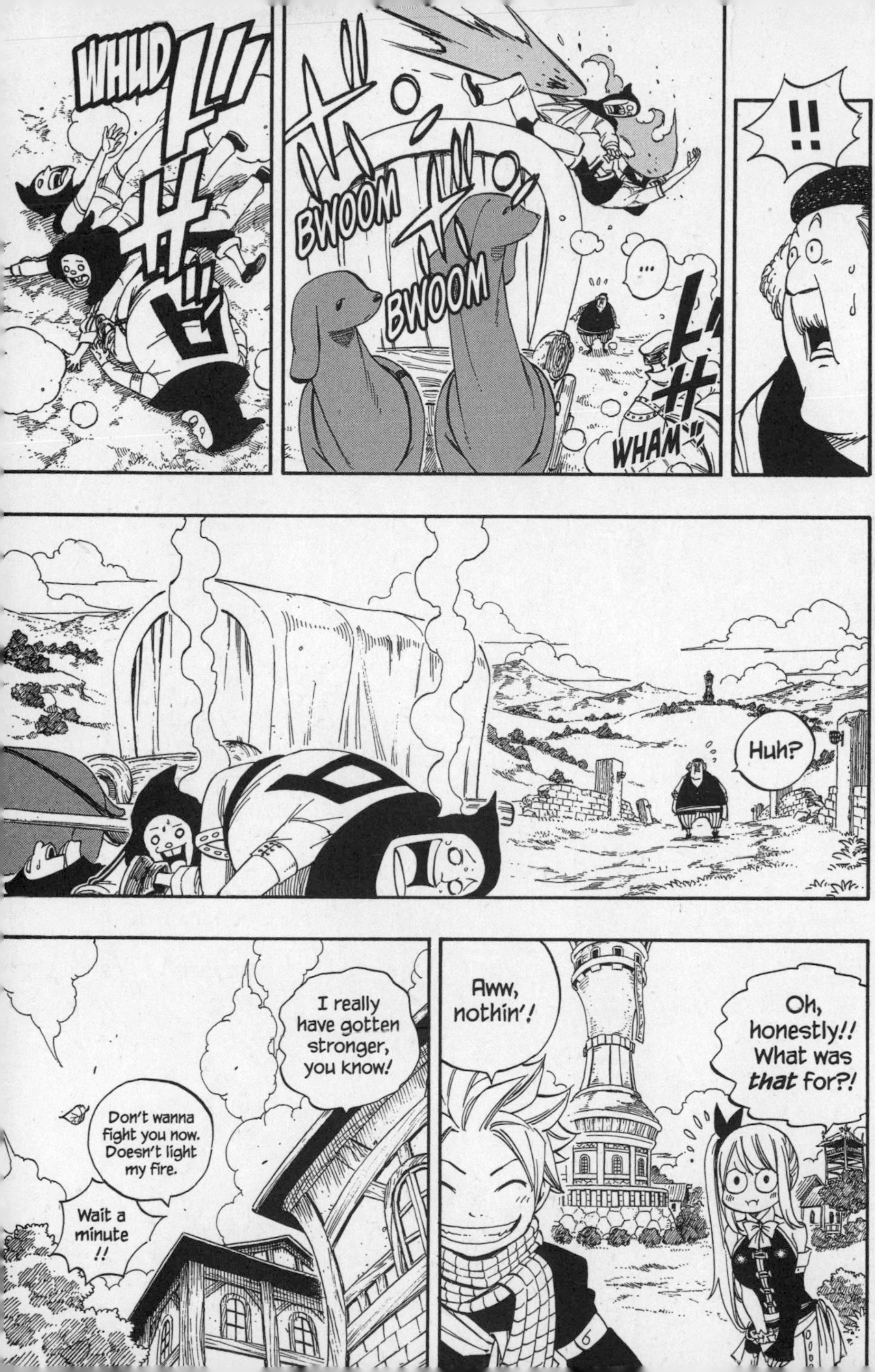
!!
...
WHAM!!
BWOOM
BWOOM
WHUD!!
Huh?
Oh, honestly!! What was *that* for?!
Aww, nothin'!
I really have gotten stronger, you know!
Don't wanna fight you now. Doesn't light my fire.
Wait a minute !!

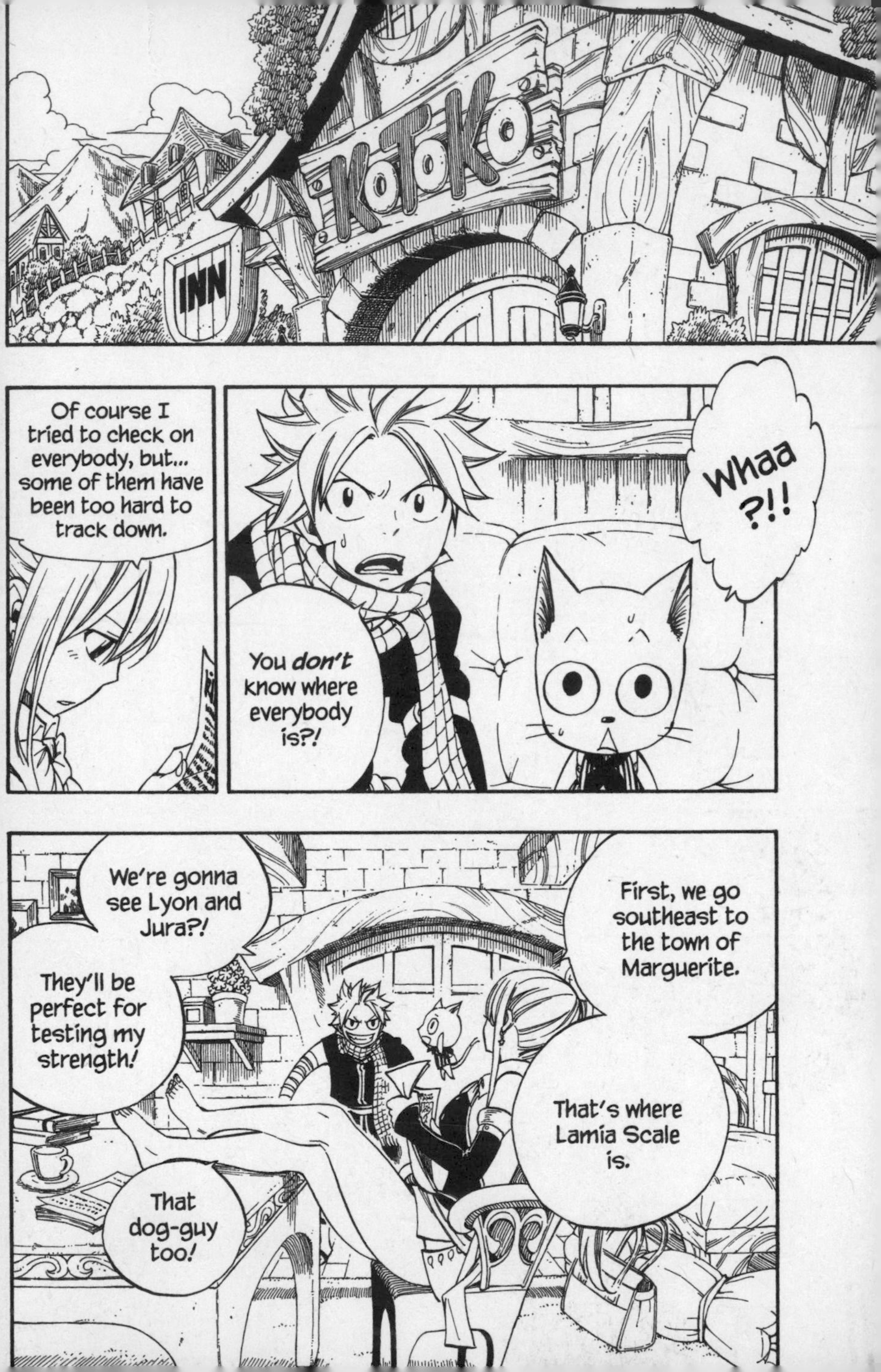
KOTOKO
INN
Whaa ?!!
You *don't* know where everybody is?!
Of course I tried to check on everybody, but... some of them have been too hard to track down.
First, we go southeast to the town of Marguerite.
That's where Lamia Scale is.
We're gonna see Lyon and Jura?!
They'll be perfect for testing my strength!
That dog-guy too!

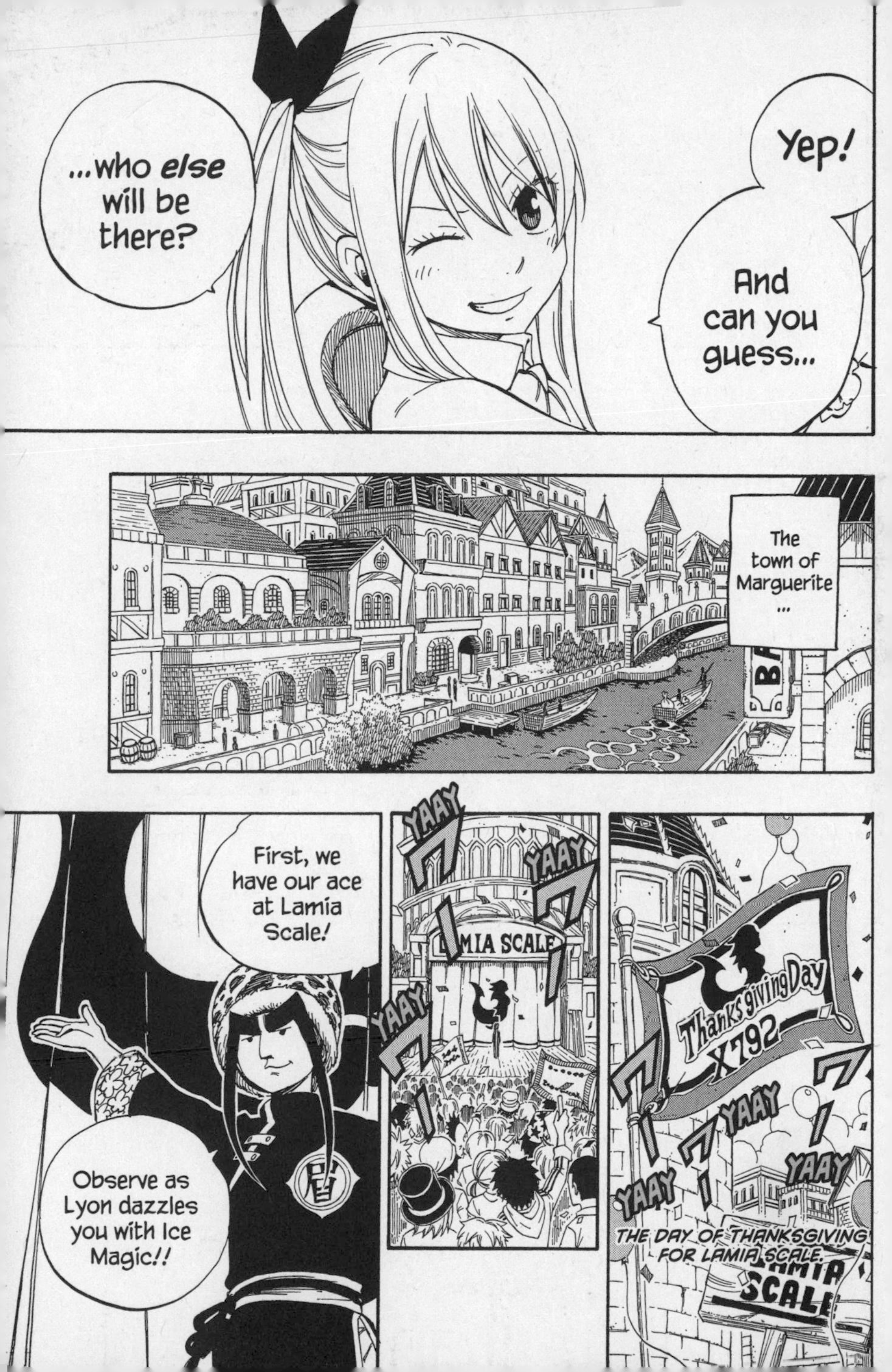
Yep!
And can you guess...
...who *else* will be there?
The town of Marguerite ...
YAAY
YAAY
ThanksgivingDay X792
YAAY
YAAY
THE DAY OF THANKSGIVING FOR LAMIA SCALE.
YAAY
YAAY
YAAY
First, we have our ace at Lamia Scale!
Observe as Lyon dazzles you with Ice Magic!!

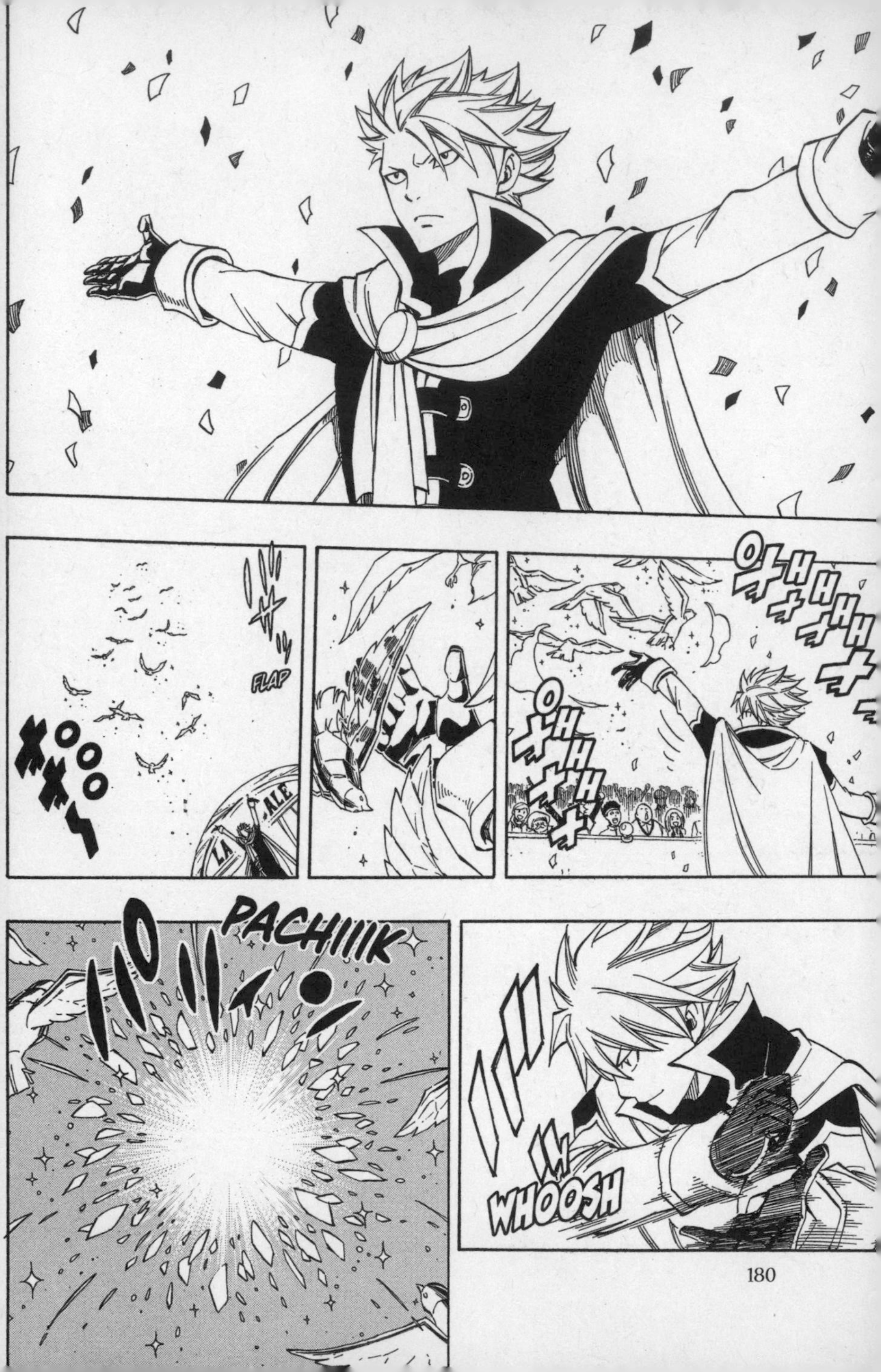
OHHHH
OHHH
FLAP
WHOOSH
PACHIIIK

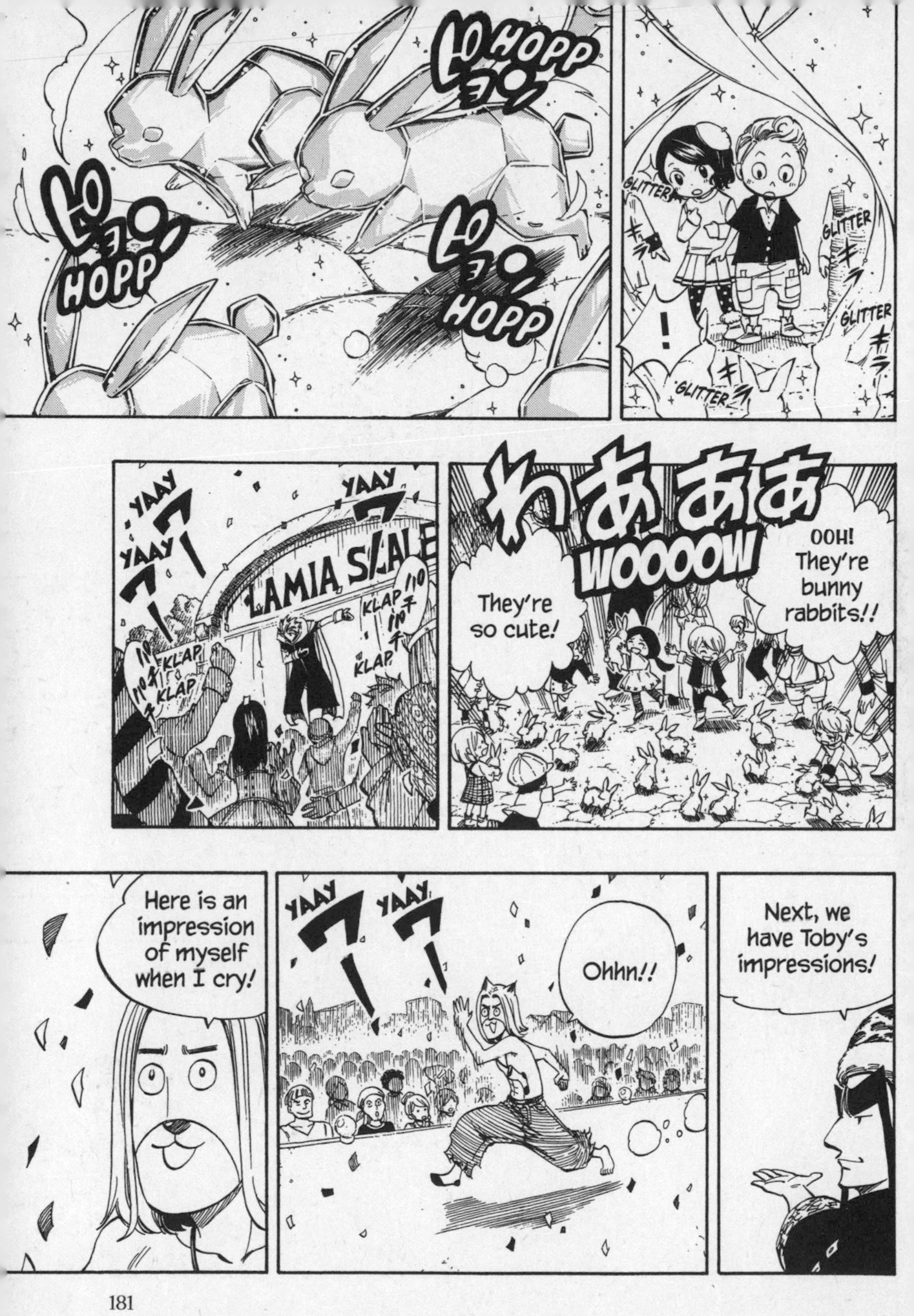

GLITTER
GLITTER
GLITTER
GLITTER
!
HOPP
HOPP
HOPP
わあああ
WOOOOW
OOH! They're bunny rabbits!!
They're so cute!
YAAY
YAAY
YAAY
LAMIA SCALE
KLAP
KLAP
KLAP
KLAP
Next, we have Toby's impressions!
YAAY
YAAY
Ohhn!!
Here is an impression of myself when I cry!

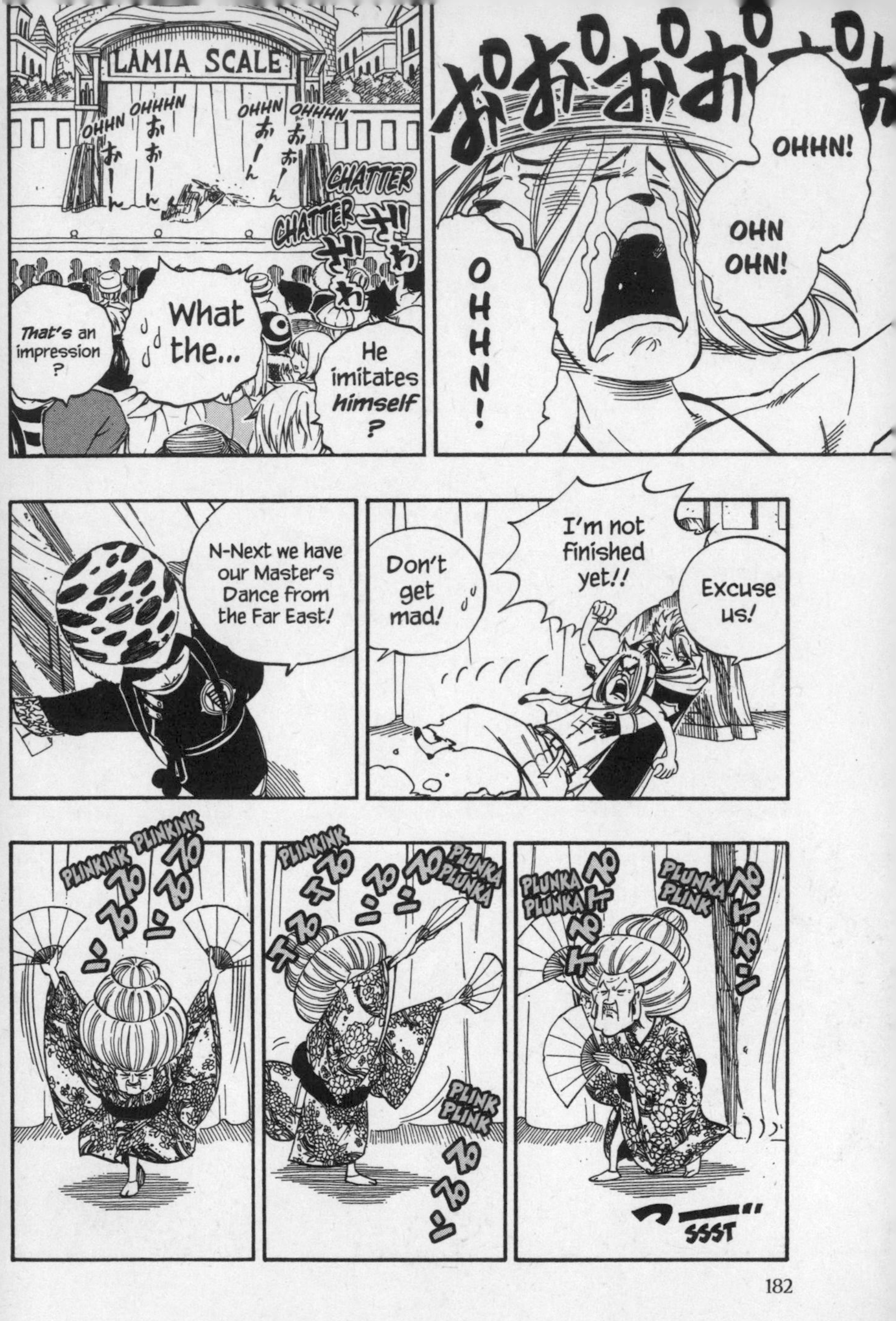
OHHN!
OHN OHN!
OHHN!
LAMIA SCALE
OHHN
OHHHN
OHHN
OHHHN
CHATTER
CHATTER
He imitates himself?
What the...
That's an impression?
Excuse us!
I'm not finished yet!!
Don't get mad!
N-Next we have our Master's Dance from the Far East!
PLUNKA PLINK
PLUNKA PLUNKA
SSST
PLINKINK
PLUNKA PLUNKA
PLINK PLINK
PLINKINK PLINKINK

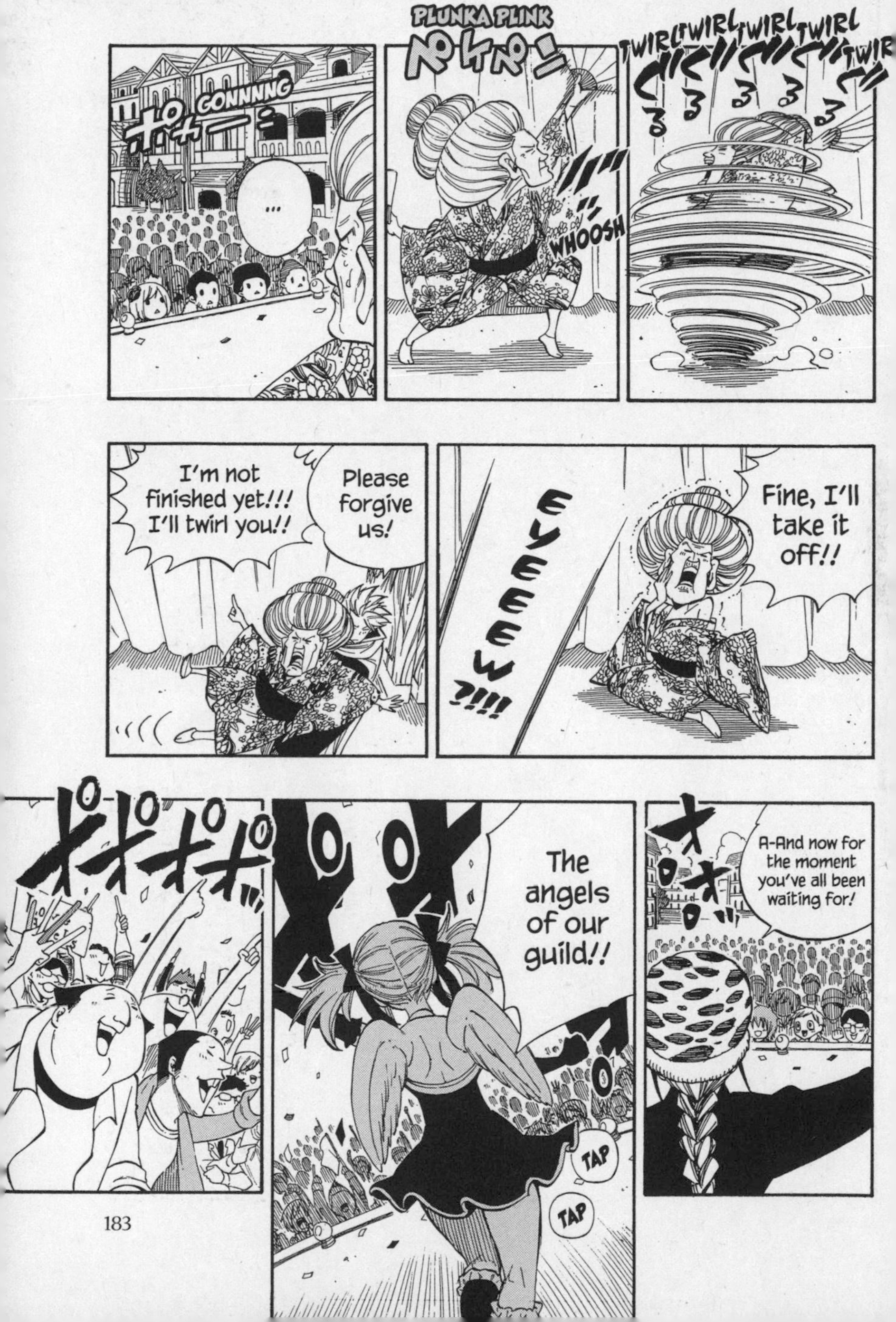
TWIRL TWIRL TWIRL TWIRL TWIR
PLUNKA PLINK
WHOOSH
GONNNNG
...
Fine, I'll take it off!!
EYEEEEW?!!!
Please forgive us!
I'm not finished yet!!! I'll twirl you!!
A-And now for the moment you've all been waiting for!
The angels of our guild!!
TAP
TAP

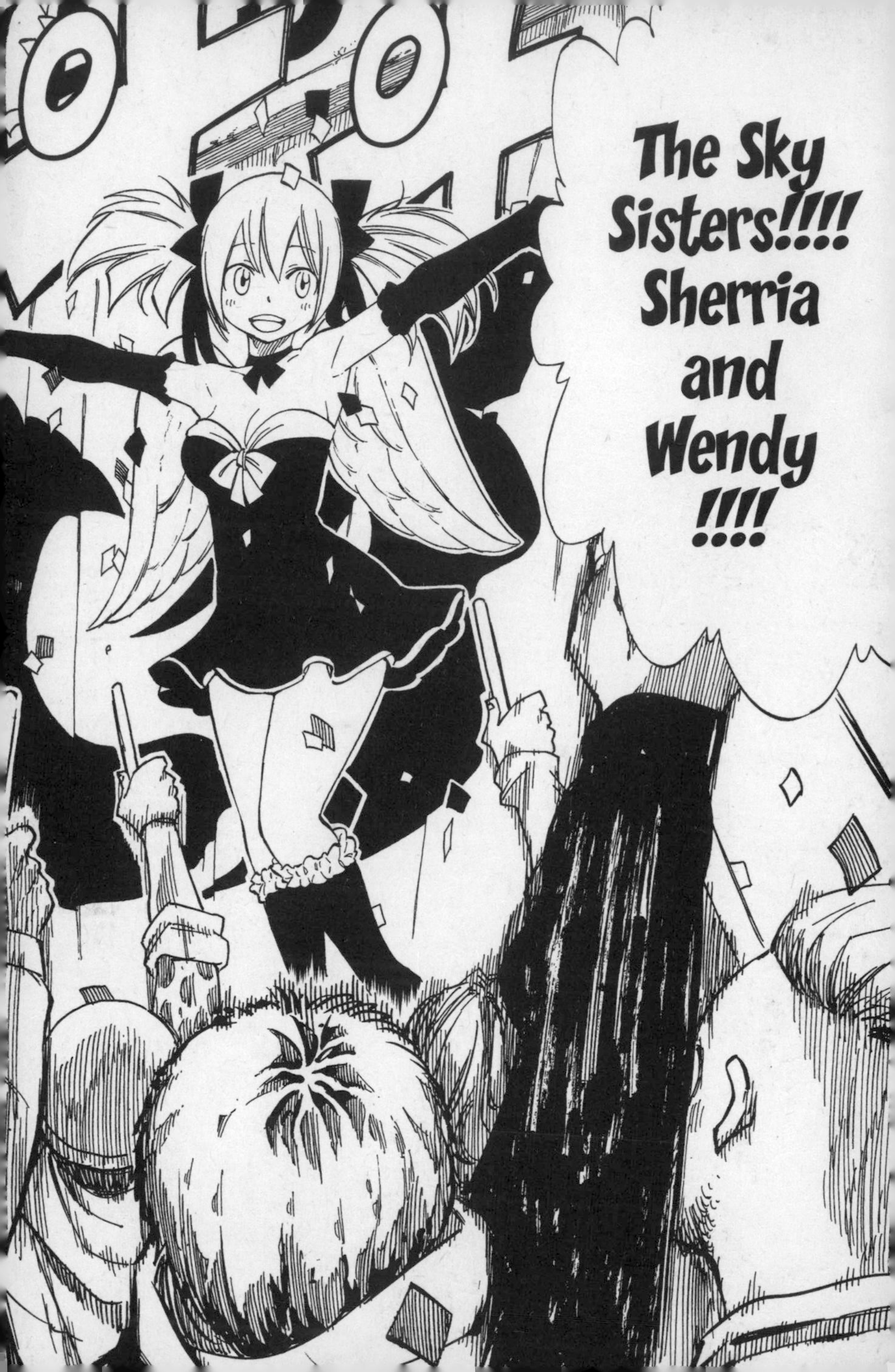
The Sky Sisters!!!! Sherria and Wendy !!!!

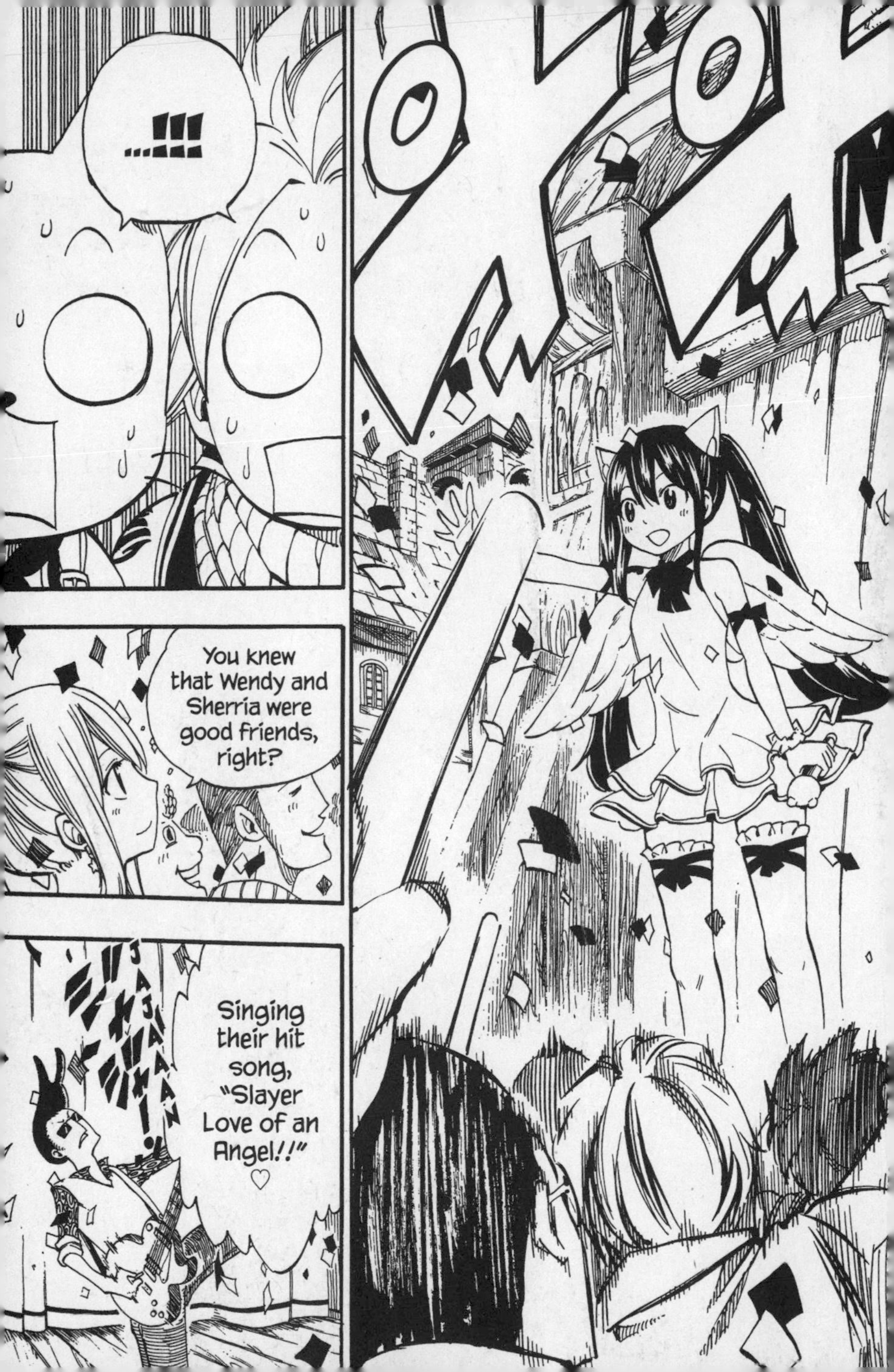

…!!!
You knew that Wendy and Sherria were good friends, right?
Singing their hit song, "Slayer Love of an Angel!!" ♡

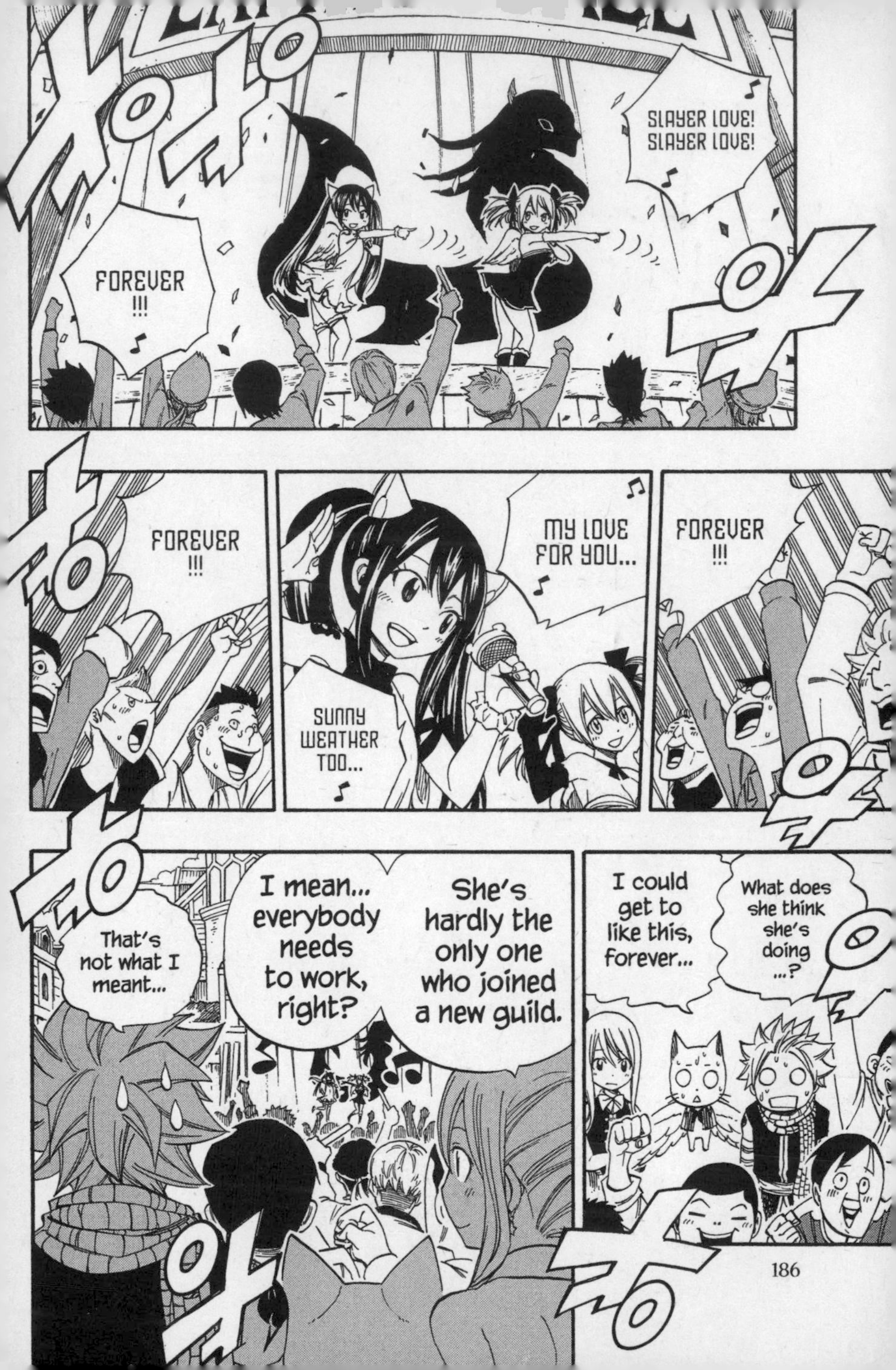
SLAYER LOVE! SLAYER LOVE!
FOREVER !!!
FOREVER !!!
MY LOVE FOR YOU...
SUNNY WEATHER TOO...
FOREVER !!!
What does she think she's doing ...?
I could get to like this, forever...
She's hardly the only one who joined a new guild.
I mean... everybody needs to work, right?
That's not what I meant...

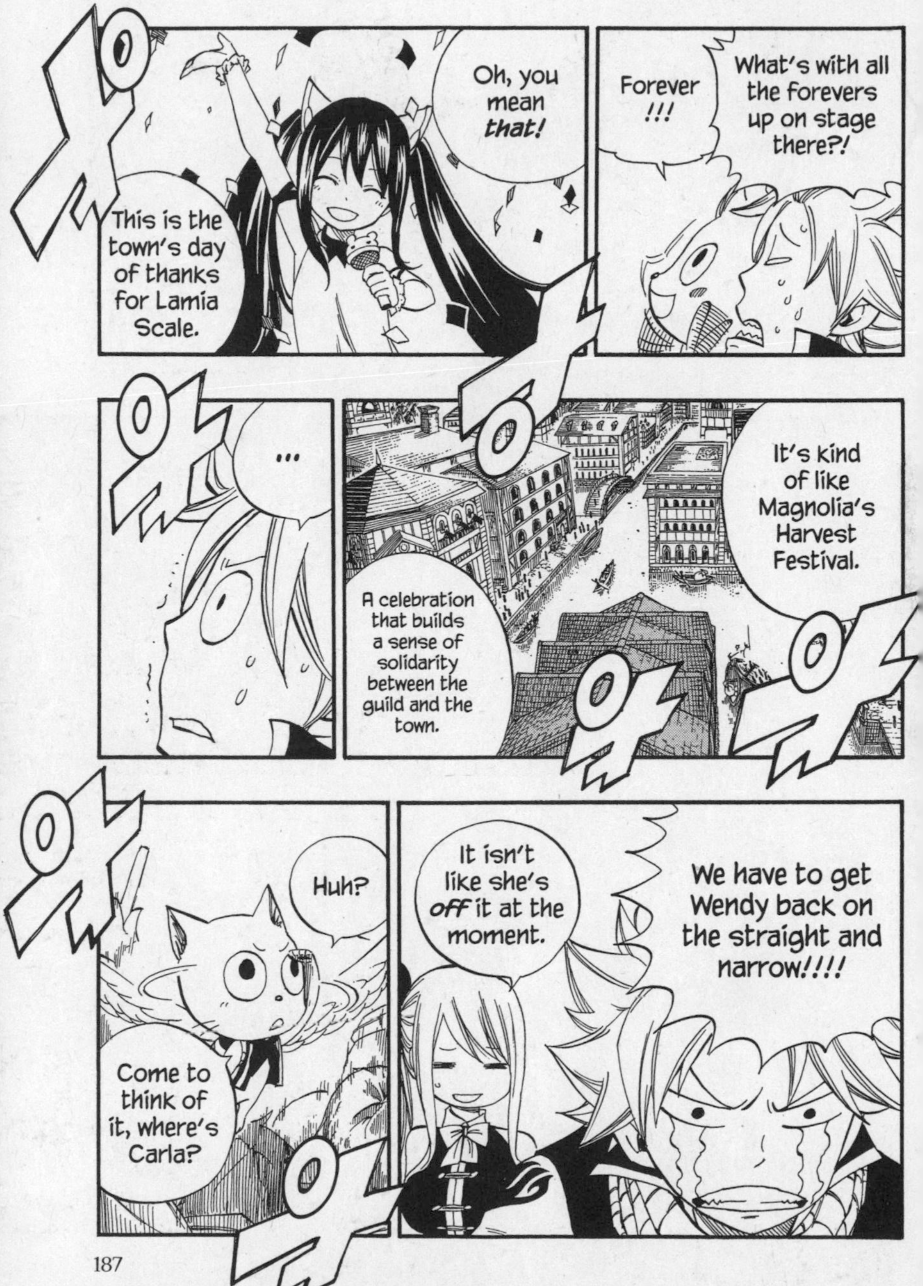
What's with all the forevers up on stage there?!
Forever!!!
Oh, you mean *that!*
This is the town's day of thanks for Lamia Scale.
It's kind of like Magnolia's Harvest Festival.
A celebration that builds a sense of solidarity between the guild and the town.
...
We have to get Wendy back on the straight and narrow!!!!
It isn't like she's *off* it at the moment.
Huh?
Come to think of it, where's Carla?

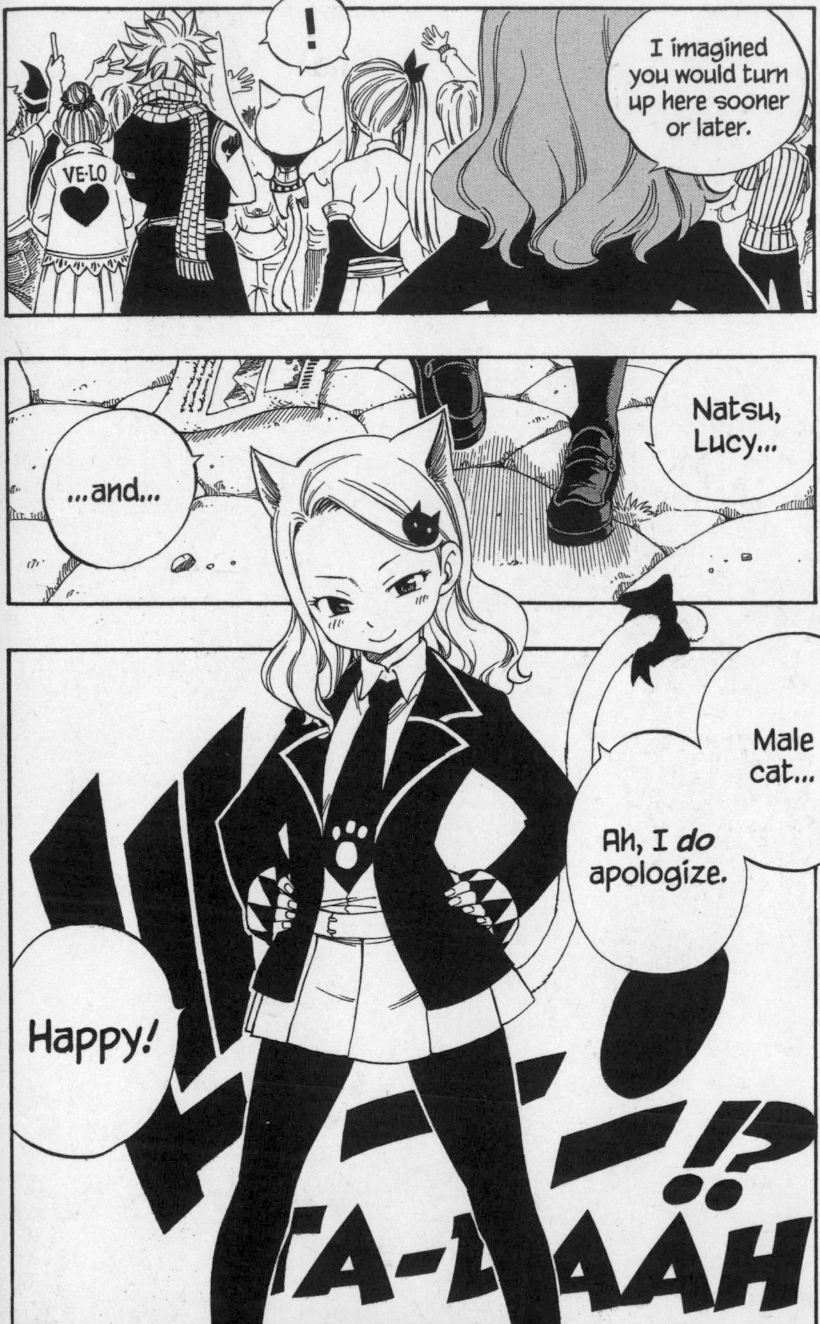
I imagined you would turn up here sooner or later.
!
Natsu, Lucy...
...and...
Male cat...
Ah, I *do* apologize.
Happy!

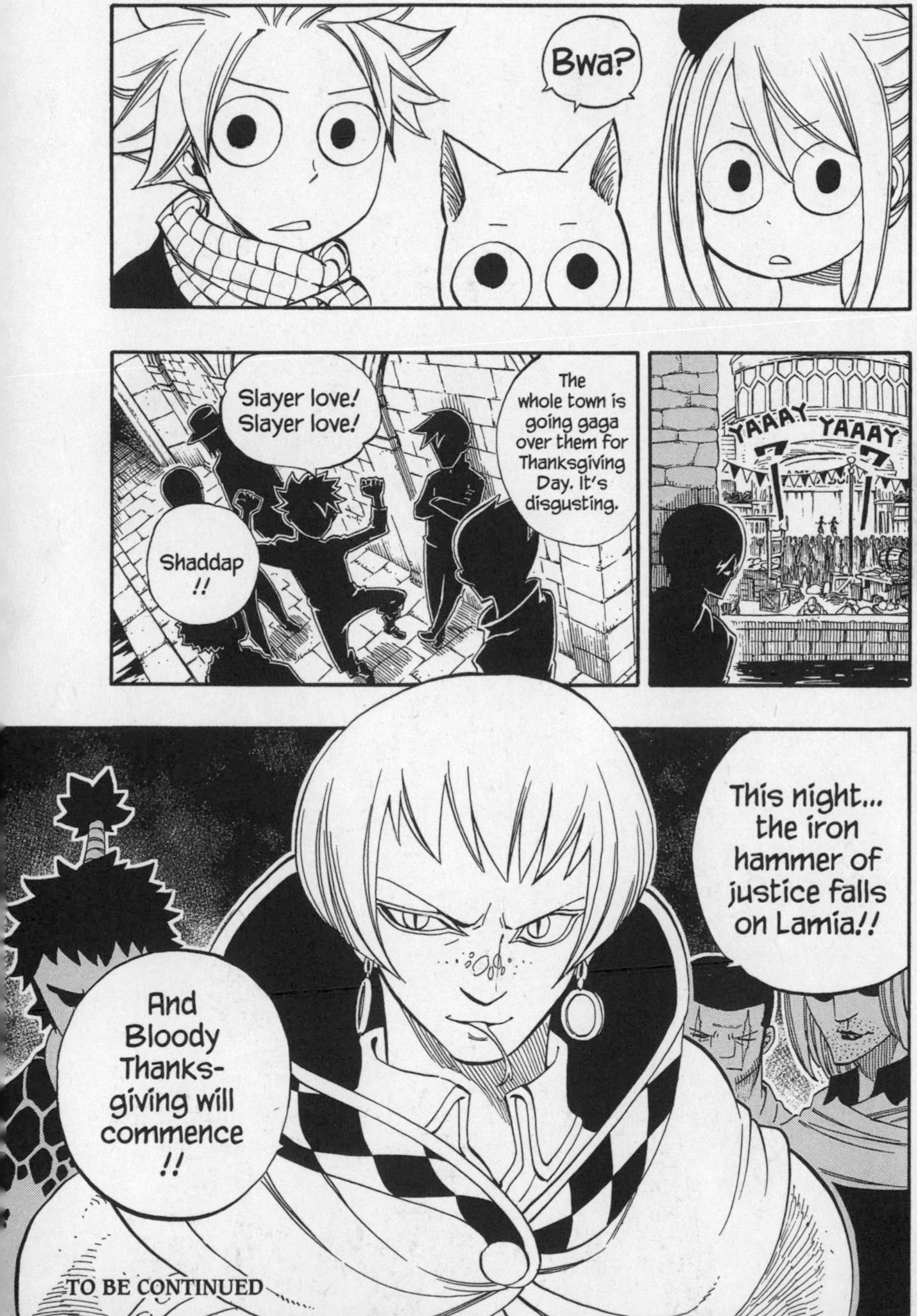
Bwa?
YAAAY YAAAY
The whole town is going gaga over them for Thanksgiving Day. It's disgusting.
Slayer love! Slayer love!
Shaddap!!
This night... the iron hammer of justice falls on Lamia!!
And Bloody Thanksgiving will commence!!
TO BE CONTINUED

Afterword

We've safely closed the curtain on the Tartaros Arc and started a brand new one. It's a little late to be saying this, but the Tartaros Arc was planned to be even longer. Well, a lot of things happened, and it was cut short, with three whole enemy characters cut along with it (cries), including a great part for Laxus. It's too bad. In exchange, we decided to make Laxus play a slightly bigger part in the anime. And I'm sure he'll get some great part to play in the new arc, too.

And so... The new arc. Who'd ever think that Fairy Tail would shut down for a whole year? People have changed, and some haven't changed. Actually, thinking while I write this about how people changed is a whole lot of fun!

There were a whole lot of sad parts and dark parts to the Tartaros Arc, so for this new arc, I've been thinking of making "hope" my theme.

So what happens next? Well, I'm actually drawing it from nothing more than a rough outline, so some of this is me feeling my way through it, but you can bet there are going to be some hot plot twists! And if not, I'll make them hot!! Stay tuned!

And so... And so... I've heard from all kinds of people on this thing with Doranbalt where he was always a member of Fairy Tail, and many of the comments were along the lines of, "There should be legal limits to the amount of retconning you can do!!" But to tell you the truth, this has been a planned part of the story for a long time now. Well, to tell you the real truth, I never got the chance to foreshadow it, and I wavered back and forth on whether to include it or not. Then suddenly the chance came, and I went for it.

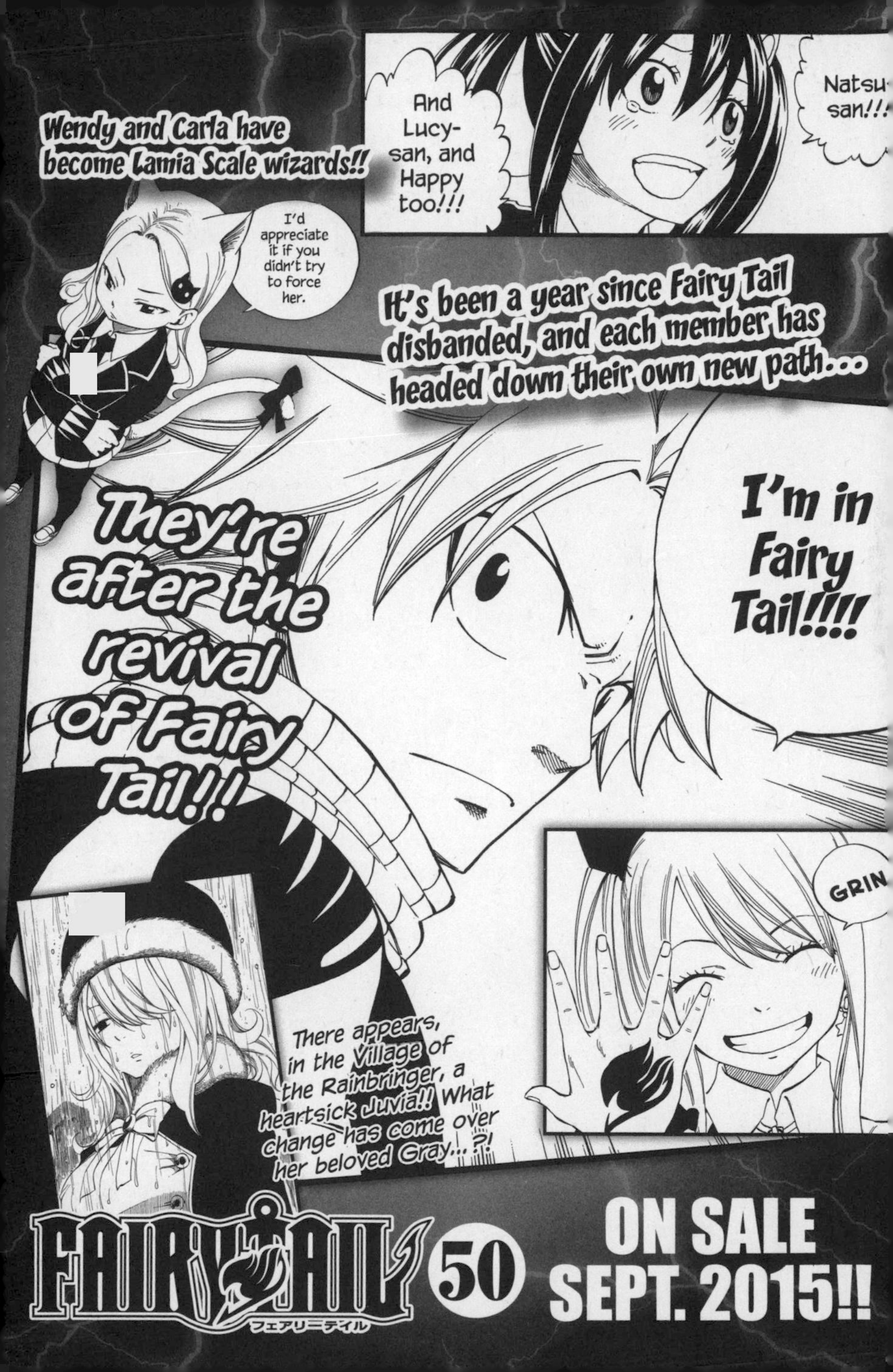
Natsu-san!!!
And Lucy-san, and Happy too!!!
Wendy and Carla have become Lamia Scale wizards!!
I'd appreciate it if you didn't try to force her.
It's been a year since Fairy Tail disbanded, and each member has headed down their own new path...
I'm in Fairy Tail!!!!
They're after the revival of Fairy Tail!!
GRIN
There appears, in the Village of the Rainbringer, a heartsick Juvia!! What change has come over her beloved Gray...?!
FAIRY TAIL
フェアリーテイル
50
ON SALE SEPT. 2015!!

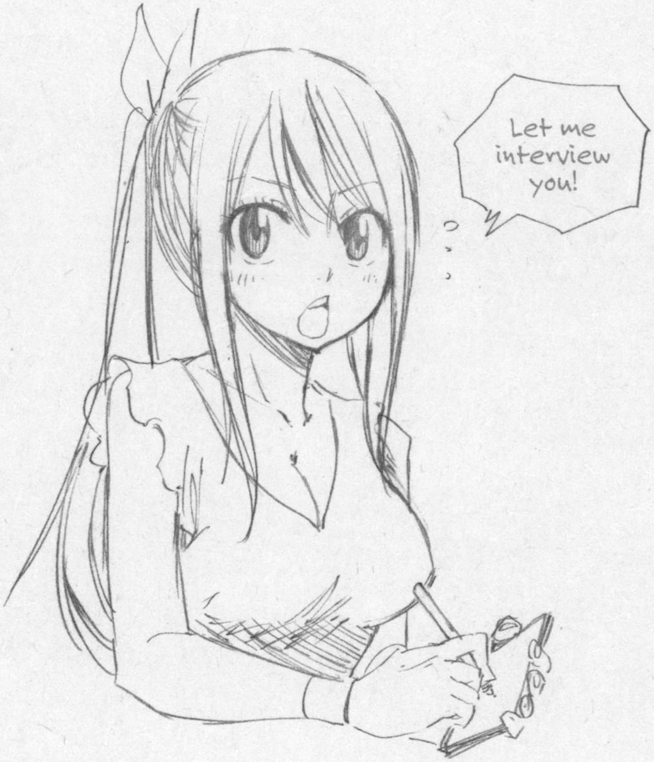
Let me interview you!

FAIRY TAIL フェアリーテイル 49

I...lost the cover...
What? Again?!

HIRO 真島ヒロ MASHIMA

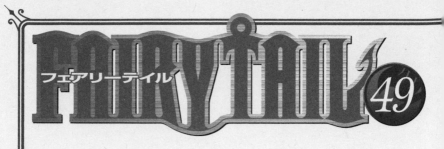

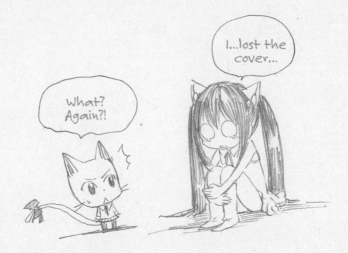

FROM HIRO MASHIMA

I didn't realize it, but it suddenly dawned on me that this is the 49th volume, and with the next one, it'll be 50!

It surprises even me!

I really didn't intend for it to go on this long, but the whole reason it's been able to continue like this is thanks to all of you!

With the new *Fairy Tail* series, there have been rumors that *Fairy Tail* is headed toward its final chapter, but in this volume we start a brand-new story arc!

We've still got a long way to go!

Original Jacket Design: Hisao Ogawa

Translation Notes

Japanese is a tricky language for most Westerners, and translation is often more art than science. For your edification and reading pleasure, here are notes on some of the places where we could have gone in a different direction with our translation of the work, or where a Japanese cultural reference is used.

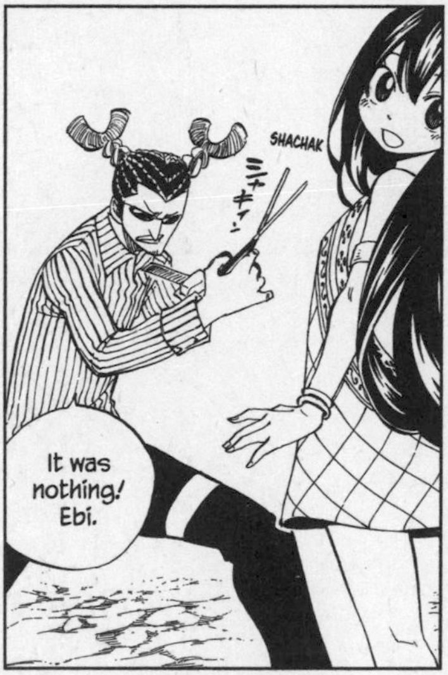
SHACHAK
It was nothing! Ebi.

Page 70, Ebi

As related in the notes for Vol. 2, Cancer is, of course, a crab, and since crabs in children's manga, anime, and some fairy tales end their sentences with the Japanese word for crab, *kani*, everyone expected Cancer to do the same. But instead, Cancer ends all his sentences with *ebi*, the Japanese word for "shrimp." He probably does this simply to be perverse.

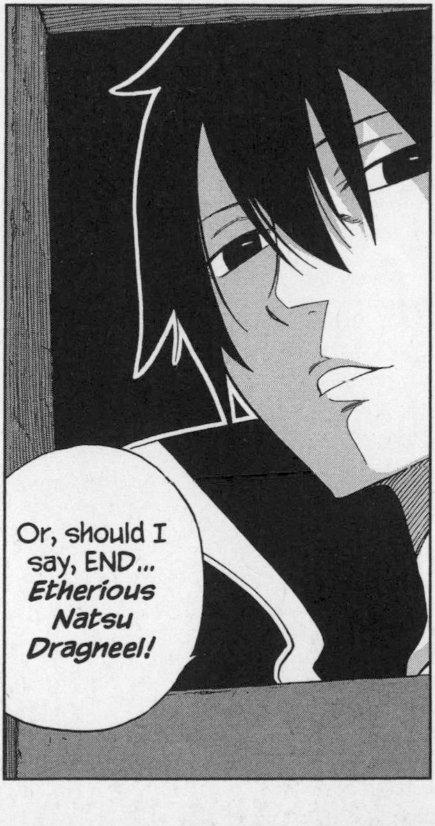
Or, should I say, END... *Etherious Natsu Dragneel!*

Page 96, Etherious

This was mentioned in the notes for Vol. 47, but there was a misunderstanding of the spelling of Etherious. While translating the first stories in which the word appeared, and with no explanation of what the word meant, I gave it the spelling I thought best suited the concept (and, as you might imagine, Hiro Mashima is far too busy to explain things to translators of every language). So it turned out that I misspelled Etherious in early printings of some previous volumes and the online publication. As you can see here, Etherious is meant to be spelled with an "E" at the beginning of it. I apologize for any confusion.

Page 122, Dullahan Head

A dullahan is a wraith out of Irish mythology that is probably the basis for the Headless Horseman of Sleepy Hollow fame. A dullahan is a large black-clad rider on horseback who whips its horse with a whip made from a human spine. In its other hand, it carries its severed head, which illuminates the dark roads that it haunts with light that comes from its eyes. Also, its mouth is split from ear-to-ear, so a jack-o-lantern is actually a pretty good representation of a dullahan's head.

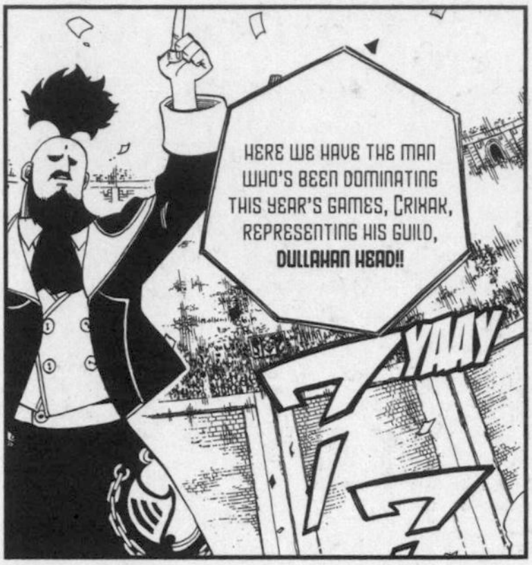
HERE WE HAVE THE MAN WHO'S BEEN DOMINATING THIS YEAR'S GAMES, CRIXAK, REPRESENTING HIS GUILD, **DULLAHAN HEAD!!**
YAAY

Page 136, Scarmiglione

Scarmiglione is one of the demons called Malebranche ("evil claws") from Dante's *Inferno*. They are assigned to the eighth circle of hell, where Scarmiglione tortures corrupt politicians by sinking them into boiling pitch. The Japanese kanji for "poison ogre's fang" doesn't seem to match Dante, but it could refer to the Scarmiglione villain from the *Final Fantasy* series. The one in *Final Fantasy IV* looks like a demon with enormous fangs.

Page 178, Kotoko Inn

The Kotoko Inn that Natsu, Happy and Lucy stayed at is a tribute to one of the singers in the idol group Nogizaka 46, Kotoko Sasaki. Apparently she is a fan of *Fairy Tail* and writes short comments on many of the new volumes on her blog when they come out. Hiro Mashima noticed, and they met in person.

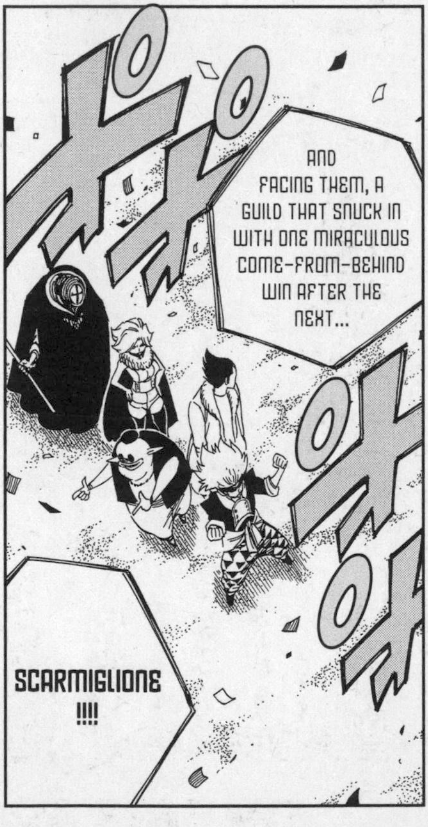
AND FACING THEM, A GUILD THAT SNUCK IN WITH ONE MIRACULOUS COME-FROM-BEHIND WIN AFTER THE NEXT...
SCARMIGLIONE !!!!

BASED ON A STORY BY **HIRO MASHIMA**

MANGA BY **RUI WATANABE**

1

FAIRY TAIL
BLUE MISTRAL

ON SALE AUG. 2015!

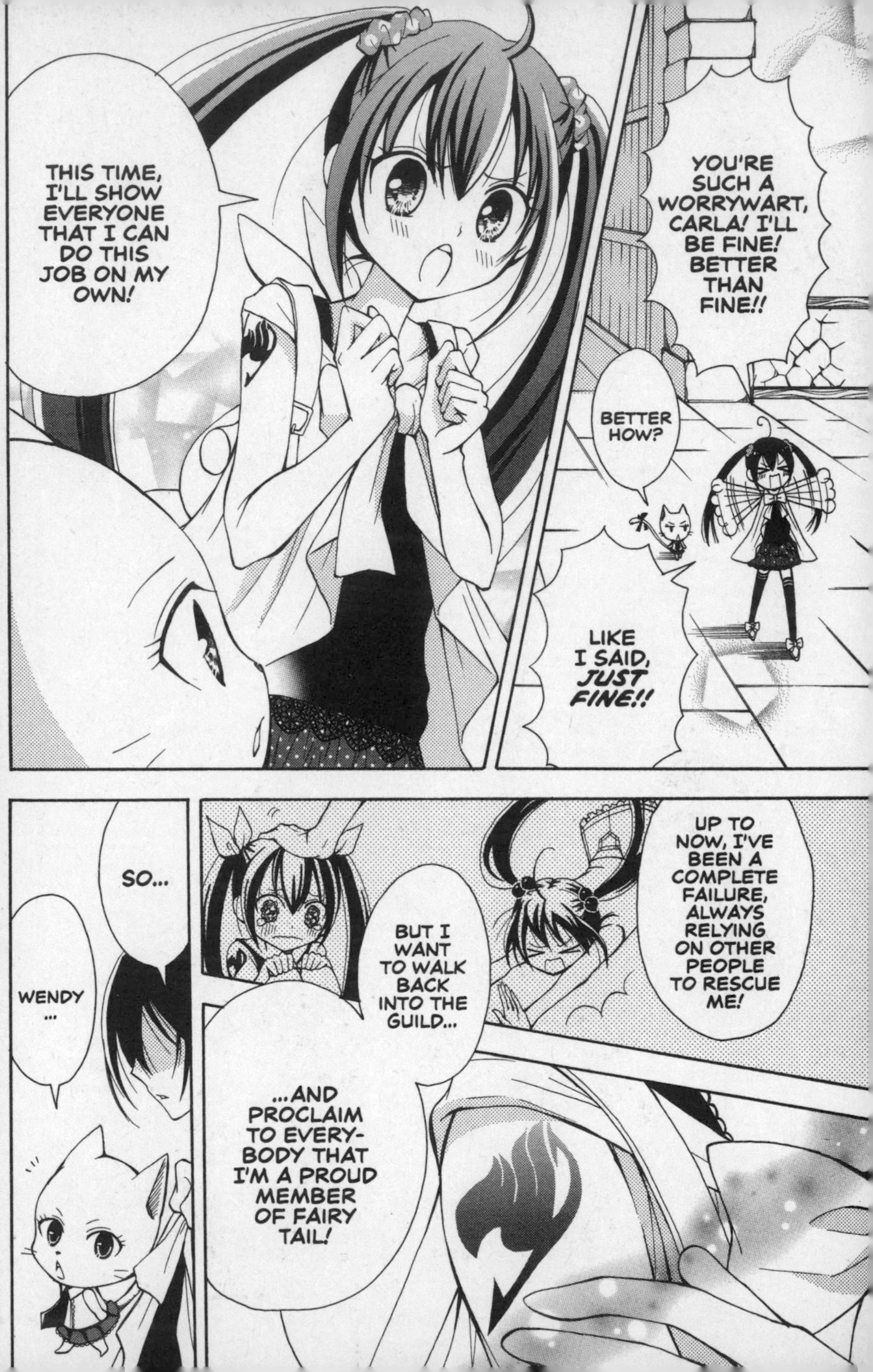
YOU'RE SUCH A WORRYWART, CARLA! I'LL BE FINE! BETTER THAN FINE!!
BETTER HOW?
LIKE I SAID, *JUST FINE!!*
THIS TIME, I'LL SHOW EVERYONE THAT I CAN DO THIS JOB ON MY OWN!
UP TO NOW, I'VE BEEN A COMPLETE FAILURE, ALWAYS RELYING ON OTHER PEOPLE TO RESCUE ME!
BUT I WANT TO WALK BACK INTO THE GUILD...
...AND PROCLAIM TO EVERYBODY THAT I'M A PROUD MEMBER OF FAIRY TAIL!
SO...
WENDY ...

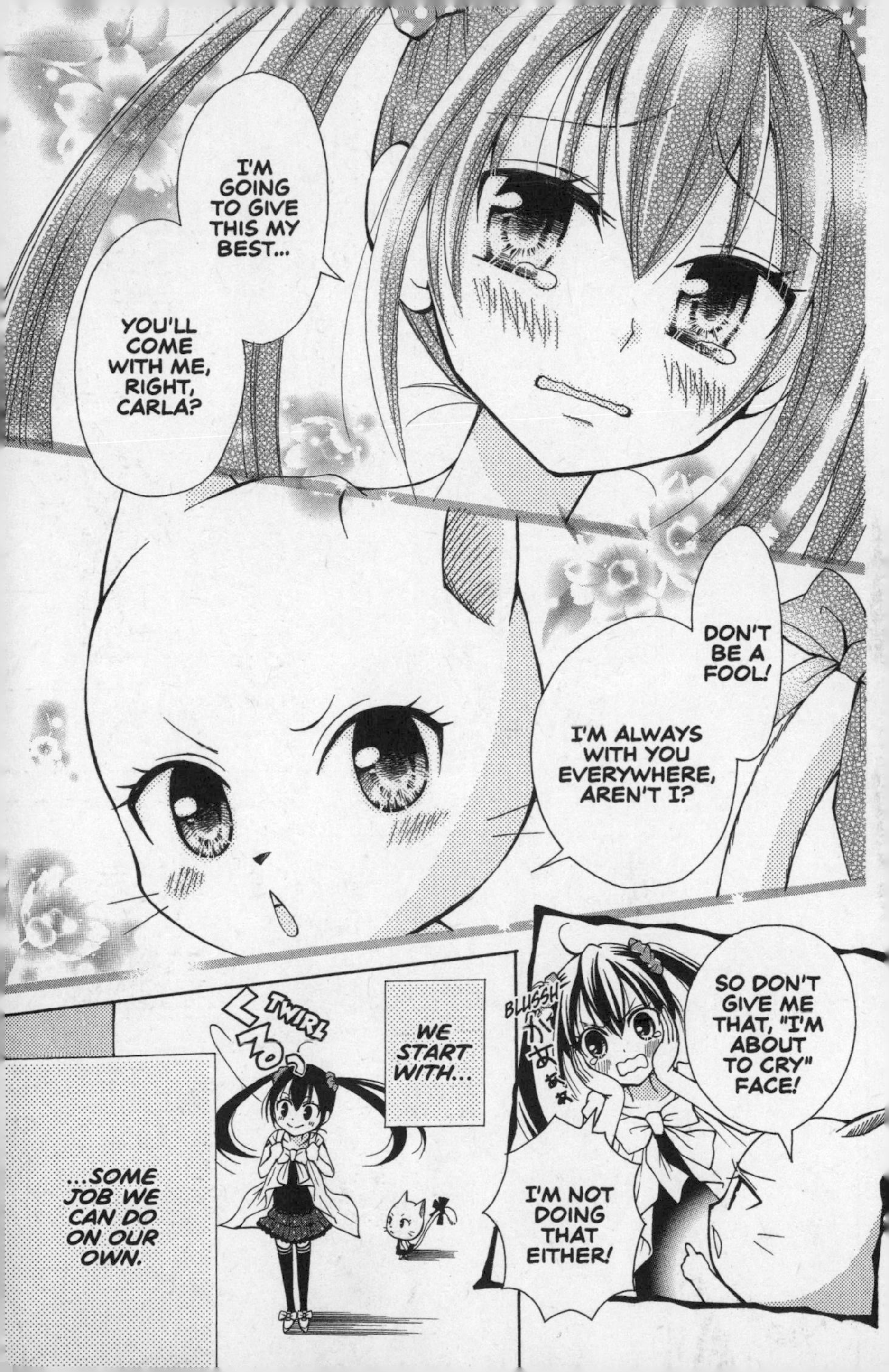
I'M GOING TO GIVE THIS MY BEST...
YOU'LL COME WITH ME, RIGHT, CARLA?
DON'T BE A FOOL!
I'M ALWAYS WITH YOU EVERYWHERE, AREN'T I?
SO DON'T GIVE ME THAT, "I'M ABOUT TO CRY" FACE!
BLUSSH
I'M NOT DOING THAT EITHER!
TWIRL
WE START WITH...
...SOME JOB WE CAN DO ON OUR OWN.

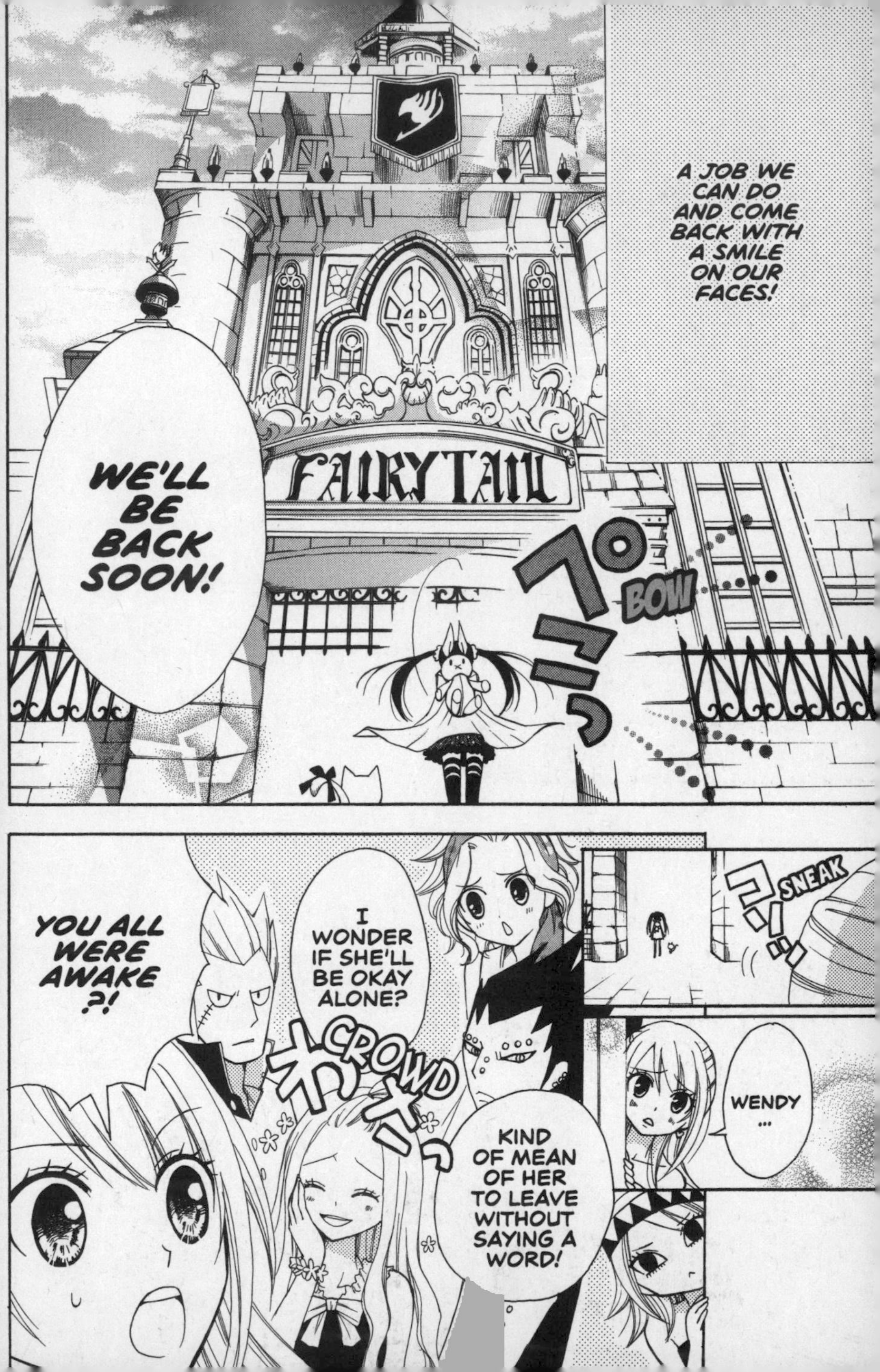
A JOB WE CAN DO AND COME BACK WITH A SMILE ON OUR FACES!
FAIRYTAIL
WE'LL BE BACK SOON!
BOW
SNEAK
WENDY ...
I WONDER IF SHE'LL BE OKAY ALONE?
YOU ALL WERE AWAKE ?!
CROWD
KIND OF MEAN OF HER TO LEAVE WITHOUT SAYING A WORD!

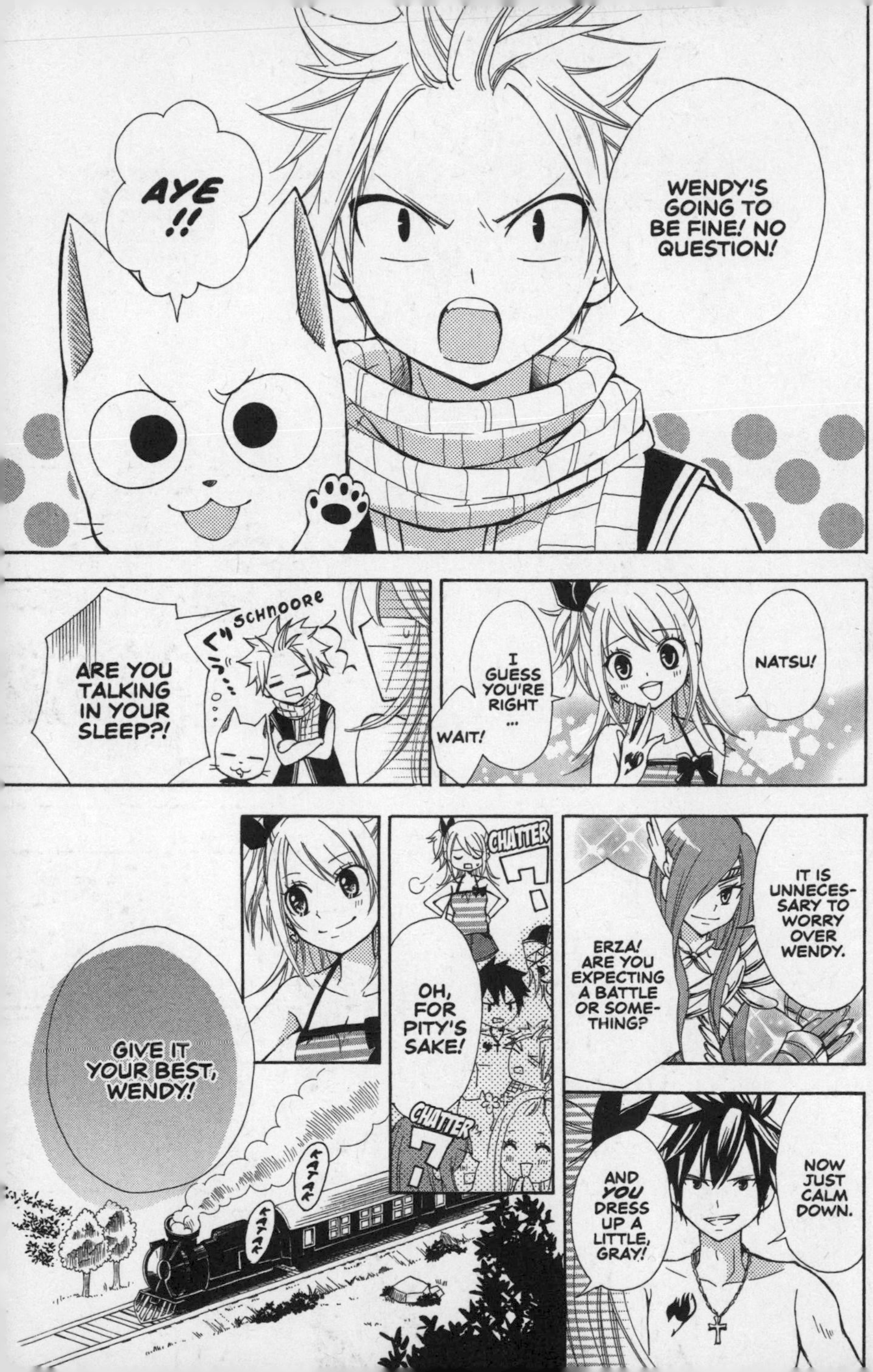
WENDY'S GOING TO BE FINE! NO QUESTION!
AYE!!
NATSU!
I GUESS YOU'RE RIGHT ...
WAIT!
SCHNOORE
ARE YOU TALKING IN YOUR SLEEP?!
IT IS UNNECES-SARY TO WORRY OVER WENDY.
ERZA! ARE YOU EXPECTING A BATTLE OR SOME-THING?
NOW JUST CALM DOWN.
AND YOU DRESS UP A LITTLE, GRAY!
CHATTER
OH, FOR PITY'S SAKE!
CHATTER
GIVE IT YOUR BEST, WENDY!

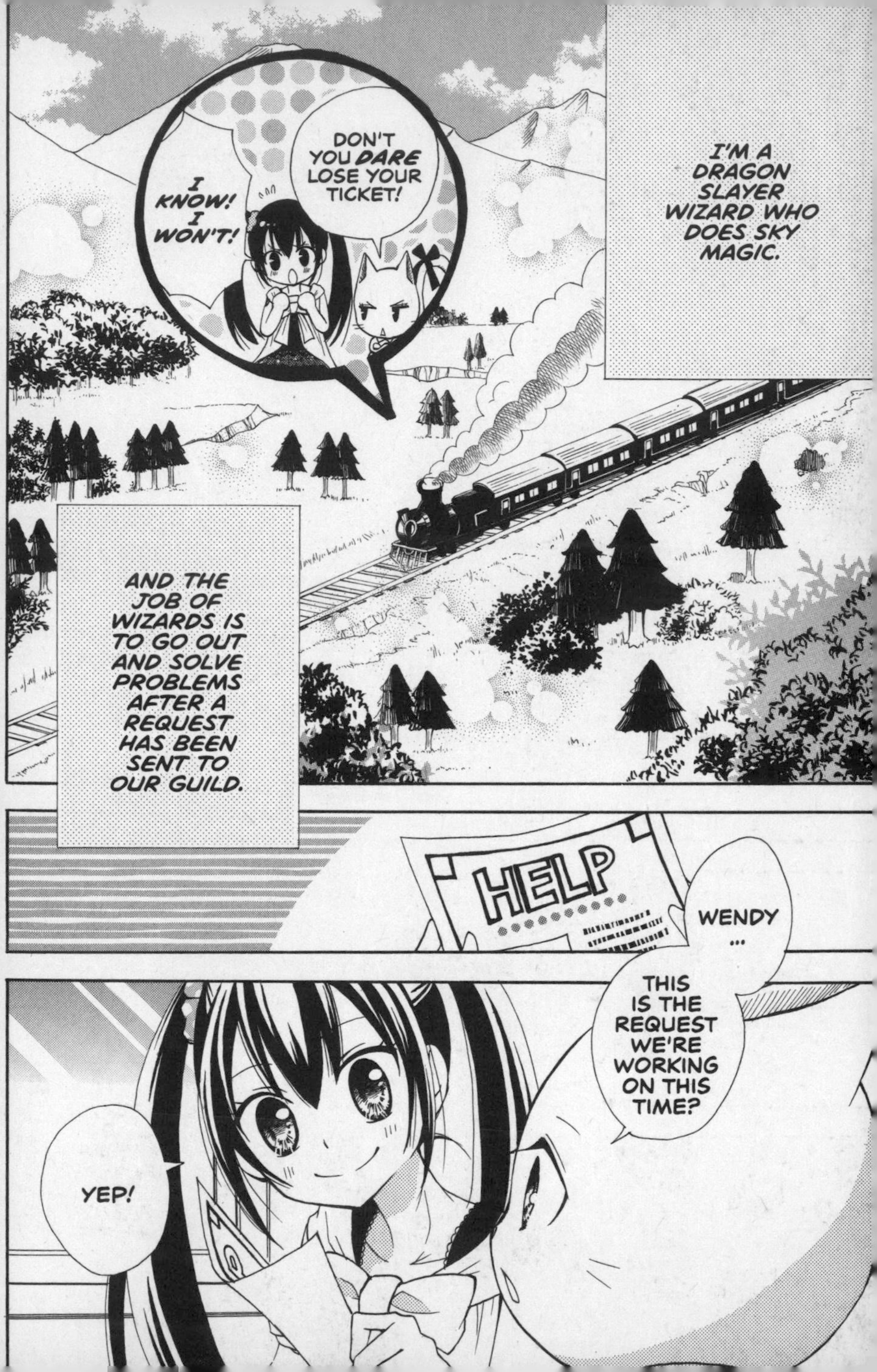
I'M A DRAGON SLAYER WIZARD WHO DOES SKY MAGIC.
DON'T YOU DARE LOSE YOUR TICKET!
I KNOW! I WON'T!
AND THE JOB OF WIZARDS IS TO GO OUT AND SOLVE PROBLEMS AFTER A REQUEST HAS BEEN SENT TO OUR GUILD.
HELP
WENDY ...
THIS IS THE REQUEST WE'RE WORKING ON THIS TIME?
YEP!

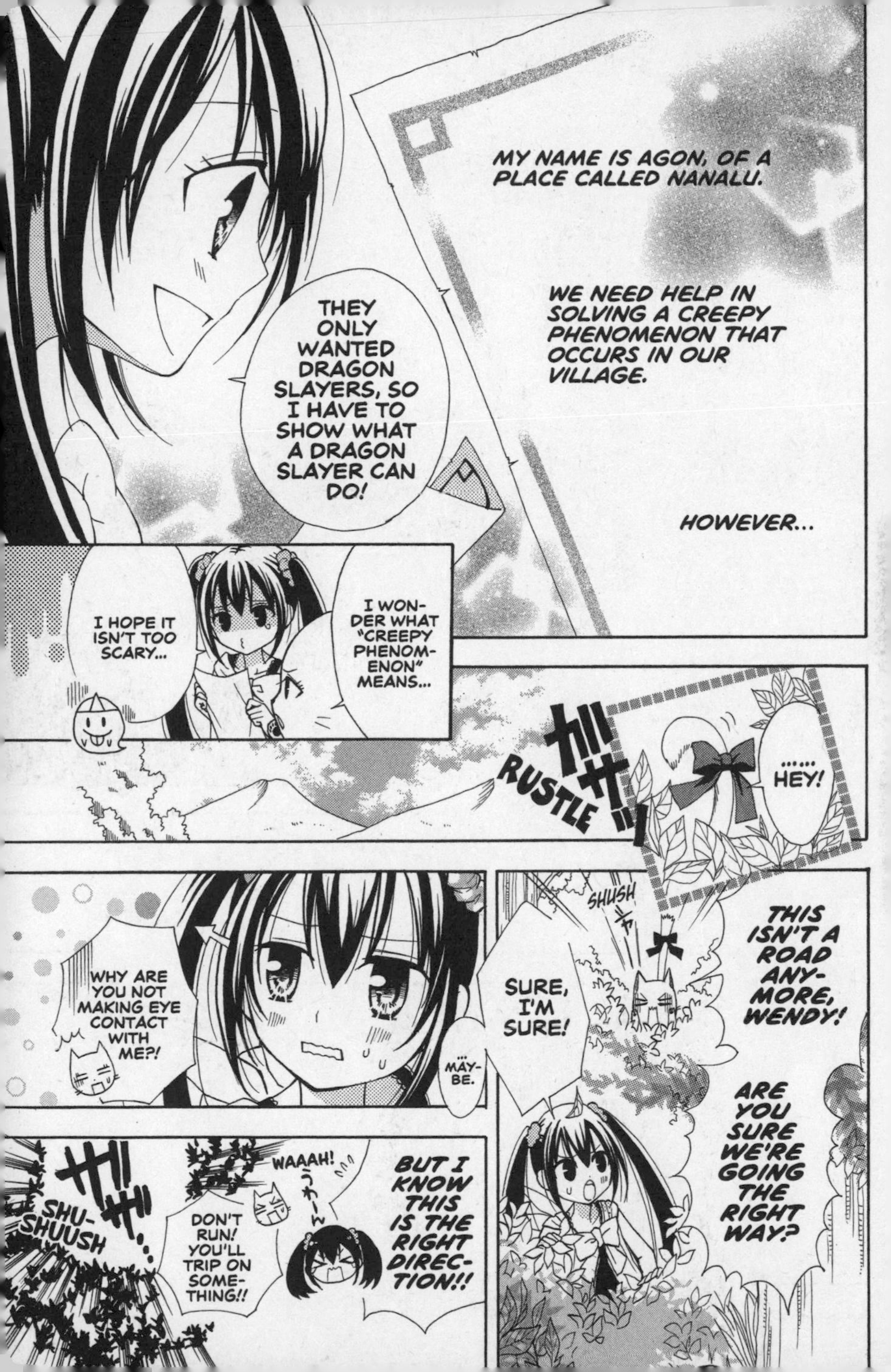
MY NAME IS AGON, OF A PLACE CALLED NANALU.
WE NEED HELP IN SOLVING A CREEPY PHENOMENON THAT OCCURS IN OUR VILLAGE.
HOWEVER...
THEY ONLY WANTED DRAGON SLAYERS, SO I HAVE TO SHOW WHAT A DRAGON SLAYER CAN DO!
I WONDER WHAT "CREEPY PHENOMENON" MEANS...
I HOPE IT ISN'T TOO SCARY...
......HEY!
RUSTLE
SHUSH
THIS ISN'T A ROAD ANYMORE, WENDY!
ARE YOU SURE WE'RE GOING THE RIGHT WAY?
SURE, I'M SURE!
...MAYBE.
WHY ARE YOU NOT MAKING EYE CONTACT WITH ME?!
BUT I KNOW THIS IS THE RIGHT DIRECTION!!
WAAAH!
DON'T RUN! YOU'LL TRIP ON SOMETHING!!
SHU-SHUUSH

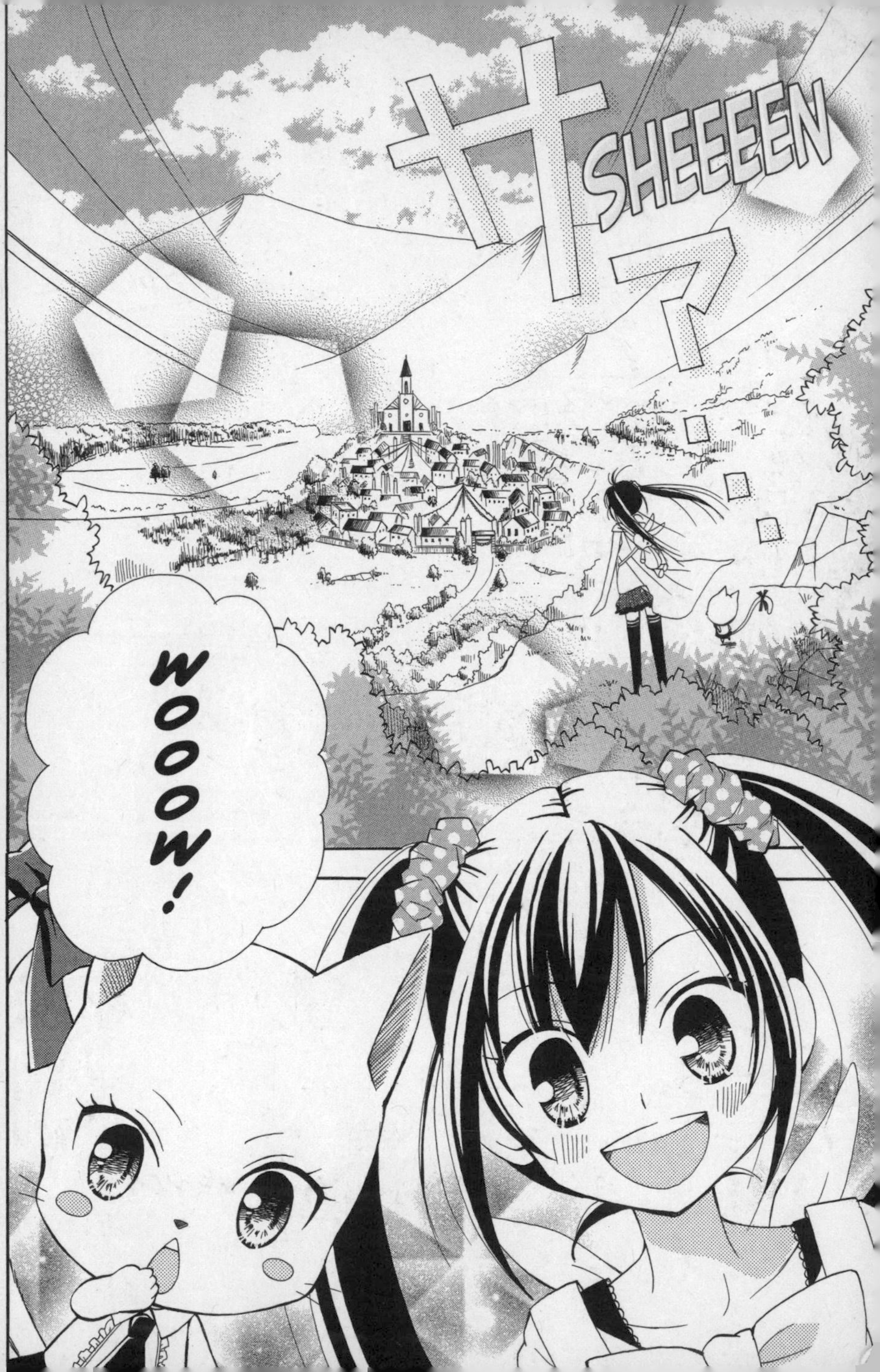
SHEEEEN
WOOOW!

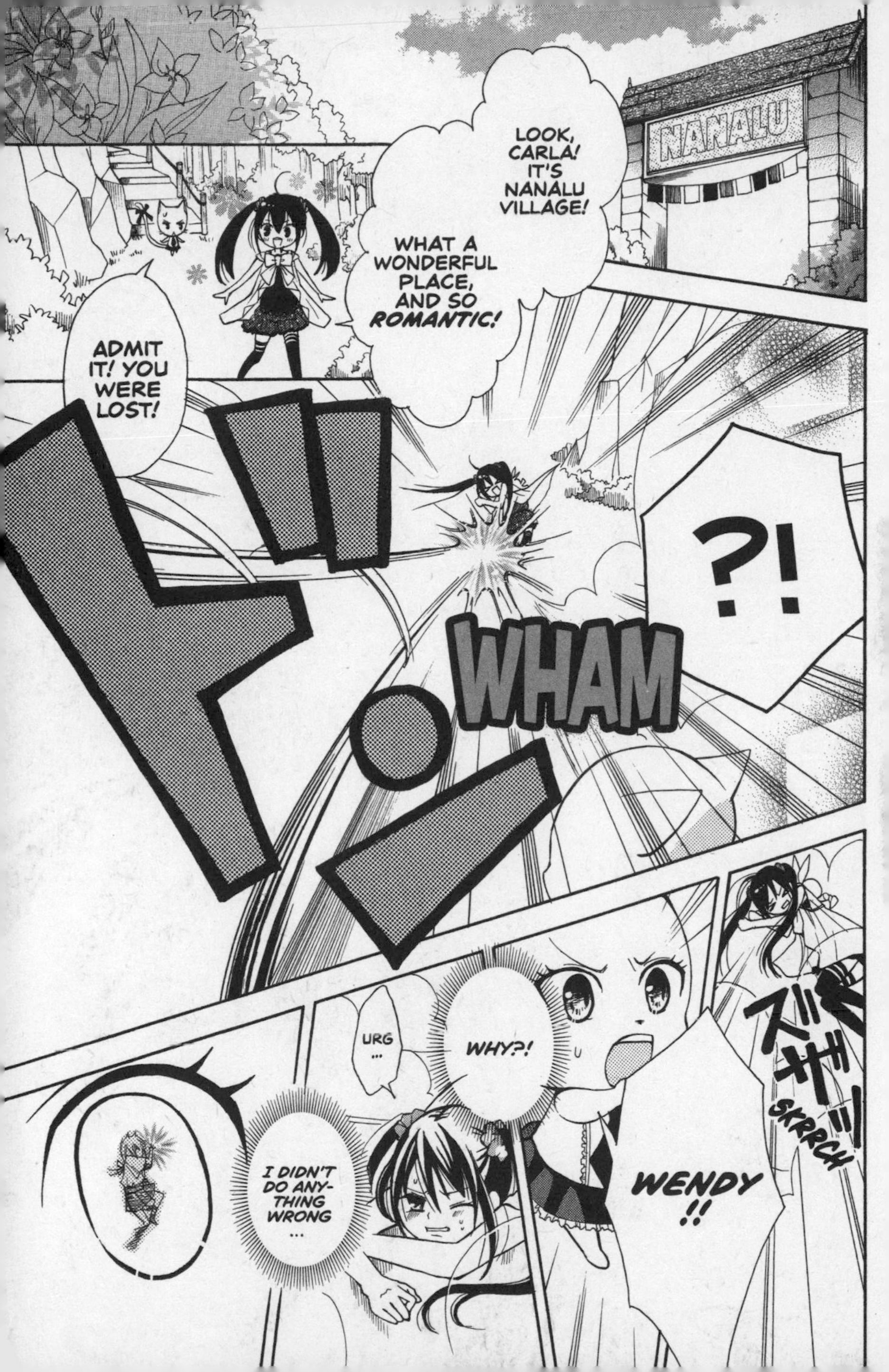
NANALU
LOOK, CARLA! IT'S NANALU VILLAGE!
WHAT A WONDERFUL PLACE, AND SO *ROMANTIC!*
ADMIT IT! YOU WERE LOST!
?!
WHAM
SKRRCH
WENDY !!
WHY?!
URG ...
I DIDN'T DO ANY-THING WRONG ...

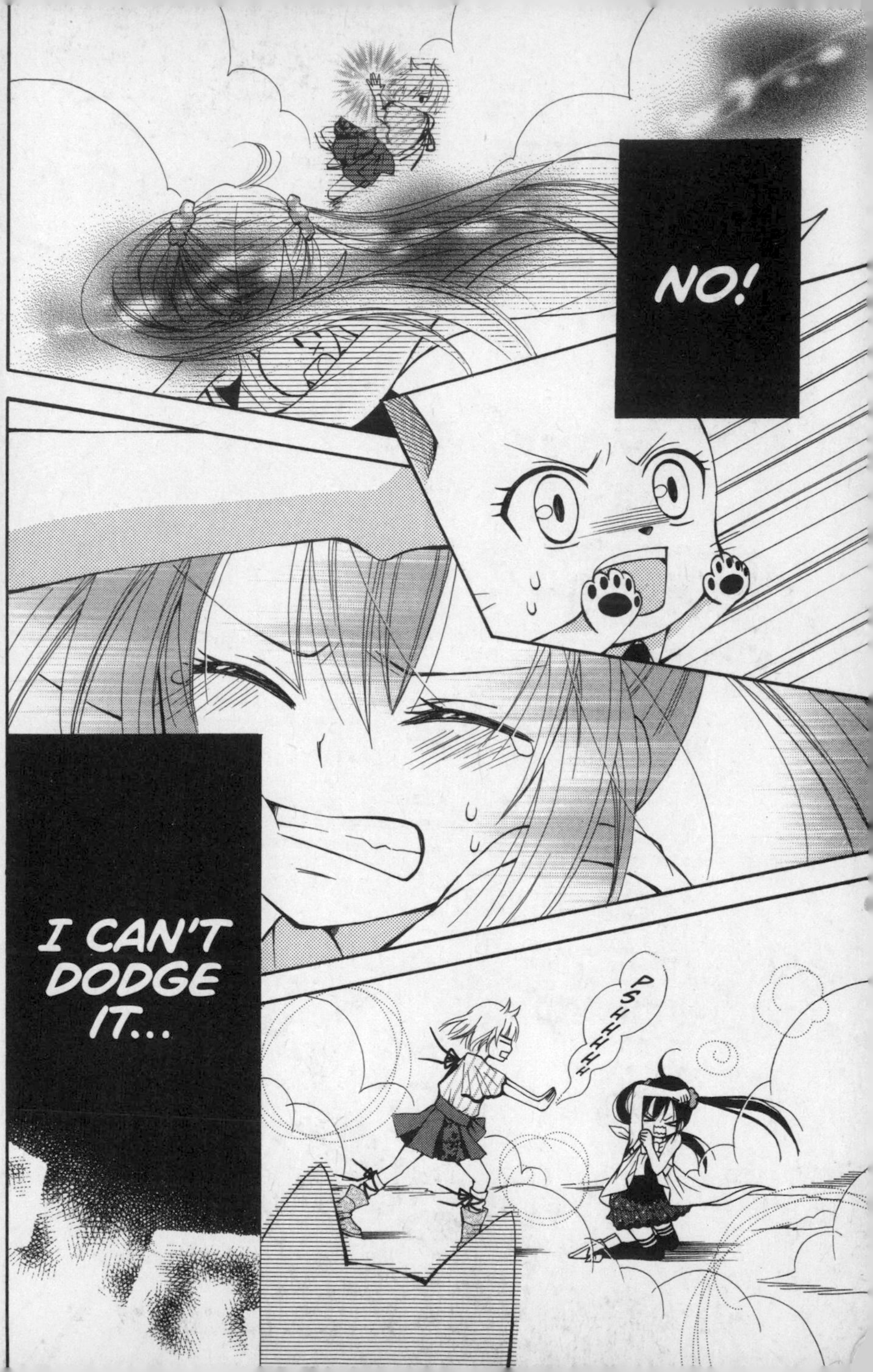
NO!
I CAN'T DODGE IT...
PSHHHHH

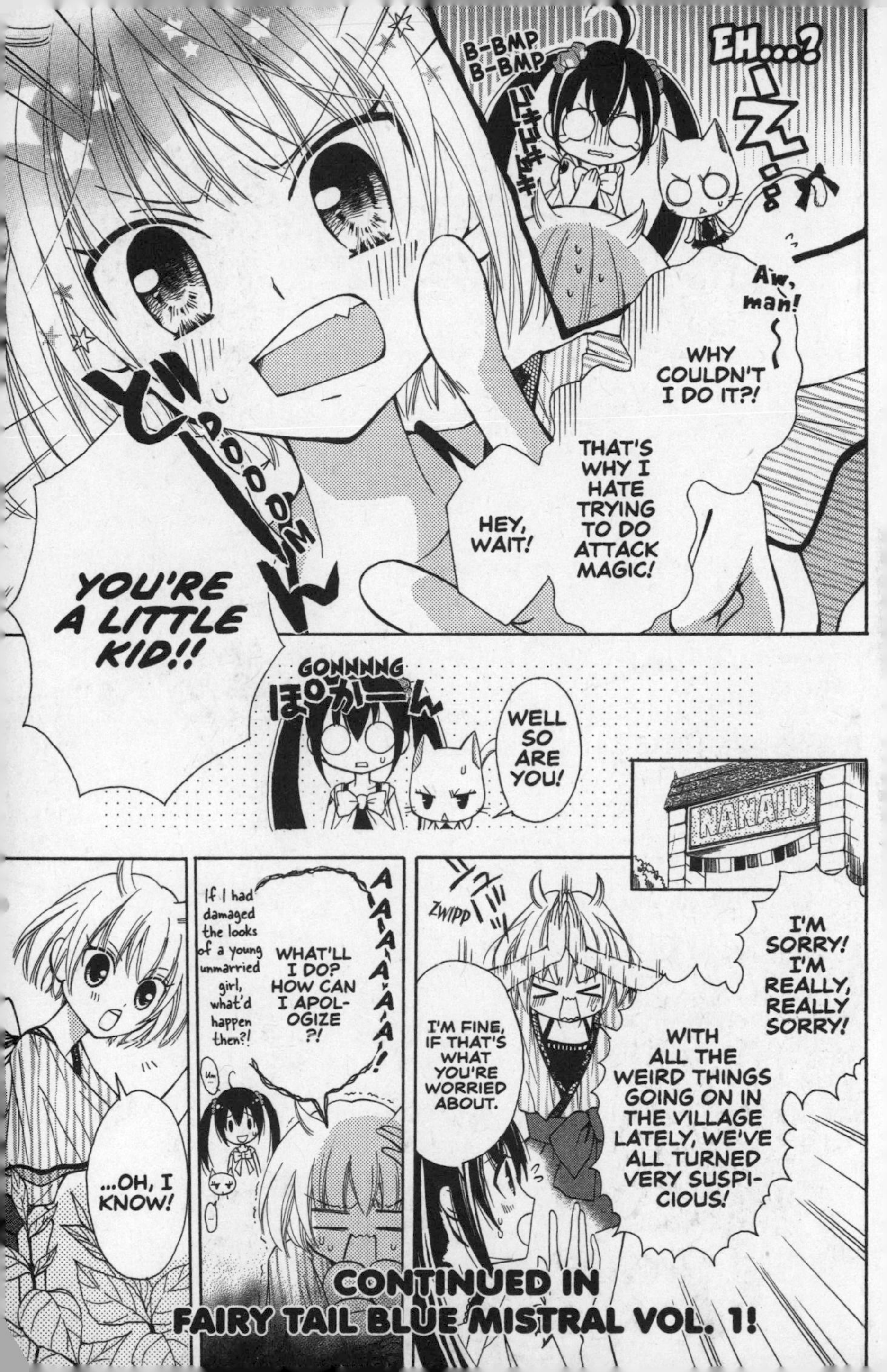
EH...?
B-BMP B-BMP
ドキドキ
Aw, man!
WHY COULDN'T I DO IT?!
THAT'S WHY I HATE TRYING TO DO ATTACK MAGIC!
HEY, WAIT!
DOOOOM
YOU'RE A LITTLE KID!!
GONNNNG
ぽかーん
WELL SO ARE YOU!
NANALU
I'M SORRY! I'M REALLY, REALLY SORRY!
WITH ALL THE WEIRD THINGS GOING ON IN THE VILLAGE LATELY, WE'VE ALL TURNED VERY SUSPICIOUS!
ZWIPP
I'M FINE, IF THAT'S WHAT YOU'RE WORRIED ABOUT.
AAAAAAA!
WHAT'LL I DO? HOW CAN I APOLOGIZE?!
If I had damaged the looks of a young unmarried girl, what'd happen then?!
...OH, I KNOW!
CONTINUED IN FAIRY TAIL BLUE MISTRAL VOL. 1!

Fairy Tail volume 49 is a work of fiction. Names, characters, places, and incidents are the products of the author's imagination or are used fictitiously. Any resemblance to actual events, locales, or persons, living or dead, is entirely coincidental.

A Kodansha Comics Trade Paperback Original.

Fairy Tail volume 49 copyright © 2015 Hiro Mashima
English translation copyright © 2015 Hiro Mashima

All rights reserved.

Published in the United States by Kodansha Comics, an imprint of Kodansha USA Publishing, LLC, New York.

Publication rights for this English edition arranged through Kodansha Ltd., Tokyo.

First published in Japan in 2015 by Kodansha Ltd., Tokyo
ISBN 978-1-61262-985-8

Printed in the United States of America.

www.kodanshacomics.com

9 8 7 6 5 4 3 2 1

Translation: William Flanagan
Lettering: AndWorld Design
Editing: Ben Applegate
Kodansha Comics edition cover design by Phil Balsman